# WANDERING SCHOLAR

# WANDERING SCHOLAR

by

## M. J. BONN

LONDON: COHEN & WEST LTD
1949

*To my friends of the Institute of International Education and of the Rockefeller Foundation who smoothed the wanderer's path.*

# Contents

# WANDERING SCHOLAR

# Prelude

•

THIS BOOK is not a history of my time, nor a full tale of my life. It is a picture of men and events, seen from a particular political angle and from a purely personal point of view. I grew up in opposition to Bismarck and to everything he stood for; I was never dazzled by the crude splendors of the Kaiser's empire. On my mother's side I was Austrian; not being a native of her country, I kept free from the traditional sentimentality that idolized the old Emperor Franz Josef, who at best was a hardworking, unimaginative bureaucrat. Unlike most Germans, I was familiar with Austria's problems.

I suppose I may introduce myself as a wandering scholar, even though as to my scholarship I am not absolutely certain. I have marched with flying colors through all academic grades —I have been Doctor, Professor, Principal, and Rector Magnificus; the one rung I missed was that of Dean; I have never been "His Spectabilitas," as this worthy was called in German universities. I have probably held more visiting professorships than any other man of my generation. I am a member of several learned societies, and I have written a few voluminous books that entailed a good deal of research. Yet I have never experienced the ecstasies of true scholarship. I dislike sitting in public libraries, however great their treasure may be; I am interested in books only in as much as I can get something I need out of them; I can enjoy early editions as works of art, not because they are old and rare. Unfortunately, I loathe detail and find it hard to appreciate the meticulous work of learned scrapmongers, though I know that without their burrowing zest my supply of material would be scanty. One of my colleagues, who justly did not like me, held me up to derision one day by reproaching me with having written nothing but pamphlets. He had once been a bookbinder's apprentice and had never quite got rid of his quantitative approach to literary excellence. At least he had rightly guessed my own proclivities, though his

I

facts were wrong. I had produced two very heavy volumes, since in those days quantitative learnedness was expected from an aspiring scholar. If I could have followed my own instincts, I would never have gone beyond slender essays. But somehow people seem to think that bulk is an essential element of truth and insist on spreading it thickly; which is all very well for the paper manufacturers. I have always felt that the sum total of what I had to say could be expressed in a few dozen pages, and that the rest was but laborious padding.

I am afraid I was never a plodding researcher. I usually guessed results before I could prove them; this guessing was the really enjoyable part of the work. They had to be carefully tested, and fortunately I was sufficiently trained to recognize this stern necessity, but the process of doubting and proving truth one already possessed was not only boring but painful. I have never become a really first-rate "specialist" in any particular line. When I had mastered the essentials of a problem, I got tired and wandered aimlessly into other fields until something new struck my attention. Yet I frequently returned to the old questions when novel developments had changed their face. What I lost as a scholar, I gained as a human being; I may not have got to the bottom of anything—as a really good scholar should do—but I managed to learn a lot about many things.

I can hardly justify this dislike of specialization by my wandering life. When I was interested in a particular problem, I thought of it and worked on it irrespective of my domicile; this was, in fact, one of the minor tragedies I had to face. I frequently pursued my studies of problems when I was removed from the scene where they were centered, and neglected the opportunities of seeing things around me, the importance of which dawned on me only when they were withdrawn from my direct observation.

In my young days, I was a homebody; I did a great deal of daring migration and exploration in my daydreams—there was a time when I was bent on becoming an African explorer—but I hated to leave home. I was very unhappy during my first university term at Heidelberg, though I had gone there with friends and though I was near enough home to spend week ends with my mother. By and by I lost this fear of a hostile world and began to look to travel as the fulfillment of dreams rather than as an ordeal. I did not realize then how fully my migratory instincts were to be gratified. Yet even after my marriage, when I had met a partner whose spirit was far more adventurous than my own, my outlook on life remained sedentary. I looked forward to the highly respectable existence of a German university professor who would do some more or less varied traveling in his ample vacations, but who was firmly rooted in the soil, though he might occasionally be transferred to another university and to a more important and lucrative chair.

Fate willed it otherwise. The outbreak of the First World War found us on the Atlantic, bound for a visiting professorship at the University of California. Ever since, I have been more or less a visiting professor, a kind of gypsy scholar. My regular duties were over and over again interrupted by foreign lecture tours and nonacademic activities. I doubt whether after 1914 I ever spent a full term at an institution without an excursion to foreign countries. My long-term appointments were at Munich, Berlin, and the London School of Economics. I was eleven times visiting professor for at least one term in American and Canadian institutions, besides innumerable short engagements. I once visited twenty-two New England colleges (Harvard and Yale not included) within three months, spending half a week in each of them—and by the grace of God I survived. This wandering life has probably made me far more superficial than I otherwise would be, or, I had better say, might have been. It agreed with me, and I really liked it. What I lost in depth, I gained in breadth. I sometimes imagined that it satisfied some deep-seated craving. It may have been the legacy of the forty years in the wilderness, which I inherited from my early forefathers. Sometimes I imagine that deep down in my comfort-craving soul, the instinct of the wayfaring Bedouin is still alive. The desert appeals to me irresistibly. To these impulses, whatever their origin may be, I owe a great deal.

During a large part of my life I have been greatly spoiled by outward conditions; I have owned homes and land, but I have lost them through revolutionary forces. Their loss has not touched me deeply, though of course it has created voids in the economic side of my existence. My wanderings have taught me to travel light. They have not made me a Spartan; I still like cómfort. But they have freed me from possessive instincts; the external objects from which comfort has to be derived have no longer a personal meaning for me. If ever I were allowed to return to my mountain home in the Austrian Alps, I would be a stranger; I still could revel in its beauty, but it would not be part of me. This is the only profound dissension between my wife and myself; she needs a soil to grow roots in; I can live on the surface.

This absence of a truly possessive instinct involves, no doubt, a kind of spiritual failure. I have missed a lot by losing it, yet it has made life easy for me. I have been at home, temporarily at least, in every country in which I have resided. I instinctively participate, for the time being, in its outlook. Yet I have never quite lost the feeling of detachment and isolation. I could have become part and parcel of my native city; I should have found it easy to serve her, as some of my ancestors and relations have done since we settled there over four hundred years ago. After I cut myself adrift, I never completely took root anywhere, neither in my many years in Munich nor in those brilliant years when Berlin was kind to me. I did not go into exile when England offered me hospitality and activities after the advent of the Nazis; I never felt like a refugee. In a way it was more like coming home, for England had always been a second spiritual home. I fitted well into English life, because the British do not like the foreign-born to pose as hundred-per-cent British. They expect loyalty, which I could give them unstintedly, but they do not believe in the possibility of complete spiritual identification. They expect from, and respect in, an alien a certain inward aloofness, and they rightly suspect those who renounce it. Sometimes this aloofness hurts those who have to practice it. They naturally share their fellow citizens' sorrows; they cannot always share their joys. This is a heavy handicap for the young and ambitious. Those who no longer desire to shape their fellow men's destinies are more fortunate. Ties are bound to snap as one gets on in life; each break hurts, however inevitable it may be. Most of the knots that bind a wandering scholar to his surroundings and to his fellow men are loose.

We are all taught that we cannot take our earthly possessions along with us; the knowledge that this must be so pains most of us pretty acutely. He is fortunate in whom the possessive instinct has died. He can leave without regret what he no longer rates very highly. And when one is held back only by a few ties, which in the nature of things threaten to snap any day, one looks forward to the end of a long migration with hope rather than with fear, even though one may not be much interested in a hereafter.

# I. The Birth of a Republican

## 1. *Frankfort*

MY FAMOUS fellow citizen Johann Wolfgang von Goethe depicted the glories of our native city, Frankfort on the Main, during the coronation of a Roman emperor of the German nation. When my day came, three quarters of a century had gone by since the last emperor laid down the Roman crown and exchanged it for that of Austria. Yet a kind of imperial fragrance still hovered over the ancient city. The city hall in which the emperors were elected, the balcony from which they showed themselves to the crowd in the market square, the banqueting hall from the walls of which their portraits looked down upon one had remained unchanged. For many centuries the empire had been a mere phantom, the symbol of a Europe yearning for unity and peace. It was a dream, no longer a power. A faint remembrance of that dream pervaded the atmosphere in the days of my youth. Somehow this smallish city—it had only eighty-seven thousand inhabitants when the Prussians annexed it in 1866—proudly recalled the days when it had been, so to speak, the hub of the universe from which the glory of the Roman name had radiated in all directions.

For half a century, 1815 to 1866, Frankfort was an independent republic. I doubt whether it was a model state; in fact I know it was not. It was narrow, self-sufficient, and arrogant. It looked down on those who were born abroad as beings of lesser status, and refused them citizenship. It was ruled by a caste of merchants who despised industry and manufactures as something beneath their dignity. It was certainly not progressive. Yet it had two great qualities. Its ruling class knew the value of independence. It possessed and practiced the art of self-government. There had been nothing above it in the days of the old empire but the Roman emperor, and in the half century of

6

republican independence even he had gone and only God Almighty had been its master.

The spirit of sturdy independence was not limited to the "patrician" ruling class. It permeated the entire population. Jew and Gentile, oppressor and oppressed had a feeling that they were something special in this world; all of them looked down upon their Prussian conquerors—a barbarian race whose rule defiled their imperial city. The pride and arrogance of these people would have been unbearable had they held a mighty empire. As they were but a small city-state, their self-inflation was purely local; it could not do much harm to others, though it may not have made them very lovable. The city with the region it dominated was so small—forty-three square miles, which included eight villages with twelve thousand inhabitants —that it had to fit itself into the picture of a larger world by sending its sons and daughters to all the corners of the earth. There was scarcely a family rich enough to provide a comfortable existence at home for all its members and descendants. My own family did not belong to the rich, but my grandfather was considered a man of means; yet all his sons but one had to start in foreign lands. My father was in business in Milan in his young days; one of his brothers went to the United States, another to England.

This very smallness of living space neutralized the narrow self-sufficiency that would otherwise have prevailed. At home the Frankfort people looked down upon everybody who was not born within the city walls. Yet all the bright boys had gone out and had made their way somewhere else in the world. They came home well seasoned, and having become affluent, spent the last years of their lives in pleasant retirement in the city of their youth. The old walls had been pulled down after the Napoleonic Wars. Their place was taken by public gardens that surrounded almost the entire city. On a pleasant autumn or spring morning one could see those returned natives taking their constitutional—leisurely strutting around their city, exchanging greetings and remarks with those of their fellow townsmen who, like them, had been abroad.

In some ways the old city had been the most international place on the continent. Long before the rise of the house of Rothschild, Frankfort had been the financial center of central

Europe. No less a person than Martin Luther had thundered against "the wicked hole from which, through which, and to which all money flowed." A good many of the world's big international financial institutions had started in Frankfort. Even after it had become a Prussian provincial town, New York, London, Paris, Amsterdam, Vienna, and Milan were at least as close to it as Berlin. In fact, to the older generation the real emperor was not William I, who had annexed Frankfort, but his Habsburg rival who sat in the Burg in Vienna. This old Austrian empire had been a real empire comprising many different nationalities, which in the western half generally were allowed to live according to their own ways. Austria stood for easygoing variety; Prussia for discipline, standardization, and drill.

Yet Frankfort felt very "national." It believed in a greater Germany that was to embrace Austria, not the little Germany dominated by Prussia. Its concepts were federalist, not unitarian. After having been the city in which the Roman emperors were elected and crowned, it had been the seat of the German Confederation. In the palace in the Grosse Eschenheimer Gasse had sat the representatives of the German governments who made up the confederation for fifty years. Here the Prussian ambassador Otto von Bismarck had first learned the trade of which he was to prove himself a master. As the seat of the German diet, to which foreign ministers were accredited, Frankfort continued to be one of the great capitals of the world, at least in its own opinion, until Prussia pricked the bubble, destroyed the republic that had sided against her, and incorporated it after having imposed a heavy financial tribute upon it. This was one of the tangible reasons why the Frankfort people loathed Prussia for a long time; and in this instance they surely were right. To require tribute from a country one was going to keep was childish. The Prussians later on recognized their mistake and never collected the spoils. They had been poor for such a long time that they hated to miss an opportunity to take cash as well as land—at least the Frankforters thought so.

There was another historic glory to Frankfort. In the ugly red sandstone Church of St. Paul the deputies of all Germany had met in the mad year '48 and tried to found a new German empire. They had failed, for after the first fright of the revolution was over, the governments remembered that they had the guns and the members of the national parliament had nothing but their tongues. The Frankfort people cherished this glorious episode that had made them for a few short months the true capital of central Europe again. When the German Republic was finally founded in 1918–19, some people suggested Frankfort as the future capital—a suggestion that might wisely have been followed.

In any case, a spirit of independence and republicanism survived in my young days, though the city had been deprived of her political glories—she was not even the capital of the new Prussian province of Hesse-Nassau. Being born into this atmosphere saved me from many illusions and disappointments. It helped my equanimity when later on I had to function in Munich and play the part of a Bavarian official admitted to the presence of the kings of Bavaria. It spared me the feeling of personal deprivation that the average loyal Prussian experienced when William II lost the crown of Germany and fled, and the German Republic had to be established. I cannot say that I was an ardent republican. Like millions of Germans, I would have preferred a parliamentary monarchy of the British type; but thanks to the Frankfort atmosphere that I had breathed early in life, I had no monarchic sentiments to get rid of. I was quite willing to wave a handkerchief to departing kings, and saw no reason to say, "Au revoir."

## 2. Hanauerland Strasse 45 . . . 1873. My Birthplace

I was born on the twenty-eighth of June 1873, near midnight, I am told, on a very hot summer day. I was my grandparents' first-born grandson, and everybody was very proud of me. I had so much hair on my head that a soft hairbrush had to be bought, which deeply impressed everybody; the brush lasted longer than the hair.

The house in which I was born, Hanauerland Strasse 45, was an old-fashioned corner house, almost opposite the small station from which the local line to Hanau started. A grocery shop on the ground floor was run by its owner, Herr Dietz. Like many people in Germany, he had bought his house by putting a very heavy mortgage on it. The rents had to suffice for interest charges, for repairs, and for taxes, which were very light in those days. The owner lived behind the shop, rent free, on what remained over. Frankfort grew rapidly after its incorporation into Prussia and again after the foundation of the empire. It lost character but gained cash. In these circumstances a houseowner was an important personage—though not as important as in imperial Vienna, where houseowners (*Realitätenbesitzer*) and their offspring were registered by the police as a kind of minor peerage. In Frankfort the well-to-do lived in their own one-family houses, not in palaces or would-be palaces as in Vienna, Rome, or Paris where they occupied the first floor, *piano nobile,* and rented the rest to members of their families or to strangers. Frankfort apartment houses were rather modest. One stayed in them until one could afford a house. No luxury flats existed in my young days.

Our landlord, Herr Dietz, was eaten up by the passion for property that animates the peasant in central Europe, with whom possessions sometimes come before family. They, not the capitalists, are the standard-bearers of private ownership, and naturally become wild socialists when they lose their property. Herr Dietz ruled the inmates of his apartment house with a rod of iron. He did not understand the purely contractual nature of his relations with them. He made arbitrary regulations as to noises, opening of windows, cleaning of staircases. He saw himself as a mighty potentate who had given refuge to homeless people whose safety depended on his good will. He was a dreadful tyrant, particularly hard on the servants. They did not sleep in the apartments. Each tenant had rented one or two garrets under the roof to house his servants. These garrets, bitterly cold in winter and hot in summer, were included in the lease. The servants came from the wretchedly poor mountain districts of Upper Hesse and Bavaria; they were farmers' daughters who had either to earn wages all their lives or to accumulate enough to make up a dowry. Herr Dietz, who had probably risen from the same stratum, had no fellow feeling for them. He looked upon them as vermin. I can still see him standing in front of his house, his legs wide apart, his feet encased in heelless red velvet slippers, his old yellow-grayish parchmenty, wrinkled peasant face with suspicious grayish eyes framed by a stubby, short, colorless beard. He ran his shop as despotically as his house; on certain days he would sell only soap and on others only starch—not because he had no supply, but because he loved to bully. After all, it was an age when even the well-to-do still thought of scarcity, and when saving was not considered mean but rather a test of character. I do not think I have ever been very careful of money, but I can be awfully mean about trifles. I am quite capable of subjecting myself to real inconvenience in order not so much to save a few cents as to enjoy the satisfaction of having been true to my early upbringing.

We lived on the first floor. From the street a broad stairway led to a glass door flanked by windows that gave light to the inner hall—a narrow, bracket-shaped lobby. Dining room, sitting room, and guest room faced the street. My parents' bedroom and my room formed one end of the bracket, kitchen and lavatory the other. We had no bathroom, but we had a tub; we did not depend on the Red Manikin, an establishment situated near the river, whence one could order a bath. Two men would carry a tub and some barrels of hot water to one's house; when one had finished, they fetched it all away. We boiled our own hot water.

My parents' bedroom housed two huge mahogany beds, two mahogany washstands and mahogany bed tables with marble tops, two quaint mahogany wardrobes, and a few chairs with plaited straw seats. The dining furniture was light-colored walnut inlaid with ebony; the small sitting room was red plush, the horrible red plush of bourgeois respectability and sleeping-car luxury. The formal drawing room was filled with chairs and settees of black ebony covered with forget-me-not blue brocade and lots of little tables inlaid with brass; there was even a spittoon encased in ebony inlaid with brass. One opened it by pressing the button of a long pole; the lid lifted and revealed a flattish basin, ready to serve its purpose; one released the knob and the lid came down. Whenever I got a chance, I handled this contraption for a purely mechanical satisfaction, and ever since spittoons have had a weird attraction for me. Their passing from the American scene is one of the minor tragedies of the march of progress.

A much neglected garden with a slate-walled garden house

was behind the house; it contained a few plots of grass, over-grown weedy paths, some lilac bushes and sycamore trees. The one and only glory of the garden was a large Pyrus japonica. That Pyrus japonica symbolized life to me. I can still see its flaming beauty against the gray slate wall of the dilapidated garden house; I wove my earliest dreams around it; it was the promise of romance. I shall never forget a little brook rambling between small fir trees not far from Baden-Baden, or a corner of the wall in the Villa Borghese, between live oaks and crumbling statues of dead gods and goddesses, or a cleft somewhere on a ridge of the Surrey Hills with a cottage and a rose garden, where a robin sings in early spring. But the Pyrus has bloomed in my memory for nearly seventy years. Was it a symbol of life? Flaming flowers but no fruits?

## 3. My Father's People

The Bonns had settled in Frankfort at least as early as 1535. An old tombstone commemorates the grave of one of the ances-tors at that date. Her name was Sprinz. This may have been an abbreviation of "Speranza." She and her husband may have fled from Spain, going up the Rhine, after the expulsion of the Jews from that country in 1482; we do not know. Or they may have come to that part of the world when Roman legions first conquered and held the country. Anyhow, the Bonns lived in this place for over four hundred years—until 1939, when the last of us had to leave. They had their ups and downs in that narrow, sunless Jewish quarter, the ghetto, in which they were huddled. They owned a house there called "The Merry Man"; perhaps it radiated the sense of humor with which some of us fortunately have been well endowed. Once upon a time they played a part in history. About 1600 one of my ancestors was financial adviser to the magistrate ruling the city of Frankfort; he was presented with a key to the gate in the wall that sepa-rated the ghetto from the town, so that he might have access to his clients at all hours of the day and night alike. Three hundred years later I held a similar position for a short time, as adviser to the German chancellor on reparation questions. After that, the Bonns receded into obscure mediocrity as small traders and bankers. They emerged for a moment in the second part of the eighteenth century, when they won a lawsuit on a contested bill of exchange against a rival called Rindskopf; for the lawyer who secured this triumph for them was young Goethe. Early in the eighteen thirties my grandfather started a banking firm. It never became important, but continued into the nineteenth century, when it was taken over by the Palatine bank. The firm as such survived and administered the family fortune. The small bank had a good name. My grandfather enjoyed a fine reputation; two of his sons, William and Leo, rose to eminence in high finance. One became head of Speyer and Co. in New York, and later partner in the Frankfort house; the other, head of Speyer's London establishment.

Grandfather, whom I remember slightly as a tall man with piercing eyes and a quick temper, had the grand manner. It was much easier to achieve in days when one strutted about in top hats and double-breasted frock coats. He cultivated it, I am told, carefully and successfully; it stood him in good stead. He was supposed to be very successful financially, which he was not. When he died—during the severe crisis at the end of the seventies—he did not leave much money, but he had managed to impress people and, not least, his sons.

Grandfather was the head of a clan whose members were trained in clannishness. Grandmother was all kindness and sweetness, but she died (I think she was older than he was) before I ever gained a clear picture of her. Grandfather had married her at the same time as his sister married her brother— Uncle Louis Schuster. Uncle Louis brought a note of healthy vulgarity into the family, plainly visible in the second set of his children—his first wife had died early. They radiated coarse vigor, had no spiritual aspirations, and associated cheerfully and successfully with Gentiles of similar disposition. The Schuster children grew up with the Bonns—there were five Bonn boys and four girls, and five Schuster boys and four girls; they must have been a lively crowd. All this, of course, was before my day.

I remember a dark house, Schützen Strasse 12 (with a corkscrew staircase), in which the grandparents lived on the top floor with Aunt Charlotte, their eldest daughter, whose husband had died early. After Grandmother's death she took care of Grandfather, and later on of her brother Philip, who was widowed. The house had a lovely garden; it stood next to a synagogue and was close to the "Philanthropin," a school to which I was sent at the beginning of my scholastic career.

When Grandfather died in 1879, Uncle Philip and Aunt Charlotte joined the westward move which most of the well-to-do families had started; the poorer and the more old-fashioned people remained in the eastern quarter. We followed only later, moving to Mainzerland Strasse 15, for at that time, my father having died, we were the poor members of the family.

Uncle Philip and Aunt Charlotte's house was the center of the family. As he stammered a little, he had stayed at home while his brothers were sent abroad, and had joined Grandfather's banking firm. He was a shrewd, practical man who had succeeded in making a good position for himself in local affairs. He was for many years on the local chamber of commerce and on the municipal council. As its financial member he had a good deal to do with shaping the city's financial policies. I never got very close to him. His main function in my life seemed to be to haul me over the coals when I had overstepped the limit and when my mother felt that she could not cope with me.

A bachelor brother, Uncle Maurice, lived with them—the bad boy of the family. He had been sent to Paris to learn business under the guidance of his cousin, the eldest Schuster boy; failing to make good, he was shipped to South Africa, where the Boers had built up two small republics across the Orange and Vaal Rivers. They bought a few European items in return for wool, skins, ostrich feathers, and ivory; trading houses in Cape Town, Port Elizabeth, and East London had established a series of upcountry stores by furnishing goods on credit to reliable young men. The eldest Schuster girl, Aunt Jenny, had married one of these traders, who was supposed to be very rich and able to finance some of his impecunious relatives. Thus Uncle Maurice established himself at Aliwal North, Lady Grey, and later on, Bloemfontein. Two of Aunt Jenny's brothers followed, Bernard and Berthold. Her husband's glory did not last long. He was decent enough to shoot himself before involving his family in fraudulent bankruptcy proceedings. Aunt Jenny had originally refused to marry him because he did not come up to her cultural standard, but she acted the inconsolable widow very thoroughly and managed to buy herself, before sailing for Europe, a complete mourning trousseau, including black-edged washrags—no small achievement in the Cape Town of a hundred years ago. Uncle Maurice and the Schusters stayed on. The former had to shoulder a gun and play a manly part standing sentry in some of the Kaffir wars. I doubt whether he burdened his conscience with the death of a native, though he used to tell me many stories of his heroic African days. He evidently got on very well with the Boers, for he was a good mixer and a kindly soul. He came back to Europe before the diamond boom with little money and no prejudices.

After his return he started various commercial ventures, none of them successful. Finally he was taken into the banking firm and entrusted with purely formal duties. When Uncle Philip died and a cousin took over the bank, the old boy was made a partner on the understanding that he was to do nothing except share the profits. Unfortunately, for a year or two they did well and his share ran into big figures. He began to spend lavishly; when the lean years came, he was short of cash and started to borrow money all round from my mother and from his sisters. So he had to be retired, which offended him bitterly. But as he did not care for work, he quickly calmed down. When he died he had saved enough to leave to each of his many nephews and nieces £100.

One cold Saturday, when the streets were iced, he passed along by the synagogue—he never went inside one—puffing a huge cigar. He slipped up—the service was just over, and two worshipers came to the rescue. They had very nearly got him to his feet when they discovered the cigar. "Smoking a cigar on the Sabbath!" they yelled, and dropped him unceremoniously. He left a dog, which we adopted, and which my sister's companion used to take out for walks. When she passed a certain house, he got very excited and strained at the leash. Being of an inquiring mind, she let him lead her. He ran upstairs, barking wildly, until a door opened and he was greeted affectionately by a lady of whose existence the female members of the family did not care to be informed. Uncle Maurice had always been a lady's man. During one of his impecunious spells he had interested himself, so he told my mother, in charities. He managed to wheedle out of her a dressing gown for a poor woman. A little later she found out that the poor woman was one of his lady friends.

My father had died a few days before my fifth birthday; a few months later, my only sister was born. To my mother, his death meant the end of her world. She had been brought up in the country and had no personal friends in the city. She had been taken into the bosom of a very large family and been taught to admire every member of it. She often told me that Father had been a very superior person; I suppose this was true. In any case, she saw him in that light, and after his death she withdrew from almost all wider contacts. The large family, imbued with the clannish spirit that permeated upper middle classes in the mid-Victorian age, sufficed her. When I first read *The Forsyte Saga,* I seemed to meet groups of cousins, once or twice removed perhaps, and socially a little more successful. Later on, when I peeped once or twice into true Bostonianism or breathed for a longer period the air of the Main Line near Philadelphia, I almost recaptured the atmosphere of some of those days long past.

Until the death of my maternal grandfather, in 1888, Mother had to live on a limited though generous income. We had no manservant as the others had, and we kept no carriage even after we had become opulent. Somehow we never went in for such comparatively cheap luxuries of those comfortable days; it meant that while the rest of the family was prospering financially and branching out socially, we remained where we had been. It was very hard on my sister when she was brought out. Fortunately she was very pretty, with a great deal of charm, and was gifted with easy social manners. Yet she would scarcely have married her first husband, the well-known Italian painter Aristide Sartorio, had she had wider social opportunities in her early life. The family was not limited to uncles and aunts—it embraced all sorts of cousins with their spouses, in-laws, and offspring; all the aunts expected to be duly kissed by me whenever I was taken around, a procedure I hated as a little boy, even when the aunts were attractive. Every Friday evening the family met in Uncle Philip's house; he tried to perpetuate the unity of the clan that Grandfather had impressed upon him. As soon as I could behave myself, I was taken around and sat with other small cousins at the lower end of the board. I have never eaten more ample or better food, but I did not become profoundly impregnated with the family spirit. Mother had deliberately adopted the whole clan and held them up to me as models of perfection. I was not impressed by many of these worthies.

What irritated me most was that they always died at the wrong time; I did not miss their presence, but Mother insisted that I, as her representative, should attend their funerals, which I thoroughly disliked. They always happened to interfere with other plans of mine. At one time I was president of a boys' riding club and we were to give a gala performance of our equestrian art at the end of the winter. I rode at their head and bossed them, as I was told later on, with ruthless brutality. Just before our final rehearsal for the great feat, at which I was to ride a kind of palomino pony and jump tandem with it and another pony, one of Father's cousins died. He was duly buried on the day of the rehearsal. I was heartless enough to ignore the grievous loss we had suffered—he meant nothing to me—and attended the rehearsal. Mother did not forgive me for a very long time.

Apart from the great Friday reunions, the family regularly dined at each other's houses once or twice a week. In summer Uncle Philip and Aunt Charlotte went to the country, to Cronberg, within easy train or carriage distance from Frankfort. They owned a big garden running down a hill, with several unassuming houses; in one of them was a huge dining room. We went there nearly every Sunday morning in fine weather, by train or in a family carriage, and spent the day with the family. I liked the country; but it was a very tame affair when compared with the Austrian mountains, where I was allowed to roam widely and mix with farm laborers.

The family's ways were very strict. My girl cousins who were of my age were never allowed to visit us except in the presence of their governesses. Some precaution was justified, as far as I was concerned, for—measured by the prevailing standard—I was a devil. One day one of my small cousins wanted to kiss me, a proceeding I greatly disliked. To retaliate, I lifted her onto a branch of a small plum tree, where she was ensconced quite safely and quite comfortably. But she could not get down by herself and raised an awful wail.

Hospitality at the "Villa Bonn" was on the grand scale. The road passing the house led to the highest mountain in the district, the Feldberg. Many Frankforters used to go there every Sunday in fine weather to train for real mountaineering. Some of them passed the Villa Bonn about ten or eleven o'clock; they got sandwiches and drinks. The next batch would come for midday dinner, followed by a few stragglers who stayed for after-dinner coffee; another batch returning from the mountain would drop in for tea, and latecomers expected supper. They rarely announced their intentions ahead, yet there was always enough to feed them royally.

## 4. *My Mother's People*

My mother's people, the Brunners, lived in Hohenems, a large village in Vorarlberg. This part of Vorarlberg is a narrow strip of land on the right bank of the upper Rhine, before it enters Lake Constance. The valley was but a few miles broad; its left bank was Swiss, its right Austrian; the river often overflowed. When the snow on the mountains melted, the Austrian fringe became a big lake. The village was situated at the foot of the mountains. Just above it were the ruins of an ancient castle, which had played its part in German literature; one of the earliest texts of the Nibelung saga was found in it. The soil was poor, partly covered with reeds; before the river was properly canalized, planting crops was too risky. In winter the mountains on the Swiss side cut off the sun. Most of the land was under grass, meadows, and coarse pastures. The peasants had little patches of boggy land on which they grew Indian corn (locally called Turkish corn), pumpkins, and beans; they kept a few cows and calves, and some had horses. Early in summer the cattle were sent to the mountain pastures, in care of the village herdsman, who used the milk for making cheese. On the first or second of October, when the cold set in on the high altitudes, the herd came down in solemn procession. The best milker was crowned as queen and decked with flowers;

the whole herd, with bells tinkling, was driven through the village streets, and each one returned to its owner.

In the center of the village, abutting the ·mountainside, the counts of Waldburg-Zeil had built themselves a huge palace; in the days of my youth it was still inhabited by one of their descendants, though their landed possessions had shrunk considerably. Under the protection of early ruling counts, who had been the owners and the sovereigns of the region, a small Jewish settlement had been established hundreds of years ago. The community had originally consisted of a few petty traders. Some of their successors, to whom the chances at home seemed too narrow, had gone to other lands. Others had stayed and become cotton manufacturers on a considerable scale. In the middle of the nineteenth century a number of cotton mills, run with the local water power, had been established. They did not go in for very high-class products, their main markets being the backward Slavonic regions of the empire and the near Balkan states, reached through Trieste. Peasant girls whose people were unable to make a good living on the land were quite willing to work in the mills.

Cottage industries flourished. The valley, on both sides of the river, was the center of the embroidery industry. On a fine summer day one could see the women working on their frames in front of every house. Later on, a special machine was constructed that fitted into the homes of the cottagers, and the men could work it. Farming had become a mere subsidiary occupation. The cottagers began to depend on their industrial output, which was sold throughout the world by merchants established in the city of St. Gallen beyond the Swiss side of the valley, until the competition of manufacturing plants and the imposition of the McKinley tariff ruined this primitive way of production. The people were very industrious, but they remained poor; in character and attitude they were more like the Swiss across the Rhine than like their Austrian fellow citizens behind the Arlberg Mountain.

My grandfather's parents were very unimportant people. His eldest brother migrated early in life to Trieste, where he prospered greatly. If I remember rightly, the main early activities of his business consisted in buying British goods in Manchester and distributing them through Dalmatia, Croatia, Bosnia, and

Albania. I knew him as a very old man who possessed many of the by no means lovable characteristics usually attributed to a successful patriarch. By and by he sent for his brothers, among them my grandfather. The young boy had to make his way with very little money from the most westerly corner of Austria down to the Adriatic. He made part of the journey on a mail coach and a little of it on the railway; most of it had to be done on foot.

In those days Austria was a Mediterranean power; she owned Venice and Lombardy. The brothers did well in their business, importing raw cotton for Austrian mills. Its nature changed in two directions. They began to sell Austrian and Swiss textiles instead of English cotton goods; and in order to do so, they established a branch in St. Gallen, which transformed itself by and by into a banking house, serving a large part of eastern Switzerland. Grandfather early left Trieste to take over the management of the St. Gallen business. He bought a large eighteenth-century house in Hohenems and went to live there, or at least his family did. His wife had died early. His five children were left in the charge of a series of female cousins, one following the other—the last one became my step-grandmother. He married her after all the children had left home. Grandfather spent the week in St. Gallen and came to Hohenems for the week end. The railroad on the Swiss side took him in about two hours to the Rhine, where his carriage met him for another two hours' drive. Before the rambling wooden bridge had been built, the river had to be crossed by ferry, and when the waters were high and a snowstorm was raging, this was no child's play.

Grandfather, when I first knew him, had retired. He lived in the huge, patrician-looking house on the main street of the village; I still own it, jointly with my cousins, now that the Nazis have had to disgorge their plunder. Behind the house was a large square courtyard, paved with cobblestones, on two sides of which were stable buildings and woodsheds. On the street side of the yard was a small garden; on its other side a much bigger garden, with all sorts of fruit trees and a lovely pergola covered with grapevines. I spent a great deal of time with Grandfather, for after my father's death he insisted on our coming and staying with him whenever we could, which was easy before my school days. Once school began, life was not as pleasant; the summer vacation lasted only a month. Usually at the end of July we had to return home and swelter until the first days of September. Then we were let off again for another fortnight, the autumn vacation. This silly arrangement had fitted in very well with Germany's earlier agrarian structure. July was the harvest month for grain crops; in September fruits had to be picked, activities in which child workers could be used. For us who lived in a city, it merely broke the vacation.

The journey was long and uncomfortable. We had to take a train to Lake Constance—three quarters of a day, or most of a night; there were no sleepers on that line—and from Friedrichshafen, later famous as the birthplace of the Zeppelins, we took a boat across the lake, which was a pleasant part of the trip. When I had not been trainsick, I was allowed to eat the lovely sausages that are the pride of Switzerland. We disembarked in Bregenz and passed the Austrian customs; this was exciting. Austria taxed heavily a good many consumers' goods; it was great fun to smuggle in a few of them and to outwit the guardians of what I considered an unfair law. I have never been able to make up my mind whether my free trade opinions originated there or in the teaching of my free trade friends. The last lap was an hour's train ride until we emerged at the village station, to be met by a porter with a long, flowing white beard. He had such a heavenly smile that one of my small cousins walked straight up to him and inquired, "Are you God Almighty?" When the greetings were over, we were packed into a heavy landau drawn by two cumbersome white horses, and four weeks of bliss lay ahead of us.

Our house still stands on the main street of the village, called, until the advent of the Nazis, Marco Brunner Strasse, after my grandfather. It is a dignified-looking town house, three and a half stories high, the top floor covered by a French red-tiled roof. Its gray front and its green and white shutters exhale a kind of civic pride—a sort of consciousness of its solid permanency, though it is only a hundred and fifty years old. One enters a dark, damp vault—there are no cellars—through a massive double door. On each side are storerooms. One ascends a steep, winding staircase and lands on a wide hall opening into rooms. There is a quaint door on each side of the wide landing, leading into a closet where firewood is stored and from which the huge white porcelain stoves are heated.

The rooms are low, the windows hardly reaching above one's knees. The floors are laid with beechwood intersected by broad stripes of stained oak. The two living floors are almost identical. The third floor has only a few rooms; it leads into a vast loft, where the discarded treasures of dead generations slumber. There was of course no sanitary plumbing. We had a contraption by which we pumped the water from the fountain to the top floor.

The glory of the place was our playroom. It faced south and west, toward the stables and the garden. To reach it one had to pass through the kitchen, with its glittering copper pans; and twice a week at least, the smell of fresh roasted coffee pervaded the air. Old Austria was the only Western land where people really knew how to make coffee. The playroom had a strawberry-colored china stove, in the apertures of which we bred silkworms. They needed the even temperature that the stove provided, and the greedy little beasts kept us busy picking mulberry leaves in the garden—Grandmother had brought the art of handling the worms with her from her native district, Bozen. From the southern windows we had a view of the Säntis, the Electors, and the Three Sisters in near-by Switzerland; even on the hottest summer day they wore a cap of snow.

Grandfather did a little farming of the subsistence type. We had a few cows to provide the household with milk, though we generally bought butter; we had hay enough to feed the horses. Oats, bran, and beets had to be bought. Early in spring Grandfather purchased a few young bullocks, to sell them in the autumn. We got chicks from a wandering peddler who carried them in a coop on his back. We kept the hens and ate the cocks. Life was simple but ample. Local stores were poor; delicacies were unobtainable. Every week a man passed by with a small barrel containing live trout. We put them in the trough of the well that ran day and night.

The contrast to my Frankfort existence was complete. Grandfather was not very social and was quite happy to be left with his family. The only regular social intercourse he indulged in was a daily visit to a small café where he went after dinner—

we dined at twelve o'clock—to spend an hour with some cronies for a game of "Tarok."

I had learned to watch for the bang of the main door that preceded by a few minutes his going to his room for a nap. He used to spread a lovely red silk bandanna handkerchief over his face to keep the flies away. I had to attune myself completely to his home-coming, for Grandmother was a strict disciplinarian, and being bent on reforming me, frequently found me in trouble. I was packed up to a room on the top floor and as punishment locked in for a few hours. No amount of yelling availed until I discovered that Grandfather's room was just below me. By saving my breath and waiting to yell until a few minutes after the door had banged, I could make sure he would hear me just as he was going to sleep. He then would run up indignantly and let me out, usually taking my side.

Life in Austria strengthened the Austrian note that Frankfort recollections had awakened in me. Grandfather, like every good Austrian, hated Prussia; especially Prussian conscription. He had spent most of his active life in Switzerland and was very keen on my emigrating there in order to get rid of the hated military service, but this did not come to pass.

The connection I did have with Switzerland was to prove very important: from my very earliest days on, I saw democracy "in being." I was often amused in later life when my North German friends discussed Austria or Switzerland from the point of view of visitors to a summer resort. In their minds, hotelkeeping, Switzerland, and democracy were identical. Fortunately, I knew better.

I stayed with Mother's family in Trieste, who had intimate contacts with Italy and the Balkans. These visits gave me a much more varied background than most people of my age possessed. They provided a counterweight to the prejudices and the narrow self-sufficiency that are indigenous to a proud city republic and even more flourishing in a defunct one.

Mother was a born romantic; all her life she lived in dreams. She bequeathed this priceless gift to me, and I became very grateful to her for it—after I had learned to indulge in this psychic form of opium eating in a moderate way. For a life without dreams is empty; a life of nothing but dreams, futile. I have kept between these two extremes. Mother had grown up in a lonely place; she had a younger sister whom she loved dearly but who had a thoroughly practical turn of mind—one of the ablest women I ever met, who could have played an important part in affairs had she had a proper modern training. But the height of female education in the sixties was a finishing school in Switzerland. Both Mother and Aunt were sent to Geneva. They learned languages and deportment, and Mother made friends with a Swiss girl. It was a friendship that lasted through her life, and which we inherited. I am always sure of a warm welcome in Berne, where I am talked to in the local dialect—which is the true test of friendship in Switzerland.

I have always thought it somewhat incongruous that people pride themselves vociferously on their nationality. From the individual's point of view nationality is an accident, the one and only event in life for which persons deserve neither credit nor discredit. They ought to be grateful to fate that they were born into a society whose accomplishments deserve recognition and have given them advantages they would otherwise have missed. I have always considered myself fortunate to have been born in a place impregnated with the spirit of an independent city republic and permeated by the tradition of a universal empire. To this combination I owe, on the one hand, a modicum of civic pride, which was little cultivated in post-Bismarckian Germany, and on the other hand, an understanding of a multicolored world-embracing universalism, which, in an age of assertive, exclusive nationalism, keeps one apart from the madding crowd.

I was equally fortunate in matters of faith. To belong to a small, not highly thought-of religious community is undoubtedly a social disadvantage. Yet the consciousness of being somewhat different from most of one's fellow citizens makes up for it; it gives one the vantage point of detachment. It may prevent one from being swamped by a craving for oneness with a more or less amorphous crowd; it contributes to a kind of personal integrity. It makes it easy to break away from hoary traditions; one has not to pay for personal freedom by being subjected to social excommunication, which might be strong enough to paralyze one's efforts. One becomes free without having to wear a martyr's crown.

# II. The Education of a Liberal

## 1. School

GERMAN CIVILIZATION, unlike English civilization, was city bred. Even in rural areas, people usually lived in more or less compact villages. Education was compulsory. Nearly all schools were day schools; one got one's fill of knowledge from them, but (with few exceptions) they were not expected to put their own particular hallmark on one. Starting after one's seventh birthday, one went for three years to the primary school and for nine years to the high school, which delivered one, after a stiff exam, to the university. One spent six mornings in the week in school, from eight to twelve, and four afternoons from two to four. One was not expected to develop a community spirit, as signified by the old school tie—though some schools did have colored caps. When we were asked to don these, we rebelled against what we considered a Prussian attempt at "militarization." I was one of the leaders in this successful agitation. Our slogan was:

"Judge them by their fruits, not by their caps."

The school was a kind of pipe line that would shoot one straight through—not painlessly—into the university. Being what I am, I was fortunate not to have had to pass through an English public school. My deep-seated hatred of militarism was not caused by its murderous aspect. Like most boys, I had collected a large army of tin soldiers, with which I fought over all the battles I had heard of; they were mostly colonial in the eighties, and of course colorful. But I loathed barrack life. Having been brought up in a house in which there was no other male, I had a highly developed sense of privacy. It has often made life difficult—I took a long time accustoming myself to the communism of the old American Pullman car. To sleep in

25

a kind of ward, with a half dozen other boys, would have been torture to me.

I was by no means pampered. My bedroom was not heated in winter; the window had to be kept open. I had to start the day with a cold shower, and when it was discovered that I eluded this by turning on the tap, which made the requisite noise, while I stood outside the curtain, a man was engaged as special supervisor who wrapped me in a wet sheet and poured cold water down my spine. This process of hardening was considered healthy. I still shiver when I think of it. But it was far better than being herded in with other boys. I am sure I would have been of that disgruntled minority who still suffer in spirit when they remember their school days, even when they have successfully followed Goethe's precepts and got rid of their bitterness by turning it into literature. I have often imagined that life under communism must be very much like being in a nationalized public school where one is taught the proper spirit. I have admired the products of English public schools, and I do not share the animosity in which people who have not been through them now indulge. I merely feel that I would have been a martyr to privilege had my people settled in London, as they would undoubtedly have done but for the early death of my father. Yet had I survived the ordeal, I might have greatly benefited from it. It might have taught me to work as a subordinate, and broken the crust of isolationism—individualism is too grandiose a term—by which I protected my sensitiveness. Nevertheless I am glad that I was spared the salutary experience—and even more glad that I never had to serve in the army.

High schools were usually maintained by municipal authorities. In rural areas they were located in the county town; boys from neighboring estates boarded with some of the teachers, which gave the latter an additional income. The standards of these county schools were generally not high; they had to graduate a certain number of students every year, otherwise taxpayers might have revolted and the central government withdrawn its grant in aid. This would have reduced greatly the amenities of local social life. High school teachers, called professors, formed an important part of local society; they did not rank with judges or with the head of the local government administration, yet they belonged to what was called the *Honoratiores*, who had a reserved table in the town's best inn or in its café. There they regularly met in the evenings, playing cards or dominoes, and discussing world affairs—always seated according to official rank.

My own school was a *Gymnasium* dedicated to the teaching of the humanities. The school ranked high among others of its type; its flag bore the slogan, in Latin, "We learn for life, not for the school." We did not believe it. Our aim was to pass exams, to get rid of the whole thing and to go to the university. Our principal was Tycho Mommsen, brother of the great historian Theodor Mommsen; the heads of the municipal education department imagined, it was said, that they had secured the services of the world-famed scholar for teaching their charges the elements of Latin grammar. Tycho, too, was very learned. I once came across his edition of Pindar's *Odes* in an American college library. He did not enjoy ruling or teaching us; we had nicknamed him "the Hedgehog."

We started at once pursuing the verb *amo* through all its tenses. I have never been able to understand why little boys, none of whom will ever make a declaration of love in Latin, must begin reciting "I love, thou lovest, he loves," when so many other verbs are available. We did history and geography, German, mathematics, natural sciences, physics, and later on, chemistry. I had no difficulty in getting along, but I doubt whether I was really interested in anything except zoology. Professor Noll was a great naturalist and a born teacher, far too good for us. I fell an easy prey to his enthusiasm. I made up my mind to become an African explorer. Very soon I had read everything about Africa I could get hold of, an intellectual investment that, unlike many other intellectual ventures, paid rich dividends later, when I was injected into colonial affairs.

As Frankfort depended on its international connections, we were expected to speak foreign languages. We had to learn French as well as Greek. I have a natural facility for picking up languages, but I loathe grammar. The only language I really enjoyed learning was English; its meager grammar enabled me to pick it up in my own way by reading and remembering words at random. Our French master, a descendant of

French Huguenots who had settled in Silesia, was an extremely bad teacher and cut a ridiculous figure. I came to know him well on account of my irascible temper. When a small boy, I had thrown a teacup at my nurse; I explained with a good deal of pride that I had done it very carefully, as, by a kind of miracle, it had not been broken. Mother tried to cure me by appealing to my vanity. She told me of an ugly red manikin who danced on my forehead whenever I got mad. I hated the little fellow; I did not want to be disfigured by him; she had merely to mention him and I attempted to control myself. I finally succeeded. I had been very naughty at home and I had tyrannized my young sister. One day Mother informed me that she had to go to Franzenbad in Bohemia to take the waters; I must board for two months with my French teacher, who would look after my mind and my morals. It was a very successful punishment. My morals were not improved, there being beside me a number of other naughty boys. But I disliked the place and the conditions prevailing in it so intensely that I decided to reform my ways.

My sister had French governesses. I had been taught in school to regard France as our hereditary enemy. Being a great patriot, I had a moral excuse for not wanting to learn her language. Yet I did pick it up, and fairly well at that, almost against my will, for one of these governesses was intelligent, and the other, who was not intelligent, was attractive. My accomplishment greatly irritated the French master, for I did no homework; I knew much more than we were expected to know. He tried hard to trip me up; I outsmarted him. I look back on these duels, fought out in front of the entire class, with a good deal of satisfaction. For I stood for the principle that it does not matter whether or not you have sweated over a subject, provided you master it. To his great disgust I always did.

My school days were not exciting. I was fortunately more intelligent than the majority of my schoolfellows. Half of them came from old Frankfort families; the others were the sons of new arrivals, Prussian officials, whom we natives greatly despised, and perhaps not without good reason. We natives were rather a lazy lot; we studied, sometimes because we were interested in a subject, but largely because we had to do so to get into the university. The sons of Prussian civil servants, judges, and army officers had a different outlook on life. They were filled with intense competitive ambitions. They were out for careers, which meant that they had to do better than everybody else. They were not more intelligent than we were, but they worked very much harder, and—what we hated most—they were subservient to their teachers. We liked some teachers and disliked others. We usually regarded them more or less as superior warders, who kept us locked up and tried to spoil our fun. The Prussians, on the other hand, saw them with the eyes of the conscript; they were their commanding officers, whom His Majesty the King had put above them, who not only deserved respect but might respond to adulation. A number of our teachers belonged to old Frankfort; they had an understanding of independence and of the dignity of human personality. They liked the Prussians as little as we did, but of course they could not show their sentiments. Others again, especially the younger ones, were genuine Prussians who had been officers in the reserve. Those who had been in the Franco-German War were rather mellow; those who belonged to a later generation were what they called *schneidig*; the word "sharp" reflects only the more pleasant aspect of their attitudes.

Prussian school administration in our city had accepted the slogan that "Prussia must make moral conquests in Germany." It sent us some good men who were enthusiastic about the classics. Yet their minds were split. They were filled with an overflowing admiration for republican Greece; they made Pericles and Demosthenes our heroes. At the same time they were loyal Prussian reserve officers, who clicked their heels—at least spiritually—when the King's name was mentioned. This combination of Greek democracy and Prussian militarism was irresistibly comic, though its basic incongruity dawned on me only much later. The best of them was Karl Reinhard, who succeeded Mommsen as principal and became a great reformer of the German educational system.

I never really enjoyed school life, except my tussles with the teacher of German, who had to acknowledge that I wrote the best essay in the class, but who was horrified at the subjects I had chosen and the views I expressed. He belonged to the group of anti-Semitic Christian socialists that the court preacher Adolf

Stöcker had founded in Berlin, and which was soon joined by Friedrich Naumann, who had come as pastor to Frankfort. Naumann later on formed a small party of his own and finally became a liberal leader. It was he who coined the term "National Socialism." I met him first as a schoolboy in his unregenerate days.

School bored me; I had plenty of time, which I spent in indiscriminate reading. I developed a habit of dreaming that I am afraid I have indulged all my life. I learned about as much as the average boy of my age was supposed to know, with the exception of mathematics, where I had very bad teachers and where I was a very bad pupil. Most of my comrades were indifferently gifted. They naturally set the pace. I could jog along without overexerting myself. Very early in life I acquired the dangerous trick of knowing (or imagining that I knew) what was essential; I picked that out and let the rest take care of itself. I had a very good memory, particularly for literary subjects. I could easily remember anything that made a genuine impression on my mind, though never quite accurately. My French friends used to compliment me later on by saying that I had a Latin mind—*l'esprit gaulois*. I suppose they meant that capacity for quickly grasping main points and not taking the trouble to master details.

The most defective part of my education was religion. In company with two other boys, I had a few private lessons in Biblical history from a very worthy but extremely inefficient teacher; I heard a little at home, and in the holidays I went to the synagogue with Grandfather. I liked the plaintive melodies, and I was riveted, on the Day of Atonement, watching old Henry Wellnamed (this was actually his name) taking the ram's horn with deliberation from under his silk bandanna, and blowing it to announce that the day of fasting was over. He had few teeth left, and he had to try several times before he managed to wheedle a raucous wail from the instrument. I was on tenterhooks, for if he failed we had to stay on, while the *Guggelhupf* and the coffee waited for us to break the fast.

But the regular Saturday service was a trial to me. I was terrified that I might be called up, as other boys were, and seated on a little stool, hold up the *Thorah* to be unrolled. I need not have been frightened; not having been confirmed, I could not be admitted to this honor. Grandfather was, moreover, never called to read the scriptures. He was the most important member of the small community, but somehow he had quarreled with it and refused to take an active part in its life.

The fact that religion was not rammed down my throat has saved me from that violent antireligious (not merely antichurch) sentiment which animated so many of my contemporaries—though the preceding generation was even worse. I have always approached religious problems in a respectfully detached, impersonal way. I have had to worry about the meaning of life and the sense or senselessness of the world as much as other people have, with the same inconclusive results, I suppose. But I have been spared the agonies of doubt about sin and salvation. Hell never meant anything to me, nor did Paradise. No doubt I missed some profound spiritual experiences; but some of them eat so deeply into one's mind that they warp it for all time to come. I have been saved from both the joys of exaltation and the horrors of despair. Curiously enough, members of other faiths have often poured out their hearts to me when the anguish of doubt gripped them; by sympathetic listening I may have soothed their pangs. Maybe I have wandered through life in a kind of "chiaroscuro." I never yearned for life everlasting, though like most of my fellow creatures, I have sometimes tried in vain to hold the fleeting moments from fading into pale memory. But the mere thought of eternity makes me shiver. Its vast emptiness makes me feel like a castaway on an arctic ice floe. It seems but natural to me that things which have a beginning should have an end, and if we can glide out of life without pain, as unconsciously as we slipped into it, finality has no terror for me—though of course nobody knows how he will stand up to the final test.

## 2. The Stage

If the essence of liberalism is respect for other personalities and noninterference with their ways, Mother was a liberal. She was one by temperament, for she had no educational principles; being convinced that her children could do no wrong, she left them alone. I sometimes disappointed her grievously, though most of my evil deeds were not very bad. Having read the story of William Tell, I once put a matchbox on my small sister's head and hit it clean with a popgun; I was very proud of this sporting achievement, but got no credit for it. Apart from such peccadillos and a little street fighting with other boys, in which I usually got the worst of it until I discovered that I could ram them in the stomach, thanks to a hard head and a strong neck, I was manageable.

Left largely to myself, I developed a shy, and at the same time ferocious, kind of individualism. I could easily be talked round by being told to be reasonable; I hated to be ordered about. I looked forward with terror to my years of military service, though not because I was namby-pamby. I was a good horseman and not a bad shot, and dreamed of nothing but dangerous expeditions into the wilds of Africa. But I hated the thought of being under the control of a sergeant who would be worse, if anything, than our teacher of gymnastics, who brandished a heavy leather strap, threatening all the time to give us a thrashing. Somehow I had managed to frighten him; he had no moral courage and let me alone.

Mother allowed me to smoke, a permission that in those years was scarcely ever given to a boy. Naturally I was not greatly tempted; I only tried it twice. I had gone to a rifle stand at the fair—the last remnant of the famous Frankfort Fair, for centuries the meeting place of north and south and east and west. I had hit the bull's-eye and won half a dozen of the worst cigars that ever came from a tobacconist's shop. I went home triumphantly. As bad luck would have it, one of my chums was waiting for me. We decided on testing the fruits of my prowess, and lit what in Germany were later called the "Stinkadores"; results were immediate, effective, and permanent.

This liberal education had its bad angles. I was frightened of the authorities. Being fatherless, I had to have contacts with officials that most small boys were spared. I was terrified when I had to face them, especially the lower grades. German postmen or railroad conductors did not ooze amiability; their salaries were low, their duties hard; by way of compensation, they were imbued with the notion that they were the local representatives of the Lords of Prussia or Bavaria, and that the last rays of the Divine Right of Kings radiated from them into the dingy offices where they had to serve the public. They were quite good-natured when one did not hurt their self-esteem; yet I always felt as did one of my Scotch terriers later on; he was a sweet-tempered dog, but he could not stand uniforms. We had to take out a special insurance policy, for whenever he had a chance, he attacked the mail carrier and tore up his pants. I am not sure whether I hated bureaucracies because I was a liberal, or whether I became a liberal because I hated bureaucracies. This childish dislike may have turned to my advantage later on when I had to deal with important affairs and was associated with secretaries of state and heads of government departments. I never felt elated, as did many of my colleagues who had come in touch with the high and mighty. I usually underrated their ability and was probably unfair to them; yet in a country like Germany where, next to the military, the civil service was "It," my attitude was salutary.

On my first visit to London as an adult, I discovered that the English capital possessed two kinds of theaters. Those called theaters were expensive; one went in full social war paint and was not allowed to smoke; the others, called music halls, were cheaper; one did not have to dress, and one could smoke. Otherwise there did not seem much to choose between them. In Germany things were different. Ever since the revival of German literature in the days of Lessing, Goethe, and Schiller, the theater had been considered an educational institution on the highest moral plane. Germany consisted of a great number of states and statelets, with an even greater number of cities. Every court and courtlet and all the bigger towns had permanent theaters. Not all of them could run to grand opera, although in pre-Wagnerian days demands on stage and scenery had been modest. Theaters performed every day, all the week round, at least in the winter months; in the fine season they sometimes migrated with their habitués to the several spas the latter patronized. One did not go to the theater, as in London or in New York, for a special treat; in the larger towns those who could afford it went three or four times a week all through the year. Tickets were cheap—through most of the nineteenth century Germany was a poor country. The better seats were usually subscribed for the season; certain weekdays were set apart for opening nights. In Frankfort, if I remember rightly, it was

Tuesday; opera was on Sunday and Thursday. The theater deficits were paid by the municipality or the court. Plays started early—generally between six and seven o'clock; businessmen went straight from their offices without dressing—towns were small and relatively clean, for there was very little industrialization. Performances were over by nine or ten. As dinner was at midday, by eight o'clock people were hungry, and during the long intermission they went to the "foyer," a kind of large room or passage, where sandwiches and light drinks were served. There they met their friends and discussed the performance with them. On a first night the foyer hummed like a beehive that has been disturbed—the disturber being the author of the play, who often got badly stung.

But the theater was not merely an important social institution; for a long time it had taken the place of the political forum. In the first half of the nineteenth century the greater part of Germany had no genuine parliamentary institutions. Books were censored; public meetings and political associations were either prohibited or severely controlled. Yet the air was full of problems that had to be discussed, and the place to do so was the stage.

Most of the problems that worried the nation in those decades were debated in more or less well-written tragedies. Long before "determinism" became a central issue in the social sciences, fate and destiny and man's incapacity to escape them were discussed in an almost endless series of plays (the so-called tragedies of fate). Since Lessing, religious tolerance had been demanded over and over again on the stage, long before it was advocated on the platform. The eternal triangle in married life formed an ever recurrent topic for an endless number of sociological tragedies. The celibacy of the Roman Catholic clergy was attacked in a pathetic peasant tragedy, *The Vicar of Kirchfeld*, at a time when the onslaught could scarcely have been made in the Austrian parliament. The stage not only reflected life; it replaced life.

Regular playgoers had the choice between the great tragedies of Shakespeare, Schiller, and Goethe and the modern problem plays. They received a generous education in the literature of most countries. Directors of theaters, who were very important people in the life of their communities, had to have their pro-

grams cover most of the year; the public was too small to allow
long runs even of a new play that had made a hit. No German
theater would have dared play Ibsen's *Ghosts* three hundred
times a year. However successful, a play had to disappear very
rapidly. The supply of good new productions was limited; producers had to ransack the dramatic literature of all nations.
German literature offered only a few good comedies—nothing
on the level of Shakespeare or Molière. So the managers had
to go abroad for lighter literature, for farces and more or less
comic society plays, often French.

An important part of my education came from the theater.
Mother had a subscription seat for one day of the week only.
But the family was large; whenever a seat was empty, word
would go around until somebody was found to occupy it.

At this time, the Social Question, spelled with capitals, was
invading the German stage. Ibsen had produced the modern
problem play. Like Shaw later on, he became a German institution. He was not sufficiently appreciated in his native country and had gone to live in Germany. Years after, in Munich,
I was shown with deep reverence the window seat he had occupied in the Café Maximilian. Ibsen had made a scathing attack on modern bourgeois society in *The Pillars of Society*,
though it was mild enough by modern standards. Sudermann
was castigating the antiquated concepts of the military caste in
his play *Honor*. These liberal, progressive bourgeois were far
outdistanced by young Gerhard Hauptmann, who brought the
proletariat onto the stage. His first play, *Before Dawn*, was a literary revolution. He became the darling poet of liberal, and
later the pride of republican, Germany. I was present at the
gala performance on his seventieth birthday. The Weimar Republic had prepared a crown of laurels for him; but it was delivered by Franz von Papen. Hauptmann did not mind the
change and calmly accepted the honors due him from the hands
of this anti-Republican archintriguer. He had celebrated the
occasion by writing a new, rather weak play that he called *Before Sunset*. Few of those present realized how near darkness
was, and how soon an all-engulfing night would fall on Germany.

On the first night of his first play, *Before Dawn*, the row was
terrific. It was a clash between two generations. The older peo-

ple were indignant that such unpleasant subjects were presented to a civilized public; the younger ones went mad with joy. My enthusiasm was not so much due to my admiration of the new art—I am not so sure I really liked it—but to the chance it gave me to join in a protest against silly conventions. I had done a lot of desultory and superficial radical reading. I had easily come to extreme conclusions. I knew probably less of actual life than most of my contemporaries. I was very much under my mother's influence, and she lived in a purely imaginary world of her own, far beyond the fringe of reality. After I had read Björnson's *A Bankruptcy,* I was quite sure that bourgeois society was rotten. I had got hold of Henry George through one of his German disciples, who wrote a voluminous book, *The Only Road to Salvation.* I was dazzled by Ferdinand Lassalle, who but for his vanity might have become Germany's great revolutionary leader. Marx loathed him, for he possessed the grand spectacular manner that the nineteenth century expected from a tribune. Naturally he appealed to a schoolboy to whom politics was identical with drama and oratory the most important part of literature. Marx, as a person, never attracted me. There was in him something of the stern, inhuman schoolmaster who meant to keep his class in order; and I disliked schoolmasters. Some of my young American radical friends call me a conservative. They ignore the difficulty of my getting excited about attacks on institutions I denounced fifty years ago when I lived in the age of innocence they have belatedly reached. It was grand to feel that one was marching with the vanguard and was a standard-bearer of a new age.

I read a great deal of poetry. Like most German boys of my generation, I wrote poems. I even worked on several tragedies. This, unfortunately, meant a sustained effort. I wasted many a glorious day of a summer vacation in writing a tragedy, which, alas, never was finished. I even started on a social comedy. A friend of the family who looked through my poems and found them fairly good gave me a piece of sound advice: "Poetry is an adorable mistress but not a good spouse." I took the hint. Fortunately I discovered early in life that I was not a literary genius of the first rank, and I was intelligent enough to realize that there is not much fun in being a second- or third-rate poet. One can be happy as a mediocre economist—most of us are in

that class—and one can even make a big income through culti-
vating one's mediocrity by writing marketable textbooks that
do not disturb youth's mental equilibrium.

## 3. Bismark and the "Frankfurter Zeitung"

From 1866 to 1890, Europe lived in the shadow of Prince
Bismarck. That shadow fell across my path when I was an immature schoolboy. My native city was a conquered state; the
older generation harked back to the glorious days of its republican independence; they hated the tyrant who had deprived
them of their political liberty—or should I say importance? By
1887–88 half of the German nation shared their views. From
the end of the seventies until his fall, Prince Bismarck had
found it next to impossible to secure a permanent majority in
a Reichstag he himself had established on the broad democratic
basis of manhood suffrage. He had started as a typical Prussian
Junker. The typical Prussian Junker was a small squire who
owned an estate in a usually not very fertile part of eastern
Prussia; he ran it with semiservile agricultural laborers, under
the direction of a farm manager (Inspektor). As he was not a
rich man, his offspring had to serve in the army and the bureaucracy in order to make a living. They despised trade; their
idea of a businessman was the small grocer in their village.
They were arrogant provincials; few of them could afford to
spend the winter in Berlin; they usually patronized and dominated the county town. They had not much use for intellectuals
but possessed a good deal of common sense. They knew how to
handle men. They respected those who dared to stand up to
them, and as long as one did not cross them, they were good-
natured. They were royalist to the core, though very independent. They needed a king of Prussia set above them as they
were set above the workers on their own estates. They were not
given to blind obedience and were ready to go into ruthless
opposition whenever their interests or their prejudices were
offended. They did not mind standing up against a misguided
king.

At the bottom of his mind Prince Bismarck shared the Junkers' contempt for everybody who was not a lord of the soil.

Like them, he held no very exalted view of mankind, its aspirations and its accomplishments. But he was only half a Junker. He possessed great intellectual powers, a large amount of political imagination and foresight, and with it all a deep-seated passion that singled him out from many of his peers in their almost bovine placidity. What in them was a rather low cunning had developed in him to brilliant astuteness coupled with sagacity. After his great triumphs in foreign affairs he became, at least outwardly, a kind of moderate liberal, and for over ten years remained so. Inwardly he had never changed. He meant to be a dictator in constitutional guise; he hated the parliamentary system. He was quite willing to lead a parliamentary majority, but he would not share power with it. He was a royalist, on the assumption that his king would back the policy that he himself considered right. Under William I this concept worked remarkably well. But the Bismarckian regime would have cracked under his successor, Frederick III, had the latter not been seized with a mortal illness that incapacitated him during his short reign. He could not get rid of the Chancellor, whom both he and the Empress, Queen Victoria's eldest daughter, hated. They were both liberals. Bismarck trembled at their advent; he saw the hand of a benign providence in the mortal affliction that freed him from a liberal master. For the Chancellor, not unlike President Hindenburg, was a primitive Lutheran. Whenever he was faced with a difficult situation that he meant to handle in not too strict observance with generally accepted moral principles, he took his troubles to his God, who gave him the strength to carry out his duties on the lines he had decided upon. He was fully prepared to leave the ultimate responsibility to the Almighty.

When Frederick III died, on June 18, 1888, I was a schoolboy. But I clearly remember the deep gloom his death cast over liberal Germany, whose hopes were concentrated on him. Had he lived, he would have compelled the great man either to resign or to accept parliamentary government. The dying king, who could no longer speak—he died of cancer of the throat—kicked out Bismarck's secretary of the interior, von Puttkammer, who had succeeded in stripping the Prussian bureaucracy of many of its best liberal traditions. Prince Bismarck had tried to get a medical opinion declaring the then Crown Prince unfit to rule. But for the energy of the Crown Princess, who secured the help of a British specialist, Sir Morell Mackenzie, who perhaps risked his professional reputation by defying the German experts, Bismarck might have succeeded. I was deeply impressed by the tragedy and wrote a funeral ode on the passing of Frederick III according to the best Greek models.

Bismarck's luck did not hold. He had deliberately impregnated German political life with economic issues by turning to protection; though the old political parties survived, they were torn internally by economic conflicts. At one time Bismarck had hoped to replace the political by a vocational parliament. He failed, but not before he had succeeded in making home politics subservient to economic issues. The Weimar Republic harvested the crop that Bismarck had sown, when democracy was turning vocational and the parties were being identified with economic interests. And he succeeded in one other respect. By deliberately depriving the leaders of the German parties of any share of political responsibility, he had made political careers unattractive to first-rate men. The second-raters, who sat on the front bench under his successors, managed to carry out the duties of an opposition to hamper and to criticize government; they had no hankering for power and were neither willing nor capable of shouldering the responsibilities of statesmen. If the German people have not shown great ability in the management of their political affairs, this was due not so much to inborn incapacity as to the devastating influence of Bismarck in preventing them from undergoing an apprenticeship. When William II had sacked him, and when he sat with bitter hatred in his heart under the tall oaks in his beloved forest, he realized his mistake. He recognized, too late, that William II could not have got rid of him had he stood at the head of a parliamentary majority. He had despised the "English influence" represented in Germany by Queen Victoria's daughter. Yet although the Queen loathed Mr. Gladstone, she had been compelled to accept him as prime minister over and over again, while Bismarck, the founder of the German Empire, the man who gave the imperial crown to the house of Hohenzollern, could be brusquely dismissed by her grandson, whose vanity would not brook a great minister.

I did not know the fundamental issues underlying events. I

felt no particular loyalty for William II—the Hohenzollerns were aliens to us in Frankfort. But I shared the feeling of relief experienced by millions of Germans when the news reached them that the young emperor had kicked out the old chancellor. In those days I could not do justice to Bismarck's greatness, especially to the moderation he had shown in foreign affairs after he had reached his goal. I saw in him only the embodiment of everything evil. Again I looked into my Greek textbook, and found the fragments of an ode composed by a Greek poet about two thousand years ago celebrating, if I remember rightly, the downfall of the tyrant Myrsilos of Mytilène. I wrote a beautiful imitation hailing the downfall of the new Myrsilos.

One great institution had developed in that small republic of Frankfort's before its downfall, which survived unharmed—the *Frankfurter Zeitung*. It became Germany's greatest newspaper—perhaps the greatest newspaper on the Continent.

After Frankfort had ceased to be the seat of the federal diet, no resident government was left that could influence the press. For this reason alone, the *Frankfurter Zeitung* was far more independent in every way than its great rivals in Vienna, Paris, or Berlin. Its owner and publisher resided in Frankfort; the social blandishments by which governments tried to domesticate obstreperous editors could not be applied effectively. Its Berlin representatives were close to the powers that be, especially after Bismarck's fall, when the foreign office had to seek support for its not always very intelligible policies. These friendly relationships did not modify the editorial attitude. The paper supported a government policy only when it approved it; it could not be dictated to from Berlin.

Its publisher, Leopold Sonnemann, was one of Prince Bismarck's pet aversions. He represented Frankfort very effectively in the German Reichstag until the year 1887, when he had to defend his seat against a Socialist and a National Liberal follower of the Prince's. No candidate had a majority, and a second ballot had to decide between Sonnemann and the Socialist. Prince Bismarck instructed his supporters by a telegram to transfer their votes to the Socialist, who was elected. Frankfort was indignant at Bismarck's shortsighted astuteness. He evidently preferred the representative of a party that was out-and-out revolutionary (at least on paper), expecting to prevent its further growth by passing antirevolutionary legislation with the aid of frightened philistines. The victorious Socialist, Sabor, was a vegetarian schoolteacher; I met him in the house of a family friend. He did not look like an advertisement for vegetarianism, nor like the embodiment of revolution. I have always felt that German and Anglo-Saxon socialists are born reformers, however loudly they may talk revolution. Even those who are not vegetarians are not bloodthirsty. The Russian breed, of course, even when extremely Westernized, is different.

Sonnemann was a South German Democrat, a member of a small party whose votes came mainly from Württemberg. It wanted a greater Germany, in which Austria was to be included, under the old imperial German colors, black, red, and gold—the flag the revolution of '48 had hoisted—not a "little Germany" dominated by Prussia and managed by a Junker. The party had only a few members, most of them with a small-town mentality. Yet they possessed the spirit of independence that frequently goes with it, and an understanding of social problems in which the far more brilliant, socially much better connected North German liberals were sadly wanting.

The upper stratum of the Frankfort electorate had become reconciled to Bismarck and was but mildly liberal. Yet a number of the well-to-do remained democrats. Many of them had lived abroad; nearly all had connections in every part of the world, especially in the Anglo-Saxon countries. A good deal of Frankfort's business, it is true, had been transacted with Austria, whose political system in those days could hardly be called progressive. Yet the city had close ties with the West; during the War between the States on the American continent, the Frankfort stock exchange had helped to finance the North. It was for many years one of the most important Continental markets for American railroad bonds.

The outlook of the *Frankfurter Zeitung* remained universal, not provincial. Its financial columns covered business transactions over the entire world. It did not limit itself to reporting them; it went into a ruthless analysis of the prospectuses it had published on its advertising pages. High Finance grumbled a good deal when reading this dissection of statements for the publication of which it had paid. Yet it could not dispense with the paper's services.

Sonnemann was a friend of my family. I grew up reading his paper. It did a great deal for my political education and for my education all round. In those days a great German daily differed very much from its Anglo-Saxon counterparts. Its service covered the globe, and its regional correspondents were excellent. But it did not limit itself to the role of a purveyor of news. It meant to be an educator. A large and able staff of editors interpreted for its readers events all over the world, and tried to teach them their proper appreciation. It did not restrict itself to political and economic events. In what was called "below the line" it published daily essays about new books, art, music, new ideas, in fact about everything worth reporting. For this purpose it had enlisted a large number of outside writers, many of whom did not share its political views. But the articles "below the line" were signed, while those "above the line" were not, and this gave the authors a wide publicity, for the paper was read regularly by influential readers in every country. Its remuneration, on the other hand, was not overattractive. If I remember rightly, my earliest long contribution netted me the lordly sum of seventeen marks, or just four dollars.

# III. Oracles and Professors

## 1. *Berlin*

CHOOSING a career seemed easy. After my maternal grandfather's death, we were well-to-do according to our standards. Mother built a large house; most of its space was taken up by a huge staircase that hung in an impressive void, which gave a great deal of trouble in the lean years of war and revolution when one could not get fuel. Apart from this, nothing changed. Mother was very generous; I could go to the university and study what I liked, irrespective of the remuneration it might or might not later bring.

I was not sure what I wanted to do. I had dreams of being a great writer, a great social reformer, and a great statesman. In the nineteenth century, politics and literature were still closely intertwined, even in Great Britain; words were frequently taken for deeds, and words were the instruments of the stage, of the press, and of the platform. I had tried oratory—we occasionally had to deliver an address in school—and failed lamentably: I mixed up too many ideas; I could not even have expressed them clearly had they not been half-baked. It took me a long time before I became a fairly good speaker—never an orator. I had to learn that one must master one's subject completely before one can elucidate it to others. Notwithstanding those failures, and they were very distressing, I was confident I would win in the end.

As to the family business, too many people around me whom I disliked were bankers, and I had no great ambition to take up their profession. But my problem became urgent when I had fallen in love and wished to marry quickly. Mother did not like the family to which my beloved belonged; I could scarcely expect her to finance an enterprise of which she thoroughly disapproved. Since bankers were well-to-do people, I thought of becoming one. My native city had hitherto been a preserve of private bankers; now joint stock banks were beginning to invade it. Some of their heads were lawyers and members of the Reichstag. I read their speeches and their articles. I might follow their example: choose a profession that would bring in an income, and besides become a statesman and an author.

At this juncture an adviser appeared, in the person of Dr. Georg von Siemens, the head of the Deutsche Bank established after 1871, who had made it one of the great institutions not only of Germany and the Continent but of the entire world. He stayed with one of my uncles, who mentioned me and my problems to him. Besides heading the Deutsche Bank, Siemens was a prominent liberal member of the Reichstag, where he represented the free trade doctrines held at that time by merchants, bankers, and shipping interests. He was a tall, heavily built man who affected old-fashioned frock coats—for he realized that his serious-minded constituents wanted a solid-looking deputy, not a well-dressed fop. The outcome of our conversation was that I should go to Berlin and consult Ludwig Bamberger, whose advice could be trusted.

Soon after this talk I set out for Berlin, provided with adequate letters of introduction; I must have been seventeen or eighteen. It was my first excursion on my own; I felt very important and I was greatly excited. I was sent to the Hotel Kaiserhof. Taking a room there and settling down in it was not an easy matter for a shy youngster. In those days the Kaiserhof was a kind of hub of the political universe of Berlin; a few steps from it were the Chancellery and the Foreign Office where Bismarck had lived and ruled. At lunchtime the great dining hall and surrounding foyer were crowded with guests, among them many leading politicians. Somebody asked me to lunch there—I would never have had the courage to occupy a table by myself among the many celebrities he pointed out to me. I felt greatly exhilarated.

Berlin itself did not impress me; everything was very new and extremely clean; streets and buildings were spacious, but there was a lot of tinsel meant to look like gold. I suppose I was unfair, for after all this was the red plush age. I had been brought up in it in Frankfort, where it seemed to be much more mellow since the shadows of the past softened its brazen glare. These were nonexistent in Berlin. The place was not unlike an oil city of the American west, which had grown up overnight and, feeling its strength, insisted on displaying its wealth; it was, of course, very much cleaner and more orderly, but not as homely and friendly. I knew very little about the history of the city. I had always looked upon Vienna as our capital; I had seen it before I had gone to Berlin and my aesthetic instincts strongly corroborated my political prejudice.* In Frankfort we held the Greek concept of wealth—not that we were great philosophers—that its possession makes a good life easy. Berlin was Roman; it went out for grab.

## 2. Three Oracles

Ludwig Bamberger lived in a quiet street of the old west end. I climbed the staircase with a good deal of trepidation. A manservant showed me into a large sunlit room—much more old-fashioned than anything in Grandfather's house in Austria. It contained a huge bookcase, a writing table, a few chairs, and a very ancient, hard-used sofa. This antedated the plush age, being covered with a kind of mauve, very faded corduroy-like stuff called rep; its Anglo-Saxon contemporary was made of horsehair. A small, bent, oldish-looking man with a pale, furrowed face, thin hair, and a thin, reddish gray beard received me and bade me sit down. His eyes were both serene and sad. He looked like a disillusioned, but extremely kind, aged fawn.

Ludwig Bamberger was a European figure. A descendant of a well-to-do Jewish family in the old city of Mayence, he had just graduated from the university when the revolution of '48 broke out. He participated in it, not in the manner of the minor intelligentsia by making speeches and writing articles; he took a gun into his hands and joined the fighting Free Corps in the Black Forest. After its defeat he managed to get across the Swiss frontier, otherwise he would have been court-mar-

* I have known all my life the ditty:
"There's but one imperial city,
  It's called Wien,
  There's but one robber's den,
  Its name is Berlin."

tialed and shot; as it was, he was condemned to death *in absentia*. He could hardly hope to return to his native country. Fortunately he had wealthy relatives and connections. He entered business and finally settled in Paris as head of one of the big international private banking firms. He recognized very early that Count Bismarck, as he then was, was not a mere Prussian Junker who hated liberals and was hated by them, but a statesman of great promise; he expressed these views in a brilliant essay in French called *Monsieur de Bismarck*. After Bismarck had defeated Austria, Bamberger returned, entered the "Customs Parliament," the forerunner of the German Reichstag, as representative of his homeland, and soon became a leading member of the National Liberal party, which in those days was genuinely liberal. He managed to become a great parliamentary debater, in an age when debates in the German parliament were on a very high level, and an open-air speaker of the first rank. In his election campaigns thousands of farmers and small-town citizens would flock together to listen with enthusiasm to this frail man who combined German sentiment with Gallic *esprit* and British matter-of-factness.

During the Franco-German War, Bamberger had come close to Prince Bismarck, who had used his great financial skill and his intimate knowledge of French affairs in the settling of the French indemnity. After the war Bamberger played a leading role in modernizing German economics. He induced the government to adopt the gold standard; the organization of the Reichsbank was mainly his work; his was the moving spirit in the foundation of the Deutsche Bank. He was a brilliant writer. His books on social questions, in which he expounded the doctrines of the Manchester School, are rightly forgotten. The essays he wrote in *Die Nation* were gems of mellow wisdom and sparkling irony.

Bamberger was one of the leaders of the "secession" that left the National Liberal party when Bismarck turned to protection. From that time on he became the Chancellor's relentless opponent, and a most irritating one, for he had the gift of coining epigrams. During one of the great debates on the tariffs, he told his opponents "Facts the gentlemen opposite cannot prove, they call practice; and facts they cannot refute, they call theory." He could not stem the tide of antiliberalism that

Bismarck had let loose but somehow he got even with him in the hundred days of the dying Emperor Frederick's reign. As unofficial adviser to the Empress he secured the dismissal of the archconservative von Puttkammer. He helped set the stage for Bismarck's fall by exposing in *The Bismarck Dynasty* the scheme to make his son Herbert his successor.

I do not remember the details of our talk; I was too much under the spell of my host. He seemed to have done all the things I wanted to do. He had become a successful banker, a leading politician, and what impressed me more than anything else, a brilliant writer. If I have learned the art of writing in simple language on complicated subjects, I owe it to him and to my friends Theodor Barth and Paul Nathan, the editors of Germany's one and only great weekly, *Die Nation*.

The outcome was that I should study political economy at the University of Heidelberg. Later on I might go to Munich, where Lujo Brentano was entering the final stage of his great career. Bamberger and Brentano were opponents on many issues, but each appreciated the other's brilliance.

My next call had no very practical purpose. I wanted to see Eugen Richter, the leader of the liberal Progressive party, the idol of all who hated Bismarck—the one and only parliamentarian the Chancellor actually seemed to fear. Richter, a sturdy, rather morose-looking Lower Saxon, was a philistine, but a philistine on a grand scale. He had qualified for an administrative career, and a small town had chosen him for its mayor; but the Prussian government, displeased with his political activities, had refused to sanction his election. Richter became what was very rare in those days, a professional politician. He was a first-class organizer, and built up an efficient party machine by rather primitive means. A great tactician, he was but a mediocre strategist.

As Bismarck became more and more autocratic, Richter grew in stature. He slipped into the role of antipope. He had no nerves, and no ambition for office. He was a consummate master of detail. He could not fight the Chancellor by constructive schemes of his own but was satisfied with mercilessly tearing to shreds the massive plans the Chancellor placed before the world. The struggle used to culminate in debates over new army estimates, which the Chancellor justified by the development of foreign affairs. Richter made himself a master of all budget details. He knew every item; generals and secretaries of war trembled at his inquisitiveness. He represented the unimaginative, upright antimilitarist attitude of the German middle class of those days, unwilling to give right of way even to the greatest statesman its people had brought forth. The Chancellor despised most of his opponents; being in a privileged position, he rather enjoyed their attacks and hit back at them viciously. Rarely was he able to sit through one of Richter's great speeches. He risked losing his temper when faced with an adversary of such imperturbability. He usually left when he saw Richter rise, who would shout after the departing Chancellor: "There he goes, it will but little avail him, he will find my speech on tomorrow's breakfast table!"

Richter and his associates owned and edited a daily, the *Freisinnige Zeitung*, the party's official organ, a dull paper but indispensable to anybody interested in German home politics. It was housed in a dingy office in one of the older parts of Berlin. To this holy of holies I directed my steps, bearing a few words of greeting from one of its Frankfort associates, eager to see the man to whom millions of Germans looked as their champion in the struggle between right and wrong. I was admitted to his presence with very little ceremony. He received me probably as kindly as he was able to do, but he certainly was not good at winning the hearts of the young. He sat at a large table covered with papers, a dour and heavy man. I tried to discuss with him some of my problems about studying political economy. He was one of those fortunate men who saw no problems and to whom everything was clear. He was right and those who opposed him were wrong. I left after a very short conversation, well satisfied with the meeting—not for the impression my host had made upon me, but for pride that I had had the courage to face the great man.

Having consulted one oracle on finance and another on politics, I turned to the academic world. A friend had arranged a meeting with Professor Gustav Schmoller, who received me in his little house in the Wormser Strasse that for many years was the Mecca of all ambitious young university professors. For Gustav Schmoller was a power in the land; nearly all appointments to chairs of economics were made at his recommendation.

Schmoller was born in one of the small Swabian cities that had been semi-independent constituents of the old Holy Roman Empire, usually ruled by a hereditary class of craftsmen and guild masters who considered themselves the salt of the earth and posed as patricians—some of their features, good and bad, have been portrayed in *Die Meistersinger*. Schmoller did not belong to this bourgeois "aristocracy," yet he represented their more distinctive features almost to perfection. The Swabians have been the best educated people in Germany. They possess a unique blend of ruthless realism and sentimental, dreamy romanticism. They have produced leading men in every branch of German life; poets like Schiller, philosophers like Hegel, religious writers like Bauer and Strauss, economists like List and Schmoller. They are typically lower middle class; even their aristocracy does not look distinguished. In their daily ways they are democratic.

Early in life Gustav Schmoller was called to a chair in Prussia. After the annexation of Alsace-Lorraine he was a leading light of the University of Strassburg, which was to outshine her French sisters. He had made his debut in economic history, in those days not yet popular, with an interesting study of the woolen weavers' guild in Strassburg. Called to Berlin, he unearthed the history of the Prussian civil service, established in the early eighteenth century by the most unattractive of European sovereigns, Frederick William I. Through these studies Schmoller fell in love with Prussia. In comparison with his Swabian home, Prussia was a large-scale state—almost a world power. To a discerning eye the expansive springiness of her later developments was visible in her earlier make-up, and Schmoller became her herald. As time went on, and as the Prussian state overflowed into the German empire, Schmoller's enthusiasm waxed more fiery, and with more justification. He had no background against which he could evaluate this novel imperial glory. He remained all his life a self-conscious provincial.

In the middle eighties the Germany of self-satisfied philistines, whose easygoing ways of living were immortalized by the Munich school of painting (Spitzweg) and have survived in that plain but pleasing furniture, walnut or cherrywood, called Biedermeier, was beginning to give way. Both reflect an age of simple living when the master of the house, after the day's

work was done, would sit with his family around a big, china
stove, his feet encased in red velvet slippers, in a Turkish dressing gown, a skullcap with a large silk tassle on his head, and a
huge tobacco pipe in his hands that had to be supported on the
floor. My Frankfort grandfather possessed and had used one;
with him the one and only trace of Biedermeier vanished from
my life. Gustav Schmoller had outwardly outgrown Biedermeier. His rise had been rapid. He had become adviser and
intimate friend of chancellors; he was made a member of the
Prussian House of Peers. Yet he always retained some of the
main features of Biedermeier. His pose of a good-natured, innocuous good mixer did not always successfully disguise his passionate temperament and his by no means amiable guile. The
historians on whose preserves he had poached called him a first-
rate economist, while those economists who understood the
complicated mechanism of modern economy praised him as a
historian. Both were wrong. He was a first-rate sociologist who
might be classified as an institutionalist, and a very brilliant
essayist. He was learned and scholarly, yet his great work, *Principles of Economics,* reads like a clever travelogue on the social
sciences—full of bright observations and of dissolving views.
For he was a superrelativist whose answer was never "yes" or
"no." He taught his pupils to look upon all economic problems
as fluid, not to say slippery, phenomena, the true inner meaning of which one could not grasp anyhow. This being the case,
the right approach was to study their history; if one was both
courageous and inquisitive, one might describe but never ap-
praise actual conditions. As to economic policies, it was wise to
be cautious and to leave them to those who were in power;
when they had made their decisions, one might provide them
with facts and good reasons to justify their actions.

The economic education of the Prussian bureaucracy was
mainly in the hands of Schmoller and of the many pupils whose
appointments he had wangled. Its results became evident in the
great economic crisis after the First World War. The bureaucracy was ignorant of the most elementary notions of economics
—there was scarcely anybody in the treasury, imperial or
Prussian, who knew anything about inflation. (In Austria conditions were different.) Schmoller's relativism, moreover, had
taught the bureaucracy the futility of asking expert advice. His

pupils had not learned to look upon present-day facts with an eye to the future; they had been trained to turn backward. They could not tell you what *should* be done; they only knew what *had* been done.

Schmoller's relativism was partly temperamental, partly opportunist. He was a master politician. He had started as a liberal and remained a liberal of vague generalities. In post-Bismarckian days he wielded great influence and identified himself more or less with governmental policies, except in university matters. Here he was firm; academic liberty, after all, furnished the platform on which he stood.

Yet in one way he was far in advance of the age. He was one of the earliest economists who understood the implications of the strivings of the working class. He disliked modern capitalism, it did not fit into the guild atmosphere in which he had been reared. He had lived through one of the ugliest phases, the great swindling boom followed by the inevitable crash of the early seventies. He rightly disliked brazen promoters. He understood very early that the more or less authoritarian type of government that he fancied could flourish in modern times only if it safeguarded the interests of the broad masses. He became one of the founders of the Association for Social Politics, which might claim a kind of grandfathership of the several New Deals all the world over.

He received me very kindly, but I did not like him and he did not like me. This dark-complexioned Swabian with his fiery, brownish eyes and grayish hair who talked to me with Prussian enthusiasm in the singsong of his Swabian homeland, and who oozed slyness from every pore, grated on my aesthetic senses. He was incongruous. Even in later life when he endeavored to show friendliness to me, I never got over this first impression.


## 3. Students and Professors

During the years when Germany had had no representative political institutions, the university pulpit was the platform from which all great national and international issues had been discussed. Professors enjoyed a good deal of freedom even in the days of strict censorship, for the men who ruled the states were shrewd enough to realize the need of some safety valve. From time to time a German government had attempted to muzzle its universities, especially when students had indulged too much in extramural revolutionary activity. In those early days students formed the advanced guard of all national and liberal movements—which at that time were thought to be identical. They were mixed up with every revolutionary move on the Continent, inflaming the masses and leading them to the barricades. Youth is naturally bored by the smugness and the snugness of its elders and either starts a new literary move-. ment, clamors for war and empire, or embarks on a revolution. The more backward a country, the greater the part its students play in political life. Progressive movements led by students are rarely long-lived, for students are age groups that pass on very rapidly; they do not form permanent classes or estates.

In my day the students no longer played a prominent part in politics. Parliamentary life had been fairly well developed; the radicals, especially the Socialist party, were not willing to submit to the leadership of immature bourgeois youngsters. The study of Marx attracted many of the more brilliant students; the third volume of *Das Kapital,* just published, had tangled rather than solved some of the riddles of the magnum opus. But the students had ceased to be a political ferment; most of them prepared for careers rather than for crusades. Much later, after the war and after the Russian Revolution, the militant students returned to the fray, at a time when everything was topsy-turvy and careers no longer seemed within their reach. They played a modest part in the Communist movement; they flocked in shoals to the Nazi standards, furnishing convincing proof that youth is at least as much interested in change and novelty as in progress and liberty.

For nearly a century the German professors had been leaders of the people. Ideas formulated in their lecture rooms had stimulated the nation. From the days when Fichte had addressed it and had prepared the ground for the national rising of 1812, to Treitschke or Adolph Wagner (he preached state socialism mixed with a little anti-Semitism), and both are among the ancestors of the Nazis, the universities were the vanguard of nationalism. Karl Marx himself, formed by Hegel, was a university product. Many of the professors were worthy of the unique place they occupied in German life. They had been among the leaders of the Frankfort parliament and had shared in the attempt to draft a constitution for a united Germany. They had failed; their failure has frequently been charged to their professorial qualities. Their critics may be right, yet nobody can deny that the world would be a very much happier place had the unity of Germany been accomplished, not by Otto von Bismarck, but by his academic predecessors.

The twilight of this great age was fading when I went to the university, though a few spectacular examples of unmitigated professorial megalomania were still alive, foremost among them Kuno Fischer in Heidelberg. Since he had no original ideas, he found a very congenial task in *The History of Philosophy,* a reconstruction of his predecessors' systems. He overdid it. He made them grow, one out of another, in inexorable symmetrical sequence; his lectures were like an organ performance, swelling in majestic volume toward the end. He was the vainest egocentric one could imagine. When discussing the lives of great men, he used to tell his class, "The sons of great men are not always great men too. My son, for example, is a mediocrity. He is a lawyer in Karlsruhe." He had written a pamphlet against a colleague, entitled *Anti-Trendelenburg.* Trendelenburg, an old man, died soon after its publication. Kuno Fischer was deeply distressed. "This time," he said, "I have gone too far. I did not mean to do this." For two terms I sat at his feet, and though he seemed rather comic, I learned the history of philosophy from him in a very comfortable way.

German universities were not meant to turn out "gentlemen." They trained professionals, lawyers, teachers, ministers, medical men, all of whom had to pass state examinations before they could practice their trade. The only degree conferred was that of doctor. The candidate turned up in a swallowtail, with a three-cornered hat under his arm and a sword at his side. Hat and sword were the property of the university beadle, who loaned them for an appropriate fee. The candidate climbed on a small platform below the pulpit occupied by His Magnificence the Rector or "His Spectabilitas" the Dean. Fastened to the blackboard were half a dozen theses, copies of which he had distributed and was expected to defend. They were sometimes serious, sometimes merely ludicrous. Their object was to start a discussion from which the *Doctorandus* would emerge triumphant. He usually had asked half a dozen friends to oppose him, and in most cases things went off smoothly, notwithstanding an occasional unpremeditated clash of opinions. One day, a Rumanian taking his degree was opposed by a Hungarian. They disagreed on some points at issue between their two nations, and finally got so mad that the Rumanian attempted to draw his sword; thanks to its venerable age, it stuck in the scabbard.

## 4. *Lujo Brentano*

Destiny must have marked me for an economist; otherwise I could not have survived my introduction to the "dismal science" during my year in Heidelberg. I fell into the hands of Karl Knies, a very great scholar, but about the worst teacher imaginable. He never finished a single sentence in the entire year during which I listened to him. He was as bored with us as we were with him. There were no roll calls; students were assumed to be interested in the subjects they had chosen. If they did not turn up in the lecture room, that was their own affair. If they managed to pass exams without any help from teachers, liberal-minded professors rather admired them. Unfortunately, I had to stick it out. There were only four of us in the class, and we did not want to desert the old man. He probably would have loved it. He never prepared his lectures; he did not need to. But we consumed many hours of his time that he certainly could have spent to far better purpose.

German students fortunately kept up a few of the traditions of the wandering scholars. Those who could afford some travel did not stay at one university. They went in search of new impressions from one place to another, attracted by great names. In my second year I decided to go to Munich to hear Lujo Brentano, to whom one of my Heidelberg professors had given me an introduction. In the summer term of 1893 he was lecturing on "The Economic History of Europe from the Downfall of the Roman Empire" and "The Industrial Revolution in England." I had not the slightest idea what the industrial revolution was, for in Heidelberg we had spent our time in splitting definitions—an extremely good mental exercise, by the way; it compels people to know what they are talking about.

On a late April morning I sat in a very uncomfortable lecture room of the old Munich University. The clock struck eleven-fifteen; a distinguished-looking middle-aged man wearing a pair of light trousers and a dark jacket walked in, stepped into the pulpit,'and peeled off his lemon-colored gloves. A darkish beard framed his perfect, cameo-like face. His ruddy complexion made him look far younger than his age. Two dark fiery eyes flashed behind large glasses. His nose was sharp and beautifully modeled; his mouth, very powerful. Had he worn an academic gown, he might have walked straight out of the Doges' Palace in Venice. We all stared, but the enchantment lasted but a few minutes. His voice, somehow, was pitched too high. Yet as soon as our ears had got accustomed to its timbre, the clarity of diction, the build of the sentences, and the structure of the lecture entranced us all. Here was a master who could bring to life times long gone by, who knew how to make impersonal institutions look like living organisms, and who inserted sharply chiseled portraits into a description of conditions. We sat there breathlessly; I remained under his spell all my life. I had not only found a teacher; I had found a master who became my guide and friend.

Brentano came of an old patrician family of Italian origin that had settled in my native city. His uncle, Clemens, was one of Germany's prominent romantic poets. His aunt, Bettina, had married another poet, von Arnim; she was a friend of Goethe in his old age. She was one of a small group of distinguished women who dominated the social and political life of Berlin in the middle of the nineteenth century; she had a great influence on King Frederick William IV. Brentano had inherited many of the traits of his distinguished relatives. His mind was a harmonious blend of romantic temperament and classic intellect. He saw things in colors and he could carve them in stone.

His father had died early. The rather troublesome boy had been sent to Dublin University, where he had passed a year or two under the guidance of the Jesuits. He took his degree in Munich and returned to England. Starting from studies of the medieval guilds, he discovered the English trade-union movement for the scientific world; the word "discovered" is the right term to use. His books on trade-unionism laid the foundation of all further inquiries; nobody has recognized this more generously than Sidney and Beatrice Webb. During his stay in England, he got in touch with the positivists, especially Frederick Harrison, and allied himself with the small progressive radical wing of British liberals led by John Stuart Mill. On his return to Germany he started as a lecturer in Berlin. He soon became full professor, going to Breslau, Strassburg, Leipzig, Vienna, and finally Munich—an appointment made possible by the accident that he was born, not right in Frankfort, but in his father's charming house in the little town of Aschaffenburg, about an hour away, on Bavarian soil. Otherwise Bavarian regionalism would have prevented his appointment to the leading chair of the kingdom.

Brentano had the natural independence of a *grand seigneur*. He disliked bureaucracies partly because they spelled routine, partly because they gave and received orders. His family was connected with the Prussian squirearchy. He took it for what it was worth; he felt none of the respect and sentimental admiration for it that blinded some of his colleagues who had come from a social nowhere. He did justice to Bismarck's genius but did not consider him a demigod. Unlike many liberals of his day, he was an ardent social reformer and an advocate, in good and in bad times, of the claims of the working class. British and German trade-unions have gratefully recognized his services. The Weimar Republic asked him to serve in Washington as its first republican ambassador. At that time he was nearing eighty. He was willing to go, provided I was appointed his counselor. He needed, he said, my knowledge of the U.S.A. He really wanted my wife's assistance, on whom he used to lean after his wife's death. The German government fortunately declined his condition. To give two first-rate jobs to two professors was too much for any foreign office. We both congratulated ourselves upon our escape. We could not have produced the miracles we were expected to perform; our failure would have been attributed to our being outsiders.

Brentano foresaw nearly all the problems that modern labor movements have had to face. He predicted that nation-wide unionism would have to be balanced by a complementary federation of employers; he insisted that these influential bodies should be held responsible to the public for the misuse of power entrusted to them.

Brentano was the last, and perhaps the greatest, academic teacher that an age of great teachers produced. He was both a scholar and an artist. Combining a researcher's inquisitiveness with a poet's intuition, he could find and group facts in such a way as to make them reveal their inner meaning. His craftsmanship showed to perfection in his courses on economic history. He was not suffocated, as Max Weber sometimes was, by the mass of information he had collected and digested. He made his facts fall into line, each representing the particular point in economic development from which the next move started—the outcome of previous stages and the cause of an ensuing one. He was not a believer in Marx; in fact he was one of Marx's earliest critics, and as a young man had a tussle with him, in which, I think, Marx was the winner. But he recognized Marx's great achievement: his attempt to formulate a theory of peaceful organic change based on definite economic laws of growth and decay to which all human societies are subject. He did not agree with the particular laws Marx claimed to have discovered. Brentano was at his best when describing the structural development of European society from the fall of the Roman Empire to the industrial revolution. To follow this course was as exciting as a preview of a master film.

Brentano taught me the art of interpretation, showing me that facts are dumb and speak only if one can loosen their tongues. He was tireless in collecting them; nothing seemed to be unimportant or was overlooked, but when he had assembled them, he carefully selected those that were essential and threw the rest out as dross. His influence on me was not always beneficial; his method fitted a genius; it did not always work satisfactorily in my hands.

I studied two years under him, preparing my doctor's thesis. When I had almost finished it, I had a term to spare before I could take my degree. So he sent me to Vienna to become familiar with another approach to economics—that of Karl Menger, to whom he was opposed in nearly everything.

## 5. *Vienna*

Menger shared with Jevons the glory of having discovered "marginal utility." From his lectures one could not have gathered that he ever discovered anything. They were on the level of American textbooks for beginners; in fact, they foreshadowed them.

No Viennese students who could afford to stay away went to classes. Only the poorest of the poor, the half-famished boys from the Galician plains, from the Carpathian Mountains, or from the sterile Alpine valleys, frequented the lecture room, partly because this was the cheapest way to keep warm in winter, and partly, too, because it gave them a chance of making a living. They carefully wrote down the professor's lectures, and sold copies for two dollars apiece to their more opulent colleagues, who turned up only just before examination. A charitable tradition had sprung up from this practice; the professor was not expected to change his lectures, for by doing so, he would have devaluated the work of these poor boys. I did go to the lectures, because I was interested in personalities; and I was richly repaid, not by the wisdom of the professor, which I could have got much cheaper elsewhere, but by meeting my fellow students. They represented the ethnic and social elements to which Austria was trying to give cohesion, and I began to understand the fatefulness of her task—since the rise of modern nationalism grown almost insoluble; far more difficult than anything Rome or Great Britain had ever faced.

Menger received me as a potential convert. He felt flattered by my coming from an opponent; he almost tried to bribe me by kindness to become one of his flock. From him I learned the art of debating. Every week about twenty of us met in his seminar to discuss the problems of the day; among them I remember the cartel question. Menger presided. One student would open the debate as speaker for the government. Then a representative for the opposition would get to his feet. At first I remained silent, for all the participants were good debaters and more advanced than I. One day I gathered courage and made the speech of my life. A fellow student told me afterward that. it had been as though a razor blade had cut through thick air. I sat down a recognized authority. From then on, I was treated as someone to be reckoned with. I still remember walking home in an ecstatic dream. I had tried, before, to speak; usually it had been a poor performance. Now I had made good: I was accepted as an equal by people who knew how to use words. I was so elated that my health became affected; whenever I rose to my feet, I had violent heart palpitations. I have never completely got rid of them. Even now, after fifty years of practice, speaking still exhausts me physically.

I made some interesting contacts. I was taken to students' unions, where I met politicians, members of the Austrian parliament, most of them of the left. Socialism was spreading in Austria. Among the leading politicians was Engelbert Pernerstorffer. He had early been a nationalist but had turned to socialism. I read a paper at a students' meeting and he criticized me, I thought, unfairly. I lost my temper and went for him in my best form. Being an old parliamentary hand, he greatly enjoyed it. From then on, he took me under his wing. I trotted behind him through Viennese beer and wine shops that he frequented and learned a great deal of Austrian politics. Marxism was the order of the day. It was passionately discussed by men trained in the subtle methods of the medieval schoolmen. They were not satisfied with culling intoxicating phrases from the Communist Manifesto—they had waded conscientiously through the three volumes of *Das Kapital*. Vienna finally became the spiritual citadel of orthodox Marxism, until Moscow dispossessed it—after having successfully destroyed its fundamental assumptions. The term in Vienna was a milestone in my life. In all its crisscross of antagonisms and hopes and ideas, I discovered myself, so to speak.

The Vienna of those days was the heart of an empire, the different races of which were fighting for equality and supremacy. But the several national fronts were indented by the Socialist movement, which persistently tried to cut across national lines of division and to make them all co-operate in a common fight for democracy. Until 1897 voting was limited to the upper classes; the struggle over its extension was very bitter.

The Viennese are among the most gifted people of the Continent. In their city, nationalities had mixed for generations; new and interesting types were in the process of formation. The Viennese had very modest standards even though they under-

stood the art of living. The city was overshadowed by a resplendent court and a proud, nationally very mixed aristocracy. It
possessed only a small upper bourgeoisie, which contained a
strong Jewish element. Below was a vast lower middle class comprised of artisans, handicraftsmen, and small shopkeepers, many
of them still cherishing medieval ideals. The small shop dominated; it was slowly being ousted by large-scale industrialism.
Many of the new industries were in Jewish hands. The economic and social struggle between the small shop, working with
little capital and no machinery, and the large plants became
partly religious and partly ethnical. Many Viennese Jews had
come from the non-German, socially backward parts of the empire. They represented Hungarian, Polish, and Slovak, not
Western, ways of living. In front of the stock exchange one
could see crowds of Galician Jews in long black gowns and black
felt hats with their traditional ringlets. The district called the
Leopoldstadt was a kind of voluntary ghetto. Modern Continental anti-Semitism was born in Vienna, where Adolf Hitler
adopted it. It was, as a witty member of the Austrian parliament, Dr. Kronawetter, called it, the moron's type of socialism.

From below and behind these motley forces a very powerful
labor movement had come to the top. Its leaders possessed
much more fiery temperaments than their German contemporaries, and they were free from the German's dogmatic quiet-
ist determinism. They believed in action rather than in the
millennium. I met many of them. A group of social reformers
who called themselves Fabians, in imitation of the British, had
been formed. They held big meetings to which representatives
of all groups and classes flocked.

Vienna was very class-conscious. The aristocracy, the middle
classes, and the working class were sharply separated from one
another. Yet the Austrian temperament was gregarious; people
mixed in an easy way unheard of in Germany outside Munich.
The heart of Vienna may have been the Burg (the imperial
residence) or the opera house; the mind of Vienna was decen-
tralized. It was located in innumerable cafés where people spent
a large part of their leisure and of their working hours. There
were a few very exclusive clubs. The bulk of the people of all
classes met in the café; many went there for breakfast and for
supper. At any hour of the day one could get a couple of eggs

or a ham sandwich. One could even get credit, for once one was known as a regular patron, the headwaiter was willing to act as banker, at a rather high rate of interest, of course. In the better cafés newspapers of the entire world were available; the waiter would reserve one's favorite journal for one's private use at a fixed hour. One wrote letters there, made business appointments, and played cards or checkers; one talked with friends, and with opponents—a practice unthinkable in Germany, where Prince Bismarck's long reign had poisoned all political relations, and where opponents looked upon each other as near criminals. The most famous of the places was the Café Griensteidl, a large establishment cut up into many small rooms. At certain hours of the day or evening particular groups had vested rights to each of these rooms, where they occupied the best tables. One had to be asked to join; after being found acceptable, one became a kind of member.

Dr. Isidor Singer, who tried to teach me statistics, had started a weekly called *Die Zeit (Time)*. Until it blossomed forth into a daily paper and met the financial difficulties daily papers had to face even in those relatively cheap days, it played an important part in Austrian affairs. He asked me to write book reviews. For the one and only time in my life I gave free play to my critical faculties. I must have committed more literary murders in that short half year than during the rest of my career as a writer. I was merciless, imagining that I was just.

There was one fly in the ointment: I discovered my physical limitations. I could stand a good deal of strain and excitement and did not feel the worse for it while it lasted, except when I got an attack of migraine, which has faithfully accompanied me through most of my life; I am very little bothered by it now, a sure sign, I suppose, of reduced intellectual intensity. But every time, when the actual fight was over, I had a collapse. It was the first warning, only partly understood, that there were things I would like to do but which I would never be able to accomplish.

## 6. *Felix Austria*

My upbringing and my family ties had prepared me for the unique chance of understanding Austria. The average North German looked down upon the Austrians; he used to say facetiously that the Bavarians, whom he likewise took lightly, were the missing link between human beings and the Austrians. He saw in them, very much as did Adolf Hitler later on, a degenerate branch of the great German family. He did not know that the Germans in Austria were but a relatively small minority, even outside the Hungarian half of the empire. He loved to go to the Austrian mountains where peaks were higher and prices lower than in Germany proper, and he found Vienna very entertaining. He did not understand why the Germans in Austria tolerated the many acts of insubordination the various nationalities permitted themselves. They should learn in Alsace-Lorraine or in Posen how to deal with obstreperous aliens and how easy it was to civilize them by a strong hand.

Long before I could grasp the nature of the Austrian problem, I had an inkling of its complexity. In Vorarlberg I had seen Slovenian hucksters go from house to house selling the hardware they carried in their crates. The half-dozen times I was close to Adolf Hitler, I seemed to discover in his face a close resemblance to these "mousetrap dealers," as the people in our mountains called them. He had the same high cheekbones, hard, lanky horsehair, and staring gray-blue eyes that they had. They lived on the German-Slav border, and most of them probably were ethnic "mongrels"—as were many Austrian subjects. Our postmaster had come from Hungary. My grandmother was born in Bozen; she always spoke of her Italian neighbors as "Welsh." My cousins in Trieste had a retail store attached to their main business where cotton goods were sold to the many tribes that lived under the scepter of the Habsburgs. Croats in their white sheepskins, Dalmatians, and Bosnians thronged it. Everybody in Trieste knew Italian, yet half an hour outside the city one was in a purely Slavonic region where the bulk of the people understood neither German nor Italian. My cousins had Moravian and Bohemian connections who wailed about the inroads the Czechs were making on the dominant position of German-speaking people in both countries. Both Prague and Brünn were becoming beleaguered cities where small German garrisons were hard pressed by Slavs. These people yearned for union with the great German Reich, where the Germans were their own masters and were not subject to Slav oppression. Had they been less enthusiastic about Prince Bismarck, I might have sympathized with them. Fortunately for me, the Bismarck they adored was the same Bismarck whom I had learned to abhor. But they made me understand the nature of Pan-Germanism. It started in Bohemia as a result of the inferiority complex of the Bohemian Germans once they recognized that the days of German ascendancy had gone for good and that they were henceforth reduced to the role of a permanent minority.

The Habsburg empire was a microcosm which reflected most of Europe's problems; it was unique, for it was composed of racial minorities. Of its eight major nationalities only Czechs and Magyars had no habitat outside its frontiers. Germans, Italians, Poles, southern Slavs, Rumanians, and Ruthenians were splinters of large nations across the border. Austria had played her part in European history; she had had a great mission. She had saved Europe from the Turks and had tried to keep western and southern Slavs within the orbit of the West.

I have always been of the opinion that Bismarck, more than anybody else, was responsible for Austria's disintegration. He had undermined the position of the Austrian Germans by driving them out of the German Confederation. They had to enter into partnership with the Hungarians. The Magyars were not content with freedom from Germanization. They wanted to impose their own not very marketable civilization on the nationalities living under their rule. They made impossible the granting of concessions which the survival of the empire demanded.

The forces that held together the old monarchy, the Crown, the Court, the Church, the Army, and the Civil Service, had been losing strength with the advent of democracy and of the machine age. They had, however, gained a powerful ally: the Socialists. The Austrian Socialists understood the economic importance of a united empire. They saw in it the linchpin of Europe; were it prised loose, Europe would fall to pieces. They hoped to level up by social reforms the backward non-German masses, and keep them within a multinational state, in which each nation was to have full cultural freedom and all members were to enjoy equal rights within the entire monarchy. The Socialists were the standard-bearers of a new Austrian patriotism. They had, moreover, a vision of "One World." Their best-known representative was Rudolf Springer, the pen name of Karl Renner, today president of the Austrian Republic.

Though I never joined their ranks, I learned a great deal from them. I became a good European who loathed the incestuous union of cultural cravings with economic graft that has made modern nationalism corrosive.

The outbreak of the First World War put an end to their hopes. That war was not due to the struggle of monopolist capitalist powers for colonial markets or for capital investment opportunities in backward countries. Austria's military chiefs had provoked it. They had used the murder of the heir to the throne by Serbian conspirators for demonstrating the empire's strength. Its impending disintegration had to be stopped by a victorious war, limited if possible to the Balkans. The issue was whether or not the empire could survive. The system of alliances by which the precarious peace of Europe had been maintained of necessity spread the conflagration. Fate, which the Austrian militarists had challenged, took her course. The empire was wiped off the map; its mission had failed. Its culture survived in a smallish farmers' republic, which found it almost beyond its strength to maintain even a shadow of the glory which had once been Vienna. It never stood on firm ground.

The void created by the fall of Austria has never been filled. When Adolf Hitler had come to the top and had recognized that the Allies would not keep Austria out of his clutches, a second war was bound to start. For once Austria was part of the Reich, Czechoslovakia, being surrounded on three sides, was doomed. She had either to be defended by a war or be re-established after a war. Neville Chamberlain unwittingly chose the latter alternative. The Second World War has freed both Magyars and Czechs from German domination; they have even got rid of their German minorities. They have become numerically unimportant outposts of the Soviet empire, who will be allowed to read Marx in their national language and may continue to enjoy their own cultural amusements such as music and dances.

I am not aware that the Habsburg government of the twentieth century interfered with these pastimes. I doubt whether Thomas Masaryk would greatly have appreciated the brand of liberty that Soviet Russia specializes in.

# IV. Victorian Twilight

## 1. *The London School of Economics*

SHORTLY AFTER my return from Vienna, I took my degree (1895). By that time, love's young dream had faded; I had dropped banking and decided on a university career. Brentano had his doubts; his influence on university appointments being limited, my chances were none too good. As I possessed independent means, he finally consented to my having a try. He suggested my going to England to round off my education by doing some research work in the British Museum. For some reason or other, the journey was postponed until spring. I spent the winter term at another German university, in Freiburg im Breisgau. Here I sat at the feet of Max Weber, who was just beginning his great academic career. I quickly learned to appreciate the amplitude of his mind and the strength of his character. Yet somehow we never got very near to one another, even though we were interested in the same subjects, and later on became political allies. His powerful intellect was thoroughly Teutonic. It had neither the clarity nor the harmony of Brentano's. It was like a huge field strewn with blocks of lava, after a terrific volcanic eruption, that had not yet sufficiently hardened.

On a day of early May in 1896, late in the afternoon, I landed in England. I had lived in London as a small boy for nearly a year when my father, in the crisis of the late seventies, and on the threshold of illness and death, had tried unsuccessfully to establish a branch of the family banking house. From this stay (I was not yet four years old when it ended) I remember that on a gray, misty autumn day the fog shrouded the Albert Memorial, making it look mean and miserable. The four animals at its base, representing the four continents, seemed to shiver in the cold. Being unaware of the nature of the British climate, I indignantly asked my nurse why it was so badly cleaned.

The year Mother had spent in London had been the happiest of her life. Her stories of London and England had made me see the city and the country with an inner eye long before I actually looked on them again. My return was favored by a glorious early-spring afternoon. The sky had the opaque pastel coloring that it has only in England and Ireland. The sun did not glare but seemed to filter through the air like golden dust. The meadows were shimmeringly green, and the white may was in bloom. It was like a page from Keats or Shelley, or better still, like the introduction to *Piers Plowman*. The sea had been calm, and I had not been seasick. I shared the compartment in the train with an interesting-looking woman with very mobile features. I exchanged a few words with her but was too shy to continue the conversation. I missed a great opportunity: she was Yvette Guilbert, the famous *chanteuse*.

As we neared London, my enthusiasm cooled. Beauty ceased where suburban Victorian England began. The endless rows of narrow, low brick houses, rubbing shoulders, with their small excrescent kitchens, pathetic back gardens, and yellow brick chimney stacks, were out of harmony with that lovely spring day.

My cousin who met me at Cannon Street station wore a top hat and a frock coat, for these were stately days. He joined the train and we went back across the river to Charing Cross. Here we took a hansom cab, which was just as queer and uncomfortable as I expected it to be from my browsing in English literature, and drove to Bond Street. He deposited me at an old hostelry called Long's Hotel, now many years gone. I did not sleep very well, though I had a double bed—the first in my life —for even in those days Bond Street was noisy. Next morning I went down to a British breakfast, also familiar to me from literary excursions, and gobbled up a meal consisting of grilled sole, a steak, toast, marmalade, and an enormous quantity of tea. (I was not so very hungry, but I had to imbibe local color.) For the first time I saw an English "boots" wearing a waistcoat with sleeves. A little later my cousin put me on the way to see the sights of London, but only after he had had me measured for the top hat and a double-breasted frock coat.

I explored the Tower and the Guild Hall and wended my way westward. I was getting depressed. I had imagined that my English was good. I had talked with many English visitors to Germany. I had had an excellent teacher, who spoke highly of my accomplishments, and I had read a good deal of English literature. To my horror, the English in England did not understand me, nor did I understand them. I summoned up my courage and walked into a restaurant called The Cock and ate a gargantuan meal, partly because I was famished, partly because I did not know how to decline the waiter's suggestions. After I was through, I dragged myself drowsily along: I did not dare to board a bus, for I was sure I would not understand the conductor, even if he understood me. In the end I hailed a cab, and managed to direct it to my hotel.

After a few days, my ears and my tongue improved. I could understand the English, and they understood me. I began to pay a round of visits and deliver my introductions.

Great Britain was the native land of modern political economy. With but few exceptions, the greatest names of the "dismal science" are those of her sons. Her universities—somewhat tardily—had taken over the classic tradition and had amplified and refined it on its theoretical side. It was nobly represented by Alfred Marshall, who formed the minds, directly or indirectly, of nearly all present-day economists. Brentano had written to him about me; soon after my arrival I went on a pilgrimage to Cambridge. Marshall had been in bad health most of his life; even an unpracticed mind like mine recognized the permanent invalid. Yet he radiated a mellow wisdom, an all-embracing, wide human understanding, which may account for his blunting occasionally the edge of his theoretic reasoning. He talked to me about the impending revolution in transportation as affecting social conditions. This was the age of the bicycle, long before the advent of the car, yet he foresaw the impact of this relatively minor invention on the life of the people, especially in the rural areas. Up to this time many of them had been tied to the soil physically almost as firmly as they had been legally in the days of villenage.

A good deal of research on economic conditions had been done in Great Britain outside the academic world—the work of royal commissions of inquiry. But for their reports, some of the great revolutionary books of the age, like those of Engels and Marx, would have been rather meager on their factual side. Most of the concrete material by which Marx justified his theories had been culled from these blue books. Academic economics had become more and more abstract. Some of its greatest representatives seemed to be almost more interested in the mathematical formulation of problems than in their practical solution.

Into this gap between theory and practice had just stepped the London School of Economics, where applied economics was to be taught. The Fabian Society had been left a legacy of fifty thousand dollars, and under the influence of Sidney and Beatrice Webb had decided to use it for such a school. With this small sum and a few grants from other sources, the school had been opened the year before I had come over. Its first director was W. A. S. Hewins, who later on became Joseph Chamberlain's chief protectionist brains truster; to him and to the Webbs, Brentano had given me letters. The school, domiciled on the ground floor in a house on Adelphi Terrace, consisted of a series of small rooms. It did not teach undergraduates but was giving advanced students and all serious persons interested in economic problems an opportunity of learning about them from experts. Apart from the director, few of its teachers were professional educators. The school tried to get hold of men prominent in government, business, and administration to give talks to its pupils. I never registered as a student; my purely academic education was completed, if not complete. I attended, however, a number of special courses, and made many contacts.

The Webbs were leaders in that small group of highly intellectual advanced social thinkers and reformers, the Fabians. The Fabians' main idea was that far-reaching social changes could be much better accomplished by piecemeal systematic reforms than by violent revolution. They reflected the British national attitude. In ways and means the English are extremely conservative; they dislike reversions, and violent revulsions; they rarely ever destroy an institution. They put a skyscraper next to a thatched cottage without being worried by the blatant incongruity. Their approach to life is organic, not mechanic. Yet all the time British affairs are in a flux. Frenchmen and Americans, while conservative in aims and ends, adore violent transformation. They are but mildly interested in slow, drab evolution; they love flamboyant, spectacular revolution. Being logical, they have a devastating contempt for the blindly groping Britisher, who prefers to trust his instincts rather than his intellect, and who, by doing so, has managed to spread the impression of being a slow-witted fool and easy to deal with. Yet they rightly suspect him, for somehow he has frequently managed to reach the goal, with seemingly small effort, just a few seconds ahead of his more nimble rivals.

The best known of the Fabians, Bernard Shaw, did not fit into this picture. He belonged to that brilliant race, full of emotional contradictions, the Anglo-Irish. They have tried hard, in their checkered career, to prod John Bull a little by instilling bright ideas into his woolly mind. They have never succeeded. Bernard Shaw chose a novel approach. He tried to goad John Bull into action by forever poking fun at him. He, too, failed. His name was a household word in Germany; he was a great sage in the United States, esteemed by the professional intelligentsia, who by now rate him almost as high as Mahatma Gandhi. Yet the English were merely amused by him. They did not mind his digs; they were flattered. He gave them a chance to show the world and themselves the wide scope of their tolerance. Had Shaw been an Englishman, they would have resented him— but an outsider was privileged to misunderstand one's ways and to laugh at them, since, being an outsider, he could not be expected to appreciate them in any case. Occasionally he got under their skin; he awoke their conscience and made them see things they would have overlooked. For this alone, it was worth while to tolerate him. I am sure Shaw would never have joined the Fabians had there been the slightest chance of their becoming the dominant party. He was a gallant defender of human rights, absolutely sincere in his social aims and aspirations; yet he would have been thoroughly unhappy had they succeeded in reforming the world completely. His genius needed an unregenerated world. I did not come across Shaw at the London School, but I had the great good luck to meet him a few years later in the west of Ireland, when during a long summer vacation he had been away from an appreciative public. For two days he let play for our benefit the cascades of his sparkling wit, which changed color as rapidly and as harmoniously as the Irish sky and the Irish landscape below it.

The second floor of Adelphi Terrace was tenanted by Miss Payne-Townshend, later Mrs. Shaw. She was a close friend of the Webbs and took a deep interest in the school. Students were few at that time. I am not sure that lectures were not more numerous. Miss Payne-Townshend acted as hostess. The students who attended more or less regularly were occasionally invited to have tea with her and the lecturer. Thanks to the Webbs, an invitation was extended to me. I met a number of distinguished people at these gatherings, who were very kind to me. One evening after I had returned from Ireland, Haldane, later Lord Haldane, asked me about my views on home rule. "If I were an Irishman," I replied, "I would be a unionist; if I were English, I would be a home ruler." I could not foresee that I would end my regular academic career, some forty years later, as lecturer at the school, after it had become known the world over.

## 2. British Liberalism

I saw the sun set on the Victorian age. A couple of years earlier Mr. Gladstone had resigned (1894); shortly afterward Lord Rosebery's Liberal government had broken up, and the party did not return to power for a whole decade. Gladstone had fallen over home rule for Ireland, the last great effort in the liberation campaign that had engaged the Liberals since the days of Richard Cobden.

The place of the Manchester School in modern history is rarely fully understood nowadays. It attempted to eliminate military physical force from political life, and to replace it by economic co-operation. Its fight against the Corn Laws was not a purely economic or even social move. Its aim was the defeudalization of Great Britain. Cobden was the first practical modern statesman who advocated a comprehensive international foreign policy, the freedom of the seas, the abolition of the right of blockade, and naval disarmament. The Anti-Corn-Law League's motto, "Peace, Free Trade and Good Will amongst Nations," was a platform, not a mere slogan. For a quarter of a century its leaders were in a position to influence political events. They very nearly convinced the greatest empire in the world that the days of imperialism were over, that colonies would soon be independent, that nationalities should not be held down by force, and that aggressive, monopolist territorialism would have to be supplanted by pacifist, free trade commercialism. Their policy was not frustrated by the British Tories, who never again were strong enough to block its advance; it was vanquished on the battlefield of Sadowa, where Prince Bismarck laid the foundation of German unity. The defeat of the Prussian liberals in the struggle with Bismarck, which was decided by the victorious campaign of 1866, heralded the eclipse of liberalism the world over. The reversion of world policies started from Bismarck's triumph; henceforth war was no longer outlawed—Great Britain reluctantly had to learn the lesson. Still, in her internal affairs she held to liberal principles, and Gladstone's magnetic personality very nearly succeeded in bringing about peace between Great Britain and Ireland. He failed magnificently.

I saw a good deal of James Bryce. He had been a member of a university faculty, and understood the problems and the troubles of a young scholar. He very kindly asked me to his house, according to the old-fashioned Victorian habit, for breakfast at nine o'clock. I have never minded rising early, but I am not a good conversationalist at that hour. I have always found it difficult both to gobble enough food and to pursue the problems I have come to discuss. It does not matter much at lunch or dinner, but at nine o'clock the choice between getting enough to eat and settling grave issues is difficult.

Bryce helped me to solve one of my problems. Liberalism on the Continent was dying; in England Gladstone had kept its flag flying. What was the reason?

Like British liberalism, Continental liberalism stood in opposition to oppressive governments. Unlike the British brand, it was generally antireligious. In Roman Catholic countries this could easily be understood. The church had attempted to rule the state. Liberals had to choose which of the two great powers they would fight. In Bavaria, for example, those who opposed church control in temporal affairs had to side with the state. Its bureaucracy, representing an omnipotent state, defended their spiritual liberty against encroachment by the church. In Protestant Prussia, things had been different. Until Bismarck degenerated the Prussian bureaucracy, it had defended the concepts of a modern government against a narrow-minded, semifeudal squirearchy that considered itself the state. Here, too, liberalism had frequently had, if not an antireligious, an antichurch note. The Prussian Junkers were not very religious—their private feelings were often enough fairly indifferent—but they used the church to support their own domination. The lord of the manor saw to it that the villagers behaved in temporal affairs; it was the job of the pastor to exercise a supplementary spiritual discipline over them.

In England the Whig aristocracy had led the fight against absolutist government; it was still strongly represented on what one might call the Liberal party's general staff, but the bulk of the army was composed of nonconformists. These people hated the state because it had endangered the salvation of their ancestors' souls by forcing them into idolatrous creeds. They looked upon the established church as a spiritual bureaucracy, and upon its ministers as unprincipled servants of an oppressor state. They knew how to secure the salvation of their souls without the help of a priesthood, a spiritual bureaucracy; they could mind their secular affairs without a secular bureaucracy, and resented government intervention in business. I had read a good deal about British nonconformity. As I really wanted to know Great Britain. I had to understand the nonconformist conscience, and see it, so to speak, in the flesh. James Bryce suggested a journey through the midlands and the north of England. He provided me with letters of introduction to Liberal election agents in important constituencies, who either were nonconformists themselves or at least were in close touch with the nonconformists who formed the bulk of the party.

On a cold spring day I started my pilgrimage through nonconformist England. It took me to Darlington, York, Middlesbrough, Durham, Newcastle, Edinburgh, Leeds, Manchester, Liverpool, and Birmingham. I cannot say that I enjoyed it. It was a grim and dreary experience. It was cold nearly everywhere; hotels were anything but comfortable; the people I met were intense, sincere, strong, and single-minded. They believed in God, and many of them even more fervently in the Devil. Mr. Gladstone to them was the vicar of God on earth, while

Joseph Chamberlain, who had split the party on the eve of its greatest triumph, appeared to most of them as the Devil incarnate. His defection was particularly wicked because he had no excuse for failing the cause, since he was a Unitarian and not an Episcopalian. I have never met such political hatred as I encountered in Birmingham until I heard some of my Republican friends in the United States talk about President Roosevelt.

The journey was a revelation to me of the stamina of the English lower middle classes. Their lives were all work and no play. The long rows of gray stone houses looked shiveringly cold. Nature seemed forbidding; the grass was bleak under a cutting wind, or grayed with soot and coal dust. On weekdays, men and women had to rise early, long before the sun was up; work started in almost Stygian darkness. One day, changing trains in Manchester at about five o'clock in the morning, I saw the station dining room crowded with men on their way to the shops, some of them breakfasting on whisky and beer in an atmosphere of smoky dampness the mere remembrance of which makes me cough. People wound up a hard day's work with high tea, a meal consisting of fish or meat and an ample supply of black Indian tea, which the British have drunk now for so many generations that their insides have become immune to the attacks of their home cooking. On Sundays, men and women went to chapel several times; if they were sufficiently emancipated, they pottered about their gardens.

As to fun, there was very little of it. "Merry England" survived in many areas, in races or in football and cricket matches, which attracted huge crowds of workers. The genuine nonconformist mind did not take kindly to these thoroughly unspiritual activities. In Manchester there was good music, mainly due to the numerous Germans who had settled there. The cathedral towns organized magnificent choir festivals, but these were generally under the patronage of the established church. One of my acquaintances took me on a Sunday afternoon to tea with his mother, a very impressive old lady who treated me with great kindness until I was foolish enough to talk about the theater. Temperance to most of them was a holy cause; and there was a good deal to be said for their fanaticism, since the havoc drink had played among the working class in England in those days was truly terrific. Yet there was another side to it. The industrial revolution had driven people from that "Merry England" in which they had been rooted; temperance was depriving them of the one and only opportunity they had of returning to it in their cups. The old saying that there is truth in wine is but partly true; there is something even more important in it for those who suffer—escape from reality.

Yet this harsh, gray world was friendly and neighborly enough, once one had penetrated into it. A certain rough comradeship continued to exist between small masters and their men. It ended only when the master graduated from the lower to the upper middle class, whence he slowly ascended toward the pinnacles of the ruling class. These reticent people were endowed with great latent strength; they were the trustworthy middle class, as their leaders used to call them. Their superb steadfastness was one of the main props of the British Empire.

In those days London, too, was pretty grim, especially on a Sunday. Old residents in the metropolis had not much to complain of. They watched the church parade on a fine summer's day—it is engraved on my memory like a page from a Victorian society novel. In the afternoon, people called on their friends for tea, for the week-end habit was not yet universal. But the fellow with few or no social connections was lost. There was little to do but go to church, which, as a mere alternative to boredom, does not strengthen one's faith. Outside the hotels, which were very expensive, one could rarely get a meal. One could not even order tea at a railway station, if one was not a bona fide traveler and prepared to present a ticket. Well might one yearn for kingdom come who shivered with cold and boredom on a Sunday afternoon in that vale of tears.

## 3. Socialism

Working conditions appalled me. I had not yet seen many factories. I was aghast at the rows of wretched hovels in which many of the miners of the north lived. I was horrified when a prominent trade-union leader in Bradford insisted on the need of children's labor in the mills: the parents who fed and housed them had a right to ask for some compensation from them.

I was struck by the crude empiricism that prevailed everywhere, and the contempt for "learning," not to say culture. Puritan nonconformity was impressive but not attractive.

But behind all this drabness, the lights of hope were shining brightly. The decades before the First World War were a golden age. Its actual achievements were infinitely below our present-day standards, but there was a firm conviction everywhere that things were rapidly mending, that the future, within easy reach, would be ever so much brighter than the past or even the present. For a golden age is in men's minds, not in their material accomplishments.

I was greatly struck by the absence of socialism. A very radical spirit permeated the north; it had nothing but contempt for soft southern England, where feudalism still flourished among what the northerners thought a servile population. But socialism meant the state, and the state had been the enemy of man's most precious possession—his soul. I saw a good deal of British socialism in London; I met a good many of the Fabians. These brilliant men and women did not impress me as very advanced. They were just getting near the positions conservative German state-socialists (like Adolph Wagner) and the so-called pulpit socialists (mostly university professors like Schmoller and Brentano) had reached long before.

The Fabians were a sect, not a party. Progressive labor was usually liberal, though in many districts Episcopalian urban workers preferred as member of Parliament a conservative rural magnate, who wielded no direct influence on their lives, to a manufacturer in whose mills they were employed. Workers were not class-conscious in the orthodox Marxist sense of the term. They were not affected by the egalitarian fanaticism prevailing in the United States. They did not try to keep up with the Joneses. They wanted to live according to their own patterns of life, which differed little from those of the shopkeepers and the smaller employers. They meant to be comfortable petty bourgeois, and did not envy their betters. Abstract ideas held little sway over Victorian England. The revolutionary impetus of the Chartists had petered out; their socialism had few adherents, that of Marx even fewer. Neither Marx nor Engels had made any lasting imprint on the mind of the British workingman. Both bourgeois economists and Fabians had but little knowledge of the explosive doctrines Marx had forged in the British Museum. The only prominent Marxist was Hyndman, of bourgeois antecedents. He was a first-rate debater; otherwise not a very attractive personality. A long, not-well-cared-for blond beard framed a sallow, powerful face, whose owner excelled in trenchant observations. He dominated completely a small socialist dinner club that met regularly once a month in a mean little restaurant. Its atmosphere was depressing. The number of members present scarcely ever reached a dozen. The regulars, besides Hyndman and Mrs. Hyndman, were Tom Mann and Keir Hardie. Both had fiery, revolutionary temperaments, Tom Mann dark and glowing with fierce passion, Keir Hardie fair, with unmistakably Celtic eyes. It is so long ago that my memory may deceive me, yet I seem to see us all on a New Year's Eve, standing round the small table, with arms interlocked, and greeting the new year with the doleful strains of "Auld Lang Syne."

## 4. Merry England

Ever since the days of the Norman invasion, two Englands have been living side by side, the England of Norman and Saxon, of Cavalier and Puritan, the England of the rural squirearchy and the urban middle class and its appurtenances. They have fought each other bitterly, but in times of national stress they have always stood together. Class distinctions were very sharply drawn between groups; they did not interfere much with individuals. During the industrial revolution, many business leaders had sprung from the working class. Their sons and daughters, and certainly their grandchildren, easily passed into the upper class.

It was my good fortune to know both Englands. A branch of my family had settled in London; my uncle, having been successful in the City, had retired and transformed himself very rapidly into a British squire. He was accepted as such by his neighbors, who were impressed, among other things, by his sportsmanship. Rather late in life he not only became a good shot but a very fair huntsman. My young cousins automatically adopted the ways of the English countryside, and looked upon life in London as a mere break, a social interlude that filled the "season," the three early summer months. Thanks to my uncle and his connections, I saw a certain amount of society. I was not very comfortable in it. I had had very little social experience at home. To many Continentals, the stringent rules of English social life were severe restrictions of their personal liberty. To have to wear a swallowtail, a white tie, and a boiled shirt in order to eat a dinner seemed to me a frivolous encroachment upon the rights of man, as I then understood them. Fortunately the conventions were so firmly established that a newcomer had the choice, either to accept them or to keep out of it. I capitulated; and in later years I often blessed the strictness of these social rules, which, once mastered, made life very much easier. In the early days of republican Berlin, nobody ever knew what to wear, and social amenities were becoming complicated. One afternoon a radical friend of mine rang me up and inquired whether I was to go to a certain party; if so, would I oblige him and wear a swallowtail? I replied that it would not be a formal party—a dinner jacket would be more than sufficient. "I know," he said, "but I haven't got one, and I don't want to be too conspicuous." So we both turned up in full war paint, to the disgust of man proletarian-minded fellow guests. In those early republican days, it was tacitly understood that class distinctions must not be encouraged, and there are evidently no worse class distinctions than a boiled shirt, a white tie, and a tail coat. Thanks to my long years in England, I got over these democratic prejudices without, I hope, being disloyal to democratic principles.

I saw a good deal of English country life, the amenities of which really came up to the expectations I had formed from English novels. It was so pleasant to be called in the morning by a valet who pulled the blinds and brought to one's bedside a steaming cup of tea, and bread and butter so thinly sliced that one could almost peer through it. He crept under the bed and unearthed a huge tin bowl, which he put on a little mat in the middle of the room. He disappeared and returned with two huge jugs of water, one steaming hot, carefully wrapped up in towels, and the other cold, and told one, "Your bath is ready, sir; breakfast will be at nine o'clock." In those days I discovered how meaningless are the definitions of democracy and aristocracy that have come down to us from Greek philosophers. They are far too vague to fit into daily life. Aristocracy, I learned, is a state of society in which a limited number of privileged people enjoy the advantages of an extremely effective domestic service. Democracy, on the other hand, is a condition of life in which nobody can afford these amenities, and in which one must console oneself with the proud feeling so tersely expressed by Daumier's swell who had to shine his own boots: "One is never so well served as by oneself." Those aristocratic days have gone long ago. The spread of sanitary plumbing and of bathrooms has made their disappearance somewhat less painful than it otherwise might have been.

I am glad I saw the twilight of the feudal age. It is so much easier to understand a social order in the midst of which one has lived—nay, it is even much more profitable. to criticize a society one has been part of than to have to direct one's outbursts of righteous indignation against institutions one knows only from a textbook whose author has never seen them at work. When I hear some of my young American friends rage, nowadays, against the rigid class stricture of England, I am almost sorry for them. It seems to me such a waste of energy to get excited about evils of which one has no firsthand knowledge, and to worry about iniquities that undoubtedly existed on a very large scale, but have been put right by the people more closely concerned. It is much easier for a low-born Briton to become a member of the House of Lords than for the daughter of a highly respected Irish Roman Catholic family, that has lived in the United States for several generations and has given the adopted homeland very valuable service, to be accepted as a near equal—not, of course, as a member—by the Daughters of the American Revolution.

My older nonconformist friends might be horrified by such statements; they might almost consider me a traitor to the liberal cause. Yet a large part of their success has been due to those members of the British upper class who were way ahead of their times, and who served their country and their own class by destroying its privileges. But for the great leaders the upper class provided, and but for its wisdom in picking out able recruits from every social stratum, liberalism in Great Britain might have been as ineffectual as in other countries. The most impressive among those I met was Sir Charles Dilke, the author of *Greater Britain*. While he looked and talked like an aggressive British Tory nationalist, he acted as an advanced progressive.

Upper-class radicals are frequently treated as traitors by their own groups. Had Franklin Delano Roosevelt's policy been started by a rail splitter, social bitterness in the United States would have been much weaker. It would not have been unnatural for a man like Abraham Lincoln, who had had no social background, to destroy the basis of what considered itself America's aristocracy. Few of my American radical friends, who foam at the mouth against British class privileges, seem to be aware that their own great leader, Franklin Delano Roosevelt, sprang from just that group whom they consider the archenemies of progress in the old country.

My appreciation of English country life—not a very original feeling on my part—remained within reasonable bounds. Though very fond of horses, I never took up hunting, even in Ireland, and the few times I went out shooting I was rather bored. I saw the feudal aspect of British civilization in the mild light, as it were, of lovely long summer afternoons. Those years before the Boer War were, after all, the last time when old England was truly merry. That war suddenly showed her her complete isolation, and the hatred and animosities that other nations had accumulated agains her; it heralded the end of the long epoch of Victorian liberalism. It was the final defeat of the Manchester School. That liberalism died as heroically as it had lived. The courage with which Lloyd George and Sir Henry Campbell-Bannerman, the leader of the party, faced the outburst of vindictive nationalism at the start of the Boer War was unlike the whimpering of modern anti-imperialists, who rave against the iniquities of systems long dead.

I watched the last pageant of that age, the Diamond Jubilee, from a window in Piccadilly. It was better than the best film. Representatives of five continents, many of them in colorful national dress, surrounded a pudgy-looking, bowed-down, old lady, who would have passed unnoticed had she not been the center. It was she whom Benjamin Disraeli had made empress of India and who had continued to rule two almost republican democracies in the Pacific and two in the Atlantic. Amid the glitter and glamour of uniforms and national costumes, she was the only almost unadorned person. This was as it should be. For Victoria Regina looked like a representative of that "trustworthy middle class" that had dominated the British Empire during her long reign.

# V. The Land of Heart's Desire
## (1896-1898)

### 1. *Horace Plunkett*

I was studying medieval economic history at the British Museum. The wealth of books and documents at my disposal made it an entrancing task. Yet somehow I did not prosper in this atmosphere. The mustiness of a large public reading room kills all my ideas.

As the summer advanced, I got restless. I was accumulating many facts that somehow would not fuse together. Suddenly I had an inspiration: why not study backward economic life in the one western country where it had been preserved? Gladstone's heroic struggle for home rule was over, but the thrill of Irish affairs was not dead. Liberals on the Continent had followed the fight with bated breath; Ireland has always been the darling of the progressive mind the world over. Great Britain—for Scotland had been in it too—had tried very hard to transform Ireland into mid-Victorian respectability. The Irish had declined the honor and had remained noble primitives. They had preferred grievances to prosperity. I decided to go over and see with my own eyes. But I had no connections in Ireland, and without proper introductions I was sure to flounder. I explained my purpose to my English friends and asked them to find a sufficiently detached person, willing to guide my faltering steps. "It cannot be done," they replied. "Every man in Ireland is a party man. He is either a nationalist or a unionist; an Ulsterman or a Southerner; a Roman Catholic or a Protestant; a landlord or a tenant. Nobody in Ireland can tell you the truth, and if there were one who could do it, he wouldn't be interested in doing so. He cannot be found." Yet he was found.

A few days later I was introduced to Horace Plunkett, who,

in spite of the difference in our ages, became my most intimate friend, and apart from Brentano was the only man who actually influenced my life. Horace, later Sir Horace, was the second son of Lord Dunsany, a descendant of Anglo-Irish barons. The Plunketts resided at Dunsany Castle in county Meath in the Pale—the Pale comprised the four counties where Anglo-Norman settlers had withstood the onrush of the Celtic flood that for very nearly eight hundred years had tried unsuccessfully to sweep them back from the native soil. They lived in huge crenelated Norman castles with impenetrable stone walls surrounded by moats, which the natives could sometimes rush but were rarely able to destroy. The country round them became a huge, grass-covered solitude, a paradise for hunting. Broad ditches divide the pastures in which cattle graze all the year round. It is a land that knows no real winter. The grass never shrivels, the ground rarely freezes, and summer is cool as spring in other lands. The grass is greener than anywhere else. Its blades have a bluish tinge, and when they wave in the wind, a silvery gleam. There is little tillage and there are few human habitations. The famine, the fall of wheat prices, the call of America, and profits from cattle breeding have cleared away the people, until the land has become a silent green sea reflecting the never-ceasing play of clouds swishing across the sky.

Like everybody else in Meath, Horace had been a keen follower of the hounds, but the soft, damp atmosphere of the country had affected his chest. He had been sent to a dry climate and had lived the life of a ranchman in Wyoming for many years, at a time when the cow country was not yet cut up into dude ranches. He was a wealthy man; on his mother's side he had inherited a share in Welsh coal mines. Moreover, he had succeeded in making money of his own on his ranch. There was nothing "British" about him, in the sense in which Americans understand the word. He had managed to pick up a complete outfit of Americanisms without ever ceasing to be Anglo-Irish. He had become one of the few Britishers who really knew the United States. He had not run through America as one of those distinguished foreigners of excellent social standing whom Americans with a pedigree and Americans with a pocketbook love to honor. He lived the life of the plain people. He understood them and he loved them. His Irish wit easily blended with the humorous drawl of the wide American plains.

His health had improved, and at the wish of his father he had come back to Ireland. It had not been easy for him; he loved horses and the free outdoor life. Yet he was anything but a he-man. One could not imagine a more gentle person. He stooped a little; his shoulders were sloping; he was extremely shy and reticent. He was the worst speaker one could listen to and the most persuasive talker one could meet. He had had many accidents and in his later years limped a bit. He was very skeptical about the medico's art and at the same time always willing to let himself be experimented upon. He had a passion for trying out diets and medical tests. He suffered more pain and physical torture than most men, and had undergone grievous disappointments, yet he never lost faith and always remained gentle and cheerful. He had what I might call a sad serenity. He had a genius for making friends, and he held many of them very close to his heart all through his life. Though his education had been defective, and he never ceased to complain about it, he had an extremely nimble mind: a rare combination of logical analysis and comprehensive imagination. He rarely pursued truth by reasoning, but when he found it, he was not satisfied until it had been proved by logical processes.

Horace had entered Parliament in 1895 as a representative of the would-be aristocratic quarter of Dublin, where the professional men and the rich businessmen lived, and where loyalists were generally sure of a majority even after the rest of the country had gone revolutionary. In those days he was a unionist. He was convinced that the prosperity of Ireland was bound up with union with Great Britain, yet he did not consider himself an Englishman. He respected the English and admired them. He loved the Irish, his own people, and almost despised them. He was quite ready to recognize the wrong done them by centuries of oppression; but he resented the equivocations and whinings by which they tried to make capital out of every grievance, and the double-dealing that clamored for its abolition—with compensation of course—and for its perpetuation as a means of levying further blackmail.

One day we were cruising among the Western Isles that stud

the coast of Ireland. We approached an island dominated by a conical mountain. One of its flanks was quite bare, where the islanders had cut off the sod and dried it for fuel; this was more convenient for them than going to the mainland to cut turf, but it was not an agricultural improvement. We were greeted by an angry, disappointed crowd. They were expecting a relief boat, a steamer bringing goods for which they did not have to pay, to save them from starvation. As one of them explained to us afterward, "If it were not for the famine, nobody could live here." Horace resented this attitude, the absence of any attempt to help themselves, the reliance on permanent grievances. He recognized that the land system established in Ireland by the English had been responsible for a good deal of Irish misery and Irish inefficiency; he fully accepted the responsibility of his own class for these conditions. At the time of my coming to Ireland they were rapidly being removed. Rent extortions had come to an end with the establishment of the rent-fixing courts, created after 1881 by the Land Acts. At that time, Victorian England had inaugurated a policy of rent-fixing as radical as anything ever attempted by agrarian reformers, not excepting Mexico. The land was slowly being returned to the tenants, the surviving representatives of the ancient Celtic populations. Thanks to the liberal use of British credit, tenants could buy farms by annual instalments nearly 20 to 30 per cent below their rents, and landlords received an acceptable, if not generous, compensation.

People imagined that the transfer of property would rapidly transform into a modern skilled farmer the inefficient Irish crofter, whose knowledge of agriculture did not go deeper than the planting of a few lazy beds with potatoes.

Horace knew better. The landed estate run by an agent for a landlord had been a social unit; it had not functioned very well; but its breaking up into separate farms owned by independent proprietors would destroy this unity. It had to be replaced by some better method: co-operation. Horace was studying co-operation as practiced in Denmark. He had started an organization—the Irish Agriculture Organization Society—to teach Irish farmers the elements of co-operation. He had found a good deal of moral support in the new chief secretary for Ireland, Gerald Balfour. The unionists had defeated home rule; they had returned to power on this issue. They had beaten it in Great Britain, but not in Ireland. They now attempted to kill it in Ireland by kindness. They offered the discontented Irish the practical benefits of the British connection. Under Parnell the Irish farmer had become a passionate nationalist after nationalism had promised him freedom from rent and the ownership of land. The unionists expected to wean him from home rule by giving him property, rightly assuming that property has a very soothing effect on revolutionary temperaments. Here, too, Horace saw very much farther. He doubted the effect of purely material concessions on the Irish mind. Yet he was convinced that such concessions had to be made, if social peace was to be maintained in Ireland, but in the end success would depend on economic progress. British Liberals had put their faith in constitutional changes. Once Ireland had received the grant of self-government, they argued, she would be able to solve her own problems. Horace knew that she had been far too deeply demoralized to do so unaided. There was no salvation in letting her "stew in her own juice," as a British Liberal leader had suggested. Ireland would boil over. She was too near Great Britain for such experiments. Horace was convinced that a social rejuvenation of Ireland had to precede constitutional changes. Since Ireland was an agrarian country, this rejuvenation had to be effected by better farming with the help of the co-operative movement.

## 2. *The End of the World*

The Irish landscape is painted in water colors, or rather, I should say, in pastels. Few other countries possess the softness of her green pastures and of her brown mountain streams that gently gurgle through her heath-covered valleys. The sky is pale blue, and though opaque, is overhung by a misty veil through which the rays of the sun radiate like threads spun from raw silk. Clouds suddenly chase along it, throwing quaint shadows over the green expanse, their contours sharply reflected in the still brown pools, and without cause or reason as quickly disappear.

Moors cover great spaces, their dank, dark tints relieved by pink and violet heather. Little red and blue two-wheeled farm carts stand in the fields, small splashes of color in a pale landscape. The wind sweeps over the plains, especially in the west; it sometimes threatens to blow the top stones off the fences dividing the holdings. The gorse, with its bright golden blossoms, frames roads and mountainsides. There is an Irish saying, "As long as the gorse is in bloom, kissing is in season," and in this land, which knows little of either summer or winter but lives in a kind of perennial mutation between spring and autumn, the gorse is in bloom all the year round.

The soft beauty of the plains becomes majestic in the sea-girt west. The mountains of Donegal, of Connemara, and of Kerry are but smallish elevations when measured by Alpine standards. Nowhere do they reach into regions of eternal snow. They rise abruptly from the sea; the peaks are often veiled in clouds and mists. The valleys that separate them are somber brown or russet slopes, covered with endless bogs or heather fields. Trees are few, for the Atlantic gales blow mercilessly over the land. Yet in sheltered nooks, especially in the south where the warmth of the Gulf Stream envelops the earth, the vegetation is almost tropically luxuriant. I have driven for hours between fuchsia hedges in the west; laurel, myrtle, and other subtropical evergreens nestle in hollows and clefts.

A thousand islets stud a turquoise sea beyond the mainland. Many of them are rocks of bare, wind-swept limestone where no tree can grow. In others, rains and sunshine have bitten deep holes in the surface in which the natives plant scanty crops. They put layers of seaweed on layers of sand and raise potatoes. If the sun shines at the right time and the rains fall when due, they get a crop. If the elements fail, famine stalks the land. The natives who live on the islands refer to Ireland as the continent. This is "the End of the World," as a medieval chronicler has called it; the part of Europe nearest to America.

I spent three summers in this fairyland, "a land where even the old are fair, and even the wise are merry of tongue," and dránk deeply of its beauty. I found what I sought: a kind of Middle Ages in being, and underneath, the remnants of an earlier tribal world. Horace had opened all doors to me; I lived in the houses of the great. I met viceroys, chief secretaries, and the heads of churches, and I saw a great deal of the plain people.

4

Ireland is a small country with clearly defined frontiers; for this reason it is an ideal subject for study. The instinct that brought me here had been right.

For nearly eight hundred years the British, or rather the inhabitants of Great Britain, have tried to conquer and colonize Ireland. First came a wave of Norman knights and Welsh retainers who subjected the natives to the king of England. All over the country, Norman castles and ruins of Norman churches and abbeys tell the tale of their might. Yet they never thoroughly broke the natives. In the days of the Tudors, the British garrison was practically reduced to the four counties surrounding Dublin. Then the tide turned. While Spaniards and Portuguese were discovering the new worlds, English adventurers under Henry VIII, Mary, and Elizabeth reconquered Ireland. Finally, under James I the Ulster clans were defeated. The Scots planted themselves firmly in Ulster. They still hold it today as an integral part of the United Kingdom. The natives rose in a terrific agrarian revolution, but were subdued by Oliver Cromwell, who planned to evacuate the Irish from the three eastern provinces and to concentrate them in the distant western islands. This is the Plantation of Connaught, which made the western province a kind of native reservation, though Irish remnants were permitted to stay in the east as workers and tenants on the settlers' land. Again the Irish rose, during the Glorious Revolution. They were defeated in Ulster with the help of Ulstermen, and ever since, the memory of the Battle of the Boyne has kept the north and the south apart.

It was not easy to get a true picture of Irish history. Each of the main groups inhabiting the country presented its own pet version. There were at least three Irelands: Ulster, settled and dominated by the Scotch invaders; the Anglo-Irish; and the Celts, who consider themselves natives. Of the three parts, Ulster was the least attractive. It was, on the surface at least, part of modern industrialized Western civilization. Belfast dominated it somewhat as Glasgow dominates western Scotland. Yet there was a harshness in Belfast, of both climate and attitude, that had no counterpart in Glasgow. Nothwithstanding the presence of large landowners, Ulster was a thoroughly middle-class country. Its real strength lay in this middle class, which had not yet been widely separated from the working class. It was a seventeenth-century urban society, imbued with hard, Calvinist doctrines. Even those of its members who no longer believed in predestination were conscious of the fires of Hell; it needed but slight provocation and fiery tongues would leap upward and devour idolators and worshipers of "the scarlet woman."

I was in Belfast in 1912 when Ulstermen and Ulster women bound themselves by a solemn covenant to rise in arms against Great Britain if British democracy dared to hand over the Ulster minority to the tender mercies of the southern-Irish majority. This passionate movement, used for party purposes by British conservatives, was the beginning of modern fascism. Mr. Bonar Law and Lord Carson, not Benito Mussolini, organized the first private armies to revolt against democracy.

I had a dim feeling that Ulster was wrong from the point of view of wise constructive policy; but wisdom is not a very powerful ingredient in the general human make-up. Even now, after thirty-five years, I recollect the profound impression made on me by this orderly revolution. It was far more imposing than the triumphant march of the Nazis twenty years later, for it was the spontaneous outburst of deeply religious, though rather narrow, passions.

Anglo-Ireland and Celtic Ireland belonged to a world I had never seen before and which no one will ever see again. Feudalism was not yet dead, though it was rapidly disintegrating. The "family" still lived in the big house; the landlord, called "himself," still held the estate and ruled it through his agent. The majority of the farmers were not yet owners. They continued paying rents. Agrarian murders were no longer everyday affairs, though some of the men to whom I had introductions were occasionally waylaid and shot at. They did not seem to mind it very much. The instrument used, the blunderbuss, is a gun whose muzzle ends in a funnel. It is charged with nails or hacked lead, and its victims are lacerated in the most horrid way. Fortunately, it is not a weapon of precision. Its repercussion is so strong that it usually bowls over the shooter, and the knowledge of this shortcoming frequently prevents a hit. Irish murderers became deadly only with the advent of the tommy gun, but even this did not seem to worry the Irish much. In the early 1930's I went over as guest of the Royal University to deliver a series of lectures. I was feted by the members of the government and taken about by them a good deal. We were usually surrounded by armed guards on motorcycles. I knew the Irish are a most hospitable people; they do not shoot at their guests. But I had no guarantee that my fame would have reached every member of the Irish Republican Army at large and that they would all be willing to forgo a chance of killing a hated minister for fear of accidentally hitting a so-called distinguished foreigner.

### 3. *The Anglo-Irish*

The Anglo-Irish gentry knew they had come to the end of their tether. The majority realized that they would have to sell out, as the wisest had already done. But many of them were too poor. They could not afford to exchange a large, though often frozen, rent roll for the paltry income they might get from British consols. For the time being, they felt relatively safe. A Conservative government was in power, after Parnell's tragic end had split and paralyzed the Irish party. But the Liberals might return any day and sell them to the traitors. This knowledge did not dim the cheerfulness of their lives, so long as they could manage to keep a horse and go hunting. As the farmers were equally fond of horses, hunting went on even in greatly disturbed districts.

The high light of social life was the Dublin horse show. It was the great event for those who bred, bought, sold, or merely loved horses. It was attended by peer and peasant, all being united for a few days by the freemasonry of horse coping. I have never seen more good-looking men and beautiful women. In the country houses I visited, I got a glimpse of what my American friends would call the "upper classes" just before the sun went down on them for good. Life, while not luxurious, was full of fun. There was always a bed for a guest and always lots of food, though usually a little monotonous. I was too superior a young man in those days to go in for hunting and shooting as I should have done. I could have learned many things from life that I had to distill from books, yet I was sufficiently close to my hosts to understand this last phase of feudalism.

I was fortunate in more than one respect. Constance Gore-Booth, an Irish reigning beauty of the day, had taken a fancy to me. She was considerably older than I and looked upon me, I am quite sure, as a very quaint freak. She poked fun at my puerile dignity and taught me, I hope successfully, not to be bumptious. She was the daughter of a great Anglo-Irish house; like many of them, more Irish than English. Her people owned a lovely place, Lissadell, on the shores of the Atlantic Ocean; Yeats often sang its beauty. With a letter of introduction, I dropped in on them and found a group of young men and women who, as I discovered later, were expecting a very learned German professor. They were rather disappointed that I did not wear the straw hat, frock coat, flannel trousers, and brown shoes they were looking for; nor did I carry a butterfly net and a tin case for collecting rare specimens. They had planned to make me report extremely primitive customs and conditions. For two days they walked about without shoes or stockings, for they wanted me to describe the west of Ireland as a poverty-stricken region, where even the upper classes could not afford such luxuries. I was not impressed. All my life I had seen people going barefooted in the Austrian mountains; I merely thought they were mad. When they realized that I was not to be taken in, they became very friendly.

Constance, like a good many women of the upper class, enjoyed the confidence of her father's tenants. He had been a rich man and a very good landlord. She took me into the tenants' cabins and made them tell me stories and fairy tales that were still alive in these remote regions. We drove tandem in a small gig over the hills where the farmers cut turf, and all along the seashore where they burned seaweed and made kelp.

Constance had been studying painting in Paris; her eyesight was bad and she was depressed by the knowledge that she would never get beyond a certain point. But she was still looking forward to an artistic career and insisted on painting my portrait; it was not very successful. Each half of my face was fairly right, yet the two would never join together properly. At last her patience gave out, and in a temper she threw the brush in my face, producing a very nice color scheme on my cheeks.

Just at this moment the first dinner bell rang and she had to wash me with turpentine in order to make me presentable. We always dressed for dinner.

Aspects of grandeur are sometimes misleading. One evening I stayed with a large party in an old Norman castle. All of us were in full evening dress. After dinner we ascended the great staircase leading to the drawing room. Unfortunately, it started to rain, and like many things in Ireland, the roof was leaky, so we ascended, each gentleman holding an umbrella over his lady.

When Constance had realized the limitation of her artistic talent, she did what women usually do: she married; and, again as is frequently the case, not the right sort of man. He was a Polish count who also dabbled in art. I saw him only once, when I called on them much later in their small house in suburban Dublin. Evidently she was not very happy, and she went into politics. She became a rabid Irish Republican, one of the leaders of the Easter Rebellion. She was condemned to death, and but for her sex would have been executed like her male companions. By and by she was released, and when the Free State was established she became a member of the Dail. A little later she died an unheroic death, caused, I am told, by a neglected appendix. She was buried in Glasnevin in the National Heroes corner. When I was last in Dublin, my host was taking me past the cemetery. I bade him stop the car as I wanted to put a few flowers on her grave. Dublin is not a very sophisticated city; there were no flower shops anywhere near. We finally had to go to a grocer's to get a handful of daffodils, which I laid on her grave. But if Dublin does not go in for flowers, it does go in for grapevines. By next day the entire city seemed to know that I had put a few flowers on the grave of a great revolutionary.

So I was asked to tea to meet De Valera. Like all fervent nationalist leaders of hitherto backward countries, he became almost lyrical about the beauty of the protection of infant industries. This being, unfortunately, my pet aversion, I may not have responded as sympathetically as I was expected to do. He did impress me by the single-minded, cold-blooded ferocity of his nationalist passion. He was the only Irish leader I met who was sternly logical: a gift he may have inherited from his

Spanish father, as it does not flourish on Irish soil; the Irish prefer a combination of incongruities. One day I had gone to Connemara as a guest of an Irish friend, with a large party of stanch unionists, loyalists to the core. A few members of the viceroy's court were among us. The evening was going very pleasantly. There were good talk, dancing, and music. Suddenly the player struck a note that seemed to change the atmosphere completely. He intoned "The Wearing of the Green," Ireland's passionate revolutionary anthem, with a swing almost as stirring as that of the Marseillaise. Like one man, all jumped to their feet and sang with deep emotion Ireland's great hymn of hate.

The life of the Anglo-Irish gentry was very much less sophisticated and formal than English country life. Conversation wah bright but rarely deep. The majority of the upper class had few intellectual interests. One day, I was told, the Irish Antiquarian Society went down to Galway to study ancient Irish monuments. The County Galway Club gave them a dinner. Each member of the learned society was sandwiched in between two local squires. The food was good, and the drink even better, but conversation lagged. The antiquarians could talk about many things, but they didn't know much about horses and hunting, and the county Galway squires knew everything about horses and hunting but very little about anything else. One of the learned men tried to start a discussion on agricultural subjects. It was just after the passage of John Bright's Land Act, protecting the improvements made by tenants on their farms against confiscation by landlords through rents. Such improvements often enough consisted of stone walls or ditches that sheltered or drained the land. The learned man inquired his host's opinion about protection of tenants' improvements. Before he got an answer, a quaking voice came from the bottom of the table. "—Talking about improvements," it said, "I've got a little mare that can jump any improvement." Conversations in country houses were not all on this level, but many were not very much above it. Yet one could always start a good discussion on home rule and other political issues, though the debate would usually be extremely one-sided as everybody was against home rule.

## 4. *The Celtic Twilight*

I met nearly all leaders of the Irish people. Parnell was dead, but I saw a certain amount of the two Redmonds, the heads of the remnant of his party. I spent some days in the company of William O'Brien and his French-Russian wife. They lived in a small cottage on the shores of Mayo. He looked like a benevolent schoolmaster, not like the violent revolutionary whose fame had become nation-wide when he had refused to put on convict's garb in the prison of Tullamore. When his jailers had deprived him of his own trousers, he strutted about the cold courtyard without any. O'Brien's breeches became a kind of symbol of national independence.

John Dillon did not take to me. He feared and disliked Horace because he rightly assumed that success of the co-operative movement might moderate the violence of the nationalist upsurge. The only genuine revolutionary among these men was Michael Davitt. He belonged to a group that had advocated the use of physical force, and had lost his arm in one attempt. He despised the constitutional separatists as West Britons. He believed in a genuine Celtic civilization, purified of all alien British ingredients. Long before the Bolshevists enforced nationalization of the soil he preached agrarian socialism. He did not want to turn tenants into peasant proprietors; he misunderstood completely the nature of a farmers' revolt: they did not want to abolish property, they merely wanted to abolish their landlords' rights and get them for themselves. He had the clarity, the logic, and the fanaticism of the true revolutionary, and a consuming passion shone through his burning eyes.

The man with whom I got on best was Tim Healy, who later became the first governor general of the Free State. He was famed for his legal subtlety and his brilliant repartee. He had to the full the *esprit gaulois*. I spent one evening with him when we recited poetry to each other instead of talking politics. He finally presented me with his copy of the poems of Clarence Mangin, author of "Dark Rosaleen." As poetry goes, they are not very good; the translations from the German are especially poor. It always struck me as somewhat queer that nearly all Irish poets who detest England do so in the language of Shakespeare, and some of them do it very well.

During the last summer I spent in Ireland, Lady Gregory asked me to stay with her at Coole, her place in Galway. She had fallen in love with the spiritual side of the Irish nationalist movement. Since nationalism had got hold of the land question and had enlisted the mass of Irish farmers, its flame was burning dimly. Parnell had recognized that even a high-minded people like the Irish would not go to war against British rule over the spelling of street names in Celtic letters, especially as the British would not have interfered with them over purely sentimental issues. Agrarianism had almost sidetracked the emotional literary nationalism young Ireland had started in the 1840's, whose leaders had either died or become respectable statesmen. By now that movement represented an early Victorian phase, much like later French romanticism and the German revolutionary poetry of '48. Its songs did not appeal to a more sophisticated literary age. But a new generation was discovering the beauties of the old Gaelic language. Erse as a spoken language had almost died out among the younger people who had passed through the national schools. The English had not suppressed it; they had just let it die. They had had the support of the greatest power in the land, the Roman Catholic Church.

The Irish, except the people of Ulster, have proved themselves most loyal children of the great mother church; but their Roman Catholicism is rather unique. They alone have accepted the teachings of the Roman church without ever having been conquered by Rome. Roman legions never set foot on the Emerald Isle; neither the Roman law nor the Roman tongue has ever permeated it. The Irish somehow remained outside the universalism of the great church; they kept up some contact with their pagan past, their heathen gods, and their heathen morality. The public attitude toward agrarian crimes showed clearly enough that they had not been completely converted to Christian saintliness built on New Testament ethics.

The revival of the Celtic language was mainly due to modern philologists, particulary German, French, and British scholars. As time went by, revolutionaries of the type of Michael Davitt, who loathed everything British and who did not want a "West Briton" republic—a kind of emancipated British daughter state —picked it up. They looked longingly back on early tribal Celtic laws as a buttress to their claims for agrarian socialism.

They had come from parts of the country where the older generation, at least, still spoke Gaelic; even in my day one could run across a good many old men and women in the west who "had got no English."

Use of the Gaelic language opened up the way to primeval Celtic institutions; their adoption would cut the country off from English domination and British civilization much more effectively than the most far-reaching constitutional reforms. Most national movements have started as linguistic revivals and coarsened later on into agrarian or political movements. In Ireland the political movements were well under way before they gave birth to a spiritual renaissance, at a time when chances of success were very poor. Gaelic spiritual life was no longer subject to oppression. The permanent irritant of language persecution, which kept up strife on the Continent, was absent; nineteenth-century British liberalism would never have permitted it. Moreover, the strength of the Irish nationalist movement lay partly outside Ireland. The British had got even with revolutionary New England by driving masses of Irish people to the United States, who turned the holy land of the Pilgrim Fathers into an Irish Roman Catholic stronghold. In doing so, they enormously aggravated the anti-British feeling that the American Revolution had generated. The American-Irish genius for political cohesion made them much more powerful than their mere numbers would have vouchsafed. They used this strength wherever possible in America for counteracting pro-British policies and for supporting by moral and financial and even by conspiratory means the Irish movement at home. Some of the great battles within Irish nationalism, in particular the struggle between the physical force parties and the moderate constitutionalists, have been fought out on American soil. A time came when the heart of Ireland beat more strongly in Boston than in Dublin; today Faneuil Hall, the cradle of American liberty, is controlled by the Boston Irish of the eighth ward.

The Irish in America were more numerous than the Irish in the British Isles, and many of them remained far more intransigent toward Great Britain. But they were lost to the Celtic cause. The United States did not forbid the use of native languages to its naturalized citizens; it tolerated a foreign-language press. But it would never allow a group of citizens to do their teaching exclusively in their native language, especially if it was a dead one. An Irish agitator at home might win votes by talking Erse in Mayo or Kerry. He would not have much success on Boston Common or in Madison Square, particularly not with a generation that had passed through the American public schools. The American-Irish were far too practical to waste energy and power on the revival of a dead language.

In Ireland, a group of highly gifted writers hoped to find new powers of expression by a return to the Celtic past. Lady Gregory, later on one of the sponsors of the Irish theater, was very close to them. She took me over to a neighboring landowner, Edward Martyn, a scion of one of the few remaining Roman Catholic landlords who had been able to hold onto their estates through the age of persecution. His home, Tullyra Castle in county Galway, was a meeting place for the champions of the Celtic renascence. He was a kindly man with a passion for poetry. I am afraid he loved art more deeply and genuinely than art loved him. His play *The Heather Field* showed a striving for beauty and profundity that did not seem to me very successful.

Among the guests assembled that evening was Douglas Hyde, later president of the Free State. He is one of the world's few great Celtic scholars, among whom Ireland's share has been rather small. He was the somber type of Celt: dark hair, deepset gray eyes, and an expression of ferocity in his face that by no means reflected his mind—it resembled the mien of "The Dying Warrior" of the Roman sculptor.

There was Martin Morris, son of a great Irish lawyer, looking, as Yeats put it, "like a blooming rose"; and there was Yeats himself, with his sharp-cut cameo-like profile, the greatest, perhaps, of all modern minor poets, the sweetest singer Ireland has produced. He had discovered the soul of the west; he could interpret its mystic beauty. Few people have ever handled the English language with more consummate skill or more subtle simplicity. His hands were so deft that he could make vibrate chords invisible to the naked eye. There is something of the strength of steel in the lilt of his songs; yet there is in them, too, an almost fleshless meagerness. He was the chosen herald of the great Celtic revival, but he did not sing to the dawn, he sang to the twilight.

The other great poet, Fiona Macleod, had not yet arrived. His entrance was the greatest disappointment of my life. I had been looking forward to meeting a perfect Gaelic beauty, black hair, lofty brow, deep-set blue eyes, with long, thin, almost ethereal fingers shaped to touch the strings of the harp. In walked a potbellied, middle-aged Scotsman with a pointed beard and a thoroughly earthly expression of self-satisfaction on his face.

They talked for days and nights of the unlimited possibilities of their movement, of the stupendous contribution the Gael had made to Western civilization and the marvelous part he would play in the near future. I was very young in those days, and as I happened to be in love with an Irish girl, I was in the proper romantic mood to accept their dream at its face value. Yet somewhere deep down in the bottom of my mind I sensed its unreality. Douglas Hyde, of course, knew Gaelic. He knew it as a spoken language and he knew it as a scholar. To him it was his native tongue, in which he expressed his best thoughts. The others had to study it laboriously. I doubt whether any of them ever mastered it as completely as we master Latin in our high-school days.

When the Free State was established and the anti-English movement had been successful, the street names in Dublin were written in Erse. The schools rightly took up the old native language and spread its knowledge widely. It is used today, though not exclusively, in the Dail. Yeats, the outstanding figure among his people, became a senator; he was wise enough to continue to write poetry in the language of the detested Sassenach. In the pantheon of great poets there may be a Gaelic section in time to come, but Yeats will not be in it.

A few years later I met Æ. He had given up his job in a department store to become Horace's assistant in organizing co-operation. He was a far more genuine poet than any of those who worked consciously for the Celtic revival. He wrote poetry, not because he wanted to write it, but because he could not help doing so. He was a natural singer, not a learned one, just as he was a painter who had never been properly trained, but who knew by instinct how to seize and to hold the soul of a landscape. His was a world of dreams, peopled by fairies. It was not a creation of literary will power, but the land of heart's desire into which he had been born and in which he moved with the unerring step of a seer to whom phantoms and symbols were reality. He did his practical business on earth extremely well; but his real home was in the clouds and mists that shrouded his pictures.

## 5. *The King of Kiltimagh*

I was fascinated by the economic aspect of the Irish west. In this lonely, wind-swept region of heather fields, bogs, and scanty pastures strewn with big boulders, economic life was almost untouched by modern developments. Farms were small and poor; tenants lived in cabins built of loose stones chinked with moss and mud. Floors were rarely boarded; the naked earth sufficed. There were no windows, only two doors, on opposite sides. The one on the side where the wind blew was kept closed. In the center of one wall was a rough fireplace, without chimney or flue. The roof was made of a few rafters covered with straw. Just above the fireplace there was a hole through which the smoke could rise if the wind came from the right side. Inside the hut, a wooden frame served as a bed; perhaps there was a table and a chair or two. The family in the cabin was often large; not infrequently the room was shared with a cow or pig. "The cow heats well," the farmer would say. Chickens and geese had the run of the place. The small fields outside the hut were sometimes enclosed by a stone wall. They consisted of a number of beds about a yard wide, of various lengths, divided from each other by a shallow furrow. In these beds the farmers planted alternately potatoes and oats, covering the seed with earth shoveled from the furrows. They rightly called these plots "lazy beds." Beyond the fields were pastures, generally very poor, and occasionally a meadow. The holdings never produced enough to keep the farmers in comfort. Even in a good year, nothing remained over after they had paid the rent; in a bad year famine stalked the land. Thousands and thousands of such farms in the west had been put under separate administration, the Congested Districts Board, which attempted to better the lot of the tenants by improving their technique, by finding them outside employment, by trying to buy neighboring pasture lands to increase the size of the holdings. I called these farms "deficit farms," an appropriate name, for yields were generally smaller than efforts. The Irish west taught me the technique of primitive economics. Few farmers used a plow; the soil was too stony and the holding far too small to maintain draft animals. These people were fairly healthy though badly fed; very good-looking, and when not actually starving, very cheerful and contented. They not only lived at "the End of the World"; they represented an earlier economic stage that had nearly disappeared elsewhere.

Among the members of the Congested District Board was a parish priest, the Very Reverend Father O'Hara. His parish, Kiltimagh, was one of the poorest of the poor. He ruled it efficiently as a benevolent despot. I used to call him the King of Kiltimagh and he loved me for it. He had often asked me to stay with him. At last I managed to find time and announced my arrival. At the station I was met by a band. I felt greatly inflated, but I had overrated my importance. The honors were not for me but for another visitor, the Right Reverend Bishop of L., who was due on a tour of inspection. He came by another train from the opposite direction. I shared his triumphal entry, but I had to stay with the curate while his lordship stayed with the priest. For two whole days I was permitted to participate in the festivities given in honor of the saintly man. They were not varied, but they were substantial. We had to inspect everything worth looking at, including a convent where they made a very good type of Irish tweed. We dined and wined frequently and lengthily with the wine of the country, hot and cold, punch and whisky. When his lordship departed, my time was up, but the King insisted on my spending a night under his roof. We had a very pleasant evening. We talked for hours, until very late into the night. I was dead tired and almost fell into my bed, but I was hardly inside the sheets when a rather penetrating scent of saintliness began to envelop me. I thought I was dreaming, but after it had continued for some time and I was beginning to get warm—it was rather a chilly night—the scent became stronger and stronger; I lit a candle and discovered the reason. I had been considered worthy to be permitted to sleep between the sheets that had enveloped the portly body of my lord the Bishop of L. I cannot say that I appreciated the honor.

Fortunately I had a rug with me. I wrapped myself up in it and spent a not too comfortable night on, not in, the bed.

After three summers in Ireland I knew what I was about. I was going to write a history of English colonization in Ireland. British colonization had been successful everywhere else; it had failed in Ireland. Why? I could not answer this question from the many books I had read; nearly all of them were violent party pamphlets. I set to work to find my own answers. I spent seven more years on it, until it finally became clear to me. The English had been successful in America, or in Australia, as the native populations could be eliminated and daughter societies could be founded. They were successful, too, in countries like India, which they ruled as dependencies by a bureaucracy. In Ireland they had not eliminated the natives. They had not ruled them by a bureaucracy. They had sent in settlers to rule the country as a garrison, and the settlers had mingled with the Irish; their sons and daughters had become Hibernicized. There remained a large, more or less native population, and there always was an English garrison. The two races never fused completely. Ireland taught me the tragedy of the composite colony where invaders and natives are bound together by almost indissoluble ties, but where they never completely fuse, and where it seems there can never be real peace until either fusion is accomplished, or one or the other of the two warring groups is eliminated. I owe a heavy debt of gratitude to Ireland for having taught me this lesson, which became the starting point of most of my future inquiries.

# VI. An Italian Interlude
## (1904-1905)

### 1. *Bleak Years*

THE YEARS between my departure from England in 1898 and my return to Ireland in 1903 were bleak. I spent them first in Munich and later in my mother's house in Frankfort. It was my last prolonged stay in my native city. My Irish book progressed but slowly. I had to cover over a thousand years of Western European history. I was an economist and a political scientist; I did not want to write history; my task was to analyze and interpret it. But I had to delve deep down into records to fill the gaps historians had left unbridged and to check their usually partisan narratives. It was a much bigger job than I had bargained for. I needed a great deal of will power to keep myself going. It is not easy to be one's own taskmaster when the goal seems to be steadily receding.

From time to time I took a vacation. I went to the Near East, and I twice visited Dalmatia. I gratefully remember a short spring idyll on its blue fjords and in the black mountains of Montenegro.

It is easy to fall in love under pomegranates and oleanders and she was a genuine Viennese beauty, her hair as golden as the sunlight which played on the walls of Ragusa. We very nearly got engaged. Thirty years later, at a London reception, a charming middle-aged woman smiled at me. Somewhat vacuously I smiled back. "You don't recognize me," she said. "I am Angela." I certainly had not forgotten her, but I was a little surprised that her glorious golden hair had turned an auburn copper shade.

From Cettinje, the capital of Montenegro, Albania could be easily reached. A horse-drawn carriage and a little lake steamer across Lake Skutari would do it. But, unfortunately, I was unable to secure a carriage, or even a bicycle—for His Royal Highness the Prince of Montenegro was giving a farewell dinner to a Russian military mission. The whole town, not to say the entire country, seemed to be attending it. Every vehicle was commandeered or hired. Spectators were allowed to peep into the royal courtyard where the dinner was served. I shared this privilege. It was funny to watch this almost Homeric meal, followed by a kind of steeplechase in which hosts and guests raced around the town in those little carriages I had been unable to hire. It did not compensate me for the lost opportunity of seeing the last vestiges of primitive clan life in Europe.

I traveled through what had been Arab Spain, and spent a few days on the coast of Morocco. When I returned, the load seemed to be heavier than it had been before. I had been considered a promising young scholar. I was taking a very long time to redeem the promises I had given. Even my friends began to doubt whether I would ever fulfill them.

I plodded on. My health was not good; I was not ill, I was merely tired. I went to the mountains, hoping for a speedy recovery in their bracing air. For the first time in my life I found climbing very hard, yet I kept on, concentrating my energy on lonely walks. Finally I had a breakdown. I had overstrained my heart. I had to go in for a lengthy rest cure.

My recovery was complete; but for the second time I had had a warning. This time I took heed of it. I recognized that I could not go full steam ahead for a very long period. I had to train myself not to be too passionate, not to hope for much, and not to fear much. Life might be a gray affair; it had to be lived somehow. I recognized that my troubles were not singular, that the problems I had to solve were those most men and women have been confronted with since the beginning of the world. I had to reduce speed, but I kept going.

Finally I returned to Ireland with a half-finished manuscript in my trunk. I stayed there almost a year, spending most of my time in the libraries. It was a pleasant year. I had many contacts and felt almost like a native. Horace had become president of the Department of Agriculture and wielded a good deal of influence.

In the summer months I had taken a cottage close to his.

Late in the autumn we joined forces. We took a house in Malahide, north of Dublin; I did the housekeeping with the help of his old butler. We went to Dublin early in the morning, he to his office, I to the library. I usually came home by an early train in time for tea and did some leisurely work at home until the telephone began to ring—Horace giving me instructions for dinner. I had always to be prepared for at least half a dozen guests at very short notice. Our dinners had to be substantial though not elaborate. Housekeeping was complicated, for Horace had a vegetarian fit and vegetables were not easy to get in Ireland. Some of our guests were spoiled men of the world who did not appreciate our fare. They generally enjoyed the talk. Horace had a marvelous gift for drawing out people and making them state their own point of view. He had a wonderful tenacity in argument, never giving up his point, but handling it in such a gentle way that the men whom he contradicted almost felt flattered. He finished his *Ireland in the New Century* in Malahide, a book whose brilliance broke his political career. I tried hard to prevent him from publishing it. But he could be very obstinate. He meant to have his say and he had it. His health was poor, and he was frequently overworked. I kept him in bed most Sundays, reading proof sheets with him, and attempted to hold back some of the barbed arrows that were all too numerous. Occasionally his beautiful cousin, the Countess of Fingall, came over with her children, and we had to make our bachelor quarters fit for lady visitors. In the soft autumn days we tramped for hours over the sands of Malahide. Horace's wedding present to me was a picture by Constance, "The Sands of Malahide."

After ten years my Irish labors were over. They resulted in two bulky volumes, *English Colonisation in Ireland,* and a small booklet, *Modern Ireland and Her Agrarian Problem.* The latter became a kind of handbook recommended to all those who wanted to understand the intricacies of the Irish land system.

At the turn of the century Ireland was the one and only unstable Western country. Her revolutionary movements had gone on almost without interruption for many decades. It was worth anyone's labor to study them thoroughly. After the First World War, the Continent had its own revolutions—less picturesque, but far more elemental and subversive than Ireland's agrarian explosions had ever been.

## 2. *All Roads Lead to Rome*

My Irish studies had been interrupted when my only sister had married the well-known Italian artist Aristide Sartorio. He was a charming companion, a delightful acquaintance. With a slight stoop, fair hair, and blue eyes, he looked much more like a romantic German professor than a passionate Latin painter. He had come from very simple people but was thoroughly cultivated. He was both painter and sculptor; the tender beauty of his landscapes in pastel was captivating, and his sculptures showed great strength. He was, if not a genius, a near genius. In any case he was sufficiently artistic to make an impossible husband. I liked him greatly. After I had met him a few times, I told my sister, "Ask him to tea, but do not marry him." The proof of good advice is generally found in its not being followed. She married him and soon there was a catastrophe. I had to take a hand in settling her affairs, and spent very nearly a year in Rome.

My sister was very attractive and had great social gifts. She lived in the heart of the section of Roman society to which foreigners are rarely admitted. I met many intellectual and artistic celebrities. I did the sights of Rome under excellent guidance—Giacomo Boni was a friend of ours; he took us round the Forum and showed us his latest excavations. I appreciated the beauty of the Colosseum and of the Campagna, but the mixture of the three Romes—pagan, Christian, and modern—confused me. It seemed to me like a very rich but badly organized museum. I am not a barbarian; I adored Florence and the Tuscan and Umbrian cities. My spiritual roots, like those of most modern men and women, go down to the Florence of the early Renaissance, of Michelangelo, Leonardo, and Machiavelli. But Rome did not appeal to me.

I was too priggish and too immature to appreciate my great opportunities. The type of society that flourished in Rome had disappeared nearly everywhere else. In Rome social life and social entertainment were not yet mere means for making life more pleasant or for speeding up its pace; they were its one and only object. It was anything but materialist. Genuine Roman society, with the exception of scions of the nobility who wanted to marry American heiresses, kept away from the sumptuous entertainments of the international set in the great hotels. It asked its intimate friends to very simple and very good dinners, but rarely gave big feasts at which people could gorge themselves with food and drink. Its great hostesses received after dinner two or three times a week. Once one had been admitted, one was expected to turn up regularly. On such an evening the huge salons with their ornate genuine Renaissance trappings were thronged, the men in evening dress, the women beautifully gowned. After the inevitable ceremonies of greeting and introduction, the guests dispersed in groups, sitting and standing about in the many rooms of the great palace. Sometimes one got a cup of tea, and on a hot June evening it might be a glass of lemonade; there never was any food. People came with the object of seeing other people and of being seen by them. Conversation was by no means profound. The great ladies were rarely well educated; they were all born hostesses. They could make small talk to perfection, frequently in two or three languages, and they looked lovely. The way they carried themselves, advancing slowly through the rooms to greet their hosts, reminded one of Greek goddesses.

I was not very happy at these meetings, yet I managed to get on. A number of men interested in affairs and in politics generally attended these receptions, and one could listen with profit. Some of the older women were very kind to me. We made some non-Italian friends. Among them was Gottlieb von Jagow, later German foreign secretary at the time of the outbreak of the First World War, one of the most honest men one could meet; a good diplomat but a bad foreign secretary, he had neither the ambition nor the vanity for the latter post. He knew he was unfit for the responsibilities of a great political office; he shouldered them from a sense of duty, knowing too well that his rather delicate health would greatly suffer.

I was bored, partly because my unfinished book paralyzed my energy; but partly too because I was merely an appendage of my sister, a young woman endowed with a natural aplomb, who spoke Italian like a native, and whose marital difficulties made her a romantic figure. She was a particular favorite with Donna Ersilia Lovatelli, née Gaétani, one of Rome's great ladies and an internationally famed archaeologist. She used to ask us to her Sunday dinners, at which she assembled local and foreign highbrows and carefully sandwiched them between intellectual members of Italian society. These dinners were followed by a huge reception, to which everyone who was anyone in Rome came.

I greatly enjoyed the friendship of Donna Giacinta Martini-Marescotti, a daughter of one of the Florentine noblemen who had played a part in the movement for Italian liberty. Her husband, another Florentine, Ferdinando Martini, was a writer, a poet, a member of the Italian parliament, and at one time governor of Eritrea. She was a sick woman. For days she had to stay in bed with oxygen on her bed table, yet she regularly received her friends in the late afternoon and talked politics with them. She was a liberal of the grand old type, a person who passionately believed in freedom and hated oppression; unlike many present-day liberals, with their tepid approach to good and evil, she had a fiery will for getting things done. She dominated her husband, who by temperament was an easygoing artist, and the many friends who assembled in her sickroom. When she was taking an interest in a movement or in a bill in parliament, the deputies whom she befriended had to turn up and sit round her bed arguing the situation with her. She usually lost her temper at their flabbiness and lack of decision and hurled instructions at them until she was seized by a fit. Somebody grasped the oxygen bottle and gave it to her; after a few moments' silence she had recovered her strength and started again. Her influence, exercised from a sickbed, was very much greater than that of the glamour girls who now infest politics because it is an even better way to publicity than Hollywood. She was the truest and stanchest friend anybody could have. A nation that has produced women of her type need never fear for its future.

I had to hire a carriage for my sister. Every afternoon we started out in a little victoria with black and red wheels and dropped cards on all the people we had met at the previous day's social functions. Nobody expected us to ask if they were in, and we would have been greatly embarrassed if they had been. We merely dropped cards, and having done so, drove leisurely through the Corso to the Pincio or the garden of the Villa Borghese. Hundreds of other carriages were making the same round. From time to time a carriage stopped a few minutes to give its inmates a chance of saying a few words to an acquaintance in another carriage. When passing, the ladies bowed to each other in a friendly or stiffish way according to social status and personal intimacies. If one felt like it, one stopped and walked a few steps to the terrace of the Pincio, from where one could look over the city and see the sunset. Here again one might meet some friends and chatter a little; then one reembarked, and passing through the Piazza del Popolo and the Porta del Popolo, one made for the English Tea Room and had a cup of tea. After these strenuous efforts one might go home, count and sort the number of cards dropped on one, and get ready for the evening's fray. Looking back on it and remembering it as one remembers a good film, I am glad to have seen it. While I lived through it, I was frequently bored to distraction —until one day when I had gone to a small reception at an American friend's.

Here I met a tall English girl, who laid down the law on most matters we discussed with such convincing energy that my arguments, however well founded, were just knocked flat. I was much impressed and somewhat irritated. I never imagined that I would spend most of my life in her company. She belonged to an early class of woman revolutionaries who were bored with the bucolic monotony of the English countryside. She had gone to Germany to study music, but by an unfortunate fall had hurt one of her fingers badly, and she felt she would never get to the top. As she was not interested in lesser altitudes, she dropped music and went over to painting and copying missals. She had domiciled herself in the old city of Siena, where she could study medieval painting to her heart's content. She was in Rome on a visit to our American friend.

We both managed to pick up the flu. While recovering from it, we were both rather lazy. So we strolled about a good deal in the garden of the Villa Borghese, sunning ourselves amid the fragments of dilapidated gods and goddesses and their imperial imitations. We discussed all the problems of the world, rarely agreeing, for we both are a bit contrary. We have now contradicted one another for a very long time; and I hope we may be allowed to do so a little longer.

A few weeks later I visited her in Siena, having had to go to Florence on business. I had never seen the austere red-brick city that had dared to challenge Florence. She had been living there for a year or two and had become part and parcel of local society. She introduced me to the Sienese aristocracy whose ancestors had ruled their city-state in the days of its glory, and who kept on living in their somber palaces long after it had departed, continuing to consider themselves the heart of the universe. They led the same social life as the Romans, only on a very much smaller scale. They had their parties, their receptions, their theater, their scandals, and their intrigues. I could only stay a few days, yet I fell completely under the charm of a life that had flowed evenly in the same deep channels dug in the ocher-colored earth in the days of the great revival.

My Italian stay was nearing its end. My brother-in-law had finally turned really nasty. He left his wife, his child, and his apartment and went to live at his studio, at the same time giving notice to the landlord; they would have to clear out at no distant day. I hired a depository for the furniture, most of which belonged to my sister, with, however, a good many pictures and sculptures he had given her; storage was registered in my name. He could not get at any of it without suing me. He resigned himself to writing me from time to time abusive letters, sometimes painted in red ink, in which he showered upon me the ample stock of insult that a proper knowledge of the Tuscan language can provide for the mouth of a Roman. I saved the furniture for my niece, for whom he never did anything except write her letters. My sister, her little daughter, and I packed our bags and left Rome. We traveled northward in easy stages, as she was very tired. She had never seen Siena, and we stopped there for a few days. She then went home to Mother and I lingered a little longer.

When I left Siena I had become engaged. We married a few months later in London, with the benediction, though scarcely the heartfelt approval, of our respective families. One of my wife's plain friends in her native county of Norfolk was wiser than the families. "We always knew," she was heard to say, "that Miss Theresa would marry a foreigner; it does not make much difference whether he has come from the Continent or from another county."


## 3. *My Wife's People*

A woman marrying a foreigner and settling down in his country needs a great deal of moral courage; but a foreigner who has to present himself to his future in-laws in a county of East Anglia needs hardly less.

My fiancée's father, Major Cubitt, belonged to an old Nor-folk family; he would have inherited the family place, had not his uncle, late in life, married and preferred to substitute a son of his own for a nephew. "The Major," as everyone round Nor-wich called him, was a veteran of the Indian Mutiny. When he retired from the army, he and his wife, the daughter of a naval officer, took up residence in her widowed mother's house. Thorpe Hall, once a seat of the bishops of Norwich in the sixteenth century, was an architectural gem. It was situated half an hour's walk from the city on a slope by the river Yare. Mighty walnut trees stood round the house, some of them spreading their branches over its roof; any roaring gale—and they were frequent—might bring them crashing down onto it. The river was tidal, and the house stood so low that drainage was difficult. It had no bathroom. But one really got much cleaner in the old-fashioned tub, which reposed under the bed by day, and emerged in the early morning with bath mat and a big can of hot water carried up by the maids. The tubs being shallow, one had to rub hard to keep warm.

The Major had gone into business, and as chairman of the Norwich Union Fire Insurance Co. had become fairly well-to-do and highly respected. As I remember him, he was a very tall man with a slight stoop; he reached the age of ninety-three in fairly good health. In his early business years he had not always had an easy time, living under the wing of his mother-in-law, who must have been a very autocratic *grande dame*. He was one of the straightest, kindest men one could imagine, who suffered greatly from his irascible temper. He could not control it, but felt deeply humiliated when he had been unable to do so. His children were much more fortunate; their outbreaks were like thunderstorms, heavy clouds rapidly gathering, terrific thunder and downpour and a great deal of sheet lightning, which rarely ever hit; then the air was clear and sweet, the sun shone, and nobody seemed to remember that there had been a tornado.

My first reception by the Major was none too warm. He was severely polite. After I had explained my situation, he gave me to understand that he disapproved of the marriage though he could not hinder it. He was too much of a gentleman to use the word *mésalliance*. "Do you really mean," I retorted, "that my English friends are going to cut me because I marry your daughter?" This clinched the situation. But for my mother-in-law, to whom I was then duly introduced, it would not have been comfortable. She had none of the stand-offish stiffness of the Norfolk families. At the time of my meeting her she was past middle age, but she had retained the spirit of youth long after the years had tired out her slender frame. She had spent all her life in the ossifying surroundings of county society, which to her keen sense of humor did not look as important as it claimed to be. She had managed with infinite tact to be an honored part of it, yet in the deep recesses of her mind she impishly had a good quiet laugh at it. Her daughter is very much like her, though somewhat less subdued. For some reason or other—it may have been the streak of Irish imagination she possessed— she took to me. Sometimes, I suspect, she must have revolted inwardly at the complacent narrowness of comfortable county life. She may have even envied her daughter, to whom I offered an escape from it. She realized, probably far more clearly than her husband, the risks involved in that venture; they increased rather than diminished its attractions. In any case, she accepted, I might even say adopted, me. Later on, on our regular visits, a strange intimacy, never expressed in words, developed between us. She loved to take me to garden parties in those parts of Norfolk we could reach. We drove round in an old-fashioned brougham or victoria, and had to be very careful not to overstrain the horses. I made many pleasant acquaintances through her in those faraway summer days before the First World War; I can still see the flowered dresses, set off against the red-brick walls, the vivid green of the lawns, and the dark foliage of the Norfolk trees—the trees of Constable. I walked under them, making small talk, and limiting myself to polite conversation.

I managed, I suppose, to graduate from the lowly position of a "bloody" foreigner to that of a "distinguished" foreigner. But however hard I tried, I remained an outsider. It was not the fault of my acquaintances—one or two of them became trustworthy friends—but of my own disposition. I was born to be the perfect bystander. I live the life of those around me, but it is not my life; it is a film I am privileged to see. But I did feel at home with the frail old lady who on our way home entertained me with her whimsical comments about the people we had met. She knew all their life stories, and her keen imagination saw through the dignified deportment with which they often enough hid their conventional inanities.

My three brothers-in-law were no more enthusiastic about their sister's choice than the parents. Two of them asked me to lunch at the old Sports Club to be vetted. It was not the place where they entertained their most distinguished guests. The eldest, Bertram B. Cubitt, had by that time reached the top of a distinguished civil service career. His brilliant mind, equable temper, and levelheadedness made him a most attractive personality. He was considerably older than I; but for my sister-in-law, we could have become intimate friends. She disapproved of me as a result of her training. As a young girl she had lived in eastern Europe on the outer fringe of the great diplomatic world, and had learned to blend harmoniously Continental and British prejudices. Yet she tried very hard to swallow me after the family had accepted me, and showed me kindness in many ways, though I did not fit into any of the niches where respectable people belonged. She cramped my style.

The youngest brother, Thomas Astley, was at that time a dashing officer with quite a record of devilry behind him. He had started in India, where he had almost gone on the rocks, and had been sent for repentance to Aden. He had joined Lugard's band of adventurous empire builders and had survived the murderous climate of West Africa. He gave us the pink umbrella (made in Birmingham) under which the emir of Kano had sat; it did not fit badly with the colors the sun rays painted on our terrace in the Austrian mountains. He was by then considered a soldier of very great promise. His active life ended as governor of Bermuda, where there was little scope for his fine talents; I always thought he was too good for the role of imperial bartender in which American tourists were inclined to see him. He and his sister were very close to one another and very alike in some ways. It was perhaps for that reason that we hit it off very well. We had few interests in common—scarcely any after we could no longer afford horses; we looked at the world from almost opposite angles, and yet we enjoyed each other's company and understood one another. I have fought militarism all my life, long before it became a pastime of tearful male and female sob sisters, but whenever I met a general in private life, I got on very well with him—perhaps because, behind my indifference, I really like a fight when I am once in it.

The luncheon at the Sports Club was not a gay affair. We all behaved like English gentlemen. We made polite conversation, discussing everything except the personal affair which was the object of our meeting.

My third brother-in-law, Julian F. Cubitt, was not of the party. He disapproved as a matter of principle, irrespective of me as a person. He was in business in the west of England. He has the most orderly mind possible; it is a kind of living card index. Yet he possesses real understanding for art, and would have done extremely well as a classic scholar, measuring and weighing syllables and interpolating commas in the right places. He lives for order and fortunately is still with us. It is a misfortune that he did not get his heart's desire early in life to go into the navy; his knowledge of naval matters is immense, and his memory for geographical details accumulated on his journeys abroad is fantastic.

On the death of two old aunts he inherited the small estate whence his paternal grandfather, a "squarson" (squire-parson), had ruled his Suffolk parish. It is a bleak, pale brick house, the nakedness of which was his own personal contribution, for he had cut down the ivy creepers that mercifully hid its ugliness; he is the last of the race of benevolent village dictators. As he is quite devoid of self-seeking, and always willing to further somebody's interest, his activities have piled up considerably and have left him just enough leisure to read *The Times* late at night.

The estate is small, and surrounded by much larger ones, but they mostly belong to newcomers, the descendants of prosperous businessmen who settled in the county fifty or even a hundred years ago, but who, in the eyes of the older natives, are not yet quite "county." He is the patron of the living—it is a little Anglo-Saxon church with round tower and thatched roof; its mural fresco of St. Christopher has gone, unfortunately beyond repair. He has to appoint the parson, with the consent of the bishop of the diocese, and is thus directly responsible for the spiritual welfare of the parishioners. It is not always easy to find the right man; the living is poor and the parish small. His neighbors have many other occupations; they recognize his generous nature, and leave things to him. He has identified himself with the people's interests and is willing to work himself to death in their service. He is like a feudal lord whose mission before God and his conscience is to force cleanliness, saintliness, and happiness on his retainers in those lonely marshes.

Our wedding, as one can imagine, was not one of the most brilliant events of the season. The parson of my father-in-law's church was a "priest" with strong Anglo-Catholic inclinations; he had scruples about putting his church at the disposal of that broad-minded cousin of my wife's, Spencer Cubitt, who wished to marry us. So the wedding took place in London, in a very unattractive church in Marylebone. There was a family dinner the night before, the excellence of which could not make one forget the drabness of the locality. The Major provided an equally excellent reception at the hotel, bustling us off as quickly as he could, for he meant to catch an afternoon train back to Thorpe. As a retribution he missed it. My cousin Max had seen me safely through the ceremony and secured our tickets. As the Major had upset our timetable, we arrived fully an hour ahead of time at Victoria. There Tom Cubitt and the cousins Mabel and William Thwaites joined us, and we had a send-off tea in the station. It certainly was an odd wedding, but was not a bad prelude to our joint life, which was never quite orthodox.

# VII. British South Africa
## (1906-1907)

### 1. *White South Africa*

MY LIFE as budding professor at a German university—I was *Privatdozent* at Munich—was not very exciting. My lecturing duties were neither very exacting nor very profitable. Having finished a cumbersome book on which I had spent nearly ten years, I was not in a hurry to tackle another big topic. Yet I was looking out for an attractive subject. I had been interested in colonial problems ever since I had written my doctor's thesis on the decay of Spain and its connection with the inflow of precious metals from the New World. My study of English colonization in Ireland had made me conversant with nearly every type of colonial venture; for the British had applied, generally with but scant success, every imaginable method of colonization to the solution of the Irish problem. My wife was beginning to be bored; she did not take very kindly to the somewhat narrow social life of a junior member of the faculty. She has her people's adventurous spirit, which has made them go to the remotest corners of the world; I am merely restless. In any case something had to be done, and we decided on going to South Africa.

I was interested in the interpenetration of native life by Western capitalism, and South Africa offered a unique opportunity for studying this problem. Two white races, Briton and Boer, were fighting for supremacy; in the gold and diamond industries, and in widely different agricultural occupations, all types of native populations and imported colored labor were employed.

I took a year's leave. The university authorities were not

convinced of the seriousness of my quest, but as they did not
have to pay me, they let me go.

After a summer in England for vacation and preparations we
embarked in Trieste on a steamer of the Austrian Lloyd, and
breaking the long voyage at Suez, Mombasa, and Zanzibar,
finally landed at Durban. There the minister of railroads took
us in hand and showed us everything we wanted to see.

We made an excursion to the tea plantations, spending a
night in Stanger in one of the worst hotels it has ever been our
lot to sleep in, or rather not to sleep in. Bedbugs from below
and mosquitoes from above joined in a pincer attack in which
we were thoroughly defeated. I needed all my energy to tramp
next day over the cane fields. Plantations and sugar mills were
worked by Indian coolies; I have never seen more miserable-
looking specimens of humanity living in more squalid condi-.
tions. Even the government barracks in Durban, where they
were received after landing, were shocking.

We proceeded to the capital, Pieter-Maritzburg, a kind of
metropolitan village, to pay our respects to the governor, and
thence to Harrysmith in the Orange River Colony on our way
to Basutoland.

Leaving the railroad, we took to a Cape cart, a two-wheeled
vehicle with a folding top and four seats in two rows; the
driver sits in front, so close that one's knees almost touch his
back. Old-fashioned Boers are very race-conscious. They will
not travel in the same railway coach with a native; they dislike
his smell, they say. But they do not mind it sitting close behind
him in their own cart, getting a whiff firsthand. Traveling in a
Cape cart in fine weather was great fun. One was bumped about
a little—but the beauty of the African veldt, its huge expanse,
its ocher-colored soil, and the bold lines of the mountains in the
background, compensated for small inconveniences. But the
storms were awful. Lightning hit the iron-flecked rocks strewn
over the veldt, the thunder crashed, the hail pelted the horses,
one never was sure whether or not they would bolt. Finally we
arrived at Maseru, capital of Basutoland. The resident commissioner kindly invited us to stay with him, and when he had to
evacuate us because other guests were arriving the resident physician took us over. We lived in a detached round house (*rond*

*hovel*) where South Africans usually house their guests, built of adobe and covered with thatch.

Basutoland is a country of towering peaks, deep valleys, and rushing streams—the mountain refuge of a valiant race. The Basuto, whom a wise native chief, Moshesh, had fused into a powerful native state, were fairly safe in their narrow valleys and steep mountain slopes where there was room only for small plots. They were well armed. They had gone to Kimberley in the early days, worked in the mines, saved their pay, and bought guns with it. They had been at war several times with Cape Colony and shown themselves formidable opponents, but they were willing to stay within their mountain fastnesses provided they were not interfered with. Basutoland was an imperial protectorate; no white settlers were admitted. A number of white traders with special permits had taken up their residence in particular localities. The only other white men within the country were government officials and missionaries. Here, too, the Basuto were fortunate. They had come under the influence of the (Calvinist) Parisian Mission, which had sent out good agents. They had learned the natives' language and understood their ways; they had converted the chief and had made him take an intelligent interest in the welfare of his people.

My Irish studies had taught me a good deal about primitive economic life and tribal law; it now came in very handy, for in Africa many early institutions such as cattle loans had survived. I saw that a sympathetic administration could preserve native customs and rule and civilize a tribe, as long as it could keep out white settlers who wanted land and white traders who sold guns and rum. Its position was precarious. Neighboring whites wanted native labor, and the natives wanted wages to buy guns and other European commodities. Yet as long as the country appeared inhospitable, strict segregation could be maintained. Once great wealth was discovered in the mountains—gold, coal, or oil—it would need a very strong government to keep out greedy invaders. So far Basutoland has weathered the storm. It is still a separate protectorate under imperial control. It is much easier for the imperial government in London to ward off claims of white land-grabbers than it would be for the Union of South Africa, whose government may depend on their votes.

Just before we were leaving Basutoland, the weather seemed to break. A cloud was rapidly approaching from the west. A huge pall of smoke blotted out the sun. It was a dense swarm of locusts; they would have devastated the region in a few minutes, eating up all crops to the last blade. Fortunately the swarm changed its course. The cloud disappeared as quickly as it had emerged.

From Maseru in a few hours we reached Bloemfontein, the capital of what then was the Orange River Colony. It was a pleasant, village-like town with long avenues of trees; it had some of the charm of a New England town, spoiled—as throughout South Africa—by buildings with corrugated iron roofs. The acting governor, Sir Henry Wilson, and his wife were hospitable and helpful; he had been at college with my eldest brother-in-law, which counted for more than our official letters of introduction. I visited some of the towns familiar to me since boyhood from Uncle Maurice's yarns of Kaffir wars and Boer folkways. I went around the country inspecting the settlements the British government had undertaken in order to strengthen the British element in the colony. Lord Milner dreamed of a white South Africa. He had induced some of the volunteers of the Boer War to settle down on lands given to them on fairly easy terms. On paper the plans were excellent; results, even at that time, seemed poor. Africa is a cruel mistress who slays those Europeans who fall in love with her. Farming is fairly safe only for newcomers with ample capital, who can replace losses that cattle pests, locusts, and other almost inevitable calamities are sure to inflict. The plight of these gallant men was very depressing. They were up against it, and however brave they were, they could scarcely hope to pull through. The Duke of Westminster had laid out a huge estate among them and built a luxurious mansion in which his hospitable administrator resided; he had successfully transplanted the English countryside to the African veldt, regardless of cost. I recognized very clearly that Africa is a black man's country, where whites can prosper only if they have sufficient wealth to back them up.

## 2. The Mines

We reached Johannesburg in the last days of the year 1906. The golden city had long passed the stage of a mining camp. Imposing skyscrapers housed her business concerns; the Carlton Hotel would have satisfied even American demands. The streets were full of the bustling life of a modern metropolis. Yet little wooden shacks and shanties with corrugated iron roofs were interspersed everywhere. Outside the central district, huts and hovels still bore the hallmarks of the callous disorder of a struggling camp  The city was the heart of a 170-mile-long mining field which stretches at the present time from the town of Heidelberg to that of Klerksdorp. Its nearest counterpart was the Ruhr district in Westphalia. An intricate rail system united the struggling, straggling towns. From the roof of the Corner House one could see a black ribbon spread from east to west: belching chimney stacks, rattling stamp mills, screeching hoists that raised and lowered cages from and to the bowels of the earth—at that time some of the mines were five thousand feet underground. The roar near the mills was ceaseless and stupefying. The country was a flat, six-thousand-foot-high plateau, to the north of which shimmered the blue Magaliesbergs. It had been a treeless plain when the first diggers had struck camp; now eucalyptus trees grew everywhere, and many residences in the suburbs were surrounded by leafy gardens. Some of the magnates continued to live in unassuming, comfortable suburban houses; others had built sumptuous palaces—Gothic, Dutch, or Renaissance, whatever their fancy.

The Rand remained as cosmopolitan as in its early days when diggers had flocked to it from all parts of the world. But mining had become a large-scale capitalist enterprise, with little scope for small operators. There were other opportunities for the enterprising—real estate, building, contracting, trading, licit and illicit, with white and colored people. Lord Bryce described the Johannesburg of his day as an Anglo-Jewish city; this remained true of the upper stratum, yet nearly all nationalities were represented. High-ranking American mining engineers with their families, a few Dutchmen from the Netherlands, and a few Germans played their part in it; one or two Afrikanders (Dutchmen) had come to the top.

The middle and lower strata were even more mixed. Half-breeds from Cape Colony lived side by side in miserable shanties with poor, uneducated African Dutchmen who despised work done by Kaffirs but were incapable of doing better jobs. Most of the twenty-thousand-odd skilled miners on the Rand at that time were English; many came from Cornwall. They were partly small entrepreneurs, partly salaried workmen. These sturdy independent fellows had hoped to make their fortunes in Africa; they had only managed to get high wages, the purchasing power of which under African conditions was pretty low. They were disgruntled and easily irritated. Mining deep down in the earth in a sweltering heat did not make for gentle tempers, and the high altitude affected people's hearts and nerves even if they did not drink.

These white miners behaved like bosses, for the bulk of the heavy manual work was done under their guidance by natives or by Chinese. They very rapidly developed the superiority complex of white masters who can order native boys about. They hated the mine owners, who got away with the swag that should have belonged to honest diggers. They did not like the solid Dutch who sat on their farms and did not believe in progress, and they despised their offspring, the poor whites who flocked to the gold fields. Most of the natives were raw, unskilled workers who came from the native kraals for half a year or so, lured from their homes by touting agents who made them all sorts of promises. They came only when they needed cash in order to buy cattle; without cattle they could not buy a wife, and without a wife they could not set up for themselves. The women tilled the mealie plot on which grew corn and millet; the men looked after the cattle. Women were investments. The standard price of a maiden in those days was about ten head of cattle. When a worker had earned enough, he left the mines for good if he could afford to do so, for life in the mines was hard. The men were housed in huge, wire-fenced barracks called compounds that communicated only with the mines; they were not allowed to leave until their contracts expired. Had they been permitted to move about freely, many would have run away and few would have survived bad outside contacts. On payday hordes of ruffians lay in wait and robbed them of their wages after making them drunk with poisoned spirits. The government tried hard to protect them, and so did the companies. This was by no means easy. On the Rand, as elsewhere, liberty and security do not always tally. The natives were well fed and most compounds were sanitary—far more so than the hovels in which the poor whites lived. But mortality was high on account of the nature of quartz mining; and it was hard for the natives to fit into the huge modern industrial mechanism.

I asked a Zulu chief why his people did not go to the mines —for from their point of view pay was good.

"I am going underground when I am dead," he replied, "but not before."

During the Boer War the natives had made a great deal of money; as long as it lasted they would not return to the mines. The recent introduction of thousands of Chinese coolies, physically well fitted for the work, was to solve the labor problem. Both British and Boers objected—this coolie competition was sure to close all avenues of social advance to struggling white Afrikanders—and agreed to their admission only upon guarantees of compulsory repatriation after termination of contracts. The Chinese were not permitted to take up any other occupation or to settle in South Africa. During their stay they were confined within huge barracks, from which outsiders were excluded; there was great fear that stray Chinese might commit crimes. The mine owners would have preferred free Chinese laborers, but they had to submit to African public opinion. British public opinion was aghast at what looked to it like a newfangled system of slavery; the anti-Chinese-slavery cry had contributed greatly to the overwhelming Liberal victory in the 1906 election.

The Chinese gave but moderate satisfaction. They were very much more intelligent than the natives, but not half as docile. The natives had become accustomed to being kicked around by a rough white boss; the Chinese had not. They gave a great deal of trouble. The experiment was but transitory; the contracts were not renewed. It was fascinating to watch three of the world's great races, 17,000 white men, 52,000 Chinese, and 112,000 black people working side by side in a modern industry that published its cost accounts. Two white men, it was generally assumed, could do the work of five black men; white daily wages were about twenty shillings a head per day, the cost of black labor (including recruiting, housing, feeding, etc.) amounted to four shillings. White labor was at least twice as expensive as black labor. It was, moreover, much more independent. A limited number of white workers organized in unions enjoyed a kind of monopoly, for colored labor was excluded by law from all skilled occupations.

On its technical side the mining industry represented a most advanced form of capitalism. Socially it was a queer compound of capitalism, feudalism, and tribalism, to which white labor added a strong tinge of socialist syndicalism. It showed the fundamental weakness of African society far more clearly than agriculture. As long as black labor was seasonal and workers returned to their rural tribal life after a short stay in the mines, social dangers were not very great. Once tribal ties were broken completely and a black proletariat had been created, depending exclusively on wages and unable to rise to skilled positions on account of the entrenched position of white labor, the situation would become very tense. Both labor groups, white and black, lived in constant fear and resentment, the whites because they had to ward off native aspirations that were bound to grow as the natives became more efficient, the blacks because they could not break through the barrier of privilege by which the whites protected themselves. The Rand showed better than anything else the difficulty of a composite society in which two races live side by side, depend on one another, cannot separate, and cannot fuse.

## 3. *The Magnates*

We soon were on friendly terms with a few leading magnates. Many of them had started life low down in the social scale and had risen to wealth and power by their own ability. They had been adventurers rather than businessmen. Nearly all of them had had to face dangers and had suffered severe deprivations before they had come to the top. They were almost classic representatives of colonial capitalism. Their wealth was not derived from exploiting their fellow men, the surplus value of whose labor they had annexed, to use socialist lingo, but from rifling a new country's great natural resources. Many were gamblers rather than men of affairs; they would run risks not so much on account of the prizes they might win as because they loved to take a chance. They never quite took to the sedate conventionalities of respectable city bankers. The King could knight them or make baronets of them; he could not turn them into gentlemen. They possessed an astounding zest and virility. In their youth they had pitted their wits against slim back-veldt Boers or cunning native chiefs. They had roughed it in the open spaces, breaking clay in Kimberley or washing pebbles on some long ago petered-out gold mine. At last they had arrived and built their fortunes on the conglomerate of the Rand, which turned out to be nearly inexhaustible. They had invaded the City and were handling and rehandling stocks and shares for the more or less fortunate investors who had followed their lead. By now nearly all of them had become outwardly respectable; a few showed that they were near geniuses whom even success could not completely conventionalize.

We met many leaders of Johannesburg society—social and business leadership coincided, not always with happy results. A few big businessmen had accepted imperial domination only because it was inevitable; they would have been quite as happy under reasonable Boer rule. The majority were thoroughgoing Britons even if not born in the British Isles. Yet most of them were turning into "true Afrikanders" and looked upon the sub-continent as their children's home. Others longed for the glories of Park Lane and the modest beauties of the English countryside. To them South Africa, its gold, and its diamonds were but the golden key that would open hitherto closed doors of Mayfair to them. Outwardly Johannesburg society was completely Anglicized. Inwardly it was not very mellow. It was torn by frictions and jealousies both among men and among women, yet society as a whole was too small to split up into permanent rival camps. As we did not belong to any faction we had a very good time.

During our stay in Johannesburg the first elections to the Transvaal Parliament were taking place. The core of the Rand was British; but the miners—frustrated capitalists—although despising the poor whites of Boer origin, were quite willing to join them in attacking the capitalists. Most of our magnate friends were candidates; we followed them round the Rand on their electioneering campaigns. They were very optimistic and expected to sweep the country; we felt strongly a kind of ugly undercurrent. Although an election campaign after the war was not the best time for knowing both sides, we did spend a few days in Pretoria and got in touch with some of the Boer leaders. The issues were rather complicated—a mixture of racial and social questions, Boer against Briton, capital against labor, liberalism against conservatism, town against country. A number of English businessmen of the liberal type sided with the Boers. They feared domination by monopolized business such as had developed in Kimberley. Their fears were not unjustified; big business in that part of the world had not yet shed its predatory habits.

In the end big business was beaten. Botha and Smuts triumphed and formed the first Transvaal government. They showed their political wisdom by declaring their willingness to remain within the British Empire. The world, and especially Germany, was almost dumbfounded. This inexplicable change was partly the reply to the generosity of the Liberal government in Great Britain, which had offered self-government to a vanquished enemy a few years after its defeat. But the main cause was fear of Germany. The native rising in German South West Africa (1904) had assumed the proportions of a major colonial war. A large German army had been sent overseas and had finally crushed the natives with the utmost brutality. It had enlisted many Cape Boers as transport riders; they brought back a good deal of information. The Boers suddenly discovered that South Africa was not an island but bordered on the possessions of the greatest military power of the age. Without the British navy they could never hope to defend themselves.

Pretoria was a somnolent country town that even the presence of the imperial government had not greatly stepped up. South Africa was an easygoing country. With but few exceptions, governments and government officials were very friendly.

Lord Milner, before his recall, had appointed a group of able young men who had just taken their university degrees. They were called his kindergarten; they looked even younger than they were. They were very irritating when they sheltered themselves behind the nonchalant boredom that has so often been fashionable at Oxford. When one had pierced this shell, they were quite human. The most picturesque of them, John Buchan, had already left for Europe. He became our close friend a little later. He had soaked himself in African lore; the result was his fascinating book *Prester John*, which established him as one of the great romancers of his time. Robert Brand (now Lord Brand) and the late Lord Lothian, then Philip Kerr, lived in a little house outside Johannesburg; the former was running the railroads, the latter was engaged in studying the poor white question and South African federation. The dinner to which they asked us on a January evening, 1907, had important political consequences; but for it the Spa Conference of 1920 might have ended with the invasion of the Ruhr under British leadership.

## 4. *The Shadow of Cecil Rhodes*

We were passing through Rhodesia on our way to the Victoria Falls. From Bulawayo, capital of what had been Matabeleland, we drove for two days through parklike, undulating country to reach the Matoppo Hills, where Cecil Rhodes is buried. The dome-shaped hill is not very high. A few huge basalt boulders—skittle balls shaped for a giant's hand—are scattered on its top. The flat space between them is Rhodes's resting place. It is as lonely a spot as a man could desire who wants to spend eternity away from the bustling crowds. No settlements and no houses are anywhere in sight. A lonely Matabele warrior silently keeps watch over the grave of the Great Chief who broke his tribe. Those who approach the grave uncover their heads; they speak with hushed voices as if they were in the presence of one towering far above mere mortals. There is nothing of that theatrical stage-play by which modern dictators have tried to inflate themselves into supermen, nothing but solemn homage to the memory of one in whom vice and virtue were strangely blended but whose greatness was proved by the allegiance of men, white and black; they fought and followed him in life; they now revered him in death.

From Bulawayo, again, we wended our way northward through ever increasing heat toward the great river. The Falls have been described many times: the vast expanse of the river before it jumps down the huge parapet (one floats over its lake-like surface in a native canoe, being warned by the guide that an inconsiderate hippopotamus might easily overturn it when it wished to get a breath of air); the rain forest below the falls, where the spray enshrouds one in percolating steam that reflects all the colors of the rainbow. But the deepest, most lasting impression was the view of the river from the bridge, crossing it toward Northern Rhodesia. It was a full moon; the African night framed the sky with a dark blue panoply descending from a silvery orb. Below it flowed the river, calm and majestic, breathing a kind of satisfaction at having accomplished its great task, a relief at being able henceforth to reach its destination and to merge itself in the sea without having to pass any more unsurmountable obstacles.

We went straight south to Kimberley, skirting the bare, yellow-brown Kalahari Desert. There was nothing to do but to sleep in the night and in the day to gaze at the glaring, empty vastness of Africa. Occasionally at a station a group of miserable huts was visible, inhabited by the Bechuanas, who seemed to be one of the depressed races of mankind; they had little in common with the proud warriors of Zulu and Matabeleland whom we had encountered.

Kimberley was the greatest company town of the world. In its way it was as much a monument to Cecil Rhodes and his dynamic strength as his majestic resting place in the Matoppos. The camp days of diamond digging had passed long ago. The place of the adventurers had been taken by the De Beers Company, which owned and ruled the town, possessing at that time the most closely knit monopoly in the world, and probably the only monopoly that has ever been popular with consumers. By maintaining the price of diamonds it attracted new buyers and protected those who owned jewels. For nobody would have been willing to invest money in a useless bauble, the price of which was declining.

The company owned nearly everything in Kimberley; it had made nearly everything but the diamonds. The site on which the town stands had been a piece of arid land. All comforts had to be artificially created. The company owned the mines, the waterworks, all other utilities; it was, so to speak, the municipality. It owned the hotel; no one could stay there who was not acceptable as its guest. It had planted trees and gardens, built houses for its employees, and made life as bearable as possible for them in such a godforsaken spot.

The mines, huge cylindrical holes going straight down into the bowels of the earth, were being deepened and widened all the time. When one stood at the rim they looked like a gigantic comb of beeswax, the core of which had been taken out, its circumference full of little niches and galleries in which men moved looking like tiny specks of sand. Huge hoists carried the load from the bottom. The clay was laid out in large fenced fields, incessantly guarded, to decompose under the sun and the rare rains. Whenever it was ripe for treatment and the market ready for another supply, it was washed on huge, pulsating screens from which the diamonds were picked.

Kimberley's great problem was diamond stealing and illicit diamond trading. A diamond is watched almost as carefully as a non-co-operator in a totalitarian state is shadowed by the Gestapo. Native workers were confined within huge compounds. When they entered them they had to leave their belongings with the guards, to be returned to them when their contracts had expired. A few days before they were released, they were taken to the detention house, where they did not work but were given laxatives; for experience had shown that swallowing was the easiest way of smuggling diamonds.

Kimberley was an almost perfect example of monopolist capitalism embedded in tribal life. Its patriarchalism made for fairly good social conditions among its colored employees. They got good pay, were well fed and well treated according to native standards (I saw a very well-equipped hospital), and were protected from wasting their money and from being robbed. They did not mind the complete absence of personal liberty—most of them, living in tribal organizations, did not know the meaning of individualism; their social system has rightly been described as Kaffir socialism. Work in the mines, moreover, was but a short interlude in their lives that enabled them to enjoy later the benefits of that leisure which their civilization wisely holds out to be man's greatest boon.

The attitude of the white employees was different. They were well paid and well cared for; those higher up had developed a loyalty to the company, yet all of them felt unfree. They could think what they liked, but it would be rather unwise to give expression to their thoughts, for the company was not only their paymaster; it was a political power. It controlled Kimberley's members of parliament and through its wealth had great weight in Cape politics.

In some ways Kimberley was a glaring spiritual contradiction. The men and women who lived on its bounty had dissociated themselves from the drab uniformity of an older civilization. They had been driven to the deserts of Africa by a yearning for freedom and adventure. They now formed part of a social life far less flexible than that they had left at home.

## 5. *The Cape*

From the arid region we passed through the Karoo, the great African steppe, crossed the mountains that divide the Cape peninsula from the interior, and on a pleasant morning arrived in Cape Town.

It was an old town; some of its houses, especially in the suburbs, retained the beauty of old Dutch colonial architecture. Its situation at the foot of Table Mountain was magnificent; the avenue leading to Parliament House was beautiful. The city proper seemed rather mean. It had little of the bustling, pulsating life of Johannesburg; its easy ways reminded me of "dear, dirty Dublin." It was a home to many races; a large part of its population was colored, the offspring of Hottentots and whites, with an occasional admixture of Malay. As colored people who had broken away from tribal life had equal rights with the whites, it was democratic. Cecil Rhodes's slogan, "Equal rights for all civilized men up to the Zambesi," was the law of Cape Colony.

A friend from my Irish days, Patrick (now Sir Patrick) Hannon, had gone out to South Africa as adviser to the co-operative movement; he got hold of me immediately after my arrival and boosted me grandly. He asked me to dinner with the most important members of the Cape cabinet and made me deliver a speech for which I was not in the least prepared. As sometimes happens it was the right sort of speech, and it opened many doors. The governor of Cape Colony, Sir Walter Hely-Hutchinson, another Irishman, took a fancy to us and asked us often to Government House. He became very fond of my wife. When we decided later to go to German South West Africa, he implored her to let me travel alone. "You'll come back with a face like an old racing saddle," he said to her, vainly appealing to a woman's vanity. Fortunately he was wrong.

The most interesting personality we met was John X. Merriman, former and future prime minister of the Cape. He was a romantic Victorian Liberal, a rare but lovable type, a dreamer who could act, for Cape Colony in the early days was not a country where one could make one's way by gaping at the moon. He was a knight crusader who wanted to free the world from evil, and a stern Puritan who was not quite sure whether it could ever be done. He hated the Rand and everything it stood for, its grabbing capitalism. He loved the land and those who worked it. In some ways he was a fervent imperialist, proud of British traditions and British character; at the same time he was a Little Englander who hated the methods of scheming, graft, and coercion by which empires had been won. Notwithstanding long political experience, he had the simplicity of a child—it was easy to eliminate him from power when the Union of South Africa was finally established. He and his equally attractive wife lived in an old Dutch farmhouse in Stellenbosch on a fruit ranch in one of those lovely mountain valleys whose replica one finds in the southern Tyrol and in some corners of California. We stayed with them several times. Through him we got in touch with the ultra-Dutch who controlled the theological seminary at Stellenbosch, the spiritual backbone of Boer nationalism. Our friendship lasted until his death. On his last journey to Europe he and his wife spent a few days with us at the Lake of the Roses in Bavaria.

Germany was represented in Cape Town by a very distinguished consul general, von Humboldt-Dachroeden, a grandson of the great Wilhelm von Humboldt. He was anything but popular with the local Germans. German colonies in foreign cities were usually divided into two camps. Those who had prospered had fused cheerfully with their hosts; the less successful ones sulked. In South Africa things were particularly bad. German sentiment had sided with the Boers. Liberals had been shocked at British militarist imperialism. German racialists looked upon Dutchmen as closely related fellow Germans (Low Germans); they never understood why Dutchmen did not desire to amalgamate with them or why their descendants in the Cape—half of whom were of Huguenot origin—greatly disliked Germany's nearness in South West Africa. They had hoped that by playing with the Boers Germany might become the dominant power in South Africa. The very astute Boer politicians saw through their game.

The first contribution to the British navy by a dominion had been made by a prime minister of Dutch origin, Jan Hofmeyr, shortly after Germany had settled down in South West Africa; he had made the first plan for imperial federation. Yet the same man had organized the Afrikander Bond, the powerful organization of the Dutch. He was the most important single personality in the Cape. He had officially withdrawn from active politics and was difficult of access, being satisfied with the role of the spider spinning his web. My meeting with him was rather futile. "Onser Jan" received me very kindly; he was willing to exchange pleasant platitudes with me. He listened carefully to what I said, but I could not elicit anything from him that would be worth quoting. He did not believe in headlines or in running politics by interviews. Many years later I was received by President Coolidge. Our conversation was not unlike my talk with "Onser Jan"—with one great difference: I am sure President Coolidge did not keep back from me any profound ideas of his own; "Onser Jan" did.

We met nearly all the important people in Cape Town, and had a chance to see the enchanting residential villages that cluster around the town. We visited, naturally, "Groote Schur," the Dutch mansion Cecil Rhodes had built. Its mellow, graceful simplicity must have formed a curious background to the violent giant who had managed to throw his shadow over the entire subcontinent while he lived, and whose name is written in large letters over the two countries that nowadays prolong South Africa almost into the heart of the continent.

Cape Town and the entire western province were not faced with a genuine native problem. The Hottentots and the Bushmen who had inhabited the country had never been numerous. The latter had almost vanished; the former had easily fitted as servants into primitive Boer life. Had the western province stood by itself, its future would have been on the American plan; it would have become a white man's country, whose structure the handful of surviving natives would hardly have affected. But the east and the northeast of the country were inhabited by dense masses of tribal populations. There had been many frontier wars, until finally all the country west of Natal had been pacified.

## 6. The Kraals

The eastern province of Cape Colony, settled after the Napoleonic Wars, bordered on broken native tribes. This area, called British Kaffraria, had come easily under British control. It had to be protected against more warlike tribes across the Kei River. It was settled after the Crimean War by the Hanoverian Legion, organized by Baron Stutterheim, which had not seen action; the members were offered land under a kind of military tenure. Beyond the border district were the Trans-Kei and the so-called Native Territories, comprising a number of powerful tribes under the control of the Cape government.

We spent some time in King William's Town, center of the German settlements. As in all colonial ventures there had been some failures, but a number of villages bearing German names had survived. Their inhabitants no longer formed a frontier militia; by now all tribes were under government control, and settlers could concentrate on farming. In these fertile districts with ample rainfall they were prospering. Nearly all of them still spoke German, though they had become very loyal British Afrikanders.

To the huge native reserve beyond, white settlers were not admitted. Small groups of white merchants, mechanics, missionaries, doctors, and officials lived in a few urban centers. In the rural areas licensed traders could rent from the natives the sites needed for their stations; they could not acquire them. There were no railroads and few hotels. We traveled by Cape cart and usually stayed at one of the trading posts, where we rented a "round hovel."

The Trans-Kei had been settled by the Fingos, a native tribe whose political unity had been broken by their more warlike neighbors. They had taken easily to civilization under the control of the Cape government. Cecil Rhodes had inaugurated in 1894 an extremely interesting experiment in a district called Glen Grey. With the consent of the natives he had split tribal lands held in common into individual farms. These holdings could not be sold, divided, or mortgaged—they were very much like the hereditary farms, that great discovery of Nazi sociologists. The breaking up of tribal property had naturally diminished the power of the chiefs. In order to replace it and to train the people in self-government, rural councils had been formed in which the natives were associated with their magistrates in the management of district affairs.

The Native Territories proper were far more primitive; here tribal life flourished undisturbed. Since tribes could no longer go to war with one another, the main outlet for their energies had been closed. They had to be taught the ways of peace; this meant a complete change of their outlook on life. The administrators of this large area governed from the Department of Native Affairs in Cape Colony. Reared in the humanitarian spirit of the missions, they combined understanding and sympathy with a firm hand, and managed to maintain peace among peoples many of whom were not far removed from the savage state. They did it by moral pressure rather than by force. The Cape mounted police, on which they had to rely in extreme cases, was a very efficient but not a very numerous body.

Mountains and valleys, brown streams, green fields, red earth, and blue hills passed before one's eyes. Each hill was topped by a number of circular, grass-covered huts forming a semicircle open toward the slope. A little below it was the kraal, an enclosure made of thorn or branches in which the cattle were kept. The settlement was the home of a native group, sometimes a chief and his family; every hummock was dotted with them.

When we had had our fill of wandering and a few more weeks in Cape Town had stretched our absence to three quarters of a year, we thought of going home. But our plan was countermanded, from a most unexpected quarter.

Germany had suddenly become colony-conscious. Prince Bülow had formed a coalition government of liberals and conservatives against socialists and clericals; he had appointed Bernhard Dernburg colonial secretary. A new colonial age was dawning. Munich University, which had not approved very heartily of our African expedition, now insisted on its being extended by a visit to the German colonies. It did not realize that traveling in German South West Africa was a far cry from the comfort of a hotel in Johannesburg or Cape Town.

In Cape Town they looked upon German South West Africa as a kind of antechamber of Hell, a huge sandbox full of nothing but pestiferous insects. The aftermath of the native rebellion was not yet over; it had certainly not increased traveling amenities. My wife's adventurous spirit was kindled by the prospect of real pioneering and of living in the vast, great veldt. By day, I was equally enthusiastic; by night, as usual, I had awful nightmares in which I clearly foresaw all dangers. But we made up our minds. We bought a camping outfit—a small patrol tent and a few other gadgets which we certainly could not have acquired on the spot later. The Merrimans saw us off on the German steamer *Kronprinz*. We left Cape Town in a terrific May gale that justified the well-known reputation of the Cape. I was terribly seasick.

# VIII. German South West Africa (1907)

## 1. Settlers and Natives

Two DAYS later we pushed through a bank of gray fog. Beyond it stretched a long line of pale sand dunes above which the roofs of a miserable-looking settlement were visible. This was Swakopmund, the port of entry to German South West Africa— an open roadstead, with a terrific ground swell. We were lowered in a chair and had to jump into the arms of the attendant boatmen; luggage was just dumped down. A few horses for the garrison were let down by strap; they enjoyed it even less than we did. We crouched in the small boat while it was being loaded; the ground swell was almost unbearable. After an uncomfortable interval we were set down at a landing stage on a sand spit, whence a few colored boys carried our luggage to a wooden structure—the Hotel Bismarck.

Swakopmund was a godforsaken place. The only natural harbor in the colony, Walvis Bay, belonged to Cape Colony. It stood on the fringe of the dune belt thirty to forty miles broad called the Namib, which stretched along the coast of the colony, waterless and with hardly any vegetation. Swakopmund's one and only redeeming feature was moderate temperature; it was fairly cool, but damp and foggy. The contraption that after a day or two carried us toward the capital was a railroad by courtesy only. The coaches, fashioned after out-of-date Prussian fourth- and third-class carriages, had wooden benches and looked like second-rate trolleys. The funny-looking little engine could go neither far nor fast. It took us a whole day to reach Karibib, the railroad junction a hundred miles inland. The inn where we had to spend a night catered to a few travelers and served as an officers' mess. Everybody glared and stared at us, full of suspicion.

One evidently did not expect anybody to come to this part of the world without sinister intentions.

We traversed once again the vast African veldt, covered with boulders and sparse, yellow grass—it was midwinter and everything was dry. Ill-tempered-looking mimosa trees pointed their thorny, wriggly branches at us. Occasionally we passed a lonely farm near a station or saw a few head of cattle. The towering mass of the Erongo Mountains loomed in the background. Above us glared the hard blue African sky. The next day we reached Windhoek, the capital, a big village with sandy streets, a complete absence of sanitary drainage, and some ugly, barrack-like government buildings. Its population consisted of a few traders, a few mechanics, some farmers, a doctor, a lawyer, some missionaries, and a few soldiers and officials. It was an improvement on Swakopmund; it had sun and water. It dozed in a kind of trough surrounded by a few stone-covered hills dotted with thorny bushes. We sat under them during our profitless stay, until we were warned of a beetle that loved to drop from them to sting the unwary. One had to put a drop of ammonia on it and it would withdraw its sting, otherwise it would remain in the wound and fester.

The governor of the colony was absent; his representative was Dr. Hintrager, a Swabian, and that dangerous type of German romantic whose mind is split, an aggressive, ruthless realism in all things practical being directed by a highly emotional, irrational, untrained imagination. Most of the junior officials were scions of the Prussian nobility who had not learned much and who were suspicious of every kind of learning. They had come out to Africa because it offered them a chance of bossing on a scale no longer available even in darkest Pomerania. All of them looked upon me and especially upon my wife as upon undesirable intruders.

Among the local worthies was a lawyer who had not flourished in Cape Colony. Like most of the residents, he breathed an implacable hatred of England. There were a few traders and a few adventurers lately arrived from Germany, who wanted to buy land and colonize the country. Nearly all were small people—shopkeepers financed by Bremen or Hamburg exporters who did business with the natives—former members of the colonial police who had retired on a pension.

The colony's natural resources were poor. It was a cattle-man's not an agriculturist's country, where farms had to be large in order to carry adequate stock; one needed considerable capital.

Moreover, there was no free land. The land belonged to native tribes who grazed it in a loose, communal way. The traders and the officials knew little native law (and the former cared nothing about it); they believed in close settlements. The colonial question in Germany had come to the front when emi-gration was assuming impressive proportions—nearly a quarter of a million men and women had annually deserted the newly founded empire. Racial romanticists insisted that lands must be found to which this stream of emigrants could be directed. A New England had been founded on the bare rocks of Massa-chusetts, a New France in the woods of Canada: why should not a New Germany arise in the temperate zone of Africa? These people did not understand that even those parts of Africa where the climate favored Europeans offered no opening for mass immigration, since all manual labor was done by natives.

Four different native groups lived in South West Africa: in the almost tropical northern belt the fairly numerous Ovambos; on the northern steppes the Hereros, a warlike Bantu tribe; in the south a sparse population of Hottentots; and in the deserts a few Bushmen, remnants of the original inhabitants. A well-watered mountainous region in the center of the country was occupied by "the Bastards of Rehoboth," offspring of Boer fathers and Hottentot mothers.

Most traders had gone into Hereroland, opening small up-country stores and providing the natives with the usual Euro-pean goods. They had given them credit on the security of their farms, oblivious, perhaps deliberately, of the fact that under tribal law natives had no private property in land. When a native had gone heavily into debt, they sued him, and—usu-ally with the consent of the paramount chief, Samuel—were permitted to acquire land. The government objected to this expropriation and issued a decree that after the first of January 1904 arrears could no longer be collected. This speeded up evictions. The chief, suddenly realizing that he had given away lands of his tribe, to which he had no right whatsoever, reversed his policy and put himself at the head of a spontaneous native rising. An agrarian revolution spread over the country. Isolated farmers who could not reach a garrisoned village were massacred; their houses and their belongings were burned. The armed police were not numerous enough to quell the movement, and the natives from north to south went into open revolt.

In Germany, indignation rose very high. Volunteers from the regular army were sent out to put down the rebellion. It took a long time to train them for colonial warfare. The plans of the commander, General von Trotha, went wrong, for the natives had not attended staff colleges; they slipped through the iron ring he had closed round them and continued the fighting. The irate general reorganized his forces and drove the natives into the desert; by guarding the sparse water holes, he attempted to exterminate them by thirst. He justified his brutality later by citing the "law of nature" according to which "weaker races must die out when they get in contact with the stronger ones." "I see no reason," I replied when his policy came under discussion, "why the German taxpayer should bear the cost of the proceedings if nature was willing to take them into her hands."

The settlers had originally applauded von Trotha's atrocities. They had cheated the natives; they feared and hated them. But they had not come out to Africa to remain lowly peasants doing their own chores. They wanted large farms like their neighbors the Boers', with the heavy work done by the natives. They advocated a policy of enslavement under which the surviving natives were to be handed over to white masters, but they did not care for their extirpation.

When we landed in the colony, the war was over. Most of the army had been repatriated. The inner story of Trotha's atrocities, which were to play an important part later on in the Treaty of Versailles, was not yet generally known in Germany, though I had gathered its outlines in Cape Town. I had visited Morenga, the leader of the Hottentots, who was interned there after he had escaped the Germans. He was a tragic figure; he knew that his people were doomed.

A few people at Windhoek were worth knowing. One of them was Colonel von Estorff, commander of the colonial troops—a Christian gentleman and a redoubtable warrior, who could match the natives in native warfare, but who befriended them after they had surrendered. His outlook, mainly military, was far more humane than that of the civilians. The other outstanding personality was the principal of the Roman Catholic mission, Prefect Nachtwey. He was head and shoulders above his Protestant brethren, most of whom belonged to the Barmer Mission. Their small-town minds had been trained in that docile obedience which was a distinctive feature of German Lutheranism; they did not dare to stand up for the rights of the natives or even for their own work. Their Catholic rival was a worthy representative of the mellow universalism of his great church, which had learned in centuries of missionary activities all over the world to handle all types of men irrespective of their skins. He was not aggressive as some of the missionaries in British dependencies had been, but he was courageous and told the truth.

Neither settlers nor officials were keen on our getting a better knowledge of the country. We were put off from day to day by promises of transport that never materialized.

When a fortnight had passed, I went once more to Government House, to tell the vice-governor that we were going home. "I was able to gather a good deal of information about the colony during my stay at the Cape," I said. "It was rather unfavorable. I doubted it and decided to test its truth on the spot. I have had to come to the conclusion that it is true; evidently you do not want me to see anything; I shall go home and tell them what I have learned." From that moment the situation changed. Everybody became helpful. The army sold us four mules and a Cape cart, though one of the mules was a little decrepit. A farmer bought two horses for us. Two native servants were put at our disposal, and the various local authorities were advised of our approaching visit.


## 2. The Trek

On a sunny winter morning our little caravan started westward. One boy drove the mule cart, the other sat among the provisions. We rode ahead on horseback. The Windhoekers had turned out to see the procession; I suppose they thought we were mad or else bent on something very wicked.

We had some trouble at Karibib; one of the native boys turned out to be unmanageable. He was sulky and frightened, for he did not understand us any more than we did him. Major Rentel, the commandant at Karibib, gave us another boy, called Ephraim, who was the perfect native servant—friendly, intelligent, helpful, and an excellent cook. All the cooking I have practiced during the rest of my life has been based on his teachings. He occasionally suffered from fits of depression, his wife, Cornelia, being a volatile lady whose good conjugal conduct could not be assumed when he was from home.

In Karibib we ran into a couple of would-be settlers from Saxony. They had some means and dreamed of being landowning magnates in a not too distant future. One of them played the gentleman and tried to impress us as a near aristocrat. The other, a loquacious, bullet-headed little man, belonged to the lower middle class at the stage when it is beginning to make big money. He was a queer blend of smartness and infantility; an almost perfect specimen of the colonial romantic whose dreams of empire building are culled from Fenimore Cooper and his very inferior imitator in nineteenth-century Germany, Karl May.

In the middle of the night the innkeeper wakened me. "We need a doctor," he said. "Mr. So-and-So is very ill." "I am not a medical man, but I'll see what I can do." I found our little Saxon in agony. The cause of his illness was easily diagnosed. He had seen a plant with huge leaves not unlike those of the rhubarb plant. Its seeds, attractive-looking blue and gray flecked grains, were contained in a prickly fruit; he picked a handful and ate them. They had a sweetish taste which he rather liked. They were the fruits of the castor oil plant. I had some opium in a traveling medicine kit that quickly restored him.

His colonial dreams came to a sad end. He bought a farm and lorded it over the few natives allocated to him as workers. He strutted round the vast land with a gun and a cur that knew as little of Africa as his owner, posing to the natives as representative of a master race. He did it once too often. One fine morning he left his shack and never returned. No trace of him was found.

His more gentlemanly companion came to grief while we were at Karibib. He had a cart and a sprightly horse, which, as he stood waiting to take my wife for a drive, kicked him and smashed his ankle. We carried him into the hotel and sent a boy for the military surgeon, who lived next door. He kept us waiting; evidently he had to consult his medical books—to little purpose. He just stared at the patient until my wife, who knew first aid, instructed him how to do the job. It was a most illuminating experience. Here was an army doctor, on whose ability depended the lives of a number of men, who had no idea of the elements of surgery. A feeling of frustration, of pettiness, and of meanness pervaded the colony—in violent contrast to the gigantic scale of its magnificent landscape.

From Karibib we trekked northward, toward the Tsumeb mines. We covered the first part of the journey in the company of a resident settler of a much better type. He carried his belongings on one of the huge ox wagons, not unlike an American prairie schooner, in which the Boers had trekked overland. It was drawn by twelve Ovambo oxen, small, graceful animals that occasionally trotted and cantered. We sometimes traveled in his wagon, which was fitted with a *katel*, a frame held together by leather thongs that served as a spring mattress. When the oxen walked slowly it was comfortable, but not much fun when they took it into their heads to sprint down a hill. We soon reached Omaruru, a small settlement situated near a watercourse, in the best part of Hereroland—an important military post during the rebellion. We talked to farmers, traders, missionaries, and settlers. Local conditions differed from place to place, but the main picture was the same everywhere. The colony was a cattle country and a poor one at that. It could not be used for agricultural purposes. It needed settlers with capital, but it had not got them. They were either small farmers bent on agricultural pursuits or former traders. Life was very hard on them. They hated the natives and did not understand them, yet they depended on their labor. They disliked the government but leaned heavily on it. The vastness and the beauty of the country was throwing its spell over them. They sensed the cruelty of Africa, yet they began to love her.

We slowly trekked northward on the rough roads the army had made. A few finger posts at the crossroads showed one where to go. Water holes were usually not farther apart than a day's ride. It was winter; the nights were bitterly cold but very blue and clear. Day and night the sky was cloudless; on a safe African horse that knew how to keep out of gopher holes, traveling in the early night was pleasant. After midnight temperatures sank very low, and the little patrol tent in which we slept did not provide much warmth. We put our sleeping bag over our "karosses" (covers made from skins). A candle stuck into an empty bottle provided light. We pulled off boots and coats and donned heavy sweaters and socks. I had gun and revolver handy; the country was not yet safe; but nothing ever happened to us. We managed to rise before dawn. Getting into the boots was a hard job—wherever we had put them, they got stiff and cold. I awakened the natives. Cold and sleep had almost dazed them; they had to be shaken several times. Our toilet was simple. We had enough water left to clean our teeth. Sometimes we had camped near a water hole and breakfasted after lighting a fire. As a rule we just packed up as rapidly as we could, having had a drink from a thermos bottle. Long before the sun was out we were in the saddle. The first hour or two were not very pleasant. We were stiff and frozen. Suddenly the sun was radiating its full strength. We were galvanized. We peeled off one coat after another until ready for the African day. We trekked on until ten or eleven, when it was really getting warm. We tried to find a place in the shade, which is not easy on the African veldt. Here we unhitched, sometimes near a water hole, and let the animals graze. At other times we had to be satisfied with the water we carried in our bags. I had probably shot a guinea fowl or a few Namaqua partridges, which Ephraim had cleaned immediately. We put our tripod, our single cooking utensil, over a fire made from thorns and boiled some tea or coffee. We rarely found a spring; water generally came from a hole in the ground on the rim of which lay the bones of a dead ox or a dead horse. The water, stagnant, greenish, slimy stuff, had to be boiled. Having filled ourselves with tea or coffee, we made the bird tender by boiling it for a few minutes. We put the stock in a tin and fried the bird in the tripod with canned butter or bacon, pouring the stock back on it. A can of peas and a can of fruit finished the meal. If we were near a farm, we had bread. After the meal we relaxed and slept during the hot part of the day. We started again in the late afternoon, and so onward till we found a camping place, where the tent was struck and another meal was prepared. Few things in my life would I like to do over again; we both would love to camp once more on the vast African veldt.

The routine of the trek varied little; it never became monotonous, even though it seemed endless. The African landscape is built on such a grand scale that one never seems to get near one's goal. The size of the Erongo Mountains, towering east of us, apparently never changed, however close to them we moved. Yet the character of the landscape altered almost imperceptibly. It became a little less arid; occasionally one saw a stunted palm tree. We were approaching a subtropical region. One fine evening we rumbled into a small settlement, "Tsumeb," the seat of the Otavi copper mines. Here we were fortunate. The wife of the resident Norwegian engineer asked us to her house; for the first time since we had left Cape Town we breathed a truly civilized atmosphere. It was not quite easy to get into it. We were encased in a crust of red earth; the little India-rubber tub we carried had to be filled and refilled five times for each of us before we dared meet our hostess. Getting dirty is a habit; the first and the second day are unpleasant. Once one is thoroughly covered with dirt, one does not mind very much. The breaking-up process, on the other hand, is sudden and very pleasant. I spent one of the happiest hours of my life in the marble tub of the steamer taking us home from South Africa. To be able to use as much hot water as one wanted was an exciting experience.

The Otavi mines were small fry. They were as primitive as everything else in South West Africa; the engineers refused to let me go underground. The natives lived in miserable huts. Our hostess and host—he returned a day later—were cultivated people; they had managed to maintain an atmosphere of genuine civilization far away from all its resources. After we left them we spent a night in the barracks at Groot Fontein, where I was almost devoured by bedbugs, and retraced our steps southward and eastward until we reached Windhoek once more. By that time my wife had become an expert mule-team driver. She amused herself by cantering our four-in-hand through the main street of the dusty town, to the utmost astonishment of the residents, who never had seen such an unladylike performance.

During our absence, the new governor, Herr von Lindequist, had arrived. He had been consul general in Cape Town—thoroughly anti-British, yet impressed with the grandeur of the British Empire and eager to ape it. He strutted about in a frock coat and top hat, which was a little funny since his capital was truly built on sand. He asked what were my impressions of the country and favored me with an outline of his plans. He wanted to make South West Africa a white man's country, the home of a dense German population, presumably of small farmers, who look for guidance to their government. My objections that the country was made for large-scale ranching and not for agriculture, and that its development depended on native labor, were pooh-poohed. I was sent to Little Windhoek to see the soundness of his schemes, where half a dozen truck farmers raised fruit and vegetables for the capital and eked out a precarious existence. Dr. Solf, who followed Lindequist later on as colonial secretary, and who had a great deal of common sense, used to speak of them as radish plantations. Both my wife and I were treated with great formal politeness; there was none of the friendliness we had encountered on our visits all over South Africa.

We sold our cart, horses, and mules and turned our thoughts homeward. We stopped in Karibib, where Major Rentel suggested a journey to the Fish River through the country of the Bastards of Rehoboth. He kindly provided us with horses and with an excellent Hottentot servant. He had been condemned to be whipped for some minor delinquency. The Major told him he might redeem himself; if he behaved during the journey, he would be reprieved.

Once again we were in the saddle, and as we had excellent mounts, we could cover long distances. Rehoboth was a land of hills, valleys, and watercourses. The Bastards, the offspring of Boer fathers and Hottentot mothers, were physically an attractive race. Their ancestors had lived in Cape Colony but had been driven out by the Boers. They were very proud of their mixed origin and gloried in the name of Bastards. The Pan-

Germans, who were very influential in the colonial party, had spread the legend that the Boers, proud representatives of the pure Nordic race, abhorred miscegenation and had never consorted with native women. The Bastards of Rehoboth were living proof to the contrary. They led the life of primitive Boer farmers; they dressed like Boers and talked the Boer language. They were an easygoing lot, not difficult to manage as long as one kept them away from drink. Their cattle were of the Ovambo type, small and quick. They used to ride their oxen, cantering along on these quaint mounts. Our excursion was finally crowned with glory. By some fluke I managed to shoot a bustard, one of the rare wild birds of that part of the world. I brought it back to Karibib and gave a dinner on it to the officers of the garrison, in whose opinion I greatly rose.

The so-called railroad returned us to Swakopmund in time for a small coastal steamer for Lüderitz Bay. Here was a kind of harbor amid the rocks, but the country behind it was completely barren. The little settlement depended on condensed sea water. A railroad was being built to Keetmanshoop, not very far, as African distances go, from the border of British South Africa. The military who were in charge took me beyond the railhead. The country was even vaster than in the north—sand, rocks, and very little grass. In this region only huge farms could subsist, and they only if a regular supply of water could be found. On our way back to Lüderitz Bay the train stopped suddenly at a wayside station, a wooden shack. We had to clear out rapidly, a terrific sandstorm was coming. We lay down flat on the floor, face downward, and covered our heads with rugs, blankets, and coats. It did not last very long, and fortunately the Lüderitz Bay Hotel had a tub; otherwise we would have remained pickled in sand. A few weeks later the first diamonds were found on the same spot, creating a boom in this arid country. We spent our last evening in Lüderitz Bay at a farewell dinner at the officers' mess, given by them to their comrades who were going home. It was a gay and cheerful party. My wife claims that I was greatly lit up: anyhow I certainly was not very happy next day riding the huge swell on our way back to Swakopmund.

This time we saw its primitive landing arrangement as seasoned spectators and not as green victims. It looked as gray and foggy as on the day when we first reached it. We had loved the veldt and the primitive life on it, but we had loathed the mean little towns through which we had had to pass. Our African adventure was over.

### 3. Colonial Reform

Our welcome home was very warm. The university recognized my having, so to speak, anticipated the course of events. I had come back an expert on problems of the day. I had published a series of articles in the *Frankfurter Zeitung* that had made rather a stir.

Colonial circles in Munich were very keen on our collaboration—until they knew my views. They all hoped for a new Germany in the wilds of Africa and looked upon natives as a mere nuisance that a superior civilization must clear out. Many of them even approved of Trotha's policy. I had come back with the firm conviction that Africa was a black man's country, where one could never establish a purely white society. One might settle a white aristocracy and prepare for insoluble social conflicts. This aristocracy would not mix with the natives; it would not even accept as equals the halfbreeds for whom it was responsible. Permanent friction between the small white top layer and the seething black mass was inevitable. The only sound way to rule Africa was by an imperial civil service with high social standards. An influx of white traders might be permitted, provided they remained under strict control. No white settlements should be organized; the land should be reserved for the natives. Experience has proved the soundness of my views. They were not popular at that time.

A women's colonial society had been founded to organize the immigration of white women into South West Africa, where they should marry settlers, become the mothers of a valiant German race, and above all prevent race mixture. They invited me to address them. I suggested they would not like my views; they insisted on hearing them. They were greatly shocked when I told them with chapter and verse that the main cause of bastardization in Africa was not the absence of white women but the presence of black ones. They never invited me again.

Prince Bülow's appointment of Bernhard Dernburg as colonial secretary had been a concession to the advanced liberal groups in his coalition of 1906. Dernburg's father had been a well-known liberal journalist; his mother, a Lutheran minister's daughter. The son had become a banker, and as head of the old Darmstädter Bank had carried off some brilliant constructive financial coups and vivified a somewhat somnolescent institution. Not much over forty at this time, in personal appearance he was anything but attractive. A broad, square body sat on stocky legs. A pallid face framed by a stubby blondish beard made him look like a Nordic Assyrian, if such a type can be imagined. With a heavy, ugly nose and pale blue heavy-lidded eyes, he looked like a very rough sort, and indeed when he was on the upswing, he could be ruthless. Yet he might be called a gentle soul. He was far more cultured than most academicians; he understood and loved the humanities. When he smiled his melancholy smile, his features lit up like those of an unworldly dreamer and became almost beautiful. He was abrupt, absent-minded, and usually not very polite, though when he suddenly remembered his manners, he showed an old-world courtesy. On his appointment as colonial secretary he was commanded to dine with His Imperial Majesty. Evidently quite unimpressed with the solemnity of the occasion, he stuck a napkin in his collar. "This is not a barbershop," William II observed quite audibly. Though Dernburg's manners were not perfect, he possessed imagination and even a speck of genius.

He had immediately taken matters in hand and gone to inspect the German colonies. He had visited East Africa, paid his respects to the British authorities in South Africa, and passed through South West Africa. He had been very fortunate, for soon after he took control, diamonds were found in the most forsaken part of the country, which were to pull this very expensive, hitherto unproductive dependency out of the red. He set to work and reorganized German colonial administration on a business basis, eliminating as much as possible the military and the bureaucracy. His advanced views on native policy had been strengthened by his visit to British South Africa. Naturally he was soon at loggerheads with Pan-Germans, planters and settlers, who looked upon the natives as beasts of burden to serve the superior race. Nearly all of them demanded compulsory labor service such as had been imposed on the native remnant in South West Africa. Dernburg made up his mind to stop it. He knew it would be a bitter struggle. The appointment of a mere outsider, a banker who had not even an academic degree, had by no means been popular in bureaucratic and conservative circles. His successful political campaigning had helped the Chancellor to win a majority; it had not endeared him to them. His abrupt ways gave them many chances to poke fun at him. He was a first-rate fighter when aroused, but his energy was of a fitful type; a spurt of combative elation was frequently followed by one of depressed exhaustion. He was reliable but not stable.

He had read some of my publications, and he probably had heard about us in Cape Town and Pretoria. In any case he sent for me and asked us to be his guests in Baden-Baden. We spent a few very interesting days with him and his wife, to whose steadying influence he owed a great deal. We drove about in his car through the Black Forest and into Alsace discussing colonial questions all the time. He asked me to undertake a systematic study of the legislation dealing with native affairs in South Africa. I had collected a large library on this subject. It now forms part of the library of the London School of Economics, to whom I gave my Irish and my African books after I had left Germany. I set to work but never finished it. A huge manuscript was among the papers in my house in Parsch near Salzburg when the Nazis occupied it.

I did a good deal to advocate and defend Dernburg's native policy. I had become a member of the Colonial Society—whose ways I thoroughly disliked, but whose platform I had to use—and Dernburg had made me an associate member of the International Colonial Institute. I was treated as an acknowledged but not a popular authority on colonial questions. I had to fight on two fronts. My main thesis was that settlers should not be encouraged to go to Africa, which should be developed as a black man's country. The colonial romantics who violently opposed me discussed issues that were already dead. For mass emigration from Germany had ceased long ago; only a few small driblets continued. Germany, indeed, had become an immigration country whose agricultural prosperity depended on a regular inflow of nearly three quarters of a million seasonal laborers from Austrian and Russian Poland.

The fight for free labor was more serious. In many parts of Africa native labor was scarce, partly because the warlike native races were not willing to work, partly because native wars and risings had diminished their numbers. Settlers and planters were in a hurry. The colonial press demanded that natives be taught the dignity of labor. Business opinion in general was not deeply interested in colonial questions. As far as it was liberal, it objected to colonies in general—a thoroughly sane attitude as long as one did not possess them. Once one had acquired them, something had to be done with them.

I have been in a number of political fights in my life. I enjoyed this battle for a healthy native policy more than any other. One day a group of East African settlers approached me and tried to persuade me to stop my activities against compulsory native labor. I agreed under one condition. "If your backers," I told them, "will guarantee to the imperial treasury the cost of the next native war arising from your demands, I am willing to shut up." They left me in disgust.

I denounced the colonial atrocities perpetrated during an earlier period, and thus played a minor part in the reform of German colonial administration. Just before the outbreak of the First World War, I was rewarded for my labors. The Royal Colonial Institute in London invited me to address them on German colonial policy. The meeting took place on the thirteenth of January, 1914. It was a gala evening. A number of prominent colonial experts attended. Lord Milner, the great African proconsul presided; he was my chief opponent. The meeting praised unanimously the work done in the German colonies under the secretaryships of Dernburg and Solf. We disagreed on my thesis that Africa was and should be a black man's country. Lord Milner opposed me, as he had to, for he had emphatically pursued a white-settlement policy. History, I think, has given the verdict in my favor. A truly white society has been established nowhere in Africa. Such white settlements as have survived form but a narrow top layer whose position is insecure and whose relations with the natives have never yet been permanently determined.

This meeting played an important part in later discussions.

When the Allies decided to take over the German colonies for very convincing military reasons, they had to persuade President Wilson. They could only do so by informing him about the atrocities the Germans had committed, especially in South West Africa. They did not tell him that these atrocities belonged to an earlier period and that German colonial administration before the war had become fairly decent under the pressure of public opinion in Germany. The slur thrown on Germany's good name by these posthumous accusations made many Germans colonial minded who before had been in the habit of decrying colonies. They drew their best arguments against these slanders from the London meeting, in which only half a year before the war British colonial experts had praised German colonial achievements though well aware of the earlier scandals. Over and over again this meeting is referred to in German propaganda literature against "the colonial slander." My statements are generally quoted as those of "a German professor." My name is rarely mentioned, for the people who wrote these apologias usually belonged to groups who disliked colonial reformers far more than colonial atrocities.

# IX. Munich (1905-1914)

## 1. *The Natives*

PREWAR MUNICH had little of the charm of those old German cities that had led a rich, almost independent civic life of their own during the Middle Ages. It possessed a few monuments of an earlier day, some of them, like Our Lady's Church, of great beauty. It had grown into a huge, provincial hamlet as the "court and residential town"—this was its official name—of the dukes of Bavaria. It was built around a court, a bureaucracy, and the army of the Bavarian state. It never was a real city and had no civic spirit.

The ruling Wittelsbach family had a long history; it went back farther than the Hohenzollerns, whom it despised as parvenus. Its great ambitions had not fully materialized; the elector had been made a king by the grace of Napoleon, but Bavaria never succeeded in becoming a leading power in Germany. Yet the dynasty obstinately retained the symbols of former grandeur.

The upper house of the Bavarian diet was styled the Imperial Council; its members bore the proud title Imperial Councilors of the Crown of Bavaria. The court maintained its stiff Spanish-Burgundian etiquette only on gala days; for most of the year it mingled freely with its fellow subjects in Munich.

Prewar Munich was almost a classless city. Its inhabitants were petty officials, small traders, retired farmers, businessmen, and handicraftsmen, some of them very skillful, for the Bavarians have a strong artistic streak. There was no sharply circumscribed lower class. Apart from the breweries the town had few large-scale industries, and its workers had neither class feelings nor class standards of living. No upper middle class was in evidence; among the leading citizens in Munich, in those days, scarcely anyone could be called a captain of industry. A few men had risen to great wealth; they had generally come from Franconia, the Palatinate, or from non-Bavarian parts of Germany. The only native plutocrats were the brewers; nearly all retained the features of their lower-middle-class origin even after they were rolling in riches. The younger among them, who were among my Trustees when I had become head of the College of Commerce, knew how to entertain in the manner of the Western world. They only did it when on official duty; it was not part of their lives. Elsewhere social intercourse outside the family was almost nonexistent. When one was asked to the house of a Munich worthy, which happened rarely enough in those days, one did not go in to a dinner. One remained in the sitting room. One was asked what one would like to have and the maid was sent out to get it. She came back with a stein of beer and some sausages, for which the guest was expected to pay.

Social life was concentrated in the beer cellars, where everybody met everybody else without class distinction and sat down where he could find a seat. In summer one went to the beer gardens in the small parks that surrounded the breweries. The brewery provided the beer; one could buy bread, cheese, radishes, or sausages at the booths at the entrance gate. An orchestra, usually from one of the local regiments, provided good music and a great deal of brassy, cheerful noise. Conversation was not very lively. The natives preferred to concentrate on the beer rather than on interchange of ideas. Yet it was easy enough to get into conversation with them provided they understood one's lingo. They were easily suspicious of those who spoke High German—these were Prussians or near Prussians, and as such to be avoided.

Living was incredibly cheap. One could get a good meal for ten or fifteen cents. In my student days I had frequented a little wine restaurant, for I never became a real beer enthusiast, where one got a four-course dinner and a glass of wine for twenty-five cents. The cheapness of life was partly due to the modest standard of living of the mass of the people; moreover Munich was the center of a great milk and cattle region.

A number of noble German families who had been independent rulers of small principalities had congregated in Munich after Napoleon let Bavaria swallow up their sover-

6

eignty. Most of them became peers of the crown of Bavaria. Below them ranked the Bavarian nobility. Both groups had estates in the country and town houses in Munich. They and a few diplomatic representatives to the Bavarian court formed Munich aristocratic society. They were neither very numerous, very wealthy, nor very bright.

The center of this small, self-sufficient, and rather self-satisfied world was the king and the court. During most of my Munich days the head did not function, so to speak. Like his romantic brother Ludwig II, the protector of Richard Wagner, who ended his life by drowning himself and his attendant medical adviser, King Otto was insane. Unable to take over after his brother's death, he had to be kept in seclusion; but he was king. A cousin, Prince Luitpold, was appointed regent and did his duty like a loyal gentleman. He was not interested in politics or in royal pomp; he could not have indulged in it, for King Ludwig had contracted heavy debts in building the monstrous castles with which he had dotted the Bavarian landscape. The regent's stipend was very meager, and his private means were slender. Fortunately he had no expensive tastes, and being a widower, could easily refrain from costly entertainments. He usually asked prominent citizens to lunch, the expense for which could be charged to the treasury. All who met him praised him as a perfect gentleman. The chase was his passion. He was not one of the royal shots who stand in a park and try to kill as many pheasants as possible in as short a time as possible. He loved to follow the chamois and to scale inaccessible crags. Every year at the annual art exhibition he made the state gallery buy a picture representing some hunting subject. I never met him personally, but his funeral gave me the first chance to become somebody in the Bavarian official world.

I had been appointed principal of the new College of Commerce that the city of Munich and the Chamber of Commerce had founded in 1910, with the blessing, as they had hoped, of the government. Unfortunately, Nuremberg had entertained similar plans and had secured the same somewhat tepid favor of the government. We had outdistanced Nuremberg and opened our doors in the autumn of 1910. As the government wanted neither to subsidize two colleges nor to get into trouble with the Nuremberg people, they gave us to understand that their favors to us would remain purely Platonic and that my status was purely unofficial. I greatly profited from this decision —my situation offered some very practical advantages. Officials admitted to an audience with the Minister of Education had to turn up in tails, a boiled shirt, a white tie, and a stovepipe. At eleven A.M., one felt slightly ridiculous in this festive outfit, especially in summertime. One of my colleagues, who had to don it often, kept it in his office for a quick change and became a kind of strip tease artist. I immediately seized the advantages of my degraded station. Thenceforth I turned up in the great man's office in an ordinary business suit, which greatly improved our relations. Independence, however, had its drawbacks. Not being an official, I was not invited to any public function. As long as my college was not represented at them, its academic standing seemed doubtful in the eyes of its older rivals.

I had not been invited to march in the funeral procession of Prince Luitpold. Whereupon I sat down and wrote a letter of patriotic indignation, complaining of this iniquity that condemned a number of patriotic professors to look at the procession from the college windows while their more fortunate colleagues shared the honor of following to his last rest the representative of the great Bavarian dynasty who had served his country in such difficult circumstances.

My protest was effective. Henceforth I was asked to all official —not social—affairs. Social affairs were purely court gatherings. Apart from the ministers of state and a few other equally elevated dignitaries, no civilians who could not boast sixteen noble ancestors attended the court ball. Wives of ministers who were not "High Wellborn" could be admitted on petition by royal favor. Public affairs, on the other hand, were matters of state, and anyone who was anyone in the state was invited. Most people in this fortunate position had a uniform of dark blue cloth braided with gold or silver according to their rank and carried a three-cornered hat under their arms. I had no rank—except as assistant university professor, and this did not amount to much in the hierarchy—and I had no uniform. I had to turn up in swallowtail, boiled shirt, and white tie. I sat with the heads of the university, the technical high school, the academy of art, and other imposing personalities, all of them either wearing academic gowns or resplendent in court dress richly embroidered with gold. Frequently I was the one and only black and white spot in a galaxy of colorful uniforms. I was young and I looked even younger, and I needed all my moral courage to carry it off. It was easier after I caught on to the usefulness of appearing odd. I was the one person who looked different. Everybody spotted me, and everybody inquired after that queer sort of animal that had managed to squeeze itself in between so many glittering worthies. I felt like an American ambassador in earlier days when he was the only normal-looking individual at a diplomatic function. It was good publicity, and it strengthened what I might call my republican tradition.

I first met the new regent—afterward King Ludwig III—at the opening of the College of Commerce. Prince Ludwig, as he then was, was a heavy-set man with a massive head framed by a whitish beard, with ruddy complexion and very blue, hard, cold eyes. He limped slightly. He was rather proud of this small disfigurement, the result of a Prussian bullet in his heel in the war of 1866. It was a personal justification for his strong anti-Prussian feeling, which naturally was not lessened by his having married an Austrian arch-duchess. The Princess may have been a beauty in her younger days; she had long ago turned into a motherly-looking German housewife who had taken good care of a large family. The financial means of the princely couple were slender; they led a very simple life. The Prince seemed to like it. He looked, thought, and acted like a gentleman farmer with the accent on farmer. He was very proud of his model farm, Leutstetten, near Munich. In Munich he lived in a wing of a red-brick crenellated structure called the Turkish Palace, which looked more like an overambitious Prussian army barracks than a vision from *A Thousand and One Nights*. Two stone lions, emblems of the house of Wittelsbach, stood at its gate. During the revolution, Red mob orators used them for the purpose served in Anglo-Saxon countries by the soapbox. I remember a screeching voice informing a not overenthusiastic crowd, "The age of bourgeois corruption has gone!" "And that of proletarian corruption has begun!" an irreverent bystander murmured quite audibly, to the intense enjoyment of most of the listeners.

The Prince had few administrative duties to fulfill during his father's life; he had ample time to represent royalty at public functions and attended them assiduously. He specialized, so to speak, in popularity. He loved farmers' meetings best. He was a shrewd man who did not share the artistic inclinations of the royal house. But he did know most things worth knowing about dairy cattle and was enthusiastic about inland waterways. Bavaria had no seaport; its nearest approach to a fleet were a few paddle steamers running across Lake Constance from the old city of Lindau. But the Prince had naval dreams; he envied the hated Prussians' industrial and mercantile development. Since Bavaria lacked a salt-water front, the best he could do was to develop her inland waterways, to improve the canal that connected Rhine and Danube—his great-grandfather had built it— and thus to join the Atlantic to the Black Sea.

The Prince had graciously consented to participate in the opening ceremonies of the new college and to pronounce his benediction and congratulations. I had to start the proceedings with a speech submitted to him beforehand. He never read it, but what made matters worse, he indulged during its delivery in his well-known habit of snoozing. Unfortunately he was a very fluent speaker who relied on inspirations. They were always forthcoming, but not always appropriate. In his congratulatory address that followed my speech he managed to say the contrary of everything he was expected to say. When he read the write-up of the proceedings in the press, he quickly saw the wide divergence among the several pronouncements. He held me responsible for it. As I was not a native Bavarian, I thought I might be forgiven; he never expected profound understanding of the Bavarian soul from a mere outsider. I soon discovered that he did not like me.

Yet he was always affable whenever I met him—and this was often the case, for he loved to tramp the streets of his capital, dragging his game leg behind him. He usually wore a frock coat that might have been built by an architect; no mere tailor could have produced a garment with so many angles and crevices. His trousers, on the other hand, famed all over the country, must have come from a bag factory. Even when he wore the uniform of his pet regiment, the Bavarian Rifles— pale blue with green cuffs—he did not look martial. His boots appeared homemade, and Abraham Lincoln would have refused to wear the top hat that crowned his massive head. He was in the habit of buttonholing those he knew, and he knew nearly everybody. If one could not escape in time by rushing to the other side of the street, one had to stand to attention, click heels, and wait for his address. It rarely failed to come forth. With me he always inquired after the college and finished up his gracious address by informing me that of course I had to remember that he did not agree with my views; whereupon I had to click heels and say, "Yes, Your Majesty."

Prince Ludwig, unlike his father, had political ambitions. He could not carry them out as regent. The insane King was incurable; he could never exercise even the slightest government function. Finally it was suggested that in the interest of the country Ludwig should be made king. It was not easy for the royal couple to accept the crown. When the Prince had assumed the duties of regent, he had taken a solemn oath to watch over the King's interest. He had to disregard this sacred obligation; he finally did so, after much hesitation, supported by consultation with and encouragement from the Vatican. He was crowned on November 5, 1913.

I was present at some of the functions but cannot recall details; their characteristic feature was a combination of stiff Spanish-Burgundian etiquette with native Bavarian unconcern. One of my friends, a member of the Bavarian House of Peers, walked down the stairs after the solemn coronation and encountered some members of the Bavarian Household Guards—they had a very picturesque uniform of white and blue—carrying a kind of huge laundry basket. It contained the regalia, the crown and scepter of the Bavarian empire, to be stowed away for the next occasion, which, alas, never came.

I was invited to the coronation banquet and to the great reception following it, when all Bavarian dignitaries, from the prime minister down to the mayor of the smallest city, were present to pay homage to the newly crowned majesties. We waited in a huge anteroom and were divided in shifts. No chairs were provided for the banquet, as there was not enough room available, and we had to take our meal standing in serried rows along the long festive boards. The food was simple, not at all royal but ample and substantial, otherwise it would not have appealed to the native-born Bavarians. Drink was excellent, for Bavaria is by no means exclusively a beer country; she grows excellent wines in the Palatinate and on the Franconian hills. We had to bolt our food to make room for the next shift. When everybody had had his fill, we were assembled in an enormous oval in a huge hall. Their Majesties appeared, the King brimming over with happiness. The Queen seemed rather tired; she suffered, it was said, religious qualms about being crowned during the life of the legitimate king. The royal couple passed along our front, the King talking to those whom he knew and honoring with a few gracious words those who were newly presented. He loved the function. Over and over again he got into lengthy conversations, to the evident distress of the aides-de-camp who had to keep the timetable. The Queen followed, generally limiting her address to a gracious smile. The royal daughters flitted about in new white dresses with the light blue ribbons of the Order of Sophia. A feeling of friendliness, understanding, and good will was about, much more impressive than any attempt at stiff dignity would have been.

Next day I met the royal couple in the family circle, so to speak. The students of the Munich colleges were offering them a torchlight procession; the heads had been invited to join their Majesties. We stood at the windows of the royal residence with them; only the royal family and the inner court circle were present. It was, fortunately, a clear night. The lights on the big square before the residence were turned out; the huge procession, each college grouped separately, began to march in, the fraternities in their fantastic half Middle-Age, half early nineteenth-century costumes, with ribbons, heavy boots, broad hats with feathers, and clanking swords, every man holding a burning torch in his right hand. The torchlights flickered with a curious red glow; wisps of smoke rose from each torch and condensed into a slight haze, broken up by gusts of wind into floating clouds that hung over the crowd. The bands played whilst the students came along in long lines until they filled the spacious square. A thousand fireflies seemed to flutter heavenward through an ever-thickening mist. Suddenly all movement ceased; stillness reigned. I don't remember whether any speeches were made. The national anthem was sung, everybody joined in; their Majesties, bowing graciously from the window, thanked the students with deep emotion and waited for the finale. The torchbearers formed a circle around an open space and at a given moment threw their torches, flame downward, to the ground. There was a quaint hissing as they died, and acrid black smoke was rising. The students intoned the *"Gaudeamus."* The old Latin song starts cheerfully enough, "Let us be merry while we are young," but after a few bars comes sadly to a halt: "And the earth shall have us." The smoke got denser and darker, the air more pungent, the last sparks quivered and flickered, and silently the crowd melted away in the all-embracing night.

The joy of the royal couple, especially the Queen, was touching. They were like little children to whom Santa Claus has brought a present of unexpected beauty. The Queen never tired of asking questions about the different groups; she wanted to know who everybody was and what every student emblem meant. The King, too, was in his element. He talked without the slightest condescension. He told us how he regretted having to leave the Turkish Palace, where he had spent so many years of his life; the great "Residence" he now inhabited was too palatial for his tastes—he really did not feel at home in it. Unwittingly he was touching on the secret of his later political failure. He had been a private country gentleman until he was past the sixties. He knew how to meet his fellow Bavarians in this role; he had enjoyed it. He had been popular by being like them. Now he became king, but he was too old to learn the kingly ways that the crowd expects. It does not mind a prince who is not different from it; from a king, it demands a kingly attitude. Neither Ludwig III nor his wife nor their daughters had it; the heir, Crown Prince Rupprecht, did.


## 2. *The Colony*

The first king of Bavaria owed his rise to kingly rank to Napoleon. He was a loyal ally, yet when the tide turned he deserted the Emperor. His timely change to the winning side secured his possessions at the Vienna Congress; but there was an end to dreams of political greatness. The second king, Ludwig I, recognized this situation and set to work to make his kingdom the cultural center of Germany. He transformed his capital, or at least its main streets, from an overgrown rustic county town into an architectural metropolis and implanted impressive copies of monumental Florentine art into his hitherto rather mean residence. He deliberately made Munich the center of German art. Though his taste was not impeccable, he succeeded in attracting a large number of artists, who thrived in the easy atmosphere of Upper Bavaria. The plain on which Munich is situated is covered with bogs, moors, lakes, and dark forests. It often looks bleak and harsh. The climate is severe—even in summer the nights are cold—but when the sun is shining, its gold is very much richer than in northern Germany, and when the south wind chases the clouds over the balloon-shaped towers of Our Lady's Church, the sky is as blue as anywhere in Italy. The natives of Upper and Lower Bavaria, mountaineers and lowlanders, are a little heavy; yet they can be highly temperamental. They respond to impulse rather than to reason.

The King's choice turned out to be very fortunate. Many of his artists were foreigners; they formed a colony, but a colony that fused at many points with the natives. His son, King Max, was interested in literature and history rather than in painting and architecture. He called a number of Germany's leading poets to his court and endowed them with pensions. The favor he showed them did not endear them to his subjects. They saw no reason why good Bavarian money should be put into the pockets of mere Prussians whose only contribution to Munich life was the cash they paid for their houses and for the bills to their tradesmen. With the exception of Paul Heyse, none of them settled down for good in Munich. The King took an interest in the university and used his influence to raise its status by calling great teachers to it, irrespective of their origin. Again the Munich people did not like it. Bavarian jobs should go to Bavarians. Moreover, most of the newly appointed North Germans were Protestants and as such worse than infidels; they should not be allowed to corrupt the minds of the young.

The unification of Germany strengthened Bavaria's resistance to everything non-Bavarian, yet it gave Munich a great chance. On the one hand, Bavarian institutions had to compete with those of the rest of the empire, which forced them to raise their standards and be more liberal in appointments in order to survive. Munich, however, became the haven of refuge for anybody who wanted to breathe a freer air than that of Bismarck-dominated Prussia. Bavaria was not a liberal country (quite the contrary). The peasant majority that controlled the government was politically reactionary. But by temperament it was oppositional. It disliked Bismarck; for that reason alone it was willing to grant hospitality to anybody who was against him as long as he did not meddle with Bavarian affairs. Under William II this tendency grew even stronger. Bismarck had been a terrifying personality; William II was a tactless meddler whose imperial struttings looked even more funny to the Munich people than to other Germans. Munich became a great residential center. After Pettenkofer had eradicated typhus, well-to-do people in search of a carefree, easy life settled in Munich. This foreign colony, as it might be called, came from all parts of the empire. They mixed with the artists and with those members of the court set who were interested in art and literature. They lived a life apart from the majority of native Bavarians, but they managed to jog along very comfortably side by side. We spent very nearly fifteen years in this free and easygoing community, which was not greatly inconvenienced by the strict etiquette dominating the court.

We had no family connections in Munich. But I had had a few introductions, one of them to Paul Heyse. He and his wife had been very kind to me in my student days—she belonged to the dark almost Italian type of beauty that is not rare in Bavaria, and which Lenbach painted in some of his best portraits. After we had settled down we saw a good deal of them. He was the last survivor of King Max's literary finds, a representative of the Germany of poets and philosophers that by then had gone for good. He must have been a male beauty in his youth, a hero of the romantic decades. He had preserved his good looks in his old age—tall and well-made, he deliberately posed as an artist. With his long hair, darkish brown beard (which by then may have been art too), and blue eyes, he looked the god-inspired poet. The creative flame had burned out long ago. His marvelous facility in writing prose and poetry enabled him to continue work, though his late productions were but words beautifully strung together, with little appeal to a more realistic generation. Nobody today can read his two monumental novels of life in Munich and Berlin. Some of his Italian stories written

in verse retain the graceful charm the author possessed in his
younger days. He was one of the few poets who could interpret
Italian life to German readers and who could interest Italians
in German literature. He had become an isolated survivor of an
earlier age. The new realism in art and literature that flourished in Munich was alien and antipathetic to him. Pictures and
poetry had to be beautiful; they should offer an escape from
life, not a mere copy. Both my wife and I have been fortunate
in enjoying the friendship of an older generation whom most
of our contemporaries despised. We were dimly aware that the
heralds who greet a new age with blaring bugles will soon be
bypassed by another, noisier generation and be limited either
to dirges or reminiscences.

Lujo Brentano's house was one of the centers of Munich
social life. Thanks to him, we were soon, if not in the midst
of it, at least on its fringes; we fairly rapidly moved toward
its center. At Brentano's one met the prominent members of
the university, with and without their wives (for a good many
of them did not shine in drawing rooms), a few of the artists
and *littérateurs* who abounded in Munich, the brighter members of the aristocracy, and odd people of leisure whose main
occupation was living pleasantly in Munich. A number of other
hospitable houses opened their doors to us. Among them were
the Pringsheims, the parents of Thomas Mann's wife. Her father was a famous mathematician and perhaps an even more
famous collector of pictures and majolica; her mother was beautiful, temperamental, and highly intelligent. Mrs. Pringsheim's
father, Ernst Dohm, had been the editor of the *Kladderadatsch*,
old Berlin's *New Yorker;* her mother was a well-known novelist:
unfortunately, a realist, who in one of her novels depicted Munich society so accurately that for quite a long time the Pringsheims were ostracized, it being quite clear that Hedwig Dohm
had drawn her inspiration from Munich and her information
from her daughter. The brilliant and independent Pringsheims
survived the ordeal.

Outside the university set, which was not always gay, for great
scholars are not too good at small talk, whilst their wives frequently concentrate on animated discussions of how to get efficient domestic help, our most interesting contact was with
Lady Charlotte Blennerhassett, née Countess Leyden. She had

married Sir Roland Blennerhassett, a large but impecunious Irish landowner, of whom I had seen a good deal during my Irish years. He had been one of the most brilliant men of his day, with great promise, combining natural Irish wit with an all-round cosmopolitan education. Somehow he had dropped out. Finally he was made president of the University of Cork, but he did not greatly appreciate its somewhat provincial atmosphere and spent a good deal of his time in contemplative isolation in the Kildare Street Club in Dublin. I often kept him company, for though in his eyes I was almost a boy, I knew the Continental world from which he was separated by two channels. His wife remained in Munich and lived with her brother, Count Leyden, who had been German ambassador to Tokyo. She must have been a great beauty in her youth. At the time we met her she was getting old but had retained her sparkling, vivacious mental intensity. She was a deeply religious Roman Catholic of the liberal school who had played a part in the spiritual movement of the nineteenth century. As a young woman she had been the friend and pupil of the great Döllinger, the protagonist in the struggle against papal infallibility. She had become the most brilliant German woman essayist. By temperament and tradition she understood the eighteenth century and knew how to portray its men and women. She never entertained on a large scale, but one always found a few interesting people in her house; its atmosphere was very much like that of the famous salons of the past.

We met some of the diplomats who represented their country at the court of Bavaria. For the King of Bavaria had not given up his sovereign rights. He maintained legations in Paris, Rome, and Vienna. Munich was a good point of observation for German affairs; it was very much less official than Berlin, and rather detached, not to say critical. One could get a lot of information that might correct Berlin impressions. For that reason Great Britain, among others, maintained a minister in Munich, though Bavaria was not represented in London.

In the summer of 1913 I was arranging a series of public lectures on the Balkan question for the next winter term. I thought it important to get the views of the Austrian Slavs and had asked Masaryk, at that time professor in Prague and a member of the Austrian parliament, to come and deliver one of them. He accepted. The program was settled at the end of the summer term. When I came back from my vacation I was sent for by the head of the Division of Education and given a severe dressing down for mixing the college in politics. When I had recovered from my astonishment, I was told that I must stop Masaryk's lecture because he was one of the leading enemies of Germany. Upon my replying that I had invited Professor Masaryk, a colleague of ours at the University of Prague for an academic lecture, the head seemed rather puzzled. So was I. Then I had an inspiration. "Am I to understand," I asked, "that the objection to Masaryk has arisen in this house?" He could not help smiling. "Did it not come from the Austrian legation?" I continued. "If so, I think I can put it right." "Go ahead," said he, "but don't give me away."

I knew the Austrian minister well. He was a kind but, as I had always thought, not a very bright diplomat. Politely received, I explained my difficulty. What would he, I asked, advise me to do? He seemed rather surprised and promised to think it over.

He had done so when I returned a few days later. He had made inquiries, he said, and had come to the conclusion that this lecture was a very serious affair that must be stopped at all costs. I replied I could not do it; I could not cancel an invitation without giving reasons, and if I did so there would be trouble. "That is your affair," he answered. "You should not have been so careless as to make such an engagement. If you do not break it, I shall have to apply to the Imperial Chancellor and ask for his intervention." "That would suit me very well," I retorted; "I shall get headlines all over the world. Besides, my position is unassailable. I shall tell the Chancellor that I do not feel entitled to censor the appointments of His Apostolic Majesty the Emperor of Austria. He has appointed Masaryk professor at the University of Prague, and that is good enough for me." The Minister nearly fell off his chair. One of the members attached to his legation in Munich had been implicated in the falsification of documents that had led to the Friedjung process in Vienna, the spuriousness of which had been exposed by Masaryk. The gentleman in question, a Hungarian, had been dropped from the Vienna foreign office and given refuge in the legation in Munich. He was naturally not very keen on meeting Masaryk.

I was quite sorry for the Minister, who really was a decent fellow. I told him that with his assistance I could handle the affair. I had to go to Vienna anyhow, and I would talk it over with Masaryk. He seemed greatly relieved.

I had a very pleasant talk with Masaryk in the Café Central in the Herrengasse. Naturally I did not tell him the inside story. I explained that Munich was a hotbed of Pan-Germanism and that he would have to be rather careful. He assured me he would do his best not to excite passions; he was very grateful for the chance I was giving him to explain the Balkan views of the Austrian Slavs. I returned to Munich and informed the Minister of my conversation. He was not satisfied. "You should have asked him to give you the text of his address." He seemed taken aback when I told him that a speaker of Masaryk's standing was quite capable of giving an address without a typed manuscript and could not be bound to stick to a text if he did not want to do so. The poor man was very distressed. "Nothing is going to happen," I consoled him, "if you will support me. I guarantee you that Masaryk will not say anything provocative, provided no previous attacks are made on him; you have to see to it that your press service does not make mischief."

Masaryk turned up on the appointed day. He gave a very scholarly but almost dull address; I am afraid my warning had been overdone.

Many years later, in 1925, I passed through Prague and called on the President. He was not in town but sent his car to bring me to tea with him in Lana. We talked of a good many old problems. I told him the whole story, which greatly amused him. The Minister in his turn was very grateful. He wrote a charming letter to congratulate me on the supreme skill (!) with which I had untangled such a delicate situation.

### 3. La Bohème

By no means all diplomats of the old order were like my Austrian friend. Most of them were shrewd observers of men and conditions. Their published reports show that they were generally wiser than the governments to whom they reported. The majority of them were keen on serving the cause of peace and not afraid of imparting unwelcome information to the home authorities. Nearly all of them had one gift in common. They managed to impress the superficial observer as a frivolous crowd who were mainly interested in social trivialities. They had learned to perfection the art of looking more stupid than they were. In this respect they formed a complete contrast to the bright boys who are now trying to shape public opinion on foreign affairs and whose looks and writings appear far more intelligent than they really are.

Their early representatives in Munich were numerous. In the north of the town was a small suburb called Schwabing. Hither had flocked the brilliant restless minds of all Germany, adding a new wing, so to speak, to the artists' Bohemia established long before. The modern cabaret that manages to make fun, and good fun, of people who are willing to pay an entrance fee for being laughed at in a smart way started in Schwabing. These bohemians were rather sophisticated. Their main object, like that of their predecessors, was to shock the philistines, but they were not satisfied with the fun of doing so; they managed to make it a well-paid profession. They dabbled occasionally in politics. By temperament they were oppositional and even revolutionary—but not because they wanted to reform the world. They made a living by poking fun at the powers that be; they would have been greatly disappointed had those powers gone. The diplomat and the smart cavalry officer, the fraternity student with his hacked face, were as essential to them as ninepins to a bowler. Many of them were very gifted. At one time the weekly *Simplicissimus* was the world's most brilliant satirical paper. It combined great art in drawing and in writing with perforating wit. The Bavarian government did not mind it as long as it concentrated its shafts on Berlin and did not hurt the church or the Bavarian royalty too badly. Munich oozed a kind of indifference that was not unlike tolerance. It was a good thing even from the imperial point of view to have a safety valve for emotional discontent far away from the center. Ridicule does not kill in Germany, otherwise Adolf Hitler, who staged in 1923 the most ridiculous revolt ever known, would have died of it A good many spiritual threads connect him with the bohemian crowd that by and by came to be known by the name of Schwabing.

Schwabing was their habitat but by no means their exclusive domain; it was really a most respectable quarter of the town. Schwabing was not unlike Greenwich Village in its more serious mood. It was an attitude, a state of mind, not a locality. It played a large part later on in the Munich revolution; in fact the short-lived Soviet regime in Munich in April 1919 was Schwabing's first great contribution to political life. Its story might well be called "Triumph and Death of Schwabing."

Great artists and writers are generally not deeply interested in political affairs. The political scene in prewar Munich was, moreover, rather drab. The struggle between church and state was practically over. The Bavarian constitution was sufficiently democratic to satisfy the mass of the people. The diet was generally dominated by the clerical party; the bulk of its members represented rural constituencies or small towns. The socialists relied on industrial workers; outside Franconia they were very much like small bourgeois. The liberals were anticlerical and but mildly progressive. The entire atmosphere was comfortably conservative. The issues were not great enough to rouse violent passions. Schwabing was really not class-conscious; it loathed the philistines rather than the capitalists; as long as it was permitted to parody anybody whom it meant to make fun of, it did not feel oppressed. It represented the minor intelligentsia and the less successful artists. It admired, imitated, envied, despised, and denounced those who had been successful. It sought feverishly after new avenues to success, partly because the old ones were closed to it, partly because the craving for novelty was in its blood. It did not take itself very seriously—though it tried hard to impress the bourgeois with its importance. It knew that it was play-acting.

As long as the old social order was firmly established, Schwabing was no real menace. It became dangerous only when the social structure—whose solidity had not been doubted by any sane person—suddenly cracked and collapsed. The political void had to be closed. The old parties and the trained professionals had not foreseen the catastrophe: evidently knowledge and experience were not essential in statecraft; intuition and creative power were. The chaos that seemed immi-

nent stimulated Schwabing. It had never believed in order—
and it had been right. Its members felt at home in that exciting
turmoil which was rapidly disintegrating most well-tested institutions. The time was ripe for experiments; the people craved
change. They wanted men who delighted in taking risks and
were not oppressed by a feeling of responsibility. Schwabing
could provide them. It had never worried about consequences;
it adored novelties; its most fundamental belief was that all
things novel were good, all things old were bad. So its sons
started lightheartedly on a series of revolutions, the last of
which was to make Adolf Hitler the master of the universe.

## 4. *The Lake of the Roses*

Our life had changed considerably after my appointment as
principal of the College of Commerce. Administrative work,
especially during the period of organization, was heavy. I had
to appoint an entire faculty, unfortunately with limited financial means. I was running all over Germany and Austria looking at older institutions and interviewing candidates. I learned
a good deal in those weeks. Some famous institutions had offered me the services of their most prominent young men because they wanted to get rid of them. I began to discover the
seamy side of academic life. Not all my esteemed colleagues
were searchers after the truth and nothing else. Among them
were inveterate schemers, including some famous men, who
loved the game of academic appointments. They placed their
favorite pupils in key positions and dominated other institutions through them. I soon got wise, after some unpleasant
experiences. I succeeded, finally, in assembling a good faculty;
some of its members had very brilliant careers.

My salary enabled us to rent a summer place where we spent
the long vacations. It was a small house with only half a
dozen rooms, situated in a garden almost at the foot of Germany's highest mountain, the Zugspitz. A small glacial lake
with dark blue-green water and a tiny island in the midst of it
covered most of the grounds—unfortunately it was far too cold
for bathing. The house had been built by an old friend of ours
as a summer residence for his lady friend, a very charming Rus-

sian. Both he and she had long ago outgrown the passionate age. She had put on weight and he had laid off passion; he had handed over the place to his son-in-law, from whom we had rented it. It was a lonely spot outside a hamlet about an hour's drive (horse and buggy) from Garmisch. It was called the Lake of the Roses. Here we settled down from June to October among the glories of the mountains. It took me about three hours to get to Munich, but I could do a good deal of my business by telephone. A number of distinguished friends came and stayed with us. Among them were John X. Merriman, former prime minister of Cape Colony, and his wife, whom we had met in Africa. Merriman, his seventy years notwithstanding, climbed the mountains of the neighborhood with me and was almost intoxicated by their beauty. John and Susie Buchan spent some time with us; he had to acknowledge that the Bavarian highlands, though different, were not inferior in beauty to his Scotch home. Philip Kerr, the late Lord Lothian, was one of our last guests before we gave up the lease. After a few quiet days I took him to some German conventions.

In 1933 I spent the last night in Germany before crossing the border not far from the Lake of the Roses. I had a few hours to spare, so I drove back to have one last look at the place. It had fallen into the hands of a rich industrialist, who had not succeeded in impairing its beauty by adding improvements. The Zugspitz towered over it as of old, in cold, majestic grandeur: its shadows covered our lake completely for half the year; no ray of sun ever reached the place in winter. But for this drawback we might have bought it.

# X. The United States of America
## (1914-1917)

### 1. Westward Ho

SHORTLY AFTER the turn of the new century, official Berlin discovered the United States. William II meant to have a powerful navy. He was intelligent enough to realize the risk of British enmity. It could be easily balanced, his advisers thought, by making friends with the United States. So his brother, Prince Henry, was dispatched on a visit to the States, where he was duly wined and dined. The United States made headlines in the official papers of 1902. Everyone who was anyone or who meant to be anyone started on an overseas tour of exploration and later recorded his discoveries in such epoch-making works as *The Land of Unlimited Opportunities*.

This sudden outburst of an intellectual pioneer spirit greatly amused and somewhat irritated me, for I had myself discovered the United States long ago. Uncle William, who had gone to the States, had presented a buffalo to our Frankfort zoological gardens; when visiting it I felt a kind of proud relationship with the shaggy animal. My native city had helped to finance the Union in its struggle with the Confederates. It had invested a great deal of money in new Pacific railroad ventures. The first American name to impress itself on my childish memory was "Denver Rio Grande"; everybody whom we knew had lost money in it, and I can still remember their wails. Uncle William's firm had financed the Central Pacific; on one of his visits to Europe he brought a sanctimonious-looking old gentleman in a frock coat and a skullcap to Cronberg, the family country place. I had to be on my best behavior, for he was a very big noise; he benignly patted my head. He was Collis P. Huntington, of California fame or ill fame, according to the side of the fence on which the moralist may be.

Before sailing for Africa we had let our flat to James Loeb. He had been a partner of Kuhn, Loeb and Company but had soon given up business. He settled in Munich and became one of our closest friends. He showed his profound interest in things that really matter by sponsoring the now famous editions of the Loeb Classical Library. We met many Americans in his house. Munich had become a favorite spot for university professors to spend their sabbatical year. A few venturesome students followed. Among them was Carlton Parker, hero of *An American Idyll*. We saw a good deal of him and Cornelia during his stay at the university. We could not give him a degree, as our rules demanded a greater number of terms than he could afford, so he took it in Heidelberg and returned to the University of California. Early in 1914 he cabled to ask whether I would come there as visiting professor for the fall term of 1914. I accepted the invitation. We left Europe on the twenty-sixth of July 1914 on the S.S. *George Washington* of the North German Lloyd.

The political situation was tense after the Austrian ultimatum to Serbia. It had been delicate so often in the last ten years that people not in the know were not much worried. Paris, where I spent a day, looked normal.

The first two days on board were restful. We got disquieting news but we discounted it. One of our fellow travelers was a major on the Prussian general staff; he was on sick leave, and he certainly did not expect an outbreak of hostilities. When the news of the declaration of war came, he burst into tears; he was missing the chance of his life. After we reached midocean, precautions had to be taken. At night all lights were dimmed. The last night before landing was very dismal. England was not yet at war, but a French cruiser might seize us. The danger was over after Sandy Hook, but the hope for peace had gone. On a very hot summer day, August 3, we landed and went straight to the old Waldorf Astoria, the one hotel whose name I remembered. Fortunately we had a number of connections. Mr. Jacob Schiff, the head of Kuhn, Loeb and Company, had been at school with my father. James Loeb had written to his brother-in-law Paul Warburg. We immediately rang them up and heard the latest news.

We spent a miserable day in New York hoping against hope

until the news flashed over the wires that Germany and Great Britain were at war. For the time being,. the continents were severed. The British had cut the cables—these were the days before wireless telegraphy—just after I had managed to let my mother know of our safe arrival. Both my wife and I had been working hard for Anglo-German co-operation as the only way to an enduring peace. All our hopes were dashed to the ground; the end of our world seemed to have come. We understood but too well the truth of Sir Edward Grey's tragic prediction: "The lamps are going out all over Europe; we shall not see them lit again in our lifetime." We now know that they will never shine with their old brightness.

We had to make a decision. Should we continue our journey to California or should we try to return? I had never been in the army; I had passed the age at which reserves were called up. The ambassador, Count Bernstorff, was on leave in Germany. The consul general in New York was one of the worst specimens a foreign service can produce. Being terrified of responsibility, he told everybody to do his duty. All men of military age should immediately return to Germany. He insisted on their running this risk, even though they were sure to end in an English prison camp. I talked matters over with the counselor to the embassy, who was very reasonable; yet the question at issue was within the consul general's competence. Most sailings were canceled; only a few people could secure passages on the available boats. Evidently officers of the reserve were much more needed than a middle-aged professor who had had no training. So I made up my mind to let the soldiers start first and wait for events. I explained my decision in a letter to the Ambassador and was greatly relieved when he fully approved it later. I met the consul general—Falke was his name—once again at a meeting of the subcommittee of the Reichstag inquiring into possible opportunities for making peace. He had been intriguing against the Ambassador and had leveled many accusations against him. The committee gave him a chance to verify them. He withdrew them completely. Needless to say, he belonged to the spiritual advance guard of the Nazis.

In a few days the term in California would begin. We started westward in terrific summer heat, spending a miserable time on the train. Once we had crossed the Sierra and were on our way down into California, we revived. The soft, cool air of the Pacific wafted round us. Early on a foggy August morning we steamed into Berkeley. Nobody had expected us at that hour. A funny-looking little trolley car took us to Cloyne Court where we were to live. The fog had not yet lifted. Berkeley looked gray and depressing. We had to carry our grips a few blocks uphill, and they were far too heavy. Life seemed very bleak indeed.

## 2. *Visiting Professor*

The passions of the East had not yet reached California. The coast was so far distant from European bickerings that it could afford a detached point of view; there was no violent anti-German feeling. San Francisco, moreover, was cosmopolitan, sympathetic, and understanding. We were very fortunate in beginning our academic career in the West.

At that time Berkeley was still a small town. The faculty was closely knit and dominated by its president, Benjamin I. Wheeler. His kindness and later on his friendship greatly eased our position, the anomaly of which turned out to be a blessing. The pro-Allied elements sympathized with my wife, and the pro-German patted me on the back. We were privileged to enjoy peace in a warring world. We fell in love with the country, some of whose features reminded us of our African days. We enjoyed the gray caressing fogs that floated across the bay and the hills the summer heat had scorched brown. Crossing the bay on the ferryboat to San Francisco was an adventure of which I never grew tired.

I had to adapt myself to American university conditions. In Germany the university may be said to have existed for the benefit of the professor, who considered himself a kind of demigod. In the United States the scales were inverted. The university existed for the benefit of the students, for the glory of the trustees and the reminiscent happiness of the alumni. I transformed myself pretty rapidly. I managed to do it without getting into hot water, thanks to my newly acquired friends on the faculty who watched my steps with the greatest kindness. They arranged some public lectures for me. Here again I had to undergo a rather severe training. I was considered a good speaker. I had talked outside the university to many German and English audiences. Yet I had to learn a lot before I mastered the art. I had to give up the supercilious, ironical tone that Continental intellectuals love, and I had to learn one essential lesson; if one is expected to talk for an hour, one should finish half a minute before the appointed time; otherwise one will be considered a bore.

The one thing that distressed us in California was the huge distance separating us not only from events but from the detailed reports available to an Eastern public. Still, we were very sad when the term was over; fortunately the ties we had made were strong enough to last for a lifetime and to keep us in constant touch with our friends.

I had accepted the Carl Schurz professorship at the University of Wisconsin. Thither we went early in the new year. We passed Los Angeles, at that time not a very impressive place, and spent a few days at the Grand Canyon. A heavy snowfall prevented us from exploring all its beauties. Its grandeur surpassed that of the Victoria Falls. In the Greek legend the giants had scaled Mount Olympus by piling Mount Pelion on Mount Ossa; the vast cleft called the Grand Canyon of the Colorado might be the place where they had dug them out of the bowels of the earth.

The change from Berkeley to Madison was hard. Winter in Wisconsin had its drawbacks, even for those accustomed to a Continental mountain climate. We had difficulty in finding an adequate apartment; neither of us was good at housekeeping. Hotel and restaurant life in Madison was not very satisfactory in those days. Only after the advent of the motorcar did restaurant feeding become easy all over the United States.

The University of Wisconsin had passed its most heroic days, during which its members had formed the original brains trust and furnished progressive ideas to the older La Follette. The pedigree of "the Wisconsin idea" is an interesting one. A young economist, Richard T. Ely, had gone to Berlin and had sat at the feet of Adolph Wagner. Here he imbibed theories of state socialism. He had gone back to the States and expounded some of them; they were considered extremely radical. Ely himself was a mild, almost timid little man unwilling to be the stand-ard-bearer of a Red revolutionary movement. His enemies had created a reputation for him; he was not inclined to live up to it. His instincts were conservative; his interests centered on land; it was but logical that he became a not-too-successful realtor in his old age. He had spent a sabbatical year in Munich and become a close friend of ours. My appointment was due partly to Ely and partly to absence of more worthy candidates, for the Carl Schurz professorship had to be filled by a German. Its purpose was to help the large German element in Wisconsin to maintain cultural ties with Germany.

When La Follette started war on monopolist private indus-tries and attempted state control of them, the university had provided him with a number of experts for carrying out his policy. Ely's knowledge of Continental social problems had made him a valuable ally. The state librarian, Charles Mc-Carthy, had formulated the reformers' concepts in a clever little book called *The Wisconsin Idea.* Theodore Roosevelt took them over from La Follette and dressed them up as progres-sivism. Colonel House saved them from the ruins of progres-sivism and put them in an atrocious novel called *Philip Dru, Administrator* (1912), in which he outlined Woodrow Wilson's New Freedom and Franklin Roosevelt's New Deal. Most mod-ern progressives are ignorant of their own origin—knowledge of previous reforms would greatly detract from the joy of novelty, which to many of them is all that matters.

The Progressives were out of power during our stay and thus the university was under a cloud. Still, President Van Hise, its last great president, managed to keep up relations with the enemy, the standpat, old-fashioned Republicans. At a dinner given in honor of former President Taft, I sat between him and the governor of the state. Both were very heavy men. Taft was a charmer, Governor Phillips a stodgy, bulky Milwaukee Ger-man. It was not a cheerful meal. It took place on the day after the *Lusitania* had been sunk. .

Wisconsin was still very German, though Milwaukee had lost many of its German features; its more successful German citizens were rapidly being Anglicized, except for the brewers and a few other well-to-do businessmen connected with them. What might be called the lower middle class and the minor intelligentsia continued to nurse German sentiments. They gathered in the afternoons in a little German café (I think it was called Café Martin) where one went for coffee and cake. They were a harmless, friendly crowd. Their cultural demands were not overexacting, though the city did have a German theater. I have talked to a good many German audiences; those in Milwaukee never impressed me deeply. I am quite sure this was reciprocal. They were enthusiastic about my colleague, Eugen Kühnemann, who stumped the country as traveling salesman for German culture, spoke to them about Goethe and Schiller, and told them about world affairs, just what they wanted to hear and in the manner they loved best. The German universities have produced a type of lecturer that can best be described as streamlined cultural Rotarian. Kühnemann was of this type. He oozed culture and he boomed culture.

The Carl Schurz professor at the University of Wisconsin had to visit German communities in the state and lecture to them in German or in English. I greatly enjoyed this part of my work. It brought me in touch with the unsophisticated, good-natured Germans in the small towns. They were passing through a tragic period. They were patriotic Americans. They or their fathers and mothers had come to make America their home. A number of them had left Germany in disgust after the failure of the '48 Revolution. They looked forward, not backward. Their fatherland was no longer the country where they were born but the land where they wished to be laid to their eternal rest. Yet they had not broken the cultural ties with the old world. Germany had changed considerably since their fathers had left her. She had become a strong, united country, respected by the entire world. The old disunity and weakness had vanished. She was no longer controlled by obscurantists. The government of William II was not a model government from the point of view of a sincere democrat; yet it was very progressive when compared to many of its German predecessors. In any case the country had become prosperous; the drabness and poverty of the old days seemed to be gone forever. William II and his theatrical stunts made good headlines in American papers; American snobs, social and cultural, had flocked to Berlin. The German-Americans were beginning to feel proud of the nation from which they had sprung. It was no longer, perhaps, the home of poets and philosophers of which they had heard a great deal. It had become the leader in social reform. Even old-fashioned German republicans were beginning to be reconciled to it.

The war had taken the German-Americans by surprise. They sided instinctively with Germany. After all, the powerful German Empire had not been engaged in a single war for over forty years. It was now fighting for its life against Russians, Frenchmen, and Britons. The average American did not like the English. He saw in Czarist Russia an enemy of mankind. Quite naturally German-Americans shared these antipathies very intensely. They had been told to be neutral; most of them understood the need of this injunction, for they wanted to live in amity with their neighbors. They were sorely puzzled when well-organized Allied propaganda swept the country with stories of German atrocities and when the German people were branded as Huns. They were greatly worried. They could understand why English-speaking Americans should side with the British, but they could not fathom why they themselves should be accused of disloyalty for showing sympathy with their German brethren. They were called hyphenated Americans. They resented the slur on their loyalty, especially when the older generation remembered how in the Civil War the hyphenated German-Americans had borne arms for their adopted country. A feeling of frustration spread among them. Almost overnight they saw themselves as a racial minority to whom equal rights were denied by a ruthless majority.

It was not easy for a guest of the United States to speak to them. They generally expected Germans from Germany to voice their grievances and to steel them to action. I was fortunate in being denied the gifts of a good spellbinder. I have addressed very large and sometimes very unruly meetings. I can only do it in conversational tones. I can't scream. I have to hold myself severely in control when I am deeply moved; otherwise I would choke. These disadvantages as much, perhaps, as a certain amount of horse sense prevented me from getting into trouble in those highly emotional days. I spoke to German audiences as a German from Germany. I tried to tell the truth; in this respect I am quite sure I sometimes was mistaken. I never said anything that might have been construed as interference with

American politics. This no doubt greatly limited my popularity among German-Americans; it increased my usefulness to them and to Germany. I gained a reputation for fairness that stood me in good stead and has enabled me to address American audiences for nearly thirty years without so far having disgraced myself.

The tragedy of the German-Americans was profound. Just when they were beginning to be proud of their native country, they had to denounce it; for the time being, the process of voluntary assimilation that they had cheerfully, nay eagerly, undergone was halted. Their loyalty, which had been spontaneous, became strained when it was made compulsory. In many parts of the country the antipathy to the Germany of William II was turned against Americans of German birth. The anti-German feeling was far more virulent then than in the second war. By that time, people had become so sick of the atrocity stories of the First World War that they refused to believe authenticated reports of beastliness which was not even denied, for the Nazis gloried in it.

Geography was even more hazy to Americans in those years than it is nowadays. We spent a few very pleasant weeks on a dude ranch in Wyoming whose owners were cultivated Easterners. When we left they expressed their pleasure in having met us. "We did not like the last Germans we had here," they said. "They were Hungarians from Budapest."

We spent the whole summer in the Rocky Mountains, mostly in Glacier National Park, and in the latter part of it we struck out into the wilds and did a fortnight of real camping. It was almost as good as Africa, though it was camping de luxe. Our guide insisted on carrying along with him a cooking stove; he had to have "spuds" every day. But the mountains and the lakes were glorious. We passed through Yellowstone Park, admiring, as my wife phrased it, the various "Biblical stunts" in which the geysers indulged, and finally wound up at the dude ranch, where I managed to kill a rattlesnake, considered quite an achievement for a greenhorn.

I had been called for the fall term to Cornell University, to the Jacob Schiff chair for German culture. Though Mr. Andrew D. White had resigned from its presidency, he still was a spiritual center. He was deeply disappointed by Germany's attitude in the war and had turned the photograph William II had given him with its face to the wall. But he and his wife were very kind to us. President Schurman was not. He was correct but nothing more. I had to lecture on a German subject, and I had chosen as my topic the expansion of Germany. He objected to it, and but for my close connection with Mr. Schiff I might have got into difficulties. Finally I delivered the dullest series of lectures I have ever given. We stayed in the house of Professor Faust, the head of the German Department and author of *The German Element in the United States*. He was aggressively and not wisely pro-German, which did not ease our position. Yet we did pull through without too much friction, as most members of the faculty were very considerate. Among the junior staff was a budding instructor whom his colleagues did not greatly appreciate. We had come across him in Munich and were delighted to meet him again. His name was Hendrik Willem Van Loon. But for the support of Lincoln Burr, the head of the History Department, he would have been a dismal failure at Cornell. We saw a great deal of him. New Year 1916 he gave us one of those delightful drawings of his in which humor and pathos are so quaintly blended.

### 3. *On the Fringe of Diplomacy*

By springtime of 1916, I had held three visiting professorships in three different parts of the country. I had learned a great deal. The animosities aroused by the war had greatly reduced the amenities of a visiting professorship. One did not encounter the hospitable deference that has so often inflated the ego of visitors. I had seen the United States with the lid off.

We had gone to Washington several times and called on the ambassador, Count Bernstorff, and his wife. They were polite to us, but as he told my wife later on, he did not like professors. Those who were running around the country presenting themselves, with more eloquence than sagacity, as ambassadors of German culture tended to increase his difficulties. Bernstorff recognized the potential strength of the United States; he had advised Berlin to refrain carefully from inflaming public opinion. He understood the President's mind and trusted his deep-seated pacifism and desire to keep his people out of the war. He was on friendly terms with Colonel House.

The military in Berlin had a low opinion of American military strength. The navy was sure they could prevent the landing of any considerable American forces on the Continent; they clamored incessantly for the resumption of unrestricted submarine warfare. The army had its doubts. Until the autumn of 1916 its chiefs hoped to win the war on land. After the Rumanian campaign they came to the conclusion that this was no longer possible; they were willing to give the navy a free hand. The Chancellor, however, managed to postpone the resumption of unrestricted submarine warfare until the result of Wilson's peace movement had become visible.

The Ambassador, who foresaw the consequences of America's entry into the war, strained every nerve to prevent it, but his influence on the Chancellor was limited. The naval and the military attachés, though personally loyal to him, were not under his control. They reported directly to their chiefs and at their orders indulged in clumsy conspiracies. The Ambassador could not stop them. He was greatly relieved when the naval attaché seriously implicated himself and had to be sent home. The military attaché was Franz von Papen. He survived his naval colleague for some time with that curious blend of *bonhomie,* irresponsibility, dash, and cunning that is all his own.

Falke, the consul general in New York, was a Pan-German; his reports contradicted those of the Ambassador, and he had to be removed. His successor, a heavy-set East Prussian of the *type Simplicissimus* had made familiar all over Germany, was cautious and cunning. He happened to have been in the same student fraternity as the undersecretary, and later secretary, of state Zimmermann, and wrote to him private letters that induced that cheerful, hail-fellow-well-met worthy to ignore the Ambassador's warning.

Bernstorff was a thorough gentleman. He came from one of the great Schleswig-Holstein families who were much nearer to the Danish aristocracy than to the Prussian Junker. He had been an officer in a crack regiment before going into the diplomatic service. He knew, understood, and loved the Anglo-Saxon world. The war between Germany and England was to him a tragedy, as it was to us. His wife was a New Yorker, a dominating personality with strong moral convictions, deep affections, and no great tact. Both of them became intimate friends of ours later on. My wife's natural impetuosity had disarmed their original distrust. While lunching for the first time at the embassy she had learned that our dear friend Horace Plunkett had arrived in the States and was staying at the British Embassy. "May I phone to him?" she asked the greatly amused Ambassador, and having obtained his permission immediately rang up a British attaché, who almost fainted when he realized where the call came from. But she established contact with Horace and we saw a good deal of him. We were to meet again in New York. When I rang him up, he said, "I must come and see you. My American host is so mad about everything German that you cannot come to his house."

The German Embassy had a financial department in New York, headed by Heinrich Albert. He figured largely in the papers when his brief case was filched in the subway. He certainly did not deserve the obloquy he came in for. I became his assistant in questions of currency and exchange. We settled in New York, and I regularly went downtown. In the summer we went to Silver Bay, Lake George, where my wife kept house for Albert and other members of the embassy. I did not have to stay in New York all the week; I could do most of my work in the country. It was a lovely summer; we swam and canoed. Yet I did feel a little bored, my work being somewhat spasmodic, until I submitted a plan to Albert.

The public in the United States had little information about economic matters in Germany. Mails were very irregular. Cables had been cut, and the newly established radio stations did not yet function very well. After the 1916 election, peace, we thought, might be waiting around the corner; preparations for it had to be made. The United States public had to be informed of the actual conditions prevailing in Germany. I suggested to Albert the publication by the embassy of a bimonthly news letter containing essential economic and financial facts about Germany. While purely factual, it would have news value, for the embassy was in a position to request otherwise unobtainable information. The Ambassador consented, and we set to work. I collected a small staff and we prepared a first issue; it was not very good, but the best that could be done at the time.

The embassy offered to send the letter to anybody who asked. We had printed only a few copies, which had been distributed to prominent business friends. Our modesty was rewarded. We were overwhelmed with inquiries. People who would have thrown the letter into the wastepaper basket had we sent it to them unsolicited clamored for a copy and studied it carefully. We seemed to have discovered an effective method of honest propaganda. But the news letter did not live long.

In the last weeks of 1916 we had become optimists. We recognized the unwisdom of the German peace proposals, which had interfered with President Wilson's schemes, but he had continued his efforts undaunted. British financial conditions were becoming serious. Some of our Wall Street friends were making financial plans for peace. One of them organized a dinner to which leading bankers were asked who had no particular sympathies with Germany but who were concerned about reconstruction. They wanted to discuss a German loan to be issued as soon as peace was in sight.

The dinner was fixed for the latter part of January. A few days earlier Albert sent for me and told me confidentially that we had better pack up. Berlin had made up its mind to resume unrestricted submarine warfare on February first. It might not mean war; it certainly would mean the end of diplomatic relations. We could not back out of the dinner engagement with a good excuse, and had to go to a party organized for preparing peace, knowing all the time that it would be war. Hoping against hope, we discussed various technical proposals that in a few days would be mere wastepaper. Our fears were justified. Berlin remained obstinate. President Wilson accepted the challenge. Diplomatic relations were severed. Our activities were over.

There was no object in staying on, for no useful work could be done in the near future. How could we get home without being made prisoners of war? I wired the University of California, at whose invitation we had come to the States. They rapidly set to work and secured a safe conduct for us. I felt complimented when I learned later that the British Embassy not only had raised no objections but seemed delighted to have me out of the way. Once this was settled, the rest was up to the embassy. We were to travel on a neutral ship, the Danish steamer *Frederick VIII*, part of which the embassy had chartered.

During the prolonged international negotiations that preceded our departure—they took about a fortnight—we had ample time to settle our affairs and bid farewell to our friends. I had to leave all my papers behind me, including the lecture notes I had brought with me, which contained the fruits of very nearly ten years' labor. I never saw them again. The State Department very kindly searched for them later. The Department of Justice, which had taken them over, knew nothing of their whereabouts. Perhaps its experts, unable to make head or tail of highly technical notes in an abominable handwriting, had become suspicious and subjected them to chemical treatment. In any case, they were lost. I might have written a few more books had the notes been preserved.

## 4. *Home-coming*

The *Frederick VIII* sailed on February 14, 1917. Controls at the pier were pretty strict, yet a number of deputations from German-American associations had turned up to take leave of the Ambassador—they had thoroughly disliked him for his aloofness from provocative German-American activities. I can still see Putzi Hanfstaengl, later Hitler's musical confidant, looking like an undertaker in his loose frock coat and stovepipe hat, presenting with that vacuous smile of his a wreath of laurels to the Ambassador. Finally we were off, heading for Halifax. We had to take a northern route to be safe from enemy cruisers and German submarines. The German navy hated the Ambassador; it would have been quite capable of blowing up the ship, "accidentally," of course.

In Halifax we were kept for very nearly a fortnight, notwithstanding our safe conduct. Our luggage was pulled out of the ship, put on the quay, and thoroughly gone into. I doubt whether much valuable contraband was found; some hot water bottles were confiscated. We were personally searched. I had to open my mouth wide to show that I did not carry contraband in my teeth. The British officers who handled us were gentlemen; they felt the meanness of the job and loathed it. We were not allowed to land. The ship was not very big. It was cold; tempers began to be very frayed. Fortunately the discussion of the iniquities to which we had been subjected served as a safety valve. I suppose the main object of our detention was to retard the Ambassador's arrival in Berlin as much as possible.

From Halifax we took a northerly course. We went near Iceland and the Faroe Islands, far off the commercial lanes and the dangers lurking on them. The sea was rough; it was bitterly cold. The company was not cheerful. About seventeen consuls and their wives were on board; all were patriotic Germans, but few of them longed to go home. Some of the men were intelligent and charming, and so were a few women, but only a few. Many were mediocre bureaucrats. They had played a part as representatives of a powerful country in the local society of their respective districts. They had been somebodies; they realized but too well that from now on they might be nobodies. The embassy consisted of the Ambassador and his wife, two counselors, and a number of attachés. Countess Bernstorff could be very gracious; she was the truest of friends to those she cared for, but she did not trouble to be nice to people whom she disliked. Consequently, the embassy kept aloof and the consuls sulked. But for the outsiders on the ship, among them some leading American newspapermen, the journey would have been very dull.

Two days before we reached Oslo I created a sensation. Dinner was over. The Ambassador had asked us to sit with him, when a bellboy loudly called my name, presenting me with a wireless. It read somewhat like this: "Please interview Count Bernstorff on exposure of Zimmermann's note proposing alliance against United States." It was signed "New York Times." I had had friendly relations with the Times, but I had not the slightest idea what this was all about. I kept the matter to myself, though everybody was eager to know all about it, until the party had dispersed. Then I went to the Ambassador's stateroom and showed him the cable. He looked very gloomy. "I will explain it tomorrow morning," he said.

Next morning he sent for me and told me the story. Zimmermann, the secretary of state, had offered Mexico an alliance against the United States, promising after a victorious war

Texas, Arizona, and New Mexico, and if Japan could be won over, a defensive triple alliance. The Ambassador had been informed of the proposal; he had certainly not approved of it. The secret had leaked out. The Foreign Office in Berlin and the people responsible for transmitting it in a code which had been deciphered attempted to make him responsible for the leak. It was their fault, not his. After some discussion we decided on a reply on these lines: "Count Bernstorff has been completely cut off from all communications for three weeks. He is not in a position to explain wireless sent to me." *

Two days later we landed in Oslo, and within another twenty-four hours our journey terminated in Copenhagen. We spent a day and night in that cheerful capital, which the war so far had treated very gently, and were allowed to buy a few provisions to take along with us to Germany. Early next morning we started on the last lap of our journey. The ferry took us across to Warnemünde. After nearly three years away, we were back in Germany. A dining car had been attached to the train to Berlin. The meal specially prepared for our benefit gave us a hint of some of the deprivations ahead; more seasoned travelers considered it ample.

Late in the evening on a cold March night we arrived in Berlin. The city was only partly lighted. We took a cab, whose driver looked almost starved, and drove to the Hotel Kaiserhof. Some of the hotel employees recognized me. They looked pinched. They had been at the front and sent home as invalids. As we carried our own soap and were provided with towels, things did not look too bad. Next morning we had breakfast —two slices of soggy black bread with a wee bit of flabby jelly and two cups of black coffee made from roasted barley.

I went out on a scouting expedition. The streets were dirty; there was little traffic. The cab horses looked starved, their drivers shriveled and shrunk. I had been fairly well informed about the situation in general; as editor of the official news sheet I had had at my disposal as many facts as the most privileged outsider. Yet the picture we had made for ourselves in New York differed from the original, which stared at us from all corners.

* I am greatly obliged to the *New York Times* for letting me have a copy of the cables exchanged between us.

The military situation was improving. The Russian Revolution was well under way; the collapse of Russia could be expected any day, yet on the morning of March fifteenth, my one. and only impression was: "Germany is going to lose the war."

# XI. The Kings Depart

## 1. *At the Foreign Office*

WE RETURNED to our house in Munich, which our servants had kept going with little coal and short rations. They had had a poor time. I reported to the government and had an audience with the King. He was, as usual, mainly interested in details. At this time he was in an optimistic mood. The revolution had paralyzed Russia's military power; the submarine campaign seemed to be going well. The King had high hopes of a victorious peace when he would claim from the Reich part of Alsace, where his ancestors had held possessions.

My report on the United States worried the prime minister, Count Hertling, greatly. "You must go to Berlin," he said, "and see the Chancellor." I considered the journey superfluous. Count Bernstorff knew the situation far better than I did. He had been shunted aside because the military did not like his views; he had to wait two months before the Emperor granted him an audience. But Hertling insisted; he would arrange an audience with the Chancellor.

I went to Berlin. As I had foreseen, I was received not by the Chancellor himself but by one of his assistants. I explained the situation in the United States—the opposition of the Republicans to Wilson, the personal feuds between leading men, the traditional conflict between the Democratic and the Republican parties. "You speak of a struggle between Democrats and Republicans," the budding statesman interrupted me. "I don't quite understand; I always thought that all Americans were Republicans." I learned from this interview that ignorance of American affairs among the leaders in Europe was as great as ignorance of European affairs among the led in the United States.

I had no desire to stay in Berlin. I wanted to go back to my college, but the Foreign Office requisitioned me. I was taken into the publicity division, where I was to work on public opinion in the United States. On this job I spent the most futile months of my life. I read newspapers, arranged interviews, and wrote articles for the neutral press. The publicity division was not highly esteemed by the policy-making division. Every scrap of paper I wrote had to be submitted to my chief, a kindly, intelligent man, who generally passed it on; the policy-making division used to hold it up. Its members were timid, without ideas, and jealous of anybody who might have an idea. They knew little about the United States. I was very bored and wrote a private letter to a friend of mine in which I described the situation accurately and not without humor. By bad—or rather good—luck it got mixed up with official papers and came into the hands of the person whom I had criticized. I was sent for and severely reprimanded. I deserved it on account of my careless-ness, but I scored on one point. I told the head of the division that I had been brought up in the belief that gentlemen did not read letters that were not addressed to them. A few years afterward he acknowledged his sympathies with the attitude I had taken. I was not kicked out, but I was quite sure that I would not be kicked upstairs. I made ready for a good exit.

Zimmermann, the hero of the offer of the alliance to Mexico, was replaced as secretary of state by Herr von Kühlmann. I knew him well. I explained to him in a memorandum that my writing up a policy of whose main features I was ignorant could do no good; I must either be taken into his confidence or be allowed to go home. Naturally I was permitted to resign. I went back to Munich and took over my college duties, having proven to my own complete satisfaction that I was a bad bureaucrat. Yet my stay in Berlin had not been useless. I had had some enlightening experience and I had made many official contacts. I had even impressed the Foreign Office. Years later, when I was appointed a member of the Gold Delegation of the League of Nations, one of the career men exclaimed, horror-stricken, "But he is so independent!"

I had written a memorandum for the Foreign Office on my American impressions. I had delivered an address on it to the Deutsche Gesellschaft, a recently founded club whose members belonged to all political camps. It established me quite unexpectedly as a great authority on the United States. Published later on in Munich as a booklet entitled *The United States as an Enemy*, it created a stir. I doubt whether the Berlin military censor would have let it pass; in Munich there was no difficulty.

By the summer of 1917 the failure of the submarine warfare had become evident. A political crisis had arisen owing to the demand of the majority of the Reichstag for a "peace without conquest." It was badly managed. It led to the fall of Bethmann-Hollweg, to the appointment of Michaelis as chancellor, and to the establishment of a military dictatorship by Ludendorff under the cover of Hindenburg's popularity. Bavaria did not like this turn of affairs. Her leaders realized that Michaelis was a mere stooge of Ludendorff. When the new chancellor presented himself at court in Munich, the minister of education summed up his impression by saying, "I won't take the trouble to remember him."

In the late summer a stalemate peace might have been concluded. Russia was collapsing, the United States was not yet ready, the submarine warfare was, to say the least, disappointing. But Ludendorff gambled on victory; he preferred the risk of defeat to a compromise peace. The Munich atmosphere was sober; official Berlin called it defeatist. My warnings of the potential strength of the United States were taken seriously; the leading Munich paper, hitherto chauvinist, had calmed down considerably. It offered me its front page for anything I might have to say. I limited myself usually to American topics. For the time being, I became the leading exponent of President Wilson's policy. I outlined it in another booklet, *What Are Wilson's Aims?*, which was widely read.

The Bolshevik Revolution gave Germany a chance to make a separate peace with Russia. Thanks to Ludendorff it was a "dictated peace." It freed Germany from military risks in the east. It ruined her morally in the west.

After Lenin's submission, Germany was in a position to break the deadlock in the west by a huge frontal attack. If it succeeded, the war, most people thought, would be over. I did not share their optimism. I was convinced that the United States would never permit a German victory once they had gone to war. Yet there might still be a chance for peace (though a very slim one) while the German attack was pending.

One could not agitate against the great offensive that was to bring victory, but one could point out that the menace of it created a favorable situation for negotiations. An appeal to President Wilson at this time, early in 1918, when the German army was ready to strike, might have had different results from the plea months later, after the German onslaught had failed. Ludendorff's friends later spoke of his willingness to accept a negotiated peace and to sacrifice most of his conquests if the civil government had compelled him to do so. As he had taken good care to emasculate the civil government, this apologia was merely an attempt at a moral alibi.

The great spring offensive was nearly successful. Yet "nearly" is an adequate consolation only when a stronger follow-up can be made. If the effort that "nearly" succeeded is final, it spells complete failure. In the early summer of 1918 it was pretty evident that the great gambler had lost. Public opinion was still optimistic, yet discordant voices were audible. I was riding a trolley car when bells began to toll announcing a victory. "Another victory," mumbled an old man behind me. "I'd much rather have a pound of butter."

## 2. The Armistice

That summer my colleague, Dr. Edgar Jaffé, requested leave for the coming winter. The high command had approached him and invited him to lecture to the army on Germany's favorable economic position, in order to raise the men's morale.

I refused. "If the army asks for you, I shall have to release you, but I am not going to assist you of my own free will in spreading deliberate falsehoods." He was rather astonished.

Jaffé was a mild-mannered little man with rather winning ways. In 1910 he had seemed to me to be the right choice for a school of business administration. He had been in business in England before taking up an academic career, and had written an excellent book on English banking. It turned out to be an excellent appointment—he was a first-rate teacher who contributed greatly to the college's growing reputation. The war had unsettled him. He was beyond military age, but not beyond the desire of playing a part. Munich was not a good jumping-off ground; business of all sorts naturally concentrated in Berlin. Jaffé tried to influence public opinion by starting a weekly magazine in Berlin (Europäische Staats-und Wirtschaftszeitung), edited by an erratic brother of his. After my return from the United States I wrote a good deal for it. I even took a hand in its reorganization when it had gone on the rocks. But the magazine was not successful enough to satisfy Jaffé's ambitions. He got in touch with the military and was occasionally sent by them to Switzerland. On one of his journeys he met Herron, who presented himself as an intimate of President Wilson and offered to act as intermediary in case the German government had anything to say. Jaffé returned to Berlin and suggested to the Foreign Office that he was in a position to send peace proposals to the President. The Foreign Office doubted Herron's importance. American diplomats resided in a number of neutral countries; they could easily communicate with the chief executive. Jaffé thought his efforts were not sufficiently appreciated.*

A little later I had to deliver a lecture in Switzerland. Herron sent me word he would like to see me. I had no desire to go to Geneva, which was a center of espionage for both sides, nor was I convinced of Herron's importance. I offered to meet him halfway; naturally he did not turn up. The amateur diplomat who takes himself seriously and is not content with the role of privileged mail carrier is a dangerous creature. By the very nature of his activities he must be "egocentric," and the less of the "I" there is in international relations, the better the results.

Jaffé's co-operation with the army had evidently not satisfied him. A few months after our summer interview this unobtrusive person, who had prematurely aged and whose natural gifts qualified him for dealing with individual facts rather than with general principles, became a rampant revolutionary.

In the last days of September 1918 the old order in Germany was breaking up. The submarine warfare had failed; pressure from the blockade was increasing; unrest among the working classes was spreading. The hopes based on the establishment of an independent Ukraine government under German protection

---

* Herron exaggerated Jaffé's importance in his letters to the President, in the same way Jaffé exaggerated Herron's influence.

had been disappointed; supplies reaching the central powers from that source were insufficient. The annexationist character of the Russian peace had shocked many people to whom the war had hitherto been a war of defense. The Independent Socialist party, which had finally opposed that peace, was gaining strength, especially among workers in the metal industries.

The astonishing survival of the Communist government in Russia had, moreover, fundamentally changed the issue of socialism. Mere doctrines could be disposed of by arguments; a socialist state in being could be damned or praised, but it could not be refuted. The future safety of the Soviet government seemed to depend on a world revolution. Germany, whose large working class was thoroughly indoctrinated with Marxism, must rapidly be made ripe for it. The Soviets had put large sums of money in the hands of their agents to carry on a revolutionary propaganda for peace. This propaganda backed by Russian cash, not American propaganda based on slogans, speeded up the final collapse of the old regime. The Wilsonian program was well known among educated people. I had been its most active interpreter. I had received a good deal of publicity, but my influence did not reach very far.

Soviet propaganda told the masses that the social aims in which they had long believed could easily be attained; it promised them peace and a completely new world order. It did not win over the majority of the organized German trade unions, who faithfully followed their old leaders, but it did affect an energetic minority. This minority had been organizing an occasional antiwar strike; it had made the going very hard for moderate Socialists. Had the Independent Socialists possessed a dynamic leader, ready to run grave risks, the outcome of the German revolution might have been very different.

The ruling powers in Germany had to broaden the foundation of the government, for the nation had to be prepared for a nonvictorious peace. Very late in the day they were adopting responsible parliamentary government on the British pattern. Prince Max von Baden formed the first parliamentary government Germany had ever possessed; all parties, with the exception of the Independent Socialists, were represented. It lasted but a few weeks. While the new chancellor was framing the outlines of his policy, the army chiefs presented him with an ultimatum. He must immediately sue for an armistice through the good offices of President Wilson or the lines would no longer hold. Bulgaria, Turkey, and Austria were collapsing. The American army had appeared on the battlefields, and the sight of these fresh, well-fed, spic-and-span battalions proved a severe shock to the tired German veterans. General Ludendorff, the man who had prevented peace negotiations at a time when the situation was favorable, forced them on his government when he had lost the war.

The news of the demand for an armistice reached us in the mountains. We were living in a country house beyond Garmisch for a week or so; we had received no mail for several days. We had gone to the inn for the midday dinner on the sixth of October. The Munich papers had just arrived. They announced in large headlines the armistice demand sent to President Wilson on October 3–4.

We were thunderstruck. I had been in close touch with the Bavarian government; I had frequently implored the Prime Minister to use his influence and to put pressure on Berlin to start negotiations. I was considered a leading authority on American affairs. My opinion had not been asked for; in fact, I doubt whether any of those who really knew the United States had been consulted by the army.

The armistice demand could have but one of two meanings. Either it was a trick to give the German armies time to extricate themselves from a menaced position, or it was a more or less veiled declaration of Germany's defeat. The Allies could not risk a faulty interpretation of this unexpected move. They could grant an armistice only under conditions that would make the resumption of hostilities impossible. They were not yet convinced of Germany's complete military collapse. They did not consider the situation as hopeless as Ludendorff did. They suspected a trap, and they took their precautions. They were irritated besides, by what seemed to them a clumsy attempt at breaking their unity. The United States was a latecomer to the war; its military achievements had not yet been considerable. The bulk of the fighting forces facing the Germans were French and English, and the supreme commander was a Frenchman. The singling out of President Wilson seemed to be another trick. It may have flattered the President's vanity; it may have filled him with new hopes for carrying out his ambitious program for peace. It made his position with his allies very difficult.

More than a month was to pass before the final terms of the armistice could be agreed upon. In these weeks fighting continued; the German lines steadied themselves again. Ludendorff had added one more miscalculation to his long line of errors. He recovered his nerve and wanted to resume fighting if the terms of the armistice were too onerous; he did not understand that he had broken German morale. Until they heard of the armistice the majority of the people were convinced that the war had been going well. They had won tremendous victories; the German armies stood everywhere on enemy soil. It was true their allies had been broken, yet it would need a tremendous effort to drive the German army back to its frontiers and follow it across the Rhine. The demand for an armistice changed the picture completely. A victorious army does not ask for an armistice, especially not for one in which conditions of peace hitherto called defeatist are accepted. It suddenly burst on the German people that they had lost the war.

They had to recognize that peace terms no longer depended on their military prowess but on the wisdom and the generosity of their enemies. The army would hold its positions until the armistice conditions had been agreed upon; it could not be expected to go on fighting if they were disappointing. The talk of a *levée en masse,* in which romantic intellectuals indulged, was but infantile babble. Under a system of vigorous all-round conscription such as existed in Germany, no mass was left over that could rise. Ludendorff should have been court-martialed, not because he lost the war but because he forced the demand for an armistice. The third of October should have been made a day of national mourning to remind the German people of the catastrophe for which its military leaders were responsible. Had this been done, Ludendorff would have gone down in German history as the man responsible for the miseries of the peace treaty. He would not have been able to start the legend that the German army was never defeated but was stabbed in the back, just when it was snatching victory from the Allies, because the German people had been bamboozled by President Wilson.

## 3. *An Impromptu Revolution*

The weeks following the demand for an armistice were ghastly. The war was lost, yet fighting on a grand scale had to continue. The lines had to be held at any cost, otherwise final terms might be too crushing. The lives lost in those tense four weeks demonstrated the futile waste of war more clearly than anything else.

The guarded phraseology of President Wilson had made it evident that generous peace terms would not be offered to William II. In the eyes of the Allies the weak, vainglorious man —who had done a great deal of foolish talking in his life, but who had generally been fairly sensible when faced with facts— had become the incarnation of everything evil. He had to go if a reasonable peace was to be secured. His eldest son and heir was not acceptable to anybody; both his private life and his public utterances disqualified him for leadership. There would be a vacuum after William II's abdication, which might perhaps be filled by one of his grandsons. They were old enough to assume responsibilities and young enough not to be saddled with a past.

Germany was a monarchist country with strong democratic tendencies. The empire, it is true, included three republics, Hamburg, Bremen, and Lübeck, which had played a large part in national affairs. Their inhabitants had a thorough republican tradition, but they were small city states that had no desire to impose their mode of government on a larger population. In cities like Frankfort, and in some parts of southwestern Germany, a purely academic republican tradition, faint traces of the Revolution of '48, had lingered on. In Bavaria, Württemberg, Baden, and even Saxony the dynasties were popular; they were an integral part of national life. The King of Bavaria had been very popular before his accession. A vicious rumor accused him of exploiting the needs of the people for the benefit of his dairy farm; yet there were no republicans in Bavaria. The Socialist party's program postulated the formation of a socialist or communist republic—at some distant date.

A parliamentary government had been installed in Bavaria; it had inaugurated liberal reforms. The leaders of the Independent Socialist party, whom the military authorities had put

under arrest as defeatists or saboteurs, had been released. Among
them was Kurt Eisner, a brilliant North German journalist. At
one time he had been editor of the Socialist party paper, *Vor-
wärts,* but he had been removed on account of his radicalism.
He was a thorn in the flesh of the trade unions who formed the
bulk of the party. He was an excellent specimen of the tribe of
litterateurs who have played a large part in Continental revolutions and who came to the front in the United States in the days
of the New Deal. He had passed through the thorough theoretic
training that Marxists had to undergo in Germany and Austria
—in strong contrast to their Anglo-Saxon imitators. He could be
very trenchant, yet he was a warmhearted, kind, almost sentimental idealist. His blue eyes and his long fair beard would
have made it easy for him to deny his Jewish origin; professional
racialists are generally not very smart in locating individuals,
for the racial types with which they are familiar are cari-
catures. Eisner was a brilliant speaker and an equally good
writer, not a man of action. He possessed the almost feminine
curiosity of the minor intelligentsia who are not so much interested in finding solutions to problems as in making experiments. The true and dangerous revolutionaries are the dour
mature men who mean to overturn existing conditions in order to assert themselves, and who use theories and doctrines
because they have to justify their actions by a semblance of
inevitability and solidity. The minor intelligentsia are "victims
of books"; they want to experiment with theories other people
have evolved, partly to test their truth, and partly, too, because
of the stimulating nature of experimenting. They are the de-
tonators that make the bombs explode, the matches that light
the fuse. They are as a rule consumed in the process of destruction and buried beyond hope of resurrection under piles of
debris, the only monument to their activities.

In normal times the Munich workers were not amenable to
destructive agitation. The Socialist party controlled their votes;
but Munich Socialists were petty bourgeois rather than proletarians. The employees in Munich's few large industries did
not consider themselves a separate class. Millionaire and workingman could be met at the same table in one of the beer cellars.
Employers and employees climbed the mountains or even followed the chase as members of the same outfit. The Munich of

the artists, the writers, and the cabarets, which centered in Schwabing, was equally democratic; anybody who had anything to contribute to its cheerful activities, whether sincere or a mere fake, could enter its portals.

But the war had changed Munich's social atmosphere for the worse. The King had grieved that the old Bavarian provinces, the core of his country, had not shared in Germany's industrial prosperity. Old Bavaria had no coal and no iron and was not well situated for exports to foreign markets. During the war the King had induced the Krupp firm to start a branch in Munich. It imported industrial laborers from many parts of Germany. They were unlike Munich workers, who were rooted in the soil, had retained their contacts with the rural areas, and were not amenable to radical "proletarian" slogans. The newcomers did not get on well with the Munich populace; their presence had made rationing more severe and had increased housing difficulties; the strain of the war frayed all tempers.

Schwabing, too, had changed. The old innocent days had gone, when one could hurl foul insults at the key men of the empire. The luxury of blackening one's own leaders was no longer permissible, but one was allowed to go, and to go strongly, for Germany's enemies. In part, Schwabing had become aggressively nationalist; in part it had turned Communist. Karl Marx was a profound thinker, which did not mean much to Schwabingers; but in his more vituperative moments he had coined phrases that appealed to them. The Russian Revolution gave them a thrill; it was like a gorgeous film—its heroic atrocities made one's flesh creep, but one was none the worse for it. It glorified the class war against the bourgeois that Schwabing had loved to indulge in when it poked fun at the philistines. Now the proletarians who were going to eradicate them seemed brothers in spirit; the "dignity of the workingman" made a good literary topic, however little one cared for toil. Besides, by its very nature Schwabing hated militarism, which meant discipline. Bolshevist Russia stood for peace among the nations— she would bring about an end of the war, and with it an end of the fear which haunted many of the Schwabing devotees that the draft might finally catch them.

Eisner had met congenial spirits in Schwabing; he found willing audiences in the masses who were thoroughly disillusioned by the length of the war and who were looking forward to peace at any price. He got support from the farmers, too. They had lost their sons on the battlefields and their help by the draft; they were willing to stand this. Since time immemorial this always had been the peasant's fate. But it was quite another matter when they had to give up their cows or to deliver their crops at unremunerative prices, when their land was exhausted because they had no labor to till it nor fertilizers to manure it. They became restive.

Eisner did not build up an organization, he merely collected a handful of disgruntled men who had come to the conclusion that a revolutionary change might be attempted. He told the story of this feat in my presence at a dinner he gave to the late Mr. Ellis Loring Dresel, who visited Munich during the armistice as American commissioner of inquiry. He explained to the horrified diplomat the ease with which his small group of irresponsible men had managed a rising. "On Monday," he said, "we discussed it, and on Thursday we had done it."

On the preceding Wednesday (November 6) the minister of education sent for me. He asked me to put a damper on the revolutionary activities of Jaffé, who was going around the town with Eisner addressing mass meetings in the most bloodcurdling language. By this time Jaffé's vanity had got the better of him; he wanted to play a role. He was a weak man; I felt pretty sure I could silence him by reminding him of his earlier offer of propaganda for the army. I could not reach him on that day. A big meeting was billed for Thursday afternoon (November 7) on Munich's exhibition ground. He was going to address it. I was sure I could not stop him when he was charged with an undelivered speech; I might succeed next day, when he had got it out of his system. I spent Thursday afternoon in my house on the other side of the river polishing an article I had written for the *Berliner Tageblatt*. It had to leave by the night mail. My secretary was to post it on the train. She rang me up to tell me that she could not get through the seething crowd at the railway station. I asked her to desist; it was not important anyhow. I was not worried and went to bed. Next morning I started for my office. I usually walked across the bridge along Munich's new show street that skirted the park. The street was deserted. On the left bank of the river I ran into an acquaintance, a lead-

ing Munich realtor, who like many in his trade was a professional booster. He seemed to have shrunk. When I asked him,
"How are you today?" he looked at me reproachfully. "Don't
you know?" he said. "We have had a revolution—a Bolshevik
government is installed in Munich." I could not believe it. Had
I actually slept through a revolution? At my office I found a
proclamation of the new government telling everybody to keep
calm.

Eisner, Jaffé, and a few others had addressed a mass meeting
and excited it to fever pitch. The mob had marched through
the town, invaded the barracks, and invited the soldiers to frat-
ernize with them. At that time the Munich garrison consisted
of youngsters finishing their training. They were terrified of
being sent to the front. When they heard that the victorious
revolution would bring peace, they joyfully joined the rebels
or attempted to go home. Eisner and his friends marched to the
office of the leading Munich paper, occupied it in the name of
the revolution, and secured a printing press from which they
could issue decrees and proclamations. Nobody resisted.

The war department immediately gave up. In the early evening the minister of war took off his uniform, put on a civilian
suit, and disappeared. For two days the war department was in
the charge of a revolutionary sergeant who happened to be on
the spot. During this time it had no contact with outside garrisons. A group of airmen were stationed at Schleissheim, about an
hour from Munich. After they had failed repeatedly to get in
touch with the capital, they sent one of their men, Lieutenant
Königsberger, to Munich. He encountered none of his fellow
officers at the War Office; they left the building severely alone.
Being the highest-ranking officer in the place, Königsberger
immediately took over and performed the functions of minister
of war until he was relieved by a government appointee. He
had no difficulty with his subordinates. They all were revolutionaries and wore red brassards. But having been trained as
soldiers, they obeyed orders.

The King accepted his unexpected deposition as an act of
God. He never thought of defending his throne. He packed up
his family and a few belongings and drove to the country. One
of the oldest European dynasties, beloved by its people for

nearly a thousand years, had gone with the wind without a hand raised in its support.

The victors meanwhile suffered agonies of triumph. They had managed to make a revolution that had succeeded because nobody opposed them. Had the fire brigade been called out at the right moment and turned the hose on them, they would have been washed under. Fortunately for them, the adherents of the old regime were not willing to fight. Once it had gone, something had to replace it. Eisner had no following; he had only a few admirers; he had a public but no program. A revolution must be organized if it is to be more than a passing event. The only people who were in a position to do this after Eisner's improvisation had succeeded were the old-fashioned trade unionists, who distrusted him and whom he loathed. They probably could have crushed him. But one could not expect a Socialist party whose members had been considered enemies of the state until a very short time ago to shed their blood for the restoration of a dynasty whose head had run away. When kings no longer believe in kingship by divine right, their people cannot re-establish this doctrine. Thrones cannot be set up by Republicans when Royalists have let them fall down.

The Socialist party had the choice between joining the new government and keeping it steady or letting it go on its course of experimentalism. After long deliberations the Socialist majority party, led by Erhard Auer, joined the government, of which Jaffé had become minister of finance.

It was a great day for Schwabing. One of their own had made a revolution. A newspaper boy had ousted a king; the bohemians had beaten the army. From the drab cafés where Schwabing had been hibernating during the lean years of the war, its representatives rushed forward and hailed the new day. A mass meeting was called at the university, where one of them addressed the students, many of whom were on the losing side, and implored them to accept peacefully the new order of things. Nobody knew what it was. The Independent Socialists whom Eisner represented were not Communists. They did not believe in Soviet methods; in fact, they might best be described at that time as sentimental ·pacifists. They had no program and no power to enforce one, for, as events showed, their hold on the masses was very slight. The majority Socialists, on the other hand, had sufficient support to carry a government. They knew how to administer, but they did not know how to rule. The people outside the Socialist party whom Eisner could win over were political dilettantes like Jaffé; he had never taken much interest in public finance; he was now called upon to run the treasury of Bavaria, a state second in importance to Prussia, of which he was not a citizen, and of whose needs he was uninformed.

I was far more depressed in the early days of this glorious revolution than after the advent of the Nazis. My dark presentiments were later justified. Eisner's coup set the stage that Adolf Hitler was to dominate fifteen years later.

# XII. The Flowering of Schwabing (1918-1919)

## 1. *The German Revolution*

REVOLUTIONS ARE supposed to be catastrophic events like volcanic eruptions. An upheaval of popular discontent breaks through a thin crust of social conventions and covers with a sheet of molten lava the remains of an obsolete social system. The great French Revolution and the Russian Revolution may have been true to this type. The two German revolutions through which I lived were different.

The republican revolution, in which I was a detached onlooker, was a "cave-in," which but for the weakness of the defenders of the established order could easily have been prevented. The Nazi revolution, of which I was a victim, was a carefully staged *coup d'état,* a blend of skillful organization and irresponsible intrigue. Neither of them made one's heart beat faster; there was no spontaneous mass upsurge behind either. The first was more like a meeting of indignant bondholders who have to take over a bankrupt concern than a passionate attempt at creating a new social order. The emotional uplift of the Nazi revolution was felt only by those who expected jobs hitherto held by liberals, Communists, Jews, or Roman Catholics, and by a handful of leaders who wanted power.

The November revolution in Munich was particularly uninspiring, notwithstanding the rapid change of scenery it provided. Yet its influence was far-reaching. The revolutionary Munich government could hardly have survived without parallel movements in the rest of Germany. These had a far more violent character; the mutiny of the navy and the street fighting in Berlin were very much more serious events; yet somehow they were overshadowed by the Munich coup. The fact that the most conservative part of Germany, in which there had been

201

little social unrest, had successfully revolted, deposing one of the oldest dynasties, created a profound impression.

But for William II's quibbling hesitancy it might have been overcome. Had he abdicated in favor of his grandson, the foundations of a liberal parliamentary regime could have been consolidated. Viewed from a traditional Prussian point of view, the imperial crown was an appendix to the crown of Prussia; an acquired taste, so to speak, of the house of Hohenzollern: William's grandfather had almost been coerced by Bismarck into accepting it. But the kings of Prussia ruled by right divine. They had inherited their crown by the will of God; they had not received it from the hands of their fellow rulers at Versailles (1871). William II was willing to abdicate as emperor of Germany; he tried hard to retain the Prussian throne and engaged in endless equivocations over the telephone from army headquarters, where he had taken refuge. He made the proclamation of a republic inevitable.

Berlin radicals were getting ready for a soviet republic. In order to forestall them, Scheidemann, the leader of the majority Socialist party, announced William's abdication and—one might say, almost incidentally—the establishment of a democratic republic. Nobody had wanted it. Scheidemann was an impulsive orator. He has often been blamed for his over-rash, undisciplined action, probably unjustly, though it may have been unfortunate. His instinct served him rightly. The sands were running out. It was too late to prepare carefully the legal transition from an old to a new form of government. When reformers are wasting time in endless discussions, they are apt to be silenced by revolutionary action, which is always more or less disorderly.

The German revolution was probably less disorderly than any other has ever been. It was sporadic and patchy rather than vehement. The German people might have accepted it as definitive had it been violent. For violence is bound to establish accomplished facts, and to these the Germans have always bowed. As it was, they associated the revolution with disorder. (Such disorders as occurred were mainly due to soldiers' discontent.) They resented it partly because it was illegal and partly because it was not quite spic and span. The English, it has often been said, love equality in liberty; the French love liberty in equality.

The Germans have only one consuming political passion, an almost fanatical love of order. They would have been quite willing to accept a revolution dressed up in legal form; their love of legalism is far stronger than their love of justice. Undoubtedly the revolution was illegal; it was sometimes even lawless. It never became really popular.

The revolution had been almost bloodless; it looked very suspicious to the Allies. They were not going to be taken in by this latest piece of Hun camouflage. Allied liberals distrusted a republic that tried to be conservative; pinks, especially those who were not quite sure whether they themselves were liberals or Communists, disliked the majority Socialists, who were neither pacifist nor Bolshevist. They had not much use for a revolution that, measured by Russian standards, was of almost early Victorian decency. No revolution without barricades and street fighting, and lacking in those spectacular atrocities essential for making good films, could be genuine.

Some American newspapermen (Ben Hecht was among them) who had come to Munich during the critical phases of this unpleasant winter openly deplored the fairly quiet, orderly aspect of a city they had expected to see bathed in blood.

Conservatives, on the other hand, were frightened by socialism. They were unable to distinguish between the purely academic doctrines of German Marxists and the thoroughgoing practice of Russian Bolshevists. They too had little love for the republic.

Immediately after its inauguration the young republic had to pay the armistice check that the dying imperial government had written; the latter's defenders laid on the republic the blame for endorsing it. The imperial government, they argued, would never have signed on the dotted line. The military had played their hand very well. A civilian, Matthias Erzberger, had headed the German delegation and put his name to this fateful document. The nationalists, whose narrow fanaticism had been responsible for the completeness of the defeat, had him murdered a few years later.

The German provisional government was formed by the two Socialist parties. Three members of the majority Socialists and three Independents represented the revolutionary masses as people's commissars. They had to carry out the obligations of the armistice, especially rapid demobilization, and to lead the nation from provisional revolution to a permanent republic. In those days Bolshevist romanticism flourished. As the Bolsheviks in their revolution had established local councils (soviets) as emergency measures, so now German committees composed of class-conscious minorities were to run towns, counties, states, and the Reich. They were the great novel contribution to the science and practice of government; parliamentary institutions were called obsolete. These more or less self-appointed minorities were the agencies that should create a new social order. They sprang up everywhere as mushrooms after rain, consisting usually of war-weary soldiers, poor peasants, and proletarian workers. A hierarchy of councils, ranging from village councils to the workers' and soldiers' central council, shot up in no time. The six people's commissars were responsible to them.

The "soviets" might be described as inverted New England town meetings, in which only nontaxpayers were to have the vote. The novelty appealed greatly to the minor intelligentsia, hitherto engaged in purely literary pursuits, and was particularly attractive to youngsters or disgruntled soldiers. They formed themselves rapidly into committees and gave orders.

The council scheme did not appeal to German workingmen, for in their long struggle against privileged minority governments they had been permeated with democratic ideas. They had learned the technique and the responsibilities of self-government in their unions, in social security institutions, and in the municipalities. They paid lip service to the revolutionary doctrines contained in Marx's miscellaneous writings, but they had put their trust in his economic determinism. Socialism would come when the economic order was ripe for it. It was wrong to by-pass important stages of economic evolution as the Russians had done. Violence might bring about an appearance of success, but it could not last, being a violation of the Master's principles. This determinism, not to say fatalism, had suited the steadily growing German labor movement very well; it had reflected the German national temperament. Labor patiently waited for the day when the silent action of immanent economic forces would put the state within its grasp and meanwhile worked doggedly at the development of democratic institutions. They had meant to be in a position to seize power at the right moment, and disapproved of the councils' undemocratic methods. Socialism and democracy were not mutually exclusive in Germany as they had been in Russia in the early days of the Soviets, for the German workers were almost certain of winning a majority in a democratic election. But the party was split. The independent Socialists distrusted both the nationalism and the opportunism of the majority Socialists. They considered themselves the true Marxist orthodoxy; they abhorred violence at home and abroad—most of them were pacifists. But they were a minority, and for tactical reasons they inclined toward the left.

A small radical group, half Communist, half rabidly pacifist, tried hard to infuse revolutionary fervor into the masses. They attacked and beleaguered the provisional government that had dared to call for a constituent national assembly. The government had to defend itself against this onslaught. It had no force at its disposal. The gray host that had carried the war to all corners of the Continent had melted away; few survivors of the great ordeal were willing to remain with the colors; they wanted to go back to their families and resume their former civilian occupations.

But there were others—individuals and groups whom the long war had unfitted for a quiet life. They had faced death, danger, and destruction for years; they were no longer frightened by them. They needed them as stimulants, as a drug fiend needs drugs. They had been trained to give and to take orders, and they were accustomed to live at the government's expense. Peace to them was a calamity—a desert in which they were lost. When the provisional government in self-defense issued a call for a new army, they eagerly responded to it. They formed a pretorian guard, enlisted and commanded by former officers. Many of these officers naturally belonged to the old military nobility; they had no sympathy with a weak, spineless republic. They held Communists and Socialists responsible for the humiliating terms of the armistice and the burdens of the coming peace. But they knew how to meet steel with steel and to handle it much better than the Communist crowds whom Liebknecht's oratory had excited.

The soldiers foully murdered Liebknecht and Luxemburg. They could not be punished for this dastardly deed, for the government dared not court-martial those who had offered to defend it. The foolishness of the Communists had compelled it to call back the military groups whom the peace treaty meant to eliminate for good. It had called them back without having called them to account for their former political misdeeds.

## 2. Bavaria Leads

The revolution in Munich had been a bohemians' improvisation. It was not unlike a comic opera interspersed with pathetic interludes, and it ended in stark tragedy. Eisner had no support in the country. He had none of the essential qualities of a Bolshevik dictator. He knew how to make speeches and even how to charm people, but he had not the slightest idea of how to run a government. He distrusted his colleagues and his officials. His one chance to keep going was the support of the revolutionary Red guards that had been formed immediately after the collapse, and the disbanding of which his moderate colleagues demanded.

Eisner concentrated his efforts on foreign affairs. He had appointed Professor Friedrich Förster his minister to Switzerland. Förster was a man of high ideals, an advocate of the strict application of ethical principles to practical politics. His father, a famous astronomer, had been the leader of the ethical movement in Germany; the son had become a Roman Catholic but had retained the strident asceticism of prudish Puritanism and was completely unaffected by the mature sagacity of his new church. To Förster and Eisner peace was a purely moral problem. Imperial Germany had been wicked; she had committed the deadly sin of going to war. Her heir, the republic, could only hope for decent terms by acknowledging her guilt, by opening the archives to the world, laying bare the depravity of the old regime and showing the desire of its successors to atone. Germany could thus purify her soul and gain just and even generous terms from her victorious enemies. Förster and Eisner were applying to politics the methods of Billy Sunday and of the later Oxford Group. Some of President Wilson's slogans did make such self-accusation promising; it greatly appealed to neurotic temperaments to whom self-inflicted tortures are a source of joy, and who completely overlooked that Woodrow Wilson was not only a prophet but a very astute political leader.

The campaign of self-accusation had drawn support from the Bolsheviks. They had opened their archives and had advertised the wickedness of capitalist governments to all the world. They had done it because they wanted to compromise their enemies, not in order to cleanse their souls. The Germans went at it, as *flagellantes,* even though they hoped to reap profit from their confession.

A commission was appointed to publish the secret documents of the Berlin foreign office. Karl Kautsky, leader of the Independent Socialists, official exponent of orthodox Marxism, was entrusted with this task. The move had no effect on the peace treaty, but it did compel the Allied governments to follow suit and to provide the historians with much material to which they would have had no access for the next fifty years. It proved, incidentally, that most German diplomats had been fairly level-headed observers, that they had worked hard for maintaining peace, and that the truly sinister figures were the men around Tirpitz, who had made an understanding with Great Britain impossible.

I had always been a critic of the foreign policy of imperial Germany. I had over and over again protested against the statement that Great Britain went to war because she feared German commercial rivalry—she could have upset it far more cheaply by renouncing her free trade policy. I had warned against German naval plans that threatened British life lines. I had greatly disliked the dramatic stunts William II played in Morocco, but I never could convince myself that Russian expansionist intrigue or Italian land-grabbing was on a higher moral level. I did not believe in self-accusation as a means of improving foreign relations; it would merely furnish gratuitous pretexts for the Allies' demands and enable them to prove otherwise unfounded accusations with material provided by the defense. I did not like proceedings in which aggrieved parties, even assuming that their grievances were well founded, transformed themselves into a court of justice and gave a verdict in their own favor. My idea of justice was different; I said so in a little pamphlet written during the winter of 1918–19 called *Justice,* in which I foretold some of the results that materialized later on.

The revolution had no immediate effect on my academic activities: I carried on my work, which was becoming more complicated through the influx of ill-prepared demobilized soldiers. I was occasionally consulted by the new minister of finance, but the problems of Bavarian finance offered no scope for constructive ideas that I might have contributed. I distrusted Eisner's foreign policy. He dreamed of making Bavaria the leader of a purified Germany, and of getting special terms from the Allies for Bavaria which would enable him to carry a campaign of moral disinfection to the rest of the country.

Late in November I received a telegram from Count Bernstorff, who was organizing the German peace delegation at the Berlin foreign office. "Would you be willing to go to Copenhagen?" Nothing more. The telephone service was insecure—cutting and tapping communications is the stand-by technique of all revolutions. I decided to go to Berlin and replied in this sense. Knowing that the revolutionary censor was sure to hold up my answer, I rang up a former pupil who had become one of the private secretaries of the Prime Minister and asked him to have it sent without much delay. He promised to do his best. A few hours later I was called to the telephone. "Prime Minister Eisner speaking," a voice said; "can you come and see me at three o'clock in the afternoon?"

Janitors and messengers at the revolutionized Foreign Office had remained at their posts; they looked a little timeworn and unhappy in this new, unceremonious world. I was ushered immediately into the Prime Minister's presence. After some cordialities—he said he knew all about me, which was probably true—he asked me point-blank, "Why do you want to go to Berlin?" Evidently he had had time to read my telegram.

"I cannot make head or tail of it," I answered. "I want to find out about it."

"You are quite right," he replied and began to talk to me about the difficulties he was encountering. As I left, he asked me to give his greetings to Haase and Kautsky—both leaders of the Independents.

"Certainly. But of course you realize I do not belong to your party."

"Tell them about conditions here. And there is another matter. I appointed some time ago a new Bavarian minister in Berlin, a colleague of yours, Dr. Muckle. We have lost track of
him. He does not report to us. I wonder whether you can find
him for us."

I duly entrained for Berlin. Winter was coming on, and carriages were not heated. My first-class compartment was overcrowded; its windowpanes were broken; one could get nothing
to eat; instead of nine hours the journey took twelve. Finally,
late in the evening, I reached Berlin.

Next morning I walked across the square to the Bavarian
legation hoping to find the lost minister. I was greeted by some
acquaintances from Munich, diplomats from prerevolutionary
days who continued to serve the new administration. They were
delighted to get news from Munich. Both the Munich and the
Berlin governments distrusted each other; they lived like cats
and dogs, if not as open enemies. I asked after the new chief;
he was in his study, they informed me, drinking herb tea, genuine tea having becoming very scarce. I was received immediately. Dr. Muckle had been a junior lecturer at the University
of Heidelberg; he had written one or two suggestive sociological books. He had not, as far as I knew, taken much interest
in politics before the revolution; he had been infected by its
emotional germs and had associated himself with the Independent Socialists. I informed him of the complaints of his
chief about his not reporting. "What for? What should I report?" he said indignantly. "At nine o'clock I talk to Haase,
who gives me a bit of information; at ten o'clock I see Ebert
who tells me the contrary; at eleven o'clock I meet Liebknecht,
whose story differs from them both. If I did send a report, I
should have to contradict myself all the time. Is it not much
better to say nothing? It saves trouble and it prevents misunderstanding." This wisdom, worthy of a Talleyrand, duly impressed me and I departed. Anyhow, I had located him.

I saw Count Bernstorff who explained to me that the job in
Copenhagen was "a listening post." We both agreed that I was
not the man for it. Then, after having called on Haase, I went
to the Foreign Office in search of Kautsky. He had become
undersecretary of state for foreign affairs and was located in
offices formerly occupied by the commercial section. The mes-

sengers recognized me, eyed me quizzically, and told me I could walk in. I did so and met a comfortable-looking middle-aged lady, Frau Kautsky, who was waiting for her husband. She had brought him his lunch, a couple of sandwiches; food in Berlin was very scarce. After a short time the Undersecretary turned up in person. He might have been the original St. Peter as portrayed by a primitive German master—a benign-looking, oldish man with a grayish-white beard and dark, protruding, somewhat astonished eyes. I gave him Eisner's greetings and we discussed the world situation. He knew all about me; he had copied entire passages from my books on Ireland and the United States into his own works, whenever they could be used in support of Marx's doctrines. For this man was the apostolic repository of the Marxist faith. He had dedicated his life to the explanation of the Master's abstruse, sometimes contradictory, statements and to the interpolation of sometimes stubborn facts into his system. He had enunciated the principles that justified the action, or rather, the inaction of his party. He was a kind of party pope whose decrees had to be accepted, even though they were not backed by force. He could never have wielded it. He was a professor in the true sense of the word, one who professed truths discovered by somebody else. He grieved at errors and aberrations. He praised and damned ex cathedra, but he certainly did not care for action. He was a very lovable man but a somewhat dull doctrinaire. Having found a rigid standard for gauging truth and untruth he applied it with an almost childlike faith to the measurement of conditions and forces that by their inherent fluidity defy all scientific tests. The Bolsheviks were to him infidels who had defiled the true faith; and he was right. For they had proven the hollowness of the Marxist assumption that the economic setup determines events. The Bolsheviks' state had been made by guns; it had transformed economic conditions by physical force. Kautsky disliked their violence perhaps even more than their attack on determinism, for he was truly a man of peace. He was gentle, a little boring, and certainly by temperament not a revolutionary. Fortunately, he took to me. Whenever I was in Vienna in later days, I went to his house in the suburbs to take coffee with him and have a good chat.

Having fulfilled my mission, I returned to Munich and reported to Eisner. Not very much later the minister of finance called me to the telephone. An unofficial American commission of nine to twelve members was to arrive in Munich that evening. How should we receive them? I suggested very modest formalities; we were not yet at peace and the commission had no official diplomatic standing. I promised to be at the station and to take them in hand.

I reached the cold, damp station wearing a business suit; I found the ministers of finance and of transportation in attendance, both in frock coats and top hats. The Lord Mayor of Munich, who specialized in receiving visitors to his beloved city, had turned up, too, in similar attire. I told them to go home, but they insisted on waiting. After a long time the train crept into the station. The lights were turned on; from the one and only first-class carriage three men emerged—Mr. Ellis Loring Dresel, Mr. John Franklin Day, and a typist. Great consternation. Where were the rest? The Bavarian minister in Berne had telegraphed full Christian names, and the Munich people had calmly assumed that each represented a member of the commission. My ministers seemed disappointed.

After the necessary introductions, I took over and drove our guests to the Hotel Regina. The government representatives had pressed into my hand a long list of persons and objects the commission should see. This I carefully kept to myself, realizing that Mr. Dresel was feeling somewhat puzzled by the reception prepared for him. I merely asked him to let me know what he wanted to see and whom he wanted to meet; we would make the arrangements.

Next morning the treasury rang me up, suggesting a dinner to be given by the Prime Minister; I was to arrange everything. Our invitation was, of course, accepted. The hotel manager was delighted. He wanted to unpack some of his hoarded treasures for the occasion. I insisted on having the same dinner that was provided for regular hotel guests: he must stick to rations, as the commission wanted to see how things were. He might produce his best wine, of which there was plenty, and we compromised on having a cup of coffee.

At this dinner the Prime Minister, arriving late from a trip to Stuttgart owing to a car breakdown, but in high spirits, told Mr. Dresel the inner story of the revolution.

With impish joy he explained the ease with which he had kicked over the Bavarian dynasty. I saw a look of horror in the eyes of our American guests. They were trained in Washingtonian traditions—they could understand Lafayette and even make allowances for Robespierre, but they had not thought it possible that revolutions engineered by a handful of stray sojourners in a Continental Greenwich Village could actually succeed. Eisner made a bad impression; the dinner was not a great success. Next day the damage was partly repaired. The guests met a number of serious-minded people, among them the Prussian minister Count Zech, son-in-law of the former chancellor Bethmann-Hollweg, and the papal nuncio, Monsignor Pacelli, now Pius XII. They continued their journey to Berlin and its much graver atmosphere.

Eisner's campaign of self-incrimination was producing no tangible results; his dream that the Allies might recognize Bavarian moral leadership in Germany was not materializing. His incapacity as an administrator was becoming very plain. He had to agree to elections for a constituent Bavarian parliament; he gained only 3 seats out of 180. The revolutionary guard was to be disbanded. The majority Socialists were gaining control. Eisner's short-lived power was waning, when a member of the Bavarian aristocracy, Count Arco, shot him down outside the Foreign Office. It was a foul murder; yet its perpetrator became a national hero to the adherents of the old order of things; his personal courage seemed to atone for the cowardice they had shown when the monarchy had collapsed. He was never called to strict account, though found guilty and imprisoned for a short time. A wave of radicalism once more swept over the country; it finally led Munich into the tragicomic soviet experiment of April 1919.


## 3. Soviet Munich

In March 1919 I had accompanied a British commission of inquiry to Berlin. Rumors of an impending revolution in Munich reached me there. I returned in time to be an eyewitness of the birth, life, and death of the Munich Soviet Republic. It lasted not quite a month.

The murder of Eisner had weakened the position of moderate Socialists. Once or twice the new Socialist government had prevented an armed outbreak, but every new shift was moving toward the left. The Bavarian elections had unveiled the weakness of the revolution and the strength of the "reactionary" forces; the Socialists held only 62 seats out of 180 and the Communists none. If the "radicals" meant to retain power, they had to adopt Bolshevik methods and establish, under the guise of the council system, the dictatorship of a very small minority. Lenin had succeeded in doing it. The Munich revolutionaries attempted a Leninist revolution without a Lenin. They represented, with very few exceptions, the type of revolutionary Lenin despised—the talkers, not the workers. Nearly all of them bore the hallmark of Schwabing and what it stood for. They were sentimental pacifists filled with humanitarian exaltation; slaves as well as masters of the word. The Red guard, which had avoided the disbanding that the moderates had tried to impose upon Eisner, were ready to follow the new, more radical leaders. They patrolled the town with red brassards on their arms, each shouldering a gun turned upside down. It seems good form for a revolutionary army to mark its uncompromising opposition to bourgeois ways by pointing the muzzles of its rifles to the ground. They were led by a few noncommissioned officers of the army and the navy. The mass of the workers remained passive. The government, presided over by Hoffman, an uninspiring majority Socialist with some leftist tendencies, immediately gave way; it left Munich and transferred its seat to Bamberg in Franconia, followed by the members of the Bavarian diet. The highly industrialized districts of Nuremberg refused to co-operate with Munich.

Munich and the few surrounding villages were left to their own devices. Toller, Gustav Landauer, Niekish, and others who had come to the top were poets, semi-poets, mezzo-philosophers, and schoolteachers. They tried to bring about a violent revolution by gentle means. They were horrified and fascinated by the ruthless brutality of the Bolsheviks, and quite incapable of imitating them. They knew neither the world they were going to reform nor the people who were going to do it. They could translate reality into stage tragedies; to turn their hazy dreams of the brotherhood of man into stern reality was beyond them.

The strength of the Russian Revolution had been the corps of professional revolutionaries whom Lenin had trained and whom he had filled with a spirit of ruthless amorality; their Munich imitators were dilettantes by profession, to whom revolution was a new literary topic. It naturally attracted the young and the immature.

Youth movements have played an important part in every politically backward country. They thrive on revolution. Their members know that something is wrong; they don't quite know what. They have not yet gone through their elders' disappointments and disillusions; they are not yet resigned and have not yet renounced. They have not yet learned to measure the distance between desire and accomplishment, between conception and execution; they have never had to carry out anything of real importance; they ignore obstacles. They naturally find their parents out of date, even if they love them. They distrust the ideals of an older generation, not because they have found them false, but because they want to live in a world of their own making. When their elders have been wise and have created a world offering safe careers to them, the young are bored by security; boredom has probably been a far more mighty revolutionary solvent than misery. Whenever the carefully laid plans of an older generation have miscarried, when uncertainty rather than security seems youth's destiny, fear takes the place of boredom.

There rarely ever was a rising that youth enjoyed as greatly as the Red April dream of Munich. The people's commissars who ruled the state knew neither what to do nor how to do it. They had seized power in a fit of exaltation; its possession oppressed them with the awful weight of responsibility. But the youngsters did not care. Overnight they were somebodies. They addressed meetings, invaded government offices, gave orders and enjoyed themselves as never before. We had let a room in our house to a charming co-ed, the daughter of a well-to-do Berlin engineer. She was an attractive girl, intelligent but abysmally ignorant. She went from meeting to meeting and talked, advised, and got excited. As the world was approaching the heaven of the proletarian age, the more gentle conventions

of life were branded as bourgeois prejudices. The house re-
sounded with the noise of her hobnailed boots when she tramped
upstairs, long after midnight, having attended some revolutionary conventicles. Her presence seemed to spread a kind of halo
over it, which she shrewdly tried to exploit in her dealings
with us.

The earlier revolutionaries had treated me with a good deal
of respect. My knowledge of foreign affairs had impressed them.
Long before they had come to power, I had done my part and
had prepared the people for the inevitable catastrophe. During
one of the many political crises, the representative of the leading Berlin paper in Munich called me to the phone and asked
in a stentorian voice:

"Are you going to accept?"

"Accept what?" I replied.

"Don't you know?" he bellowed. "In a short time you will
be asked to take over the Bavarian Ministry of Foreign Affairs.
What are you going to do?"

"I shall think it over when the offer has been made to me," I
replied. Whereupon he furiously banged down the receiver.

The invitation never reached me: I suppose my disrespectful
attitude on the phone may have been responsible. In some ways
I regretted it. I suppose I have made a fairly good university
professor; I know that trade in and out. But I learned from
long experience in at least three countries that a good professor
usually makes a bad political executive. Giving advice and carrying it out are two very different propositions. There are, of
course, many exceptions; and the rule must not be inverted. A
bad professor makes even a worse executive, of which there are
many examples. Yet it would have been very flattering to receive
that invitation, solemnly to thank those who made it, declare one's willingness to ponder over it for twenty-four hours,
and then modestly decline. I was not smart enough to secure
this triumph to my vanity. I may have been very fortunate. I
suppose my wife would have prevented me from accepting the
offer and from making a fool of myself. But one is never quite
sure of one's own limitations if one's vanity is sufficiently tickled.
The matter did leak out, however, and I felt greatly flattered
when Theodor Wolff, chief editor of the *Berliner Tageblatt*,

8

mentioned the rumor, adding that in his opinion I was too intelligent a person to accept such a position at such a time.

Those halcyon days had passed. The revolutionaries no longer believed in Wilson; their God was Lenin. I was a Westerner and no good to those who worshiped Eastern saints. In November 1918, I was looked upon as a peacemaker; in April 1919, I had become an antediluvian fossil. Yet I adjusted myself rapidly to actual conditions. As soon as the Munich Soviet government was established, I assembled my colleagues, my students (there were few of them because it was vacation time), and my employees, and asked them to elect a soviet for the administration of the College of Commerce. I was unanimously elected president. I declined the honor, explaining that the job of the council would be to control rather than to support me, whereupon my chief accountant, my janitor, who was an old noncommissioned officer in the Bavarian Horse Guards, and a shell-shocked Communist student were elected. The student did the speechmaking, the others did the work. We carried on the administration as we had done before, my loyal assistants transmitting to me the orders we had agreed upon. This gave me complete liberty of action for other purposes. My council gave me a passport and an identification card, which were respected by the Red guards and enabled me to go unmolested wherever I liked.

Having secured my college from the risk of undue interference, I had to tackle a much more difficult job. The new government planned a complete reform of the university system. They appointed a commission of six students to work out adequate plans. The university asked me and two colleagues, whose progressive views were known, to represent them before the commission. For almost a month we met daily. The reformers, if revolutionaries may be called reformers, had no plan. The membership of their commission changed continually. The first group had been fairly moderate and had had some knowledge of academic problems. By and by they either resigned or were ousted and replaced by more radical colleagues. Finally we were confronted with an almost Communist group, the most bloodthirsty member of which was an extremely unattractive girl from Saxony. She made the wildest speeches of the lot.

I soon found out that speechmaking and debate usually satisfied our opponents' energies; they meant to dismiss the entire teaching body and to reappoint only those who were fellow travelers if not comrades. Fortunately, they shared the most conspicuous quality of German radical youth, fear of responsibility. They were quite willing to decapitate any professor, however eminent, provided my colleagues and myself proposed his dismissal or at least agreed to it. They tried very hard to make us do it by dangling before our eyes the eminent positions to which we would be called if we lent our hands to this great work of reform.

One day the Saxon girl made a passionate appeal to us in the name of the proletarian classes. I replied that they ought to be intelligent enough to recognize, if not to respect, our own class-consciousness, which made it impossible for us to sacrifice our own academic comrades. "Don't be cowards," I shouted at them. "Have the courage of your convictions, act and dismiss us, but don't expect us to take the responsibility for your actions." They rather liked this speech; it appealed to their dramatic instinct. Nothing happened but a comic intermezzo.

A professor in the veterinary department had a grievance; he had not been promoted, he thought, according to his merits. He went to the revolutionary commissioner of education and demanded an inquiry. The student commission, acting on this suggestion, asked for the files. They were informed that they were in the custody of the rector, and being of a confidential nature, could not be shown to outsiders. The commission insisted on interviewing him. The regular rector, a weak-kneed professor of philosophy, the official exponent of Roman Catholic metaphysics, unable to face a revolutionary storm, had resigned; Friedrich Müller, a physician of international reputation, had accepted the thankless task of steering the university through the straits. The commission and my colleagues went to see him. The commission demanded the key to the file cabinets. The rector refused, whereupon they threatened violence. "In that case," Müller replied with studied dignity, "I shall give in under protest."

"Hand over the key," said the commissioners.

"Wait a moment," said my colleague Rothenbücher, one of the best representatives of German political science. "This is an important affair that has to be done in proper form. We have to make a protocol."

He dictated a most solemn declaration, stating that Friedrich Müller, Rector Magnificus of the University of Munich, was handing over the keys to the files of the Department of Veterinary Science to the revolutionary commission under protest, acceding to the threat of bodily violence. We signed this important document and the revolutionaries added their names; the key was handed over to them. They were rather disappointed; the files contained nothing out of which they could make political capital.

A few months later, when the Red ghost had long since been laid, a young woman came to Rothenbücher's study. She was very excited and burst into tears. He calmed her and elicited the following facts. Her sister had been the wildest member of the Communist student commission. When the White army approached Munich, she had been entrusted with the guardianship of the key and had been wise enough to decamp, charging her sister with the mission of handing it over to the authorities. The sister, being innocent of political activities and ambitions, had been overawed by the burden of her responsibilities. On a dark night she had gone to Munich's public park and had thrown the key into a little brook. Her conscience smote her and she had come to confess her evil deed to Rothenbücher. He consoled the young woman and got in touch with the authorities. They lived up to the reputation for which the German bureaucracy has been rightly famous. They dredged the brook and found the key.

## 4. *The End of the Red Republic*

The Red republic was not always funny. The majority of the Munich people quietly went about their day's business, rather glum, but docile as they had always been. Yet there was a genuinely revolutionary underground swell, which became more and more threatening.

In the beginning nobody had believed in the duration of the experiment. One could not establish a soviet regime in an isolated city that had to get its food, its coal, and everything it needed from outside. The radius of soviet rule was only a few miles wide; it comprised no important agricultural areas. A few miles behind my home was a little village called Riem. It was in possession of the White enemy. White advance guards held it strongly, yet connections were not completely broken off, for it was the site of the Munich race course. Easter Sunday has always been a great racing day for the Munich people. They are a very conservative lot; they do not mind political revolutions as long as they do not interfere with their daily lives and their holiday amusements. Both sides seemed to understand this. On a bleak Easter Sunday—spring came late that year—I could see from my study window an endless stream of cars and hikers making for Riem, eager not to miss the races. In the late afternoon the same procession returned in the opposite direction.

Yet isolation was growing more stringent; coal and provisions merely trickled in; an army was approaching from the north, and Munich was slowly being surrounded. One could no longer communicate with the rest of Germany, although the line to Vienna, considered a Red city, was open. I managed to write an article from the beleaguered city for the Vienna *Freie Presse* that reached its editors without difficulty and was duly printed.

On a Sunday morning about a fortnight after the establishment of the Soviet Republic, we heard heavy guns from the other side of the river. A group of young lawyers, mostly moderate Socialists, who had been in the army, had taken off by train from Nuremberg, reached Munich station safely, and set out to capture the city. They occupied the square in front of the station and might have succeeded had the Reds not possessed a flame thrower. The invaders had not expected this sort of defense and quickly withdrew. Having been wise enough to keep up steam, they managed to start their train just as the Reds rushed on the platform, and got away safely on their inglorious return journey, followed by a few futile shots. They had suffered no losses, but victory had gone to the Reds, who naturally were much elated. At the same time they were getting frightened.

A few revolutionaries of the genuine Bolshevik type had come to the top in Munich, among them a man called Levine, a somber, rather sinister person who did not suffer from the sickly sentimentality of Toller and company. These genuine revolutionaries were now getting ready for a last stand. They were taking hostages to safeguard themselves if worst came to worst. Tension was increasing from day to day; at any moment the comic opera might be turned into a tragedy. The ground on which one stood was no longer firm.

In the early days of the revolution my secretary at the college, who had been with me for nearly ten years, had left me. I found it hard to replace her. First came a girl student with rather advanced ideas who immediately plunged into the political fray. She called herself a moderate Socialist, but her sympathies belonged to Bolshevism. She rapidly picked up the double-barreled loyalty of the Communists, which the Nazis later on developed so successfully, and in a conflict, loyalty to what she considered her principles got the better of her loyalty to her employers. I shifted her to the research department where she did useful work but compromised the institution by underground activities of which I only heard later on. Her successor was a good-natured mediocrity married to a semi-intellectual. They naturally called themselves Communists. I did not mind their brand of communism. They were so naïve and outspoken, so proud of parading their convictions, that one could hardly consider them dangerous. One had to recognize that one could no longer trust those to whom one had to extend one's confidence. But for the support of my young friend Dr. Carl Landauer, whose steadfastness, common sense, and integrity of character I learned to appreciate, I would have been very isolated. He kept me in touch with the majority Socialists in Bamberg who were the legal government of Bavaria. We had, moreover, some good friends among the plain people. My wife received warnings from several reliable sources that I was on the list of prospective hostages.

It would have been easy for me to leave Munich; my pass from my "soviet" would have seen me through the Red guards. I had a decent pretext for absenting myself; I had received a call to join the German peace delegation at Versailles. But I did not want to leave Munich. I am no hero; whenever I have been in a tight place I have been thoroughly frightened, yet somehow I have always managed to stick it out.

I had to take some precautions. The Reds' technique was copied from Russia. They arrested "suspects" in the middle of the night. The best way to avoid these unpleasant proceedings was to decamp—"address unknown." If my own house was unsafe, few others would be much safer. None of my German friends could offer me an asylum. So I decided to spend my nights with our friend James Loeb. He was known to be a millionaire, and as such, one would have thought, an object of Bolshevik expropriation. But he was an American citizen. No German Bolshevik, I was convinced, would dare to molest anybody who could wave the Stars and Stripes in his face. Jimmie Loeb shared this view and offered me his hospitality. I spent my mornings bickering with the commission at the university; in the afternoon I went to my house, and just before sunset I went back to the city to my hiding place at Loeb's. It was a hard life, as public transportation had almost broken down. To use a taxi when regaining my asylum would have been foolish. So I had to foot it. Sometimes I stopped on my way to have a chat with our friend Princess Oettingen, a daughter of the famous Pauline Metternich, the wife of the Austrian ambassador in Paris in the days of the Third Napoleon. Princess Oettingen had been wise enough to offer her house to the Red Cross; she was fairly safe in the two rooms reserved for her own use. Here I met occasionally the papal nuncio, Monsignor Pacelli, and his secretary, Monsignor Scioppa. Pacelli looked like a prince of the Renaissance stepping out of one of Titian's great canvases. Monsignor Scioppa had had some rather unpleasant personal experiences in those Red days; the recollection of them may have made a lasting impression on his chief, who later became nuncio in Berlin, Cardinal Secretary in Rome, and is now Pius XII.

Among the functions I had to take over in those hectic days was the chairmanship of the Council of Brainworkers. My teacher Professor Brentano, who had been its first president, had resigned and wanted me to take his place. I disliked the job from the beginning and I handled it very badly; I am not cut out for the part of lobbyist, whatever the lobby may be. Some of our meetings took place in the Royal Residence, where many central government agencies had been housed. The day before the downfall of the Red republic, as I was leaving the building, a friend saw me and said, "You are a lucky man to have escaped

from this place; they might easily have kept you as a hostage."
I had never given that unpleasant eventuality a thought.

A little later another friend rang up the college and implored me to get the release of her son who had been taken as
a hostage to one of the improvised barracks. It was late afternoon, everybody had gone home except my Communist secretary, nobody could be reached by telephone. A deep moral
depression had settled on the city. I could not go in person—
I probably would have been asked to keep him company. My
secretary volunteered. She was a member of the Communist
party, and she had a bicycle; she was sure she could get him off.
A little later she telephoned triumphantly that he had been
released. It was in the nick of time; shortly afterward the other
inmates were shot by panic-stricken Red leaders who realized
that the game was up. They were dilettantes to the bitter end—
they did not understand that dead hostages serve no purpose,
except revenge.

The "White Army" sent from the north was surrounding
Munich on all sides. Some of the Reds fought very courageously.
The issue was never in doubt; the final assault was retarded
by the natural desire of the encircling forces not to destroy
Munich. Thus some of the leaders had ample time to save.
themselves. Actual fighting was not very severe, yet it is not
pleasant to hear heavy guns barking a few hundred feet away
from one's house, sending their missiles into a city where one
has spent half of one's life. We were very fortunate; only one
bullet went through one of our windowpanes. My wife, con-
ducting a lame friend of ours, was in the street when a volley
crossed her path; she was not hurt, nor was the dog she was carrying under her cloak; none of our friends was.

The Red dream was over; the Soviet Republic in Munich had
collapsed. The aftermath was awful. The futile murder of the
hostages had turned an infantile enterprise into a stark tragedy.
The northern regiments—the hated Prussians—behaved fairly
well; they had recovered a proper military bearing. The Bavarians under Colonel Epp acted very differently. A mingled feeling of shame and hatred made them see red. The revolution had
been an outrage perpetrated on Bavaria by foreigners; there
was some truth in it. They could not get hold of all the foreigners—some had managed to escape. So they shot down in-

discriminately many a harmless, well-meaning Bavarian—
especially among the trade unionists—whom somebody had
denounced as Communist. Some aristocratic refugees who had
left the city when the Reds got control returned with Epp and
played the part of revengeful heroes as spectacularly as they
could to make their neighbors forget their cowardly flight. Decent people were shocked. Frifri von Geyr, née Bonaparte, related to two of Europe's former ruling dynasties, who lived in a
distant Munich suburb, rang me up in despair and implored me
to do something to stop the White terror that raged around her.
She had no sympathy with the Reds, but she did not want to see
her neighbors murdered. I could do little but get her in contact
with the representatives of the government, who had few means
of controlling the fury of Epp's free corps. The Bavarians are
an easygoing, good-natured people, but when they get mad they
are far more brutal than the Prussians, because they have much
less self-control and discipline.

A few days later all was over; I departed for Versailles. By
the time I returned, not quite two months later, the atmosphere
had changed completely.

The Socialist period in Bavarian history was as good as over;
a revengeful, reactionary Roman Catholic party was ready to take
control.* They planned to make Bavaria the orderly center of
Germany whence the forces of restoration were to radiate over
the Red north. The shame of having submitted to a Socialist
rule that had no real strength behind it had burned deep into
their hearts. They were going to avenge that humiliation. They
had always been "Bavarian" not "German" patriots; many of
them would cheerfully have accepted a separate peace could
Bavaria have had one. They were now grooming themselves for
the role of German superpatriots. They had been antimilita-
rists. They now offered a refuge to Ludendorff and looked upon
him as their great inspiration. Being Roman Catholic, they had
always believed in internationalism, at least in the spiritual
field. They now became the most narrow-minded nationalists.
They had been far more democratic than the north; they now
vetoed democracy. They planned to re-establish the monarchy,
to restore the Wittelsbachs and perhaps make them emperors

* It did so in March 1920, at the time of the Kapp Putsch.

of Germany. The Munich Soviet Republic made possible the return of Ludendorff to a role of political importance. It had created the atmosphere in which Adolf Hitler could sprout from a paid army spy to a spellbinder of national importance and dimensions.

As for my own work, I had to realize that my days in Bavaria were numbered. The Red carnival had not destroyed my reputation, but it had weakened my position. No outsider who holds a good job has ever been popular in Bavaria. I was not a Bavarian. I had been fighting battles for Bavaria and I had done my best for her, especially for the university; I did not expect much gratitude from it, for I had learned very early that gratitude is the expectation of favors to come. But while there was no room for me any longer on the local stage, my position in the German theater had greatly improved.

# XIII. Versailles

## 1. *The Atmosphere*

A FEW days after the liberation of Munich, I left for Versailles; the German delegation had already preceded me. I traveled through Berlin to resume contacts, having been out of touch with affairs for over a month.

Count Bernstorff was at the head of the Preparatory Peace Commission in Berlin—I probably owed my appointment to him. He took me to a meeting of the cabinet, where I was presented to President Ebert, to Philip Scheidemann, the chancellor, and the other leading members of the government. The Foreign Secretary had already gone to Versailles. Hugo Preuss, friend and colleague of mine, was secretary of the interior; he was drafting the Weimar Constitution. The cabinet meeting was very informal. I took quite a lively part in it; I now remember it with horror.

I have a faint recollection of having flatly contradicted Matthias Erzberger (who had signed the armistice), probably the most energetic minister serving the Weimar Republic. He had come from a small village in the Swabian Alps, inhabited by a score or so of small Catholic farmers and a few equally poor Jewish cattle dealers. He had been a schoolteacher and had joined the Catholic party. His restless energy and unlimited capacity for work had made him an influential member of the old German Reichstag, where he was feared rather than respected. Quick in the uptake, somewhat inclined to intrigue, loquacious, indiscreet and tactless, he had one gift rare among German politicians: he could make up his mind and come to a clear, rapid decision. A deeply religious man, completely at peace with God, he lightheartedly shouldered responsibilities that others shied at, and took rash steps that he had not the slightest qualms in retracing when he recognized his mistake.

He was an unattractive speaker; his pathetic phrases ill fitted the common sense that oozed from all his pores. This stoutish, rather flabby-looking man with small cunning eyes did not impress me very favorably. I am quite sure this antipathy was mutual. I have been on friendly, not to say intimate, terms with many of the leading members of his party; yet I never established personal contact with him, though we worked in the same field. I did, however, recognize his great ability. I wrote his biography for the *Encyclopaedia Britannica*.

Ebert, Noske, and Erzberger were three republican leaders who were not afraid of their own courage. Noske had suppressed the Communist revolt. His intellectual gifts were limited, but in his early days he showed the supreme quality of leadership, the will and the ability to strike. Both Ebert and Erzberger possessed it; both grew in stature during their relatively short political lives. Erzberger was assassinated because he had signed the armistice—he was the first middle-class victim of the counterrevolution. Had he lived, he might have ripened into a truly great statesman, once he had got rid of his soapbox mannerisms and learned the importance of discretion.

Immediately after the cabinet meeting I left for Versailles with messages for the members of the German delegation. Once again I reclined in a plush-covered carriage of the international sleeping-car company. I traveled under French auspices across northern France. I did not see much of the battlefields on this slow journey; I passed those regions in the night. At the Gare du Nord an official car with a little yellow pennant met me. The French had very tactfully chosen yellow for the German delegation; it denotes pestilence on board. I was whirled through Paris and taken to Versailles.

The German delegation was housed in two hotels, the Hôtel des Reservoirs, and the overflow in the Hôtel Vattel, where a room was reserved for me. The two were separated by a short stretch of the main road. We had to walk in the road when going from one to the other, for the sidewalk on both sides was boarded up with huge planks and reserved for the native population. The purpose of this segregation was obviously to avoid friction; passions were supposed to be running very high, and the German delegation was to be protected from the populace. But this boarding up had a curious, probably unintended, psychological effect. The people on the sidewalks could look down on the Germans walking in the middle of the road; they may have felt some moral elevation in doing this. In any case, the Germans thought so and were greatly humiliated. The anguish of defeat and the sense of guilt with which some propagandists had tried to impress them had created a kind of inferiority complex from which most members of the delegation suffered.

They were a motley crowd. Once the treaty had been analyzed paragraph by paragraph, many of them had little to do but be in attendance. From time to time an answer to an Allied inquiry had to be made; there was feverish activity and they were busy night and day. When the spurt was over, they could relax. There were few opportunities for healthy recreation. Part of the park of Versailles was fenced in and reserved for the delegation; within its limit they could move freely. The space was sometimes expanded and sometimes contracted. It was big enough for exercise in normal circumstances. In the early spring the park was very lovely; but after the first favorable impressions had worn off, it became a kind of prison yard to most members of the delegation. They had fervently accepted the new democratic faith, some because they had felt attracted by it, others because they expected it to pay. Many had hoped that the foundation of the republic would quash the indictment against imperial Germany, and had fancied they might be greeted by the Allies as long-lost brother democrats. They were horrified at the isolation imposed upon them. They could not quite understand why they should be ostracized after having gotten rid of all imperialist wickedness. Few were aware of the hatred that the military occupation of an enemy country is bound to arouse, even when carried out in a humane way. The German army had been harsh; a number of pretty bad abuses had occurred. The people at home had not heard much about them. Their representatives at Versailles did not understand the practical reasons for this segregation, which turned out to be superfluous. For the Versailles people behaved very well until the departure of the delegation was announced, when they feared that it would not sign the treaty. The members of the delegation, accompanied by French guides, were allowed to go shopping; without exception shopkeepers were polite, though German buyers who were starved for goods must have been rather a trial to them.

The situation did not worry me very much. The thought that we were treated like wild animals in a zoological garden, visited by crowds gaping through the grills, who were warned not to irritate the dangerous animals, appealed to my sense of humor. I enjoyed myself when walking from one place to another, listening to the good citizens of Versailles exchanging observations with one another as they looked down from their moral elevation. I particularly remember one incident. I was wearing a shabby, battered panama hat, which among other things had seen a year's service in Africa, and which had reached that advanced stage of decomposition in which it could safely be put into my pocket. "Who is the fellow with the panama hat?" I heard one man ask. The other looked at me very intently before showing his profound knowledge of international relations: "He's probably the delegate from Panama."


## 2. *Brockdorff-Rantzau*

Ulrich Count Brockdorff-Rantzau, foreign minister of the German Republic, headed the delegation. He was a career diplomat. He came of an old aristocratic family of Danish origin. He showed no trace of the roughness and directness of the Prussian Junker. He had the charming—in his case perhaps a little too oily—friendliness for which the Danes are rightly famous. He had been William II's minister in the Danish capital during the war and had succeeded in maintaining excellent relations.

A little stooping, of moderate height, with a sharp-cut aristocratic head on a slender body, he looked not unlike the picture public opinion has made for itself of the smooth, well-groomed, somewhat effeminate diplomat. He was a liberal by temperament, not by conviction, as many of his more intelligent colleagues have been. Being an individualist of almost anarchist proclivities, he disliked bureaucrats and soldiers. A courtier rather than a statesman, he was far better fitted to deal with persons than with problems. Not being deeply interested in the latter he was free from many prejudices. He could work equally well with Communists and conservatives, pacifists and nationalists, provided they respected his sensitive ego. For he did not identify himself with a cause; he identified the cause with himself; everything with him was personal. His ambition was limitless—he would have liked to be German chancellor or even president of the Reich; he would not have minded the political color of the party that chose him.

Rantzau had not got on very well in imperial Germany; his clear though shallow intelligence had early foreseen the impending catastrophe. He had had a hand, it was said, in managing Lenin's journey to Russia through Germany. Not being of old Prussian origin, he was not encumbered by the traditional loyalty that bound the Junker to the house of Hohenzollern, and he had not found it hard to throw in his lot with the republic. He got on much better with people he considered his social inferiors than with his peers, for with them he was quite sure of his position. He had a smallish store of actual knowledge, but possessed quick perception and limited intuition. Being something of a "decadent," he liked to get up late in the day, preferably just before lunchtime, and he hated to go to bed. The nearer midnight, the brighter his light was shining. He was a brilliant conversationalist as the hours went past, with those he liked and trusted.

I saw a great deal of him after his resignation. I appreciated his trenchant remarks about men and his delight in naughty epigrams. Many a night I have sat up with him in the Victoria Strasse in the flat he shared with his brother, who loved and admired him, imbibing large quantities of brandy. He needed a stimulant, and the more he consumed, the clearer and brighter were his observations. I could not keep up the pace with him in this field, but when one refused to go on, he became irritated and suspicious. I had to fill my glass over and over again. His brandy was excellent; I enjoyed it in moderation. Rantzau was very fidgety; he walked up and down the rooms all the time, and when he turned his back I offered a libation to the gods in true classic style and emptied my glass for their benefit into one of two high China vases. It was a great pity and a terrible waste, but not too high a price for enjoying the company of an extremely interesting personality who needed but a small amount of common sense and a little less egotism to achieve actual greatness. He was a lonely man; few people trusted him. He had an inclination to intrigue, and his extreme sensitiveness made personal intercourse difficult. To disagree with him on an important issue was a personal insult. As he never took any exercise (he despised walking), he had no way to get irritation out of his system by mere bodily energy. I remained on intimate, even confidential, terms with him until the Rapallo Treaty was concluded—to a considerable degree at his instigation.

He took the Treaty of Versailles as a personal affront. The slight he had suffered as head of the German delegation had made him thoroughly anti-Western. He could write very concise, pungent notes, but when he had to deliver an address, even from a manuscript, he was nervous and trembled visibly. For this reason he remained seated when rejecting the accusations with which Clemenceau had presented the treaty terms to him. He did not mean to be discourteous; he was far too much of a courtier not to understand the value of politeness. But he did not want the Allied statesmen to see a Count Brockdorff-Rantzau tremble before them. It did not occur to them that a man who had had the moral courage to face the ordeal he was undergoing was too nervous to read a prepared speech. So he stuck to his armchair, read his reply, and aroused the violent wrath of the Allies, who saw in his behavior only the brazen challenge of unvanquished Prussian arrogance. Their loud denunciations made him a national hero.

The German people were thunderstruck at the harshness of the terms; they saw in this nervously twitching figure a valiant knight who defended their dignity against the insults that had been heaped upon them. He was delighted with this unpremeditated effect of his constitutional weakness. It made his name a household word in Germany; yet, somehow, it really broke his career. He deeply offended the Allies. He could, of course, easily have explained his attitude, but not without destroying the legend that had grown around him. Whenever he was mentioned for the highest office, his enemies alluded to his unpopularity with the Allies. He had facilitated his elimination by his trenchant, very undisciplined tongue. I once warned him of the danger of coining epigrams, which amused many, but hurt a few, generally very influential, people. "You are doing the same," he replied. "Yes," I retorted "but there is one difference; I have no ambitions. I do not want to get to the top; you do. I can afford the fun; you must give it up."

He did not give it up. When he was finally appointed ambassador to Russia, he used his position to get even with the wicked West and tried to strengthen co-operation with Russia. If the two bad boys of Europe stood together, they would not hang together. He enjoyed playing the role of the Red nobleman. I disagreed with his policies and he knew it. He had always sent for me on his visits to Berlin, even when he stayed only a few days. After Rapallo, he ignored me completely; I never saw him again. Having opposed him was equivalent to having betrayed him.

But at Versailles he was very kind to me. I reported a few details to him that he did not yet know. I often dined at his table and occasionally accompanied him on his afternoon drives. He had originally distrusted me as a friend of his cousin Bernstorff, of whom he was very jealous. For this reason he had received me with particular friendliness, for he believed that flattery can win everybody. By and by his attitude changed. I was neither a diplomat nor a soldier nor a bureaucrat—merely a private person who responded to his repartee and could be as trenchant as he was. There was not the slightest chance of my becoming his rival. Once he recognized this, he became almost affectionate and used me to good purpose.

## 3. The German Delegation

The German delegation was a huge body. Besides Brockdorff-Rantzau, it consisted of six delegates plenipotentiary.

The ablest of them, Karl Melchior, was a partner of the Warburg banking firm. He was one of the rare men in whom character and capacity are harmoniously blended; his advice was never influenced by personal or business bias. During an important discussion Hugo Stinnes once turned round to me and observed contemptuously, "Surely they cannot expect me to give them advice that would hurt my interests." Karl Melchior acted differently. He had not a creative mind. Being completely devoid of egotism, he was always ready to take up other people's ideas, to weigh them carefully, to formulate them so as to make them practical, and, if there was a chance of doing so, to persuade other parties to adopt them. He stood firm in matters of principle, though willing to meet opponents halfway. He became Germany's most influential representative in reparation negotiations. The Allies trusted him almost as much as the Germans. Any proposal sponsored by him was taken seriously.

The other five plenipotentiaries were representatives of political parties: Landsberg, a brilliant lawyer and a courageous man of action, and Leinert, a shrewd trade unionist, of the Socialists; Bell and Giesberts, two complete nonentities of the Center party; and Walther Schücking, of the Democrats, professor of international law, and ardent pacifist. He should never have been allowed to go into politics, as I had ample opportunity to find out. When later he was my colleague at the College of Commerce in Berlin, his crude naïveté never ceased to astonish me. Whenever a member of the faculty planned a dirty trick in appointments or otherwise, he first secured Schücking's support. It needed a great deal of persuasion to undo this bamboozlement and make him see what was really the matter. He could never believe that human nature could be so depraved. He was not a practicing lawyer, yet he consented to represent several German dynasties in their financial lawsuits against the German Republic. He never understood that they had enlisted him as a highly respected representative of German democracy and not as a smart attorney. He would have been horrified had he seen through their true motives.

The rest of the delegation represented all groups of German life. Bankers, merchants, industrialists sat side by side with labor leaders from the three main groups of Germany's trade unionism. All departments of the central government and most of the states had sent members; some were old-fashioned civil servants, others flotsam the revolution had carried to the top. Every special interest and every special group had its experts or its advisers. Army and navy had delegated technically excellent staffs. A few professors were added as experts on historical, legal, or economic problems. The most prominent were Max Weber, Hans Delbrück, and Albrecht Mendelssohn-Bartholdy, who shone by the charm of his personality.

I have never been able to find out why I was included. I suppose my knowledge of American affairs counted for something; yet I always suspected that I was on tap as a superior scribe. Most members of the delegation could write an intelligent memorandum on subjects with which they were conversant; few were able to address an enemy in his own language and make an impression on him. My job, I suppose, was to translate minutes suited for interdepartmental circulation into international documents. It was an important task. Most papers presented by the German delegation were lamentably unimpressive, even when their contents were fairly correct and after they had been submitted to the criticism of the many newspapermen who completed the delegation. I was asked once or twice to do a job of this sort. I wrote a draft of a reply to the covering note which accompanied the treaty in its final form. It had the ring that the occasion demanded: I suppose for that reason it was not used.

After the treaty had been presented to the German delegation and had been studied for a few days, it was broken up in sections. Each section was handed over to a particular committee. These committees had to work very hard; nearly all of them sat at the same hour; one could only be a member of one or two committees. I would have liked to serve on the financial committee, which had to deal with reparations. But this was reserved for bankers and industrialists. It was evidently assumed that people who did not know the difference between a balance of payment and a balance of trade were best qualified for handling problems connected with them. Melchior, Warburg, and a few others knew what it was all about. Most experts indulged in making plans that showed great knowledge of particular trades, coupled with complete ignorance of economic theory. The seed sown by Gustav Schmoller had ripened. His historical school had produced few scholars who could teach the elements of modern economics to businessmen or civil servants. I saw several of these memoranda when their authors asked my help in formulating them; they were at the same time both arrogant and childish.

The pick of Germany's businessmen were assembled at Versailles either as members of the delegation or as occasional visitors. I talked to most of them. I took long walks with them in the park of Versailles; my knowledge of English and American conditions of life made me of some value to them. Being a good listener I learnt a great deal from them as long as they stuck to their own business. On general issues, most of them were rather dumb. Some old-fashioned Prussians turned out to be highly cultivated men, though their attitude to labor was antediluvian. Few only, foremost amongst them Eduard Arnhold, had an understanding of world problems on the human as well as on the technical side. The majority had very crude ideas about the mechanism of international trade. "When they hear of *valuta* [the German term for foreign exchange]," Max Warburg used to say, "they think it is a glamour girl."

The labor delegates were moderate, modest, but rather timid. They might be able to meet captains of industry as their equals on wage boards or in conciliation councils; in a wider social atmosphere they were rather subdued.

The delegates were naturally gloomy. They had not expected such a harsh treaty. Most of them naïvely identified their private wealth with public welfare, and acted as representatives of their own particular groups, not as advisers of the nation. I used to tell them at a later date that I was the only genuine expert. "I am the only person in this room," I explained, "whose income will not be affected by the advice he can give. You are not expert advisers, you are highly skilled representatives of particular interests." Many private groups would be hurt by territorial amputation and delivery obligations; those affected had to be listened to, and their wails were pretty loud. I met Fritz Thyssen only once, during a discussion of the demand for delivery of the Rhine coal barges to the Allies. He threatened the government with separation of the Rhineland if they dared to comply with this nefarious request. He would not understand that republican Germany had not picked on him as its victim for sacrifice to the Allies, but that it had to pay the bill for the lost war, for whose prolongation he and his associates had been largely responsible.

I encountered everywhere highly skilled specialist "technicians" who were unable to understand and unwilling to learn the elements of economics. When I resigned as reparations expert, a rather humorous undersecretary of state asked me in a somewhat condescending tone, "What are you going to do now?"

"I am going back to my academic work," I replied, "but I am starting a new venture. I am opening a beginners' class in economics, for secretaries of state and captains of industry." Alas, I never had any pupils.

### 4. *The End of Isolation*

My stay in Versailles had been very instructive but not very satisfactory. I had three good meals a day, which I had not had for a long time, a comfortable room and a bath, a good deal of talk, and a certain amount of exercise in the park. I was not doing much useful work; I was beginning to be bored, when something happened.

The Allies had had great difficulties in coming to an agreement among themselves. In order to safeguard their unanimity, the German delegation was not allowed to meet any representative of an Allied government. One day as I was walking by myself in the park, I ran into a distant connection of mine, who recently had led the British commission to Munich and Berlin. I naturally called "Hello," but I was severely reprimanded. "You must not speak to me," he said, and I naturally left him to himself.

But a new development was taking place. Alexander Redlich, a brilliant German journalist, was propagating economic co-operation between Germany and France. While most republicans favored an understanding with the Anglo-Saxon powers, he advocated friendship with France. The French responded. Redlich, a German industrialist, and an important member of the French foreign office met from time to time clandestinely and discussed the future industrial co-operation of the two countries. Brockdorff-Rantzau was a little suspicious of their activities. He asked me to attend their meetings and to report their progress to him.

I was not an expert on coal and steel which formed the center of these discussions, but I had no ax to grind. I had met the French representative before; he is playing a very important part today in his country's affairs. I had not much sympathy with the plan, but I faithfully reported my observations.

This had been going on for some time when I once more

encountered my English friend. He got very angry when I greeted him, repeating that he was not allowed to talk to me. "I don't see why," I replied. "I talk to a French representative every second day." He was dumfounded. "Can you give me proof of this?" he said. "Certainly I can, if you will wait outside the Colonel's lodge." A French colonel was in charge of the German delegation. All arrangements passed through his hands. I had promised the French representative a paper on the coal situation in upper Silesia. It was ready in my room. I went to my hotel, picked it up, and returned to the Colonel's lodge, outside which my British friend was waiting for me, now reinforced by another British officer. I showed him the address on the letter, walked into the Colonel's office, and asked him to deliver the letter. "Certainly, monsieur," he replied with the courtesy of old France. The two Britishers in the background were craning their necks like hungry giraffes reaching out for a particularly savory leaf on a very high tree.

Next morning we met again in the park. "I have spoken to the Prime Minister about it," my British friend informed me. "He did not believe it at first, but I have convinced him. We are not going to kick up a row; we are not telling the French that we have found them out, but from now on we can talk." Soon afterward an important member of the German delegation got in touch with his British counterpart.

This accident established my position with Brockdorff-Rantzau. He used me occasionally for more or less delicate missions. These interludes had no effect on the situation. It was clear and simple. We might get some concessions by written negotiations; the main principles of the treaty would stand. Were we going to accept it?

The army was of the opinion that resistance in the west was impossible, but they were prepared to give a good account of themselves in the east and give the Poles a licking. Brockdorff-Rantzau had made up his mind to reject the treaty. The majority of the delegation adopted a similar attitude; so did the government in Berlin. I knew that the war could not be resumed; but I knew, too, that a refusal to sign the treaty would greatly have embarrassed the American and the British governments. They, too, could not continue the war, and they had no desire to occupy Berlin. Even the French military had some doubt about the wisdom of such an advance. I would have preferred a declaration by the German government regretting their inability to accept a treaty many clauses of which could not be carried out. They had no intention of offering resistance; they would make preparations to hand over the government of Germany to the Allied powers—a train would be in readiness at the German frontier to carry Marshal Foch and his staff to Berlin, where they could take over the administration of Germany. I still think that there was some sense in this suggestion, but the German parties were frightened. They feared a surrender to France might bring about the complete permanent disintegration of Germany. A spontaneous separatist movement had in fact started on the Rhine and in Bavaria.

Erzberger was telling everybody that the treaty must be signed. A few days before a decision was reached, Professor Haguenin, one of the leading French experts on Germany, paid me an unannounced visit in my room at Versailles. He was a friend of Germany as far as a patriotic Frenchman could be friendly to the great, dangerous neighbor. "Use your influence," he said to me, "to make your people accept the treaty. If they refuse to do so, we will dismember Germany. We will exonerate every German state from its share of reparation payments. Many of them will accept this privilege, and German unity will be destroyed."

"An excellent idea," I replied, "especially if you carry it a step further and apply it to each Prussian province. They will all secede. Germany will be cut up into a number of independent states, none of them will pay a penny of reparation, and after twenty-five years they will all reunite." I reported this conversation immediately to Brockdorff-Rantzau. He was very much amused by it.

By this time a decision had to be taken. The delegation went home. Brockdorff-Rantzau asked me to stay on for a few days. The Berlin government had resigned. A new government had been formed under Erzberger's guidance, prepared to accept the treaty. I remained behind with nothing to do. When it was quite certain that the treaty would be signed, and when the new plenipotentiaries were on their way, I asked leave to return. I had no desire to be present at a ceremony for which I had neither direct nor indirect responsibility. The government that had appointed me had ceased to exist; it was time for me to go home.

# XIV. The Resurrection of Militarism (1919-1920)

## 1. *The Committee of Inquiry*

WHEN I returned from Versailles to Munich in the first days of July 1919, the revolutionary spook was over. A Socialist government was still in office, but power had passed into the hands of a reactionary, resentful bureaucracy. The change had taken me by surprise, for in Versailles I had not been able to keep up with the rapid shifts of the political scene at home. The same people who had been cringing at the feet of Red troopers, and who had implored me to intercede for them, appealing to my well-known liberal opinions—they seemed to them a kind of insurance policy against revolutionary accidents—now gave me the cold shoulder. It was an unpleasant, though a salutary, lesson. For when the Nazis came in fourteen years later, and many supposedly stanch republicans suddenly dropped the mask, I was neither greatly astonished nor deeply grieved. Man, no doubt, is a political animal; he is not a very spirited one. In the summer of 1919 this discovery depressed me. The world of abstract theories in which I had grown up had gone to pieces. The realities of war, peace treaties, revolution, and reaction had shattered them; my education was being completed. The summing up was painful. Living conditions were still rather hard. My wife only slowly recovered her strength after an operation from which she had nearly died. I spent a restless summer and autumn in our house, little imagining that never again should I live in it.

Brooding over the problems of a greatly unbalanced world, the worries of which had got mixed up with my own life, I received a wire from my cousin, Dr. Julian Triar, who was attached to Erzberger's secretariat. It asked me to join as an expert

238

the committee the National Constituent Assembly had set up to inquire into the responsibility for the loss of the war. I accepted with delight.

To the German people the war had been a war of defense. They saw themselves encircled by a world of enemies, in which they could rely only on the Austrian Empire. The survival of that ramshackle empire was a matter of life and death to them. They saw in the Serbian agitation the spearhead of a Pan-Slav movement for its destruction. In this respect they understood European problems much better than romanticizing philologists and novelists in Great Britain, who rightly extolled the noble qualities of primitive Balkan races but forgot that proud warriors do not make good pacifists. Few Germans liked or even understood Austria. Many of them disapproved of the Kaiser's policy that had led to Germany's isolation and to her compulsory support of Austria, but they could not break the vicious circle. They accepted the war as one accepts the bursting of the clouds and the first streaks of lightning, when the long threatened storm has broken at last, and a feeling of exhilaration replaces fear. Their innermost thoughts were much more clearly expressed in the peace resolution of the Reichstag of July 1917, demanding a peace without annexations, than in the programs of Pan-German annexationists; the treaties of Brest Litovsk and Bucharest, which the high command had imposed, were a great shock to them.

War had never before been considered a crime. Germans suddenly were faced with the puritan concept of political "sin." It appealed to a small fanatical minority that, following the Bolsheviks' lead, were keen on attributing the responsibility for all terrible happenings to a wicked imperialist order.

The coupling, in the treaty, of reparation payments with this war guilt gave a practical angle to an otherwise abstract issue. It was felt that a vindication of German political honor—however honor may be defined—was not only necessary for setting Germany's political conscience at rest; it might, if successful, liberate her from a heavy financial burden—an utterly naïve attitude, for indemnities are not the result of moral guilt (which is not automatically proven by defeat), but of defeat.

I had not liked the Allies, an interested party, setting themselves up as an impartial court of justice. I greatly disliked the introduction of the technique of revivalist camp meetings into the political field, for the soul of a nation cannot be saved by some of its representatives' taking the sawdust trail. But I was deeply interested in placing political responsibilities where they belonged.

For over one year after the peace resolution of July 1917 had been sidetracked, the government of Germany had been an irresponsible military dictatorship in the hands of Ludendorff, who had sheltered behind the popularity of Field Marshal Hindenburg, and the shadowy authority of the Emperor. For over a year he had set his face against any attempt at making a "stalemate" peace, assuring the army and the people that one more final effort would win the war. Even after the bogging down of the spring offensive, he would not give up hope of victory, until, in the early days of October, he completely broke down and compelled the government to sue for an armistice.

An inquiry into the role of the high command during the war, a demonstration that its interference with, and finally its control of, policy had caused the loss of the war, would discredit the dictatorial militarism that Ludendorff stood for. It would establish beyond doubt his responsibility for the armistice and its consequences, and thus prevent a resurrection of militarism. The Germans have an innate belief in the soundness of military leadership; if they could be made to see its dismal failure, they might be on the road to recovery. I hoped that the third of October, the day of the demand for an armistice, would be made a day of national mourning, and that the memory of a great military defeat would be coupled with the name of its author for all time. If one could but convince the German people that war did not pay, a great step toward peace would have been made; this surely would be easier than to teach them that war was a crime—when all nations of the world, including the foremost democracies, had committed it over and over again and still celebrated the anniversaries of successful sinfulness in church and chapel.

## 2. Mismanagement

The National Constituent Assembly had appointed a committee of twenty-eight to inquire into all matters connected with responsibilities, for and during the war; it divided the work among four subcommittees. I was attached as expert to the second subcommittee; it was to answer the following questions:

> "What opportunities existed during the continuance of the war for bringing about peace parleys, and why did such opportunities come to nought?"

During what might be called its dramatic period the subcommittee concentrated its efforts on the Wilsonian peace move. It had to inquire into and report facts, and could compel witnesses to give evidence. It was not a court of law, but unfortunately it was made to follow the rules of procedure of criminal courts. It could not pronounce judgment, though its findings might call later on for prosecution before a not yet established national high court. Public opinion was inclined to mix up guilt and responsibility; so did many witnesses, who were afraid of inculpating themselves by their evidence. The allusions to the penal code in setting up the procedure of the committee, and the Allies' demands for the punishment of war criminals, gave them some cause for uneasiness. As representatives of a fallen regime they did not expect fair treatment at the hands of the new men.

As a matter of fact these fears were groundless. While most members of the subcommittee were severely critical of the imperial regime, none of them was vindictive. The chairman, Warmuth, a judge by profession, was a nationalist deputy whose sympathies were all with the fallen order. Though he presided impartially, he may well have been in collusion with some of the witnesses. The committee's moving spirit, Hugo Sinzheimer, was by party affiliation a moderate Socialist, by temperament a radical. He did not mean to insult witnesses, yet his unfortunate habit of blending unctuous pathos with rasping aggressiveness made them see red. His colleague Dr. Oscar Cohn, representing the Independent Socialists, was one of those gentle dreamers whose hatred of oppression drives them steadily toward the physical-force groups of the left, whose brutal methods they condemn and condone. Both Sinzheimer and Cohn, being Jews, were easy targets for anti-Semitic vulgarities.

Our first witness was Count Bernstorff, the former ambassador to Washington. The committee offered him an opportunity for refuting the charge of duplicity raised against him in the United States. He could easily prove that he had been honest in his attempts at collaboration with the United States; the home government had not been equally so. Though eager to avail himself of his chance, he was too much of a gentleman to mention the intrigues in the German Foreign Office against him, and too reticent where a fuller statement might have inculpated colleagues or subordinates. He never succeeded in silencing suspicion completely.

Bernstorff was followed by the former chancellor, von Bethmann-Hollweg. He had had neither the ambition nor the ability to play the part of dictator that the Iron Chancellor had bequeathed to his unfortunate successors. An honest, conscientious administrator slowly ripening into a statesman, he had desired peace as earnestly as Grey or Wilson. But he was not a strong man; no strong man could have maintained himself between an emperor who played with absolutism and dallied with war, and a parliament groping for power. He should, of course, have resigned when army and navy had overthrown his antisubmarine policy. His remaining in office threw doubts on his sincerity. He justified it as a patriotic duty—he did not want to raise fears as to the outcome of the submarine warfare campaign once it had been decided upon. His sacrifice was useless; the high command managed to squeeze him out anyhow a few months later. His predecessor, Prince Bülow, did not credit him with such unselfish motives. Long afterward I suggested to him at a luncheon party that Bethmann's international reputation would have been greatly enhanced had he resigned. The old cynic smiled condescendingly. "You do not understand, my dear Professor, and you cannot understand. You have never been a Prussian minister on the dust heap; you do not know what a mean position it is."

I saw a good deal of Bethmann during our meetings. He seemed to sense my disapproval of Sinzheimer's questioning. He suffered visibly under it. He had either to acknowledge his weakness, which was his only guilt, and exculpate himself completely—or to defend a policy he had pursued under military pressure very much against his will. The atmosphere of the sub-committee unfortunately had made him feel like a defendant. Instead of separating himself from Ludendorff and the navy, his "judges"—that is how he began to envisage them—treated him as the army's fellow conspirator. Yet he accepted the situation and tried to answer questions truthfully.

His former deputy, Karl Helfferich, had been the most outspoken opponent of unrestricted submarine warfare. He, too, had remained in office after his advice had been rejected and had defended the new policy with the same skill with which he had formerly opposed it.

I remember calling on him after my return from America. Having converted himself to the navy's views, he was full of assumed optimism. The submarine warfare was going well. The British were in grave difficulties; scarcity of timber for their coal pits was seriously reducing coal production, and the collapse was bound to come soon. "There are lots of trees in England," I ventured to suggest; "the British will cut them long before they give in." He gave me a withering glance of pity. I was not greatly surprised later on to see the trees still standing in most of the parks. Helfferich's conversion had forced him into an alliance with the militarists, and made it difficult for him to come to terms with the republic, whose advent his own miscalculations had accelerated. He hated it with the vitriolic hatred of the renegade. In order to justify himself, he had to defend the policy of the army against his own former arguments.

After having treated the committee to a somewhat distorted version of the Wilson peace move, which he found hard to maintain in cross-examination, he suddenly sprang a carefully prepared coup. He refused to answer a question put to him by Dr. Cohn. "If I were sitting here before a court I would object to Dr. Cohn as a judge, and would have the right to do so under the criminal law"—his reason being that Dr. Cohn had accepted money from the Soviets to organize a revolution at a time when Germany was making her hardest fight against her enemies. Though Cohn's rejoinder to this accusation in the National Assembly may not have convinced everybody, the matter had nothing to do with the proceedings of the subcommittee. Helfferich was staging a ridiculous legal farce.* The committee fell for it. For obstructing the proceedings he was solemnly fined seventy-five dollars, and continued his evidence next day, after presenting a carefully worded legal protest. The nationalist chairman, doubting the legality of the fine, resigned.

The subcommittee blundered, and had made Helfferich a national hero at the cost of seventy-five dollars. A carefully prepared propaganda praised him for having saved Germany's honor from those who were slandering her statesmen and soldiers for the benefit of that archhypocrite, Woodrow Wilson. After this, even Bethmann-Hollweg became restive and excused his having given way to the army on the ground of the tremendous pressure of public opinion; he resented bitterly the statement that he had not properly informed the public and the Reichstag.

The republic suffered a setback. A few days later it underwent a heavy defeat at the hands of Ludendorff.

## 3. *Ludendorff's Return*

The antimilitarist passions of the early revolution had resulted in a few bestial murders of officers; Ludendorff, who was rightly considered the embodiment of militarism, had thought it wise to disappear. In civilian disguise, with a false beard and spectacles, he had escaped to Sweden. He was soon back, but he lay low. The republic, animated by a spirit of good will toward all men, and a hatred of bloodshed and persecution often akin to weakness, had left him alone.

His return to the public stage was cleverly planned. Called by the subcommittee, he had expressed a wish to have his testi-

---

* Helfferich's argument was legally untenable even from his own point of view. The committee was not a court; Helfferich was a witness, not a defendant; and even a defendant cannot object to a judge halfway through the trial; the right to decline him must be exercised before proceedings begin. The chairman ought to have advised Helfferich of the actual position, but he was a member of his party. Dr. Cohn ought to have refrained from defending himself in the subcommittee. He should have told the chairman that as member of the committee he meant to elicit the truth from a recalcitrant witness, who evidently desired to cloud the issues; that he would henceforth address his questions to the witness through the chairman, and deal with Helfferich's calumnies in another place.

mony taken in the presence of Hindenburg, whose mantle had covered so many of his sins.

The committee need not have acceded. Its rules did not permit a witness to lay down conditions under which he was prepared to appear. It could easily have risked Ludendorff's refusal and excused him on the assumption that he evidently feared to incriminate himself. As to the Field Marshal's testimony, it was not needed; everyone knew that in all political matters he had been Ludendorff's speaking tube.

But even after Helfferich's coup, the subcommittee did not realize the magnitude of the political battle in which it was engaged. Some of its members enjoyed the wide publicity given to it; they were puffed up at having the war lords appear before them as simple witnesses.

We sat in one of the large chambers of the Reichstag. All the earlier witnesses were present; many members of the assembly and of the diplomatic corps attended; the representatives of various departments had turned up. The press, of course, was there in full force, eagerly expecting a gala performance.

Everybody rose when the Field Marshal and Ludendorff entered.

Many years ago, Heinrich Heine had predicted a future German revolution. It would ruthlessly execute kings, but it would lead them to the guillotine with the utmost deference. The poet understood his countrymen.

The Field Marshal was in uniform—a massive statue rather than a man; both face and figure gray, he might have been a somewhat humanized idol of a pagan Prussian tribe carved in stone. He moved almost like a robot, with stiff, heavy steps. I had occasion to say a few words to him. His face was sad, not unkind, almost without expression; his eyes were very old, lusterless, almost dead. He was like a living corpse, whose limbs went on functioning, but whose soul had withered long ago. He seemed a survival of an earlier geological age, when all creatures were built on a larger scale, and on a somewhat simpler plan.

Ludendorff, in a business suit, looked like the choleric manager of a big industrial concern. He was tense and vulgar, excitable and excited, for he was playing for high stakes—his comeback.

Both were treated with deference going beyond courtesy. The Field Marshal responded to this reception; he said many things that were offensive and irresponsible, but he did it in a dignified manner. After all, he was a gentleman, and Ludendorff was not. They prefaced their testimony with the same stereotyped legal reservation that Helfferich had formulated. A number of questions had been forwarded to them, to which they were expected to reply. By some fluke they had not reached them in time. It did not much matter. Neither meant to give evidence. They were here as propagandists, not as witnesses. They insisted on telling their tale as they thought fit, indiscriminately mixing fact, hearsay, opinion, and even a little fiction.

The gist of their story was that they had concentrated on their military job and left all political matters in the hands of the Chancellor. Interruptions by the chairman or questions by committee members were brushed aside as irrelevant. Both were evidently well prepared, not to say well coached. They did not stick to the topic on which they were to be heard—the Wilson peace move. They spent a good deal of their time explaining that the military catastrophe was due to the moral breakdown of the home front, caused by internal agitation. Droning monotonously, the Field Marshal launched the legend of the "stab in the back" by stating, "An English general has said with justice, 'The German army was stabbed in the back.' " He was not even asked the name of the general and the question would have disconcerted him greatly. For he was not given to reading foreign writings and was merely repeating a story he had memorized. Ludendorff took up the same line and violently attacked the Socialists. The more sloppy the evidence, the better was the propaganda.

Finally Ludendorff lost his head and attacked Count Bernstorff. He accused him of having failed in counteracting Allied propaganda (Bernstorff was too magnanimous to reply that propaganda is not easy when army and navy instigate silly conspiracies). He reproached him with having sent over insufficient information about the American situation, declaring at the same time that he attached no weight to the Ambassador's reports, as his contacts were exclusively with the Chancellor. He finally protested against a gross calumny by the Ambassador who, he affirmed, had stated on his oath that he, Ludendorff, did not want peace. With the fury of a raving lunatic he declared that all his life had been dedicated to getting peace for Germany.

I was anxiously waiting for the Ambassador's reply. His hour of destiny had struck. He held all the winning cards. He had but to get up, repeat his original statement and refute Ludendorff's imbecile interpretation. For the issue was not whether Ludendorff wanted *peace*, but whether he wanted *a peace acceptable to Wilson*. He had insisted on a conqueror's peace; all his ranting showed this plainly enough, and so did the peace treaties of Brest Litovsk and of Bucharest, his opposition to the peace resolution of the Reichstag in 1917, and his elimination of von Kühlmann. He had decided on unrestricted submarine warfare in the hope that it would get him such a peace within three months; he had gambled on it and lost. He had objected to Wilson's mediation when he could have had it on the basis of a peace without victors, and he had clamored for it after he had lost the war. His demand for an immediate armistice was the real stab in the back that broke German resistance.

Count Bernstorff was unmoved, merely disgusted by Ludendorff's outburst; he replied with great dignity. But dignity does not dispose of a mad bull; one could not argue with Ludendorff, one had to shout him down. At 2:15 the meeting was adjourned. Ludendorff was too exhausted to attend an afternoon session. Public indignation was roused to such a degree that sittings could not be resumed before April 20, 1920— five months later.

On that day the subcommittee reassembled and questioned Bernstorff on the points Ludendorff had raised. He had no difficulty in refuting them and in vindicating his statements. By that time it was too late. Ludendorff's ravings had carried the day. The legend of the stab in the back had taken root. An excellent Nationalist propaganda pictured the venerable Field Marshal and his faithful companion in arms as victims of pacifist, Socialist, and Jewish persecution. They had heroically defended themselves and had beaten back the Red rabble who had been responsible for Germany's defeat. Early in 1917 the two great military leaders had saved Germany from the iniquities of a Wilsonian peace. As the result of the stab in the back—

9

the revolution—they had had to accept it in the autumn of 1918. (Actually, of course, Ludendorff's demand for the armistice, October 3, had preceded the revolution, November 9, by a full month.) The peace of Versailles had proved Wilson's mendacity.

The republic was beaten. I walked home with Count Bernstorff; I could not hide my disappointment at his having failed us. "One need not work in the stockyards," I said to him, "if one cannot stand the blood, the stench, and the squeals; but if one does go into that business, one must not mind killing pigs."


## 4. *The Kapp Putsch*

The pacifist interlude was over. The militarists were again in the saddle; an almost hysterical nationalism swept over the country. Owing to the recollection of the local soviet regime, it was strongest in Bavaria. The debacle of the subcommittee had laid bare the weakness of the republic; it seemed easy for a handful of political adventurers to dispose of it completely. Under the leadership of an East Prussian administrator, Kapp, the corps of a treacherous general, von Lüttwitz, assisted by troops employed in the Baltic provinces, rebelled and occupied Berlin (March 13, 1920). Fortunately they failed in securing the government or the president.

A general strike was proclaimed; for once it was universal, not limited to manual workers. From the permanent heads of the Foreign Office downward the entire civil service joined it.

It was not easy, however, to make liberal bourgeois support it. A general strike meant to them the end of social order—the beginning of revolution. I spent a good deal of my time in the Democratic Club, where a center of resistance had been organized, explaining to our members the legality of a general strike ordered by a legal government. I implored them to come in, all of them, otherwise the working class would justly claim the victory of a republic that was but partly its own. The argument appealed to their reason—not to their hearts.

Kapp claimed to have acted with the approval of the British government. The story, widely spread, could not be denied, for the British high commissioner, Major General Sir Neill Malcolm, had not yet returned from England. By a stroke of good luck I managed to intercept him and secured a categorical denial, the effect of which was very salutary.

All German revolutions had a comic side. One day the Kapp men had hermetically sealed up the Democratic Club. I had wisely refrained from entering it and was watching proceedings from the corner of the street when suddenly General Max Montgelas, in mufti, emerged. The guards naturally stopped him. He spoke a few sharp words; they clicked heels and presented arms. "I merely told them who I was," the General explained. "Prussians always know a general, if you talk to them in the right way, and of course they love to obey."

The days of the Kapp Putsch are among my few proud recollections of the republic. They were not comfortable. Life is not pleasant when public utilities do not function and lavatories no longer flush. There was little actual fighting, only a few brawls. The invaders paraded the streets in full battle dress, hard, haughty, brutal faces—the forerunners of the Nazi host. But the people did not seem to notice them. Nobody talked to them; they were completely shut in by an impenetrable wall of icy contempt. They had looked forward to a triumphal entry, the consolation for that victory parade of which the armistice and the peace had cheated them. They had come as liberators, and they were universally shunned. They could not stand it; their leaders collapsed and capitulated.

But the republic was not strong enough to punish them. "Soldiers do not shoot soldiers," said General von Seeckt, who extricated the army with great skill. But Communists did not mind shooting bourgeois. They rose once again—as if they meant to help the Nationalists—and compelled the government to use the army against the workingmen; it could always be trusted to shoot Communists.

All over Germany the first military conspiracy had collapsed. Only in Bavaria had it succeeded. Herr von Kahr, who later played with Hitler in the beer cellar putsch and was murdered by him in 1934, became prime minister.

It might have been wiser had I not joined the committee. Nearly all my personal friends, even my wife, disapproved of my participation. I minded her dissent much more than the warnings of personal danger I received from several sides. I did not consider myself of sufficient importance to be singled out by an assassin. I have lately reread (in a rather cumbrous English translation) the proceedings and reports of the subcommittee. I now know that I was right. I had both grasped the danger and seen the opportunity for meeting it. I was not responsible for the failure, which was due to that peculiar maladroitness that seemed to dog the steps of republican statesmen. But one does not get much satisfaction out of "I told you so," apart from the discovery that one's own judgment and one's own conscience are fairly trustworthy guides.

# XV. The Tribulations of an Expert

## 1. Making History (1920–1921)

In the spring of 1920, at the suggestion of Heinrich Albert (at that time head of the Chancellor's secretariat), I was appointed adviser to the Chancellor on the reparation question. I enjoyed the good will of most members of the cabinet, yet Albert had to fight a battle royal before he could break down departmental jealousies. I had to give up my positions in Munich. In return I was promised, after the work was done, the choice between the post of financial adviser at one of the three great Western embassies or an academic post of the same standing as the one I was vacating. It was my good fortune that I had not to depend on this promise.

Germany was entitled to make proposals of her own up to May 1921. The better part of a year had gone by after the treaty and nothing had been prepared. My first duty in Berlin was the drafting of a memorandum outlining Germany's capacity to pay. Starting from this point, I suggested a definite bold offer to the Allies, high enough to be attractive and to make its refusal difficult, and at the same time within the limits of Germany's resources. I attempted to connect it with a stabilization of the mark.

To the evident relief of the government, the need for making a proposal lapsed. The Allies invited us to an international conference in July 1920, at the small Belgian watering place, Spa. My chief, Chancellor Fehrenbach, the foreign secretary, Dr. Simons, and a few other heads of departments were to attend. Dr. Fehrenbach, a member of the Center party, had played a dignified part in his native country, Baden, before he had become president of the German Reichstag. He was a good figurehead for the hinterland, for he had the warmhearted, slightly lachrymose eloquence beloved by plain people. He had no knowledge of international questions, and no ambition to play a role on the international stage. A modest, loyal man, he accepted the advice of his staff and of the abler members of his cabinet. He would do his best.

I was not included in the delegation. I do not know whether my omission was due to the jealousy of the Foreign Office or to the intrigues of powerful experts who feared I might not play the game according to their rules. By the time I arrived, on a later train than the delegation's special, my opponents had managed to occupy all the rooms in the hotel reserved for us and to put me into an annex. Suspicious bureaucracies always fight outsiders in accordance with a set pattern. Their first move in the game is to dispatch him to a room far away from the main office, and to provide him, if possible, with an inefficient secretary. Their brave attempt to keep me away failed, however. I rapidly moved into the center of events. For two days I actually helped to make history—it never happened again. Two years later at the Genoa conference I was asked to unmake history, a task, I am afraid, as hopeless as unscrambling eggs.

I spent the first days of the conference hanging round in the lobbies with other similarly unoccupied delegation members, talking to journalists, looking important, though we knew we were not, and generating the atmosphere of excitement, intrigue, and boredom that characterizes most international conferences, at least for their minor participants. By and by the reparation question came to the fore. I was suddenly requested to outline an index scheme to be presented to the Allies. A standard rate of payments was to be agreed upon and to be raised or lowered automatically according to certain objective tests of increasing or decreasing German prosperity. At a moment's notice I was asked to propose a plan to the Allies. Nothing of that sort had been prepared; yet I managed to get a few points on paper. I developed them later on and constructed an index scheme very much like the one embodied in the Dawes Plan. I was not called to present it at Spa, and had nothing to do with its insertion in the Dawes Plan, although if any German delegates had a hand in shaping it, they are sure to have copied my earlier draft.

The conference was soon to explode. While I had been sweating at my index scheme, Hugo Stinnes, attached to the delegation as an expert, had risen and addressed the chiefs of the Allied governments on the coal deliveries stipulated in the Versailles Treaty, in which Germany had fallen short. He gave them a bit of his mind, and a terrible upset followed. It was at Spa that the importance the peace treaty had given to industrial magnates suddenly burst upon the world.

Hugo Stinnes was in his way a great man. He came of an old Rhenish coal-merchant family that had gone into the mining business. Inheriting the parental firm, he had expanded it into one of the most powerful coal and steel combines of northwestern Germany. He might have been a belated offspring of the great merchant adventurer dynasties who had built up overseas empires by a rare blend of calculation, imagination, and boldness. He showed none of that boisterous hail-fellow-well-met comradeship that successful businessmen in both hemispheres love to display. Plainly dressed, he impressed one as a rather modest, somber puritan. A sharp-cut face with aquiline features reminded one of an Assyrian king. He argued almost silently, scarcely ever raising his voice, suppressing his passions. The clarity of his exposition easily won over opponents. He had the *esprit gaulois* so rare in Germany except in some Jews, though Frederick the Great had possessed it. Stinnes's friends assured me that he took no interest in politics, that all his energies were devoted to problems of economic reconstruction. In some ways they were right. Deep down in his heart he felt that Germany was doing well if Hugo Stinnes and Company were doing well, and that the growth of his firm was the most important contribution to Germany's welfare. He dreamed of a Germany composed of a number of huge combines, a country divided into economic provinces, its center the Ruhr, the home of iron and coal, to whom the ownership of the national railways would give control of all central Europe. He was not a reactionary, not even an authoritarian; he relied on his marvelous gift of "persuasion." He had been elected to parliament, but played no part in its open meetings; he disliked platforms and lobbies, preferring the conference room. A passionate ambition and perhaps an even more passionate vanity lurked behind his engaging modesty. He sought satisfaction for both cravings in well-advertised semiobscurity. Yet sometimes a sudden outburst, a blend of passion and self-interest, broke his reserve—it did so at that meeting at Spa.

The meeting was adjourned at once, the Allied statesmen taking counsel with one another. The German delegation was perturbed.

Its leader, Dr. Simons, the foreign minister, was an ideal civil servant. A subtle legal mind, untiring industry, and an unbiased intellectual integrity had fitted him admirably for the secondary posts he had hitherto held. He had been Brockdorff-Rantzau's right hand at Versailles, serving the peace delegation as conscientiously as he had served William II. Born to carry out the will of others, he was incapable of shaping a foreign policy of his own. This cultured, gentle bureaucrat was no match for Stinnes, who but a short time ago had been among his employers. For after Versailles, Simons, despairing of the public service, had become managing director of the German manufacturers' association. It never entered his mind to call Stinnes to order and to tell the Allied governments that he was merely an undisciplined expert who had no right whatsoever to speak for the German government.

The scene made excellent headlines. All over Germany, the news flashed that Stinnes had "given it to the Allies." He became a national hero; Stinnes getting up on his hind legs was even better than Brockdorff-Rantzau sitting down on his buttocks.

National heroes who tangle up international conferences are expensive luxuries. The Allies very soon presented the German delegation with a bill making it clear that Stinnes's cheap heroics had been extremely costly. Germany was served with an ultimatum insisting, among other things, on the prompt deliveries of coal that Stinnes had meant to invalidate: sabotage by the Ruhr industrialists would not be tolerated. If the German government did not accept the ultimatum within seventy-two hours, an Allied army would occupy the Ruhr, the industrial heart of Germany.

Consternation reigned in the German delegation. A meeting of experts was called to hear the Allied ultimatum and offer advice. When my turn came, I asked Stinnes what the French desired us to do. "Make them march into the Ruhr," he said. "In that case our policy is clear. It seems to me but common

sense to do the contrary of what the enemy wants you to do."
Fortunately the majority of the delegates had spoken in a similar way. My argument had evidently contributed to the result,
for Stinnes walked up to me and expostulated very angrily with
me. "I may not know the details of the coal situation," I replied,
"but you do not understand the essentials of politics."

With the delegation split, the government was at its wits'
end. The Chancellor had no opinion of his own. He was merely
unhappy. Simons understood that Germany had no choice; she
could not reject the ultimatum. But he dared not go against
Stinnes. In the eyes of the heavy industries and in his own,
Stinnes was a patriot who was freeing Germany from the humiliation of the lost war and the shackles of the peace.

While various groups hung around discussing the situation,
I walked up to the Foreign Secretary. "Perhaps I can do something to ease the situation. Philip Kerr" (later the Marquis of
Lothian, and at that time Lloyd George's private secretary) "is
a friend of mine of long standing. I have not seen him since
before the war, but I am sure that I can get in touch with
him." Simons thanked me and retired with the members of the
cabinet. We continued the usual chitter-chatter. Late in the
afternoon I was sent for by the Chancellor and given a paper to
hand to Philip Kerr for the consideration of Lloyd George. It
contained a number of questions about the nature of the ultimatum. Germany evidently would have to give in, but she
might obtain some modifications to make its acceptance bearable in the face of the patriotic storm that Stinnes had un-
leashed.

My arrival at British headquarters naturally aroused the
curiosity of the newspapermen waiting for Lloyd George's
return from the golf links. They tried to find out what I was
doing there. I told them I had an appointment with an old
friend, and talked with them about other things. After some
time there was a commotion. The Prime Minister had arrived,
followed by Kerr. I managed to get near Kerr and whisper to
him, "I have to see you." With a nod he gave me the number of
his room and went along. I returned to the hall and did a little
more chatting with the journalists. As nothing seemed to have
happened, they dispersed. When they had gone, I walked up to
Kerr's room. European backwardness has its advantages; had

the building been a skyscraper with forty floors, the Prime Minister would surely have occupied the penthouse, and the elevator boy would have known where I was going. As it was I found Kerr's room without too much climbing. I gave him the Foreign Secretary's letter, and in a short time he returned with a reply; I went back to my delegation. The reply covered only a few points; it required an answer. Before the answer was ready, dinner was announced. I had no time to sit down to it, so Simons ordered a couple of sandwiches and wrapped them up for me with his own hands—the only token of recognition I ever received from him. I munched them in the car on the way.

Late in the evening I came back with more notes. That night I did not sleep very well. For the time being, some of the threads from which the web of history is woven were running through my hands. I very nearly had a severe attack of megalomania. Next day, I repeated my journey several times. The German delegation and Mr. Lloyd George were holding a mutual "Information Please" contest. By asking questions, by insinuating interpretations and formulating replies, the two parties finally succeeded in arriving at a compromise. The ultimatum was to be complied with, but Germany would be granted certain important concessions, among them a cash advance, the only loan ever extended to her before the Dawes Plan. In about forty-eight hours, if I remember rightly, everything was finished. I was sent down with a letter addressed to Lloyd George containing the German government's acceptance of the modified terms of the ultimatum.

The answer had to be delivered by noon—before the Allies' started marching into the Ruhr. I arrived at the conference hall a little after eleven o'clock. The lobby was almost empty. The Allied governments were in a private meeting. Only a few Belgian guards hovered round; I could not entrust my message to them. No member of the British delegation was in sight. The sands were running out. The letter in my hands secured the peaceful solution of the conflict. Could I deliver it in time?

I had greatly enjoyed the preceding days, when I had played at making history; I now discovered a sterner side to that game. I very nearly sweated blood. Suddenly I saw a pair of long legs dangling from a club chair in a distant corner of the hall. I walked up to their owner, who sprawled in his chair with the nonchalant insouciance that only a native Britisher can muster. I looked him over. He bore the hallmark of the British civil service. I told him my name, mission, and predicament. I asked him to go into the conference room and hand my letter to the Prime Minister. He sized me up rather suspiciously. "It is really important," I insisted. "A great deal depends on its reaching him immediately." Finally he relented, took the letter, and disappeared. A few minutes later he re-emerged, minus the letter. He had delivered it into the hands of the Prime Minister. I was sure he had done so, but I had no proof. A few more anxious minutes passed. It was nearly twelve o'clock when a Belgian messenger turned up and handed me an official receipt. After all I had managed to be on time and had saved the peace of the world!

In the meantime, Hugo Stinnes had got busy and organized a storm of indignation against the weak-kneed government that had been sold to the British by some foolish experts. He did me the honor of singling me out by name and a good deal of abuse concentrated on me. I do not remember that the government stood up either for me or for the other experts whose advice they had followed. It would not have been difficult. The delegation had been successful: it had prevented the occupation of the Ruhr, and had secured a loan. The financial situation was improved; the dollar fell from 60 to 35 marks. Yet the delegation was greeted in Berlin with a loud chorus of indignation. It did not have the courage to defend itself, or the intelligence to tell the German people that the situation would never have become desperate but for the arrogant intervention of an ignorant businessman. After all, in the field of international politics Hugo Stinnes was but an egotistic dilettante.

Some of my friends high up in the banking world expostulated with me and warned me of Stinnes's enmity. I replied that I felt greatly honored by it. Being a little inflated, I enjoyed the unpopularity with big business that I was encountering. The Chancellor's office and the Treasury supported me loyally; not so the Foreign Office. I had stepped on its toes without knowing it. I had not only had a bright idea, which outsiders are not allowed to have, but I had carried it out, a function generally reserved for the junior members of the service. Career men do not like such intervention. I was not wise enough at that time to anticipate the impending end of my official career. I had been right, and for once I had been successful, a double crime which neither my business opponents nor my foreign office colleagues ever forgave me.

After Spa we had a short, almost quiet, interlude. The mark remained fairly stable. An international monetary conference at Brussels in September 1920 passed off successfully. A little later (December) an experts' reparation conference assembled there. I took part in a good many of its meetings, acting sometimes as translator to the German treasury representative and to the president of the Reichsbank in their private conferences with members of the British delegation. The atmosphere was fairly good, for experts on both sides realized the natural limitations of the problems. They racked their brains to find a solution. We separated for the Christmas vacation, hoping to meet after the holidays and reach some practical conclusion. We never assembled again.

Politics had once more come to the fore; technical advisers were shelved, and another international conference, somewhat on the lines of Spa, was called in London. I was informed ahead of time that I would not form part of the delegation, for Hugo Stinnes had refused to join if I were taken along. Dr. Simons showed his gratitude for my having helped him out of an impasse into which Stinnes had led him by siding with Stinnes. I was naturally indignant, though I should have been jubilant. After all no greater compliment could have been paid me than Hugo Stinnes's insistence on my absence. "If he comes along," he said, "he will sell us to the British." Nobody retorted that Stinnes had tried to sell Germany at Spa, and would continue selling her for about two years more.

The London conference (March 1, 1921) was a gigantic failure. Dr. Simons opened it with a carefully prepared speech which suffered from one great flaw. It did not fit the situation. The Paris plan of January 24 now became an ultimatum. It was dramatically rejected, the returning delegation being greeted with unbounded enthusiasm. A few days later (March 8) a number of German cities were occupied by Allied troops, and not evacuated until the terms of the ultimatum had been complied with. I had been very fortunate in not going to London. I would have been asked to disentangle a hopeless situation, and I certainly would have failed. I would have been branded as a traitor by people who were specializing in economic high treason.

A few weeks afterward the reparation commission finally determined Germany's total liabilities at 132 billion gold marks. She was to issue fifty billion gold-mark bonds and to pay annually during their currency two billion gold marks and 26 per cent of German exports. She had to accept this proposal under threats of occupation of the Ruhr. German resistance collapsed. The Fehrenbach-Simons government resigned.

I was on very good terms with the new chancellor, Dr. Wirth, with whom I had got on very well while he was minister of finance. I thoroughly agreed with his policy of fulfillment. One could not hope to reduce Germany's obligations by trying to wriggle out of them; one had to make serious efforts to carry them out before one could convince the Allies of the need for rearrangement. But the Chancellor's secretariat was reorganized; Albert resigned, and without his support I had no backing. Walther Rathenau became minister of reparation, and as long as Wirth was under his spell, there was no room for a less spectacular adviser.

So I threw up the sponge, realizing clearly that I had not been a success, even though I had been right. I accepted with gratitude, not, however, unmixed with grief, a call to the College of Commerce in Berlin on very favorable terms. Once more I was independent; it seemed unlikely that I would ever be important again.

I was wrong. As adviser to the Chancellor I had had little influence; no party and no economic group was backing me. My advice had often been ignored. I could write reports and memoranda, but I could not even insist on their being read. Now the situation was changed. I had made many contacts; I not only knew who was who, but, what was much more important, who disliked whom. When the more intelligent bureaucrats no longer saw a rival in me, they became confidential. Moreover I was no longer tied down by official secrecy. I could say what I wanted to say, where and when it suited me. The front page of the leading Berlin dailies, the *Berliner Tageblatt* and the *Vossische Zeitung* were at my disposal whenever I desired to air my opinions. Since I did not abuse their hospitality,

I was becoming a favorite with the public. After I had reconciled myself to being a nobody, I suddenly bobbed up as somebody.

## 2. *"Reconstruction"*

When Leon Trotsky visited Munich in January 1905, he stayed with a friend of his, a Russian exile named Helphand, who had settled in Germany, and was playing a part in the left wing of the German Social Democratic party. At that time the party was split into two camps, the revisionists and the orthodox, of which the latter had the better theoretical arguments, while the course of events favored the former. Trotsky greatly admired his friend, who wrote under the name of Parvus, and who initiated him into the mysteries of the concept of the "permanent revolution." In Trotsky's eyes, "Parvus was unquestionably one of the most important Marxists at the turn of the century. He used the Marxist methods skillfully, was possessed of wide vision and kept a keen eye on everything of importance in world events. This, coupled with his fearless thinking, and his virile muscular style, made him a remarkable writer. His earlier studies brought me closer to the problems of the Social Revolution and for me definitely transformed the conquest of power by the proletariat from a final goal to a practical task for our own days. And yet there was always something mad and unreliable about Parvus. In addition to all his other qualities, this revolutionary was torn by an amazing desire to get rich: 'What we revolutionary Marxists need is a great daily newspaper, published in three European languages. But for this we must have money and lots of it.' Thus were thoughts of revolution and wealth interplayed in the heavy fleshy head of this bulldog."*

The outbreak of the 1905 revolution inflamed Parvus's imagination. He rushed back to Russia to take part in these stimulating events. He evidently enjoyed them. He was so carried away by a revolutionary play that he bought fifty tickets for the next performance, which he meant to distribute among his friends. But he was arrested, and these treasures were found in

* George Vernadsky, *Lenin: Red Dictator*, Yale, 1931, pp. 72-3.

his pocket. They greatly puzzled the police, "who did not know that Parvus did everything on a large scale," * and who sent him promptly to Siberia. By 1907 he was back in Germany and Austria. With a man called Lehmann he published a book, *Starving Russia.*

The Balkan wars brought Parvus to Turkey. A number of small Socialist papers had combined and sent him to Constantinople to cover the wars. He did not, if I am rightly informed, limit himself to reporting, but became a successful war profiteer who made money in the grain trade. He repeated this feat in the First World War, when he was said to have earned a handsome fee by negotiating a deal between Danish co-operatives selling butter and pork to German trade unions, who paid in coal. He became a rich man whom inflation rapidly made richer. He used his wealth generously for the party. He loved good living, wine, and women, but as his standards were not very high, he had ample cash to spare for all purposes. He steadily moved toward the right.

The party had always accepted rich men in its ranks, though never quite sure whether to respect or suspect these apostates from capitalism; but it did not like its members' going in for the accursed game of making money. It disapproved of their actions but accepted their donations. A rigid doctrinaire like Trotsky would not compromise with such evil ways. He drifted away from Parvus, even though he had been his spiritual guide and had given him his most fertile idea, "the permanent revolution." He evidently, as is shown by his autobiography, retained an affection for him, even though Parvus continued to pocket the wages of sin and managed to fulfill his dream of wealth.

Yet Parvus never became a bourgeois, either in habits or in outlook. He remained a Socialist and played an influential part in the party as a contributor of articles and of cash. In the second year of the First World War he discovered his mission. It was, as he expressed it in the periodical *Die Glocke,* "to serve as intellectual link between the armed German and the revolutionary Russian proletariat." ** Both the German army and the Russian workers had the same enemy: the Russian autocracy.

* Trotsky, *My Life,* p. 167.
** Vernadsky, p. 140.

Like Lenin, Parvus wanted to use the German army to break Czardom—but unlike Lenin he favored a German victory. It seems likely that Parvus, through his commercial representative in Stockholm, furnished funds to the Bolsheviks. Almost certainly, he was one of the men who organized Lenin's journey through Germany, for he was at that time in a position to approach the German military authorities, through his connections with the heads of the party. Quite naturally Lenin, after profiting from Parvus's good offices, denied all connection with him. It was hard enough to explain the deal with German militarism, without which he could not have got to Russia. The end had justified the means, but he could hardly be expected to acknowledge his obligations to Parvus. The latter remained in Germany and made more money. With the advent of the Socialists to power his influence grew steadily.

I never knew why he suddenly got interested in me. I had always refused to join the party, though I was on friendly, almost intimate terms with some of its members, especially Breitscheid and Hilferding. I had neither a revolutionary temperament nor much sympathy with the petty bourgeois atmosphere in which even its most revolutionary firebrands had to move. "What a pity," Brentano used to say to me, "that the people who are good company are not good society, and the people who are good society are such bad company." My Socialist friends were good company; they became rather pitiful when they got into society. Parvus, however, had no social ambitions. He craved power. One day through a mutual friend he asked me to lunch, though we had never met.

I met a somber, saturnine giant standing on tiny feet, extending to me an incongruously small hand. His face, framed by a sparse beard, topped by a bald cranium, and lit by dark sleepy eyes, looked like a Tartar death mask—he may have been a crossbreed between Tartar and Jew, yet nobody seemed to know whence he had originally come. After a very good meal in his rooms at the Hotel Kaiserhof—later Adolf Hitler's headquarters—he proposed my joining him as publisher of a weekly to be called *Reconstruction*. It was to be published in half a dozen languages. The dream he had divulged to Trotsky was to come true, though by now it had lost some of its earlier revolutionary glamour.

As far as I was concerned, Parvus had struck the right moment. After my short excursion into history making, I was a little bored with purely academic duties. The role of guiding spirit of an influential international organ naturally appealed to me. Yet I had my doubts about collaboration between a Marxist and a Liberal. I was quite sure he did not mean to use me as a decoy—at that time I was highly unpopular with big business, which Parvus evidently meant to propitiate. His ultimate aim, if I read him rightly, was a collaboration of captains of industry with trade union leaders, the two groups jointly to rule the world. He had a sneaking admiration for Hugo Stinnes. He may have dreamed of an alliance with him, the one controlling the capitalist, the other the socialist battalions. I was an outsider in both camps, which perhaps attracted him. We talked things over thoroughly, and finally I accepted. If we could not agree, I could always choose the right moment to resign. In the meantime, I had a platform.

I saw a good deal of Parvus in the first half of 1922. His more puritanically minded party friends regarded him as a wicked libertine. Though one of the ugliest men imaginable, he was supposed to be attractive to women—those whom I met at his parties did not look like sirens. He had taken one of the loveliest country places round Berlin, Schwanenwerder, where he entertained in summer on a sumptuous, rather heavy scale. He meant to give a good time to his old cronies and to their wives, by letting them have the best food, the best drink, and the most expensive cigars money could buy. Yet the atmosphere was thoroughly solid petty bourgeois. The men were frequently well-informed, though not always cultivated, but the women remained what they had been before their husbands had set their feet on the long social ladder. The parties I went to did not justify any aspersion on Parvus's moral character. They were at least as dull as most of those I attended in highly respectable houses.

*Reconstruction*, however, did not prosper. We were always in arrears with our translations, and as we could not issue our German edition before the other editions were posted, we were always behind events. I wrote a good deal about inflation, and my figures were usually wrong, for when my articles reached the reader, the fall of the mark had outdistanced my most pessimistic anticipations. I felt uneasy. I drew a big salary, and nothing was accomplished. I finally told Parvus I could not go on if we did not get a different editor. But as Trotsky had said, Parvus did things on a large scale. He was willing to give the editor another chance and lose a great deal more money. So we separated. We parted good friends but soon got out of touch; I finally lost sight of him. He had, as I heard later on, over-reached himself. Like many a gambler who knew how to profit from inflation—Hugo Stinnes was one of them—he could not turn round quickly enough when stabilization was succeeding. He died a few years later in Switzerland, a relatively poor man.

To have known him was a revelation. He was a figure from a Balzac novel. I owe him a good deal more than gratitude. He gave me a platform at a time when it was very useful to me; and I have ample reason to assume that he had vigorously pulled wires for my benefit behind my back. His influence with President Ebert was considerable; whenever he rang up the President, the latter picked up the instrument without the slightest delay. Parvus wanted me to attend the Genoa confer-ence, from which he expected great things, and at which *Re-construction* should be represented, not by a mere reporter, but by a member of the German delegation—and to Genoa I finally did go.

## 3. *Unmaking History*

The Genoa conference in April and May 1922 was to lay the foundations of a new economic order for Europe. Germany was to participate in it as an equal—a position she could have se-cured at Spa, but for Hugo Stinnes's ill-timed intervention. Bolshevist Russia, not yet recognized by the Western powers, was to be readmitted to the comity of nations on condition that she acknowledge her prewar debts—an assumption not too well founded, repudiation of loans being both a sacred principle and a financial necessity of the Bolshevists.

A few days before the German delegation left for Genoa the chancellor, Dr. Wirth, had asked me to join him as personal adviser. I did not take his invitation very seriously, though I knew that Parvus was very keen on my being on the spot. I went to Meran in the southern Tyrol to spend a short vacation with my wife, who was recovering from a severe illness. After a few days I got a wire requesting my immediate presence in Genoa. Evidently Parvus had pulled wires successfully.

When I reached Genoa, the conference was not yet in full swing. The atmosphere among the German delegates was depressed. They had been in Genoa nearly a week and nothing had happened. Lloyd George had not yet sent for Rathenau, by then foreign minister. Were the Allies preparing another kind of Spa conference, and forming an alliance against Germany?

For the time being, recognition of Soviet Russia was the most pressing issue; her prewar debts overshadowed for the moment Germany's postwar debts. But the Germans had not fully realized this; nor did they comprehend Lloyd George's difficult position. Poincaré had tabooed the discussion of reparations at the conference, though an economic world conference at which the reparation problem could not be openly dealt with was very much like a performance of Hamlet without the prince. Lloyd George was putting a good deal of pressure on his French allies to change their minds. In the meantime he preferred not to meet the German delegation, a fact that greatly perturbed Rathenau and Wirth. They knew that the Allies were having conversations with the Russians. They themselves had had negotiations with them in Berlin but had refused to sign an agreement. Were the Russians coming to terms with the West?

The foreign minister, Walther Rathenau, was the most attractive, and at the same time, the most elusive personality in modern Germany. His father, a prominent engineer and a very able businessman, had founded the German General Electric Company and become very wealthy. The son, trained as an engineer, had succeeded him, and presided with exquisite dignity over shareholders' meetings. One of the most cultivated men of his age, he would have shone rather as a professional writer and lecturer than as a businessman. A very striking figure, tall and broad, he loved to talk, or, rather, to sermonize. A messianic undertone pervaded his utterances, whether he was vaticinating things to come or winding up his address to the Genoa economic conference with a deeply felt, and at the same time histrionic, appeal for peace. He was mystic rather than profound, understanding but not discerning. He sometimes underlined his Jewish origin; yet he suffered intensely from this martyr-dom of his birth. He yearned to be a Teuton. He had renounced with eagerness the freedom from illusion that is part of the Jewish inheritance, and deliberately cultivated the haziness of professional German transcendentalists. He could have sympa-thized with the more abstruse of the Nazi philosophers, had his race not prevented him from joining their ranks; but he would have been horrified at the brutal application of their principles, for his was a world of words, not of deeds.

He had brilliant flashes of practical intuition; the organiza-tion of raw materials for German industries in the First World War was due to him; the military had completely overlooked it, and without it Germany would rapidly have collapsed. Yet he preferred to dwell among abstract conceptions. He was meant to be the gallant outsider, the great columnist, who accepted the happenings of this world with profound understanding, and interpreted them to his more shortsighted contemporaries from the angle of eternity, with a gentle tolerance born of mellow skepticism. Yet he had an irrepressible urge to be in the fray, not because he loved the din of the battle, but because he wanted to be seen. He had little genuine ambition; neither power nor money really attracted him; his one devouring pas-sion was vanity. His sad eyes betrayed his utter loneliness. He disliked the crowd and despised the people after the manner of great philosophers, not so much as the great unwashed, but as the unlearned, who could hardly appreciate the nuances of his resounding verbal output. Yet he could not do without them; they were the echo which brought back to him the sound of his own voice. The revolution had compelled him to take sides; he had become a member of the democratic party, but the party managers did not appreciate him. They preferred lobbyists to seers, and never sent him to parliament. Yet they felt flattered that he was one of them, especially as he asked no favors. They loved to hear him at their party gatherings, not so much for what he said, as for how he said it. Outsiders treated him as one of the great captains of industry of the age. His con-frères in that select fraternity had no great opinion of his de-tached dreamy attitude to business problems, though they were under the charm of a personality that both irritated and cap-tivated them.

Our contacts had been few and pleasant before Rathenau became minister of reparations. They continued so after he had taken office. But we were not meant to do teamwork. He approached all problems as an aesthete and a mystic, while I relied on mere reason. Discussing currency and monetary issues with him was like talking to a dreamer who does not care to understand facts but is in search of material for prophecies.

He had captivated the gifted but inexperienced chancellor Dr. Wirth, and overshadowed his somewhat untidy mind with the monumental spaciousness of his own speculation. As his emissary he had gone to London. Here he had accomplished a far more difficult feat: he had impressed Mr. Lloyd George. The Prime Minister had met all sorts of men and known how to handle them. But here was something novel. A prophet of Israel, meticulously groomed, who discussed complicated practical issues with a sonorous fluidity, evidently gained by an intuitive insight denied to the average mortal. To deal with such a man was a great relief after one had had to do business with tearful municipal councilors and legalistic bureaucrats, which seemed all republican Germany had been able to produce by way of statesmen. But long before the Genoa conference Mr. Lloyd George's enthusiasm had cooled down. The repetitive melancholy of this male Cassandra depressed his springy optimism. His common sense recoiled from the opaque vagueness of this gloomy seer, who took himself and his problems so seriously. Mr. Lloyd George had frankly got bored, though he had been polite enough to keep this feeling to himself.

Rathenau had inwardly recognized the unwisdom of a Jew's being foreign minister when humiliating conditions would have to be accepted. He was a politician who did not believe in politics. Over and over again he had expounded his favorite theme: two hundred businessmen at the head of their concerns held the fate of the world in their hands. He now had to prove it. In this respect he was a genuine exponent of German industrial capitalism, whose leaders asserted the supremacy of economics over politics long after the socialist workingman had got rid of this spook.

I was attached to the conference's second, the financial, commission. Its labors centered on a resolution demanding the balancing of budgets as a preliminary to currency stabilization, for we still lived in the days of financial orthodoxy. President Havenstein of the Reichsbank demurred. In his opinion the main cause of currency depreciation was an unfavorable balance of trade, which could not be corrected by budgetary measures. As his mastery of English was incomplete, I had to translate his unconvincing statements; I toned them down a little. After a private tussle with him, I made him agree to inserting a clause that some countries could not balance their budgets without external help. This concession in the resolution passed by the commission was important; it implied recognition of the need of a foreign loan to Germany.*

After the meeting, the undersecretary at the Foreign Office, von Maltzan, drove me back to our hotel. He told me en route the startling news that on the preceding day (April 16) we had come to terms with the Russians. They had advised the German delegation of their negotiations with the Allies and of the very tempting offers that had been made to them; they preferred, however, to deal with the Germans, who must make up their minds very rapidly.

A section of the German Foreign Office had always advocated co-operation with Soviet Russia. While German workers distrusted the Soviets, some soldiers and diplomats were taking an opposite view. The Western powers were bent on ruining Germany; they had shown themselves equally hostile to Soviet Russia; Russia and Germany should stand together. Their co-operation would neutralize Germany's eastern neighbors; Poland, especially, hemmed in between, would not dare to be aggressive. Brockdorff-Rantzau favored this policy. The Western powers had forced him to sign the peace treaty or resign. They had become his personal enemies; he hoped to get even with them through Russia. Within the Foreign Office, von Maltzan had advocated it; so far, not successfully. The German delegation had gone to Genoa with strict injunctions not to recognize Russia separately and prematurely. Conditions in Genoa, however, favored von Maltzan.

The hopes the Chancellor had put on Rathenau's contact with Lloyd George had not immediately materialized; both he and Rathenau were worried. Rathenau's close business associates were looking for an understanding with Russia, which in their

* The text is in J. Saxon Mills, *The Genoa Conference,* p. 362.

eyes meant contracts; I had met Chicherin, Lunacharsky, and Litvinov at dinner parties in the house of Rathenau's partner, Felix Deutsch. Rathenau himself preferred co-operation with the West, if he could get it. But if the British did not make an offer and the Russians did, the Russian move had to be met. Yet he did not want to act rashly.

A halfhearted attempt was made to get in touch with the British delegation. Mr. White, who handled its Russian contacts, was called by phone but could not be reached. Maltzan, who meant to come to terms with Russia in any case, let it go at that. Finally Rathenau gave in. His intellect disapproved; his mystic fatalism bade him accept the inevitable.

Thus the Rapallo Treaty was signed. Maltzan outlined it to me. He talked about it as if it were a more or less technical matter. He did not realize that the Russians had outmaneuvered him: Germany had not only recognized the Soviets and renounced all claims to her prewar investments and loans in Russia—she had broken the front of the capitalist powers and the unity of Russia's creditors. She had blown up the conference; I found that out next morning.

On my arrival at the finance commission's meeting, an English member, a friend of long standing, took me aside and asked me point-blank, "Were you aware of negotiations with Russia, when we passed yesterday's resolution?" I had no difficulty in convincing him of my ignorant innocence, yet I had to recognize that my personal position had become almost untenable. It could not stand the blend of clumsiness and underhanded astuteness practiced by the German Foreign Office.

I saw the Chancellor and asked permission to leave, since I could no longer be of any use to him. He was greatly perturbed. His main reason for consenting to the Russian treaty was fear that the British had turned round again; he, the Chancellor, could not afford to go home without having achieved something. Moreover, he said, a refusal of the Russian offer would have made the solution of the reparation problem next to impossible. For the Russians were entitled under the Versailles Treaty (Article 116) to add their claims to those of the Allies, and the burden would become unbearable. "An argument," I suggested, "that bears the hallmark of the Foreign Office legal division. Nobody else would worry over this menace. The

Western Allies know that they themselves will never be paid in full; they would not give priorities to the Russians, whose claims must be tacked onto the tail. Since the tail will be cut off anyhow, its length does not make the slightest difference—whether or not that part of the bill which will never be paid is increased by a few dozen billions need not disturb anybody's slumbers." The Chancellor begged me to stay on. He promised to mend his ways and to keep me informed of all future steps.

The German delegation had to get in touch with Mr. Lloyd George. I was suddenly rediscovered and sent to him as the Chancellor's private representative. I saw one of my old friends and told him my object. He went to Sir Edward Grigg, now Lord Altrincham, warning me that I would not get a cordial reception. He was right. I was in for a fierce outburst of indignation. When the storm was over, I meekly said, "After all, I did not do it," and we laughed. The British, naturally, would have liked our canceling the Rapallo Treaty. I favored this solution, for the Russians had deliberately deceived us, and I suggested it on my return. The Chancellor and Rathenau deeply regretted their hasty action, yet it was next to impossible for them to denounce it. My mission was quickly finished. As soon as contact had been established, the Foreign Office took over. Rathenau ignored me.

A little later I went again to the British delegation, this time at Mr. Lloyd George's request. I found him in the garden of his villa, surrounded by cabinet colleagues and members of his staff. They were seated in a semicircle open toward the sea. I was placed on a chair in the center facing them, looking, I suppose, somewhat like a guilty prisoner on whom the judge is about to pronounce sentence.

The Prime Minister addressed me. I doubt whether, in his long career, he had ever spoken to a meeting composed of a single, not very important, individual. He showed none of his familiar platform mannerisms; he did not throw back his head and shake his leonine mane, or raise his voice beyond purely conversational tones. He talked to me as one talks to a wayward child whom one wants to rebuke gently for having strayed from the path of virtue. The child was Germany, or rather the German government; I was only a transmitter. The tenor of his speech was very simple. If the German government did not mend its ways, he would wash his hands of it and Great Britain would withdraw from the Continent.

I was under the spell of his caressing voice, and of that captivating smile which hovered round his eyes. I dimly sensed the underlying gravity of the situation, hidden behind his serene appearance—if the conference failed, Lloyd George's reign was over. Yet it looked to me like a perfectly set stage play. I was the lonely spectator at the preview: the soft spring tints of a formal Italian garden, to which, as everywhere along the Riviera, the palms added a note of theatrical vulgarity, the hoarse crackling of their leaves interfering with the soft murmur of the Mediterranean behind me; and in front of me the little Welshman, the spokesman of the British Empire. He was striving desperately to save his political life by using me as a speaking tube.

I could faithfully report the scene to Rathenau and Wirth. I could impress upon the latter its dramatic character—I did not know, then, that I could not approach the former, for after Rathenau had recognized his fatal mistake, he sulked with those who could have prevented it and would not talk to me. But I knew that even a prime minister cannot unmake history.

On my way out I remarked to Sir Edward Grigg, "I am awfully sorry that I am only a messenger boy who has no right to speak."

"What would you have said?" he inquired.

"I would have expressed my deep regret at the Prime Minister's threat of withdrawing Great Britain from Europe. 'You can do many things,' I would have continued, 'but there is one thing you cannot do; you cannot remove the British Isles.' "

The conference dragged on, though after the conclusion of the Rapallo Treaty it was doomed to failure. Germany's recognition of Russia and her acceptance of Russia's repudiation had strengthened the Soviets' position enormously. They had secured recognition and needed no longer to settle their debts. They were quite willing to make some payments provided they got a large loan in return, but they would not recognize their obligation to do so. The Allies did not expect much cash, but they would not give new money to a customer who did not recognize that he had "hired" old money.

The failure of the conference had greatly weakened the Wirth government. Berlin was sinking into deeper gloom. A few weeks after his return Rathenau was foully murdered. In an outburst of righteous indignation the Chancellor charged the Nationalists with moral responsibility for the crime. "The enemy stands to our right," he exclaimed. Unfortunately the country did not respond to his call; even moderate Nationalists never forgave him for this attack, the justice of which it was hard to deny. I have often wondered what Rathenau would have been able to achieve had he been spared. His own fate proved the futility of his pet theory that economics decide the destinies of the world. The shots of three besotted fanatics pierced it beyond mending. But they made him a martyr and a figure of historic grandeur.

# XVI. The Great Inflation

## 1. The Shadow of Inflation

THE BREAKDOWN of the Genoa conference greatly complicated the reparation question. It justified French fears of the dishonesty of Germany. Stinnes's explosion at Spa could be explained as an attempt by a particular group to sabotage reparations. The Rapallo Treaty seemed evidence of the fickleness of a government of the left, pledged to a policy of fulfillment. Germany, a creditor of Russia, had condoned Russia's repudiation, evidently with the intention of following her example as soon as the opportunity presented itself. As long as these suspicions prevailed, neither a loan nor a moratorium was obtainable.

Naturally the mark declined rapidly; Rathenau's murder accelerated its downward course. The dollar jumped from 317 marks (average June 1922), to 1135 (August) and to 3181 marks (October). The decline of the mark held up both the balancing of the budget and the reparation settlement, which depended on a moratorium or a loan, or a combination of both. Without them, the mark could not be stabilized permanently; on the other hand, without a balanced budget and stabilization, loans or a moratorium were unobtainable.

The issue was quite clear. Could inflation be stopped before reasonable reparation terms were fixed, or had one to wait until claims had been scaled down and a moratorium and loans had been arranged? I had no doubt that stabilization must come first in order to show Germany's good will, and to dissipate the atmosphere of suspicion Spa and Rapallo had created. I understood the social danger of inflation earlier than most people. Already in my doctor's thesis, *The Price Revolution of the Sixteenth Century and the Decay of Spain,* I had depicted the social dislocation bound to follow a sudden serious rise in prices due mainly to monetary causes. I saw in inflation the real world revolution.

Having come from an old banking family, I never felt the mysterious charm of money and banking to which some of my colleagues succumbed, and had turned away to other studies. Yet almost against my will I was always brought back to monetary problems. They emerged from textbooks—where I could have ignored them—and became social issues that had to be faced. First it was the bimetallist controversy—the great depression in the 1880's and early '90's was attributed to a scarcity of gold. Recently I was told that a memorandum I wrote on the subject during my early stay in England had gone to the Board of Trade, and even circulated among the British cabinet. The great gold discoveries in South Africa soon settled that question. To its great relief, the world discovered it had not been nailed to a cross of gold, and cheerfully went about its business. Modern writers on money have been ungrateful to William Jennings Bryan and the American populists: they blazed the trail to plenty by siphoning money in and out of circulation. The Keynesians ought to venerate them as their patron saints.

For a while I succeeded in avoiding monetary problems, not even returning to the fray when Georg Friedrich Knapp startled experts with his *State Theory of Money*. This was an extremely brilliant modernized statement of the medieval concept that the value of money is due to the will of the government, and not to any intrinsic material qualities. The germs both of complete economic nationalism and of central planning are contained in it. (Perhaps it was no accident that John Maynard Keynes busied himself in arranging an English translation of Knapp; some of the correspondence went through my hands.)

German bureaucrats had next to no knowledge of economics. Their training, especially in Prussia, had been exclusively legal. Yet they considered themselves capable of running any department, whatever its problems might be.* The president of the Reichsbank, Dr. Havenstein, was an able adminis-

* After the loss of the colonies the colonial office was out on a limb; its personnel was shifted over to reparations. The most ticklish questions of international finance, such as the settlement of private debts through the clearing system, were entrusted to a jobless administrator who might know how to run a small island in the Pacific, but was like putty in the hands of business experts advising him on these intricate subjects.

trator; he had managed the placing of the war loans very skillfully. He deserved credit for having maintained the level of the mark fairly high, and for having salvaged a considerable gold reserve from the vicissitudes of war. But he did not understand monetary theories, except those of Knapp. (I doubt whether he had studied Knapp, but Knapp had justified in advance the course of policy he was pursuing.) Havenstein attributed the decline of the mark to an unfavorable balance of commerce, which resulted from forces beyond anybody's control —especially if one had to pay reparations—and had little to do with unbalanced budgets. As his foreign colleagues rightly held his character in high esteem, the Allies had imposed a statute on the German government early in 1922 making him practically immovable. Later they discovered with horror that the bank president whom they had meant to protect from the unchaste demands of extravagant governments understood inflation even less than the most wasteful finance minister.

Before the Genoa conference I had published, with the blessing of the Treasury, which had at last grown frightened, a pamphlet on *The Stabilization of the Mark.** The public response was not encouraging. Heavily mortgaged landowners did not mind inflation, nor did manufacturers shy at the reduction of the weight of their debt charges. Labor was not worried. Money was plentiful, and industrial activities expanded; unemployment was declining. As labor was strongly organized, wages followed the rise of prices pretty rapidly. The people who suffered immediately were bondholders, beneficiaries of other fixed incomes, and house owners. For rents had been frozen early in the war and had never been raised. Since many houses were heavily mortgaged, their owners' gains on their debt charges offset their losses on rents.

In the summer of 1922 the Reichsbank had ample means for granting the government a gold loan that could have siphoned out of circulation a large amount of notes and would have provided a revenue for temporarily balancing the budget. Three quarters of its reserve would have sufficed to dominate the market and to make selling marks short very risky. I convinced the Chancellor that temporary stabilization was possible. He had invited a committee of experts to Berlin to discuss it;

* The First National Bank of Chicago arranged an English translation.

Keynes, Vissering, and Cassel were among them. After the customary intrigues I was asked to join them. They proposed the formation of a billion-mark gold pool by all central banks, with which the stabilization of the mark could be amply supported against bear movements. Havenstein refused to participate in the plan; he was willing to risk only a small portion of his gold —he could not see that a small pool would rapidly be exhausted, while a large pool was bound to succeed without loss of a single gold mark. He took me to task for siding with the Allies' experts and breaking the united patriotic front. "It is not my duty," I replied, "to support the unwise policy of an unbroken national front."

I was well aware of the risks of provisional stabilization if it were not soon followed by a moratorium. But I was convinced that the Allied creditors would not dare to foil a successful experiment once Germany's good faith was proved. Poincaré was sure to refuse co-operation in return for a *promise* to undertake stabilization. Would he have dared to upset an actually established equilibrium? The risks of a bold policy were great. In the absence of an alternative, they should have been taken. As usual, caution triumphed. Wirth resigned in November 1922; the new government adopted a timid stabilization plan, conditional on far-reaching prior concessions that the Allies were unwilling to grant.

## 2. *The First Fruits of Inflation*

The heavy industries and their political allies had failed in their direct attempts at invalidating the treaty through sabotaging coal deliveries; they had merely increased the burdens, and destroyed the moral credit of the German government abroad. In the eyes of the French people the republic was ruled by the masters of the Ruhr. Yet like many events in history, inflation in the beginning was not made; it was not the result of deep Machiavellian machinations; it just happened. By and by the shrewder industrialists discovered the political use they could make of it.

Inflation was bound to ruin the Reich. While it would wipe out the government's heavy internal debts and free taxpayers from an unbearable burden, it would raise the weight of the reparation charges; the fall of the mark would continue and finally bankrupt the republic. A bankrupt debtor cannot pay. His creditors must negotiate with him, and in the long run accept a reasonable settlement. When the reparation debt had been wiped out by it, industrialists would stabilize the mark, repatriate their foreign funds, and restore Germany's economic life. Once this government controlled by the unwise masses was financially exhausted, it could be reduced to harmless impotence and easily be robbed of its few remaining assets, especially the railroads. If one could get hold of them, one could fix remunerative prices for the products of the heavy industries, and organize distribution all over the country by the control of rates. Acquisition of the railroads was Stinnes's great dream; it very nearly came true.

Inflation was wiping out the debts of the producers, into whose hands the government was to fall. It put a premium on exports. Rents, frozen at prewar rates, had become almost a negligible item in the workers' cost of living; money wages could remain about 20 per cent below normal standards; in any case they were rising more slowly than prices. Thus at the expense of German house and mortgage owners, German exports to foreign countries were subsidized. Every fall of the mark reduced imports and, for a limited period, stimulated exports. These devaluation profits vanished as soon as internal prices had caught up; they reappeared with the next downward plunge —which could easily be brought about by selling marks. Exchange control was not very strict; it could not be enforced in the occupied areas. The banks shared the blindness of the Reichsbank. They lent marks in ever increasing quantities and at cheap rates to customers who then bought goods, securities, or foreign exchange, and repaid their loans in depreciated marks. Each downward move of the mark made repayment easier. Industrialists borrowed marks in order to sell them, and they sold them in order to depress them. Stabilization would have terminated this highly profitable game. The players might even have been caught "short."

From the industrialists' point of view, inflation was really a blessing in disguise. It enriched the businessmen on whom the economic welfare of the country depended, and freed them from the control of shortsighted democratic consumer interests. The captains of industry were staging a capitalist variant of communist expropriation; they robbed, not their "class enemies," but the broad mass of their own supporters.

What really mattered to them was the welfare of the "enterprise," i.e. of the men who managed it, not of owners or creditors. Bondholders were parasites, bloodsuckers whose claims threatened its stability; shareholders were profiteers whose greed might sap its expanding vitality. A leading banker, presiding at a shareholders' meeting of a prosperous concern, voiced this new concept in almost classic simplicity. "Why should I throw away my good money for the benefit of people whom I do not know?" he replied to a shareholder who asked for payment of dividends from the corporation's ample profits. Entrepreneurs no longer needed the savings of the little man; they financed themselves from the undivided surplus they retained in their own hands, and treated investors as the "idle rich" who had to be "soaked." They vehemently opposed stabilization as premature, using of course their customary patriotic arguments. Their resistance had to be broken. When I had suggested temporary stabilization to Dr. Wirth, he made this very clear to me:

"I'll do it," he said, "but you must go and persuade Hugo Stinnes."

"There is only one way of doing that," I retorted. "Arrest him and try him for high treason."

## 3. The Struggle for the Ruhr (1922–23)

The German government's inactivity toward the inflation danger convinced Poincaré of its complicity with the Ruhr magnates. If the German government could not break them, he would see to it that France was paid. He would occupy the Ruhr and use the great producing area as collateral for deliveries and payments. Once he held it firmly, he would be willing to talk to the Germans. He had not long to wait before the government of Wilhelm Cuno gave him his chance.

Few men could wear a frock coat and a cutaway with greater distinction than Cuno, the son of a petty German official; none had a more charming way of talking and listening. He would have been a superb reception clerk in the most exclusive hotel. Unfortunately perfect manners were his main stock in trade. After Genoa, Cuno had gone to Berlin to voice his indignation to President Ebert at the foolishness of Wirth and Rathenau. The President, greatly perturbed by the Rapallo Treaty, was deeply impressed by him. He singled him out as a future chancellor who might be able to extricate Germany from the many complexities into which Rathenau's somber genius had evidently led her. It was Ebert's gravest mistake. For Cuno knew less of the clash of governments and of the struggle of parties than an average trade union leader who had tumbled into a minister's chair. He was now called to the most difficult task that could confront a statesman.

He and his government saw the danger. Yet so great was their ineptitude that they furnished the French with legal, though pitiful, pretexts for invading the Ruhr. Through purely technical mishaps, due to bureaucratic mismanagement, deliveries fell short on a contract for 125,000 telegraph poles and on 12 to 16 per cent of the coal and coke quota. It was mean of the French to avail themselves of these trifling irregularities; it was criminal of the German government, whose fate hung in the balance, to let them occur, and to provide France with the pretexts she was waiting for. All through the life of the German Republic, somebody bungled and furnished its enemies with good pretexts; the perpetrators were usually men who prided themselves on the clarity of their patriotic vision: Stinnes at Spa, Maltzan at Rapallo, Cuno in the autumn of 1922, and again Curtius in the ill-advised move for a customs union with Austria.

The reparation commission decided, against the British vote, that Germany had failed in her obligations and that the French were entitled to occupy the Ruhr. Great Britain dissociated herself from the enterprise completely.

The news of the invasion sent the mark down from 8,000 marks to the dollar (early in December) to 50,000—a fall of more than 600 per cent. Germany could not fight, though the military organized a "black army"; she had to rely on passive resistance, on cessation of mining, non-co-operation, and finally on highly efficient sabotage. The French could not raise coal with bayonets, but they could and did arrest recalcitrant officials, industrialists, and workers. The German working class, whom nationalists had so often accused of cowardly internationalism, put forth its entire strength against the invaders. It supported, if it did not practice, a large amount of industrial sabotage. In the long run its heroism was of no avail. It received no thanks for it. Thyssen's incarceration and Schlageter's criminal proceedings made them national heroes and martyrs; the silent sufferings of the working class were soon forgotten. Mass misery never lends itself to impressive propaganda.

I used to meet Foreign Minister Rosenberg, General Groener, and other members of the cabinet at the weekly dinners of the Tuesday Society. I never could understand their optimism. They pinned their faith to Anglo-Saxon intervention. Yet from the beginning the struggle was hopeless. Neither Great Britain nor the United States could do more than show their disapproval.

As time went on, the economic activity of the Ruhr became weaker and finally the industrial heart of Germany almost ceased to beat. Most of the workers were on a dole, paid by the Reich with newly printed notes. Circulation had risen from 770 billion marks in November 1922 to 3,530 billions in February 1923. Early in January the dollar had climbed from 8,000 to 50,000 marks; a few days later it fell to 20,000 marks.

For the Reichsbank intervened. It would not pool its gold in a stabilization experiment that was bound to succeed and might have prevented the invasion; it risked it in an attempt that was as foolish as it was bold. Its large purchases of marks reduced circulation; it could even rebuy considerable quantities of foreign exchange from frightened "shorts." Yet this was a purely technical maneuver, for the budget could not be balanced, and the note circulation rose from 3,530 billions in February to 6,500 billions in April. One cannot stabilize a currency and simultaneously increase a deficit. The bank generously discounted commercial bills from industrialists, who sold their proceeds against foreign currencies, which they carefully hoarded. German investments in foreign currency finally amounted to nearly one and a quarter billion dollars.

The Chancellor and his advisers evidently waited for a miracle. Early in February, I had come to the conclusion that sometime in April the end was in sight—the turning point was actually reached on April 18. Within two short months one would have to come to terms with France before the mark should completely run out of hand. I sent a memorandum to Dr. Hermes, the minister of finance; he did not even acknowledge it. I pressed for an interview and he accused me of defeatism. I had prepared a plan for using the railroads as collateral for future payments—this was done later in the Dawes Plan. He waxed patriotically indignant. In May, when defeat was clearly recognizable, the government made a timid, muddled reparation proposal.

After half of its reserves had gone, the bank had to stop intervention. In July the dollar was quoted at over 350,000 marks; its rapid fall offered new opportunities for temporary control. Yet technical intervention was of no use as long as the printing press could not be stopped. The Chancellor had made new, much more concise reparation proposals to France and her allies on June 7; he did not understand that the battle had been lost. The signs of social dislocation were becoming visible everywhere; all political parties took fright; they eliminated Cuno on August 12. He disappeared completely from politics, yet he should always be remembered for the disastrous battle for the Ruhr, the inflation catastrophe, and the birth of the spirit of revenge, which was finally embodied in Adolf Hitler.

## 4. Stabilization

No attempt at stabilization could succeed as long as the drain from the Ruhr continued. Its stoppage involved calling off passive resistance. Gustav Stresemann, the new chancellor, had the courage to liquidate the hopeless adventure.

Stresemann's father had been in the retail beer trade; the son owed his rise in the political world to his remarkable gifts as a speaker, manager, and organizer. In person he was unattractive; his face was pale and pasty, his voice raucous. The pathos of his early oratory, reflecting his literary inclinations, suited neither his speech nor his realistic approach. His political past was not blameless. Once, during an election campaign, I had called him a man of proved unreliability. During the war he had seen eye to eye with the supreme command and had been a rather violent annexationist. He had so compromised himself that the Democratic party, the successor to the old radical-liberal party, refused him admission after the revolution. It was a grave mistake, for in many ways Stresemann was a better liberal than some of the party's most influential members. His somewhat emotional liberalism stemmed from the German literary classics, whose importance for statesmanship he used to stress. His claim to greatness is based on the moral courage he showed in August 1923, when he assumed the responsibility for Cuno's bankrupt inheritance. He had to sue for peace after the war was lost. He had to order cessation of passive resistance as a preliminary to negotiations; he had to accept unconditional surrender.

In the meantime the struggle over stabilization, or rather over the creation of a stable mark, continued. The groups who had opposed timely stabilization were not willing to let go the benefits they had secured. They had succeeded in destroying the Reich's credit and the national currency; they were now planning a new currency, which they meant to control. Their spokesman was Karl Helfferich, whose hatred of the republic had made him the leader of the Prussian Junkers. Inflation had wiped out the debts of farmers and industrialists (3 billion dollars' mortgages and $1\frac{1}{2}$ billion dollars' industrial bonds). Landowners and industrialists were now going to register mortgage bonds on their estates and their plants, and therewith establish a new bank which was to issue mark notes against the bonds, somewhat on the lines of the old national bank system in the United States. The value of the new mark was to be the equivalent of a fixed quantity of rye; its purchasing power would fluctuate with the price of rye and guarantee a fairly stable income to the rye-producing Prussian Junker.

My share in the battle was determined by my relations with Rudolf Hilferding, the new minister of finance, one of the few surviving orthodox Marxist theorists. We had met in our Vienna student days but had not kept in touch. He had given up medicine, though he had served as a physician in the Austrian army, and turned economist. His book *Finance Capital*, published early in the century, had become almost a classic; Lenin and other anti-imperialists had drawn many of their inspirations and a good deal of their substance from it. After the war, he had settled in Germany as editor of *Liberty*, the official paper of the Independent Socialist party, which represented Marxist orthodoxy in its international purity. He possessed an Austrian's capacity both for abstract reasoning and for thoroughly grasping economic reality. This realism made him respect the actual setup of the capitalist world, including the men who managed it. They were important phenomena that one had to understand before one could dispose of them. Their administrative ability, the rapidity of their decisions, the obtuseness with which they ignored ultimate consequences fascinated him; their naïve economic generalizations, whose center was cost of production in a purely physical sense, amused him. He saw in them a kind of adolescent Marxists. He liked to consort with them; he hoped to train and educate them; they on their part, observing his Viennese love of good living, expected to conciliate and corrupt him. Indeed, one could put Hilferding into a very pleasant mood by admiring his wife and by giving him his favorite Viennese dishes; it did not have the slightest effect on his political actions. After the advent of the Nazis he sought refuge in Switzerland and finally in France. The Pétain government surrendered him to the Germans, who put him in a concentration camp, where he died by his own hand.

Hilferding's appointment as minister of finance filled me with dismay. The new government would have to balance the budget and to stabilize the currency. This implied cutting expenditure to the bare bone, and ruthless imposition and collection of new taxes. It was unwise to entrust this task to a Socialist, thus providing the propertied classes with a pretext for calling the heavy taxation imposed by him "confiscation." To defraud a treasury run by Socialists bent on expropriation would seem to them a patriotic duty. I managed to impress my views on some of my Socialist friends, who had never thought of these dangers. We scoured the Reichstag in search of Hermann Müller, the party leader, but we could not find him; in any case it was too late.

Next day the new minister sent for me. I openly told him my misgivings; naturally he did not share them. So I did my best to put him wise. He would have no authority in his department, I told him, if he did not assert himself immediately, reorganize it, and put a single secretary at its head (there were three of them), removing at least one of the other two to a sinecure. "Pick one of the younger clerks as your private secretary and you will have an expert at your disposal on whose loyalty you can rely, for after his sudden elevation his colleagues will not be too kindly disposed toward him. Once the department has accepted you as its master, it will give you cheerful, faithful service. The civil service is accustomed to take orders. Its members are not cut out for the role of impartial advisers." A week later, he sent for me again. He had thought over my suggestions but found them unnecessary. His officials, he said, were giving him loyal support; it would be unfair to remove them. Seeing that I was of no use in Berlin, I went on vacation to my country house in Bavaria. A few weeks later Hilferding sent me an urgent wire. I found him a changed man; he had received none of the help from his staff he was looking for. They were loyal inasmuch as they carried out his instructions faithfully; they liked him against their will, but they did not look up to him. They were born detail-mongers, who knew how to kill an idea by specific objections to it. They had to go outside their departments for inspiration, and they got it from their former head, Karl Helfferich.

I participated in some of the discussions on the "rye mark." I naturally objected to a plan under which the people who had destroyed the state-created paper mark should be the guardians of a privately issued new mark. I soon convinced myself that Hilferding could not solve the problem, and returned to my hilltop. In September the dollar was worth 99 million marks. A little later Stresemann resigned. Hilferding retired. Luther, former mayor of Essen, became minister of finance; he possessed the needed ruthlessness.

The old mark was dead. A new bank of issue, the Rentenmark Bank, was established (October 15, 1923). Its notes were covered by mortgage bonds based on the assets of German agriculture and German industry but were not tied to rye. They appealed to agriculturists, who were refusing paper marks, and who did not mind undermining the hated republic. The issue of the Rentenmark Bank was limited; its management was indirectly turned over to the Reichsbank; yet the new mark could not remain stable unless the budget was balanced by ruthlessly slashing expenditure and by collecting taxes on a gold basis. Balance could not be achieved without stopping the Ruhr subsidies and compelling the magnates to come to terms with the French. But these magnates had a shield—the immovable Reichsbank president, Havenstein.

German industrialists had accumulated 1½ billion dollars in foreign currency. They were not willing to disgorge them as long as the Reichsbank gave them mark credits, with which they bought additional dollars. While the dollar in Berlin was kept stable at 4.2 trillion marks, it rose in Cologne to 11 trillion marks (November 26)—the paper mark had been stabilized at one trillion to one gold mark. Havenstein had recoiled from putting the screw on patriots. He was unwilling to resign, for he was conscious of his mission. For once Providence intervened in favor of the Weimar Republic; he died after a short illness at the decisive moment (November 20, 1923). After a bitter struggle, the republican candidate, Dr. Schacht, was made president against the violent opposition of nationalist and industrial Germany, which favored Helfferich. I pulled wires for Schacht as hard as I could. He was the man of the hour. He turned a deaf ear to the industrialists' demands for credits; he caught the bears in the occupied areas at their own game and compelled them to sell their foreign exchange hoards to him. The bank's gold and foreign exchange reserve rose from below 500 million marks in January to over 900 million marks in October 1924. He completed what since has been called the miracle of the Rentenmark. It was no miracle. The success was due to balancing the budget (which implied abandonment of passive resistance and cessation of all subsidies), to the limitation of the new rentenmark issue, which stopped further note expansion, and to the repatriation of hoarded foreign exchange —the result of putting the screw on private borrowings.

I had insisted that unconditional temporary stabilization would have to precede any reparation settlement, and had maintained that it could be done *temporarily* without foreign aid. It was not attempted at a time when it would have been fairly easy, yet it had been carried through successfully in the most trying circumstances. Its permanent success depended on a reasonable reparation settlement. The Dawes Plan, the first and only sound attempt at solving the reparation muddle, outlined it. My thesis had been proved.

## 5. The Last Phase of Inflation

One morning I arrived in Munich on my way to the country. While strolling outside the station, I ran into an acquaintance, a charming woman, who almost embraced me in public. "Do give me something to eat," she said, "I am famished. I went to the country," she explained, "with a supply of five-dollar bills. Yesterday the mark broke so rapidly that nobody could change one for me. I had no dinner; I took the earliest train to town this morning; I am waiting for the banks to open, and hope that they have enough marks to change a five-dollar note. I would have had to go without breakfast, if I had not met you." During the late phases of the inflation such experiences were common. Anybody who had foreign exchange was rich, provided that his money was in sufficiently small denominations to make an exchange possible. Germany was invaded by hosts of profiteers, by no means all of them from countries with high standards of solvency. Czechoslovakian, Italian, and even Austrian currencies circulated freely; they possessed a fairly high purchasing power when converted into marks. Germany was a rapidly decomposing corpse, on which the birds of prey were swooping down from all directions.

We had rented a farmhouse in Bavaria, where my wife lived most of the year, and where I used to spend my vacations. We kept one or two cows and had a vegetable garden; fields and pastures were leased. Our neighbors were farmers, owning isolated holdings on the top of hills similar to ours. They depended mainly on dairy farming and the sale of young livestock; they grew few crops. Each of them possessed a piece of timberland, and in the winter the young men went lumbering in the state forests. These farmers did not suffer badly; they had got rid of their surplus crops against cash, in order to make a few purchases, and to pay taxes, which were not very heavy. They had been accustomed to take in a few summer boarders, who helped them to eat up their surplus stuff. Now if they liked them, they let them come again, and even accepted their cash. But they would not sell anything against marks, though they did a lively trade by way of barter. For a pair of old flannel trousers or a few leather straps we could buy grain to feed our cows. Moreover we were in a privileged position. My wife had a small sterling income of her own, and at that time I was very much in request as a contributor to American papers. We always had a few legally acquired dollars or pounds to spare. My wife, living on the farm all the year round, was on friendly terms with the neighbors. They visited her and asked her to their family feasts, whereas I, being only a summer guest, remained a "city dweller," quite a low type of human being. They were more than eager to sell goods against foreign currency, the acceptance of which was forbidden—but nobody cared any longer for the law. In these faraway mountain villages, every well-to-do peasant followed eagerly the quotation of dollars, of Dutch florins and of Czech crowns. He was not so keen about sterling, for the conversion of a pound sterling, being equal to four dollars, into marks represented a larger transaction than he was willing to go in for. In these last stages inflation seemed to affect even the animals; cows no longer gave surplus milk, and chickens refused to lay eggs, as the peasants cut their output down to their home needs. Goods were becoming much more valuable than money.

Shopkeepers were never sure of covering the cost of replenishing their stocks, irrespective of the prices at which they sold the goods; many goods had completely disappeared. Factories were no longer interested in selling to the home market against money, the value of which was rapidly vanishing. Foreign goods were scarcely obtainable. Manufacturers were permitted to acquire foreign exchange in order to buy raw material abroad for keeping their plants and their workers employed; mere consumers were disregarded. Shopkeepers treated their customers almost as enemies—they deprived them of stock which could not be replaced. Buying, like kissing, went by favor. In the late summer of 1923 the mark had ceased to function even in these rural areas.

Artisans and tradespeople in our village were very much worse off than farmers, since they could not get sufficient food from their small plots of land. Raw materials were scarce, and they had few opportunities for making goods. One day the village authorities approached my wife. A truck of potatoes, the village winter supply, had arrived at the local station. Since ordering the load, prices had risen so rapidly in paper marks that the village had not enough cash to pay for it. Would she lend them a couple of pounds or so and ensure the potatoes' being unloaded? Naturally she gave them the desired amount, and the village hurriedly raked in its potato supply.

In the big industrial cities no one was self-supporting. Yet people were no longer willing to carry on their transactions in marks, especially as they frequently encountered technical difficulties in getting a sufficient amount of them. Big industrial concerns made their own money to pay wages with it; it was accepted by the local business community. Municipalities printed notes, which circulated freely within their confines but were not valid in neighboring areas. Emergency money to the amount of 200 billion paper marks was in circulation. In July 1923 the cost of living index had risen 39,000 times. An unskilled metal worker, whose weekly wages before the war (1912) had been 24.44 marks (6 dollars) was getting only 73 per cent of his former income's purchasing power: his weekly wage amounted to 531 million marks in September 1923.

Workers were not the chief sufferers. Thanks to strong trade unions, their wages were regularly revised upward, though generally with a lag. In the earlier stages, before the Ruhr invasion, unemployment was low, as it always is during the inflation upswing. For this reason labor had not strongly insisted upon stabilization. Accounting was becoming a nightmare. Before the war a weekly wage of ten dollars was written in two numerals; it now took seven or nine. An army of clerks had to be recruited, and as many of them were inexperienced, business became very involved—prices were being quoted in millions, a habit that continued in Austria long after inflation had stopped. Banking activities were feverish. Most banks added new floors to their buildings to house new employees. Yet they were no longer keen on getting customers. The handling of an account of 100,000 marks was expensive when its gold value had shrunk to 25 dollars, so they asked depositors, frequently in rather peremptory language, to take away their accounts. Wages were adjusted at least twice a week according to dollar quotations; so were salaries of civil servants. Most of them asked for cash and rushed immediately to the shops to buy such goods as were available. A few hours later the mark might have gone down another 100 per cent, and the purchasing power of their salaries might have been halved. Those who had spare cash or credit gambled in stocks. As shares were supposed to represent stable physical values of a tangible nature, such as factories or stock piles, their quotations followed, and sometimes even outran, prices. A good many members of the middle class made a precarious living by gambling on the exchange. One of my colleagues was regularly late for his eleven o'clock class. He had to telephone instructions to his brokers before the exchange opened, and he rushed back to the phone as the clock struck twelve to give new orders. Big industrialists like Stinnes were habitually borrowing money from the banks, with which they bought up shares, enterprises, properties of all sorts, and created huge combines, many of which, being without internal cohesion, were mere gigantic junk shops.

Universities and colleges were overcrowded. Tuition fees had been but slightly raised; the only actual expense was the cost of transportation; fares were frozen and raised only slowly. For the time being house property had little value. Rents had been "ceilinged" early in the war, and had not been moved; by and by they amounted to next to nothing. Notwithstanding a housing shortage, little new construction was under way. Rents of new houses were not controlled, and were by comparison exorbitant, for building costs had gone up with prices and wages. The shortage of private dwellings had led to severe rationing. In order to hire an apartment, one had to have a ration card issued by local authorities. When I was called to Berlin as adviser to the Chancellor, I had not looked into the housing question. I had assumed that, being appointed to a high office, I would have no difficulty in finding a suitable apartment; but the housing authorities were local and did not take the slightest notice of me. Yet I was very lucky; an elderly widowed banker, who owned a beautiful house in one of the best parts of Berlin, gave me a small apartment in which I lived comfortably for nearly three years. Thus he was spared compulsory tenants, who might have been less desirable, and I had the advantage of a private home at an almost nominal rent. But for the housing shortage, a large part of the smaller "idle rich" would have gone to the wall completely. The value of their investments, insurances, and life annuities had been wiped out; apartments and furniture were often enough the only wealth which remained to them. They generally lived by subletting, payment to house owners being purely nominal. House owners defended themselves as well as they could by making no repairs, or by insisting on the tenants' paying for them. As most apartment houses were heavily mortgaged, owners defrauded creditors while tenants defaulted on them. Owners of mortgage-free homes who had let them to tenants fared worse. They either had to pay for repairs or let their property go to rack and ruin, and they had no creditors whom they, in their turn, could defraud.

The so-called *rentiers* were almost wiped out—though they got a pitiful compensation later on. By 1925 their real income had fallen from over 2 billion dollars (in 1913) to 300 million. They were not the victims of socialism, for the working class, too, had lost heavily, since their savings and their social insurance contributions had vanished (the reserves of the social insurance institutions had been invested in government bonds and mortgages). Their destroyers were the producers, the active businessmen. They had successfully expropriated investors; they had secured additional "tangible values" (they called them values of substance), such as land, houses, stock piles, shares, by systematically making new debts, which they paid back in rapidly deteriorating marks. Many of the huge combinations they had assembled disintegrated rapidly when the Reichsbank, under its new leadership, refused them the credits with which they had been in the habit of exploiting their fellow capitalists.

When it was all over, the social structure of Germany had been profoundly altered. The steady middle class, closely connected, though not identical, with the professions, was proletarianized at a time when the rising working class ceased to consider itself proletarian and was ready for incorporation with the middle class. It was a genuine revolution, far more devastating than the political collapse in the autumn of 1918 had been.

# XVII. Indian Summer

## 1. Pomp and Power

THE STABILIZATION of the mark and the acceptance of the Dawes Plan terminated the troublesome postwar period. From 1924 to 1929, the world experienced a respite. It looked as if it had really gone back to "normalcy." These five years might be called the Indian summer of the old European order. They were pleasant years for me. My work at the college kept me busy, but not so busy as to preclude other activities.

The downfall of a monarchy is bound to upset the social life of its capital. A court, the center of sumptuous spending, disappears, and with it vanish all those who for various reasons were attached to it. This shrinkage was most painfully visible in Vienna, where the wealthy feudal aristocracies of the many colorful nations that comprised the empire had outvied the dynasty. The old emperor had led an almost spartan life—the short reign of his successor covered only a few war years—but the nobility had pursued a life of stately magnificence in the spacious palaces they inhabited in the winter months. All these splendors had gone. A few members of the old generation still clung to their Vienna residences, if they could afford their upkeep; the majority stayed in the new capitals, willing, if they were intelligent, to sacrifice titles and position in order to retain property and influence. Vienna died with its court and its cavaliers. To those who had known it of old, it had become a city haunted by the ghosts of a dead past.

Berlin was more fortunate. The old Prussian court had been a soldiers' court, in which an impecunious lieutenant, even from a provincial regiment, might expect to cut as good a figure as an imperial count from one of the new provinces. William II had tried hard to outdo Vienna and London by pompous splashing. He lacked the elements for success. Rich South German or Saxon peers preferred their Munich or Dresden courts, where they could shine more exclusively and at less cost than in the more expensive Berlin climate, where they had to compete with a new plutocracy. Only Silesian and to a lesser degree West-phalian and East Prussian magnates were rich enough to live on the scale of their Viennese compeers. Few Prussian Junkers could afford a town house in Berlin—never a palace. They really did not care very much for the cultural pleasures of a sophis-ticated metropolis.

Part of Berlin society, whether admitted at court or not, had always been bourgeois. In the first half of the nineteenth cen-tury a few brilliant Jewish hostesses received intellectual Ber-lin in their usually very modest salons. Peers and gentry, soldiers and statesmen flocked there and connected them with the royal court. Under William II money had come into its own. Leading bankers and foremost industrialists—sometimes ennobled—were competing in entertainment with the relatively small number of wealthy aristocrats who thought it worth while to waste cash on urban, purely social entertainments. Most preferred to spend it on their estates, where they exercised their influence on William II when he came to shoot their stags, and they often managed to "bag" a few ministers they did not like. All this had gone with the revolution. Only bankers and industrialists remained on the stage. Peers and Junkers retired to their country places.

The new men knew little about social life. In the earlier phases of the republic they despised it as the main occupation of the "idle rich"; evening dress was considered taboo. This spartan renunciation of festive garb soon vanished, except among the hangers-on of the Russian Embassy. At one of its big dinners (it was the only embassy that went in for social mass production) some two hundred guests might be assembled. Among a crowd in full social war paint a few handfuls of gen-uine "comrades" showed their contempt for bourgeois society by disporting themselves in Russian blouses or open shirts with turned-down collars. The setting would be brilliant, the long table laid with lovely china, silver, and cut glass dating from Imperial days. Huge blocks of ice filled with caviar, sturgeon, and sterlet, and plenty of vodka started the feast. The Russians seemed convinced that bourgeois society was corrupt and could be bought cheaply with these delicacies. I almost shared their opinion when I saw professional anti-Reds, whom only official duty compelled to attend, washing down huge lumps of caviar with copious drafts of vodka, their eyes brimming with ecstatic joy.

In the absence of a national center, social life crystallized round the embassies. Here the Westerners naturally set the tone. One might almost say that they educated the new republic in the use of Western standards. Ambassadors, however, found no well-organized society with which they could immediately take up contacts according to the protocol. Everything had to be improvised. When Lord D'Abernon arrived in Berlin, Ludwig Stein, leader writer of the *Vossische Zeitung,* met him at the station. He offered him his good offices and proposed to put him in touch with anybody he might like to meet. Having secured a courteous reply, he set to work and told a number of people that Lord D'Abernon wanted to meet them in his (Stein's) house, and started to give a number of luncheons for him. In this way Stein became an important "society broker," and served a really useful purpose.

Few members of the government had social training or ample private means. This being so, official life tended to become bureaucratic and departmental. The various ministries entertained under the leadership of the Foreign Office, which naturally delighted in the resumption of some of its earlier functions. A few private houses began to fill the gaps left by the collapse of the old order. By then bankers were outdone by industrialists, who in many ways had been the beneficiaries of the revolution. One or two of the hostesses, like Frau Deutsch, wife of Felix Deutsch, the head of the General Electric, set the style the new times demanded. She used to mix her guests irrespective of the protocol, trying to give each a chance to enjoy himself by meeting people he would not have encountered elsewhere. When an ambassador, oversolicitous for his country's honor, once complained to her about not having been given the seat he was entitled to, she expressed her regret at his feeling slighted and told him he need not come again.

The troubles through which Germany was passing attracted an uninterrupted flow of bankers and financiers to Berlin, making new investments or looking after old ones. The Dawes Plan had domiciled a number of financial experts in Berlin who were to watch over its execution. They enjoyed diplomatic privileges and, being well paid, could afford to indulge in diplomatic hospitality. The many new states born of the peace treaties were eager to show that they counted for something, and went in for a good deal of display. As governments changed rapidly, the newcomers and their wives had to be drawn into the social network. And as most members of a defeated government had a good chance of coming back, the wiser embassies did not strike them off their visiting lists. A few exotic figures had emerged from nowhere, who had amassed a pile in the inflation and had not lost it during stabilization. They went in for sumptuous, indiscriminate entertaining to celebrate their arrival and to make sure that they would stay.

An interesting personality, Antonina Valentin, had succeeded in establishing an important center. She was a Galician Jewess, no longer quite young, without any particular background. She did not aspire to the role of political siren, to which so many simplifiers of history have ascribed the fall of the French Republic. She merely used what might be called a superb instinct for current events to gather round her people engaged in shaping, or at least discussing, them. In the semiobscure privacy of her paneled drawing room, politicians of all sorts met newspapermen, diplomats, or business acquaintances and held their ears to the ground without having to squat on the floor. Deals could be prepared that would not have prospered had publicity shortened the period of their incubation. It was here that Gustav Stresemann practiced some of the steps in high statesmanship that Lord D'Abernon was teaching him.

President Ebert had learned the social tricks high office demanded very rapidly, though his beginnings had been unpromising. I remember a pleasant small dinner in the house of a new minister where he enjoyed himself thoroughly but too long. This was hard on a few old-time diplomats, whose high professional standards forbade them to depart before him. At that party, I sat next to Frau Ebert. She spoke longingly of the good old days in Bremen where she and Fritz had had a little house and she had to whitewash its steps. She certainly was not seduced by the pomp of power.

The old field marshal, who succeeded Ebert, owed his election to the Communists. They had refused to throw their vote to the republican candidate, Wilhelm Marx, whose election they could have secured. I naturally voted for the latter. After the meeting of the Committee of Inquiry, I distrusted Hindenburg. I did not doubt his sincerity, but I doubted both his motives and his intelligence. I probably underrated the latter. He had that instinctive cunning which border populations acquire in the long course of their tortuous history. He had, moreover, that facile Lutheran faith which throws the responsibility for everything one does on the Almighty. On the night before election day I tramped the streets of Berlin as one of the huge republican host, yelling with them at the top of my voice, "Vote Marx, vote Marx," rhythmically tapping the pavement with my heels. Marx was a liberal Roman Catholic, a worthy son of the Rhineland. His candidature was a compromise in which the conflicting forces shaping the new Germany were finally united. Our opponent was a mere symbol, the symbol, seemingly, of a dead past. But as has happened before, the hands of the dead past strangled the hopes of the future.

Hindenburg contented himself with official functions. His great age gave him ample excuse for keeping out of a world which was not his own. He had personal dignity, and his palace naturally became a center from which a sort of etiquette radiated. He kept up private contacts with old friends and cronies, aided and abetted by his son, whose implication in somewhat shady deals contributed to the fall of Brüning, who was inadvertently uncovering them. The foundations of a "camarilla" were slowly being laid.

Hindenburg's secretary, Meissner, had managed to turn a purely clerical position into a high office with the rank of secretary of state. Assisted by an attractive wife he had established a salon. It became a very important political clearinghouse, where gossip, intrigues, and stock exchange news were cleverly shuffled by the adroit hands of its master. I never entered it. As long as I was a private individual, I could indulge my archaic instincts for political cleanliness. Meissner, who played a sinister part in bringing the Nazis to power, served Ebert, Hindenburg, and Hitler with the same flexible loyalty.

Berlin had always been an intellectual and cultural center. Though its university no longer dominated German thought, as it had done in Hegel's days, it still boasted a number of great personalities, Harnack and Meinecke among them. Its natural science department, and the Kaiser Wilhelm Institute, where Einstein was at work, were world famed. Berlin had never excelled in music and painting as Vienna and Paris had done, but its standards, always very high, were well maintained. In literature, or rather in the dramatic arts, it led. Its radical, and at the same time selective, experimentalism was not so much tied up with financial considerations as was the stage in New York or London. The average German was a regular theatergoer. The theater meant to him what cricket meant to Victorian England, and baseball to the United States. The Berlin public was unemotional, unlike its Viennese counterpart; it went to the play in a stern, judicious frame of mind, given to dissection rather than to enjoyment. In Max Reinhardt it had found the ideal producer, who managed to combine an appeal to its traditional literary values with loving attendance to the realistic details its cantankerous spirit demanded.

The capital of the republic had lost both its court and its provincialism. It became a truly international city with something of the American go and splash in it. It was the meeting place of East and West. Vienna had failed in its historic mission of reconciling Slav and German; Berlin had become its heir. By now it was much more a question of finding a common meeting ground between opposing social creeds than between nations. It was hard to enter the Soviet state and even harder to see things there visitors were not meant to see. Berlin housed a strong Soviet agency, for the most fervent hopes of Moscow converged on the return of the Marxist homeland into the fold of true believers. The German Communist party, strong in numbers and fervor, was led by a particularly dumb lot; they were mere speaking tubes through which the Moscow masters issued commands. For that very reason one could gather Moscow views from them as one can study a face from its reflection in a mirror. After Rapallo there was a kind of short-lived honeymoon-liaison which, owing to incompatibility of temperaments, never led the parties to the altar. Yet one met leading Russians all the time. German structural industries, which hoped for large orders, were on much more friendly terms with them than even leftist Socialists.

The Weimar Republic was extremely tolerant. One could have lunch with the Chancellor, dinner with a rampant Nationalist, and then go and spend half the night with Reds, pinks and lesser shades of revolutionaries without becoming suspect. Diplomats, semidiplomats, and plain travelers loved this free and easy city. The Junkers had often denounced Berlin as a modern Sodom, a cesspool of iniquities—and such were certain quarters to which they used to flock in masses during the annual agricultural festival. In general the city was physically clean, with a more daring, open-minded morality than that of other metropolises. Foreigners enjoyed a place where they were not held in check by the traditional taboos of their own countries, and where a new society had not yet crystallized its own; they, and the natives associating with them, had a merry time. Berlin did not compete in organized yet temperamental sexual laxity with Budapest, which in the eyes of many adventurous-minded Anglo-Saxons was the attractive red light district of Europe. In Berlin amateurs prevailed over professionals.

Sometimes this reborn metropolis did seem to justify the German ditty:

> You are raving mad, my child,
> To Berlin you go,
> Where all the madmen are,
> There should be your show.

In the late twenties, social reformers rightly tried to provide fresh air for the cooped-up urban masses. So Berlin's Lord Mayor approached his colleague of the City and inquired how the week-end movement in London had been organized. It must have been very hard for His Worship to compose a suitable reply. Whatever its tenor may have been, Berlin set to work. Grants in aid were offered for building summer cottages; but they had to be constructed in such a way as to preclude their use in winter.

I did not plunge deeply into the social life. I am not in my element at large parties, and the absence of my wife during most of my Berlin stay handicapped me. She disliked city life and was repelled by some of the crudities of Berlin. Yet from time to time she did turn up for a few weeks, and we went in for a social splurge. I continued to live in a small, old-fashioned four-room apartment, where I regularly did a good deal of intimate entertaining with the help of an excellent housekeeper cook.

I had the entry to the Western embassies; I knew nearly all the leading politicians, most of the civil servants, the bankers, some industrialists, and last but not least, the intellectuals within and without the colleges. Scarcely a week passed without a visitor from abroad presenting himself; and thanks to the help of Grata Schlomka, my devoted secretary—she committed suicide when the Nazis drafted her into a road-building battalion—I had a system through which I could put our guests almost automatically in touch with the persons they wanted to see. Some of my younger English and American colleagues did part of their work in my institute for finance. I was leading a pleasant, and as it then seemed, a useful life.

I was near the center of events, a privileged spectator, yet sufficiently detached; I had no political ambitions. I am endowed with a goodly portion of vanity, but it has fortunately been held in check by indifference, shyness, and common sense. Only once I consented to stand for the Reichstag, to oust the sitting member of my own Democratic party, Carl Friedrich von Siemens, one of the most prominent industrialists. He no doubt shared his family's cultural liberalism, but I knew by then that it did not matter to which party big industrialists belonged; their actual achievements had shown them to be lacking in political sense—in this respect they were far inferior to the Junkers.

Siemens was very unpopular with genuine liberals. Yet his great wealth, his position, and his name had induced the party managers to nominate him, and nomination in Berlin meant election. I never expected to be nominated. But I hoped to split the party to such a degree that it would prevail on Siemens to decline nomination, if I too would withdraw. My supporters were eager, decent, very naïve, and quite unbusinesslike. We got a really good licking. However, I spoiled Siemens's fun at playing the game of politics. He did not stand at the next election. He preferred to accept the presidency of the Reich railways, which were very good customers of his own firm. Public opinion in Germany was very indiscriminate. It yelled corruption whenever a prominent trade unionist profiteered on the stock exchange by a tip from some unsavory acquaintance. It never thought of insisting that big business should be disinterested. It did not expect the chairman of a government-owned enterprise to retire from concerns with which it was likely to do business.

## 2. *Williamstown*

Twice, in 1924 and 1926, I visited the United States as guest of the Institute of Politics in Williamstown. The first time, I gave a series of lectures on "The Crisis of European Democracy." They were published in German and in English. At that time of comparative quiet I diagnosed some of the impending changes much more clearly than I did a few years later. I pointed out the serious dislocation among the powers brought about by the war; I used in this connection the terms, "have" and "have-not" nations, which later became so popular. I was not greatly worried about the territorial losses which Germany had suffered; as a Westerner, I did not share the Easterner's hatred of Poland, and as a democrat of long standing I had to recognize that German rule in Alsace had been a failure. But I was profoundly disturbed by the economic consequences of breaking up the Habsburg empire into relatively small states. Their nationalism was bound to prevent any intelligent economic co-operation. The highly developed small states of western and northern Europe have been among the torchbearers of modern civilization; their less advanced counterparts in the east and the south have preferred to generate heat rather than light.

The inversion of the international balance sheet had made an impoverished European world the debtor of a rapidly enriched United States: it raised very grave issues. I stressed these points during my second visit when I presided over a round table. I gather from the records that for once I was far ahead of the show: I predicted as inevitable the impending fall of prices. Most experts contradicted me; unfortunately I was right.

The institute in Williamstown has played a very important part in international affairs. Under the guidance of the late President Garfield and of Professor Walter McClaren, both of

Williams College, it awakened an interest in foreign affairs all over the United States. It was the forerunner and pattern of the many institutes dealing with such problems that sprang up later on. It enabled European visitors to get in touch with those strata of American public opinion that were interested in foreign affairs. Some were misled by the enthusiasm they met. They did not recognize that their public was an elite and did not represent the outlook of the average American.

I was fortunate inasmuch as I had known the West and the Middle West during the war. I had sufficient contacts all over the country to get into close touch with all sorts of audiences. The foreigner who is on a speaking tour in the United States will learn much more about them by addressing Kiwanis and Rotarian clubs in small towns than by talking to highbrow organizations at universities or in urban centers. I had, moreover, found out long ago that the only way to bring home to an average American audience the true inwardness of European issues was through one's willingness to learn from it the essentials of American life. I had never before lived in New England, though I had of course visited Harvard and Yale. Williamstown opened my eyes to its unique though limited beauty, and brought me into contact with many prominent Americans whose friendship and sympathy I have been allowed to enjoy ever since.

The outcome of these tours was several books on America, which had a great success in Germany; some were translated into English, French, and Spanish.

My lectures centered in the problem of the permanent minority. How can a racial, religious, or social minority that has no hope of ever becoming a majority, and is permanently subject to the will of a majority, be protected? The various means hitherto devised had not been very satisfactory. In the last resort, its security depends on the moderation and tolerance of the majority. Yet the danger that a minority menaced by an intolerant majority might violently seize power and institute a dictatorial government was always present. The sudden advent of democracy in Central Europe, and its strong socialist tendencies, made me fear a dictatorship of reactionary groups, especially as the Bolshevists and their admirers had justified, not to say glorified, the use of violence by minorities. During the era of "permanent prosperity" that Americans were telling mankind was within its reach, these somewhat pessimistic views seemed groundless.

By 1927 I had become a member of the European Center of the Carnegie Foundation. Twice a year we held meetings in our hotel in the Boulevard St. Germain in Paris, which our excellent secretary, Earle Babcock, had organized on the basis of luxurious comfort. Some of my colleagues, Count Carlo Sforza, Gilbert Murray, Alfred Spender, A. G. Gardiner, Henri Lichtenberger, and Senator André Honorat (founder of the Cité universitaire) were very distinguished men, and their friendship was very valuable. But our work was disappointing. We were supposed to advise the New York trustees on policies to be followed in Europe. We often saw them announced in the papers before they had ever come under our consideration. I disliked responsibility for acts I was not cognizant of. Our president, Nicholas Murray Butler, did not fancy the old-fashioned constitutional scruples I expressed. I fell into disgrace with him, even though I had but gently opposed him.

The world is fortunately not run by original thinkers, though their thoughts may revolutionize it fifty years after their deaths, when they are no longer applicable to existing conditions, as had happened with Karl Marx. Nicholas Murray Butler was well aware of this fact. He carefully kept away from anything smacking of originality. But he was a marvel. He used to address our annual meeting for a short hour or so, treating us to facts we all knew by heart, and to ideas that might have sounded novel in our college days. Yet there we sat spellbound, while in well-chosen words and carefully structured sentences he told us nothing worth listening to. He managed to get it cabled all over the world and had it reprinted in innumerable addresses, which the foundation distributed in great quantities, and which everywhere were received with respect. He was probably the greatest platitudinarian who ever lived. In the intellectual field he was the leading representative of mass production on the running belt, just as Henry Ford was in the industrial sphere.

## 3. Irrational Rationalization

The Dawes Plan put Germany under a kind of receivership. A young American, Mr. Parker Gilbert, was appointed reparation agent; for a few years he became the central figure in international economics. The success of the plan depended on a regular inflow of foreign capital to Germany, for the country needed new equipment on a gigantic scale to fulfill its treaty obligations and to satisfy the needs of its people. If this borrowing were overdone, Germany would have to default either on her reparation payments or on her private debts. The authors of the plan had undoubtedly foreseen this and were prepared for a potential crisis. Its outbreak would inevitably lead to new international arrangements, which would scale down payments sufficiently to prevent its recurrence—but it would hardly enhance the reputation of the reparation agent. One could not expect a brilliant young man to wait for it and to wreck a great career deliberately because the Allies at Versailles had not been wise enough to make reasonably definite financial arrangements. Mr. Parker Gilbert attempted to put on the brakes.

In those halcyon days American businessmen were rather pro-German. They loved to come to big German cities, especially to Berlin, adoring the combination of modern sanitary plumbing with effective personal service. To many an American, especially to newspapermen, the bar of the Hotel Adlon seemed the hub of the universe. Parker Gilbert was an exception to this rule. He spent his working hours in Berlin, but he preferred Paris. He established few of those friendly personal relations that most of his assistants found useful and pleasant during their long stay in Berlin. He wrote excellent scathing reports; their documented criticisms naturally irritated German officialdom; they would have hurt much less had they been amicably discussed round a luncheon table. At one time Treasury and reparation agent were not on speaking terms.

Fortunately Professor Edwin Seligman was then visiting Berlin. His reputation had penetrated even to the permanent officials of the ministry of finance. I invited the minister, Dr. Köhler, to a luncheon with Seligman; he was delighted. I asked him whether he and the heads of his department would mind sitting down to lunch with the reparation agent and his staff, who naturally wanted to meet their famous compatriot. Politicians are generally good mixers; he accepted. Mr. Parker Gilbert was in Paris, but his chief assistants turned up and met again their opposite numbers. Thanks to the genial personality of Edwin Seligman, the party was a general success.

The Dawes Plan had entrusted to the Reichsbank the supervision of all financial operations necessary to keep the mark stable. Thanks to the moodiness of the Treasury, Dr. Schacht, the bank's president, had established close relations with Parker Gilbert and had concentrated a good deal of the reparation business in his own hands.

I had known Schacht for many years. His family was of Danish origin; yet he managed to look like a compound of a Prussian reserve officer and a budding Prussian judge, who is trying hard to copy the officer. His high wing collar, his upturned mustache, his curious stiff gait, the parting of his hair, his flattish face, and the pince-nez sitting on an upturned nose made him an excellent target for cartoonists. He was smart enough to understand their usefulness to him. He was a curious blend of shrewdness and naïveté. Both his ambition and his vanity were boundless; his imagination was fervent but rather hazy. In his younger days he had been deeply interested in colonial affairs, yet his colonialism was essentially romantic. He looked upon the world as Hjalmar Schacht's particular oyster, and was very sensitive to public criticism. Having clashed with many strong and ambitious personalities in the German banking and business world, he was full of resentment against colleagues who had at some time outdistanced him. Once he had arrived at the head of the central bank, he gloried in being their boss. His knowledge of monetary theories was not profound; he knew that his opportunist inclinations might lead him into difficulties. For this reason he was always willing to take advice—in private. I did not stand in his way, and I got on with him extremely well. I never attacked him in public, but I frequently argued with him in his office. Being hopelessly egocentric, he did not always foresee the impression his measures would make on the public. One day I said to him laughingly, "You do not need my advice about what you ought to do, but you had better let me tell the reasons why you are doing it."

Schacht favored an inflow of foreign capital, but he tried to limit it to purely private business enterprises. He objected unsuccessfully to borrowings by public bodies, who often spent them indiscriminately on public works. In this era of permanent prosperity, the capital markets of the world, especially of the United States, were overflowing, while rates of interest in Germany were high. American institutions that had never before gone into international finance attempted to get a share of this easy wealth. Their agents, often inexperienced men, overran the Continent, asking chance acquaintances the name of a firm to whom they might sell a loan. Few public bodies in Germany could resist such temptation. "If I can get a loan without having to take much trouble about it," replied the Lord Mayor of Frankfort to me in a public debate, "I am going to have it. It takes the unemployment problem off my hands." It did, as long as he could secure a second loan to pay the interest on the first. The *theory* of public works may be a discovery of the New Deal, or rather of its spiritual protector Lord Keynes. Its practice was familiar to every impecunious municipality worried by unemployment in republican Germany. I supported Schacht's policy; but I objected to indiscriminate borrowing of any sort. The danger from malinvestment by private industry seemed to me greater than that from municipal wastefulness. Nobody expected foreign exchange from a lavishly built municipal swimming pool. But foreign creditors looked forward to regular returns from their overseas industrial investments. It was all very well to rationalize a plant that was fairly sure of its future market; but wholesale rationalization in a country where labor was cheap and credit was expensive would court disaster. The so-called rationalization, however, became a craze. Even the cartels, whose main object had been restriction of production, so as to secure the survival of the weakest concerns by keeping up prices, were caught by it and advised their members to increase capacity by scrapping old plants, irrespective of the cost of borrowed money. As long as this wholesale spending for more and better machinery went on, wages and prices naturally rose and unemployment decreased. Lord Keynes's "multiplier" ticked merrily as long as foreign loans, granted indiscriminately and spent lavishly, were inflating purchasing power. Nobody worried where the final consumers of additional products were to be found later on.

I did not make myself popular by my warnings of this borrowed prosperity, which I denounced as *irrational rationalization*. Economists who predict the bursting of the bubble are never greatly appreciated. When their help is required later on, and when they cannot resurrect the dead whom captains of industry and labor leaders have slain, they are called impotent.

The United States was the center of this streamlined paradise. I was there in the summer of 1926, when the era of permanent prosperity was dawning. It intoxicated everybody, even those who had not yet been toppled over by the equally exhilarating stimulants of Prohibition. As usual I was deeply impressed by the marvelous technical strides America was taking; yet I was disturbed by its cocksure optimism and its carbonated swagger. My friends assured me that the second industrial revolution had found the key to permanent prosperity; but when I asked to have a look at it, nobody could produce it. Behind all the braggadocio and the boasting, I could hear the still small voice of fear; when people had time to think they were worried. Some of my Continental colleagues, who had come to the United States for the first time, were swept off their feet. One of them felt bound to write the customary book on America, rightly called *The American Economic Miracle,* for he could neither understand nor explain it.

When a hard-headed business nation was going off its chump, and solemnly assuring one that yields no longer mattered, that one had to concentrate on appreciation, debt-ridden Germany could not be expected to remain sober. In the inflation struggle the old commercial code, that debts must be paid, had been scrapped. Leading industrialists almost prided themselves on having cheated their bondholders and outwitted their shareholders. They did not intend to default on their new foreign obligations; but in their eyes bankruptcy was no longer immoral. A London City banker considered himself the trustee of his clients whose money he had invested in foreign bonds; a German manufacturer felt greater responsibility to the workers whom he had to employ, and to the concern he had built up, than to alien creditors. Bankers knew that confidence was a tender plant; manufacturers did not mind trampling on it. Inflation had impoverished the banks and enriched manufacturers. Once debtors were no longer afraid of default, their creditors' hold on them had gone. Banks were rarely in a position to refuse a loan to an important industrial customer and let him go for it to a rival. They had to finance, and to finance liberally, the malinvestments their manufacturing clients were bent on. The day of finance capital was drawing to its close.

I had predicted the impending catastrophe in a small book entitled *The Destiny of German Capitalism.* It closed with the words, "Surely the fate of German capitalism is in very weak hands." Four years later the book was republished in an enlarged edition. Though a great literary success, it had no influence on those to whom my warning was addressed. Jeremiah is never listened to when he talks ahead of time.

Schacht, of course, saw the dangers; he neither could nor would face them. Had he attempted to stop private borrowing, both capital and labor would have accused him of sabotaging the Dawes Plan. At that time, he believed as fervently as President Coolidge that hired money must be returned. He did not yet entertain those plans for fraudulent bankruptcy in the execution of which he later so distinguished himself.

## 4. *The New Plan*

As Germany's indebtedness on private account grew heavier, investors were becoming worried. Would they be allowed to convert German marks into dollars after the reparation agent had stopped doing so? The French were frightened. They could not make payments in dollars to the United States if they got only blocked marks from Germany. They desired a revision of the Dawes Plan. Gustav Stresemann agreed to a bargain; he knew he was dying. He had a very low opinion of his possible successors, and wanted to secure the evacuation of the Rhineland before he had gone. The French were willing to withdraw before 1935, the date fixed by the treaty, in return for adequate compensation. I used to warn my friends in Paris: "At present," I told them, "there is no great danger from Germany. If the two nations cannot be reconciled, danger will come later on. If you clear out earlier with a *beau geste,* without asking for ransom, the Germans may be grateful to you. If you have to be bought out, political friction is bound to result." They might have listened had there been in Germany less popular clamor for an early evacuation. It would have been far more patriotic to suffer the burden of occupation, which was no longer unbearable, than to cry for speedy liberation, which had to be paid for by the scrapping of the Dawes Plan.

I opposed both loans and premature new arrangements in a booklet called *Loans or Liberty*, but again nobody listened. Schacht had been won over by Parker Gilbert. He saw in Gustav Stresemann a successful rival. With a little patience he could have deprived him of his last triumph, the evacuation of the Rhineland, for he knew that he was dying. But Schacht could not resist the temptation to draft a plan that would free the German population from French control and at the same time greatly reduce the burden of all German taxpayers. He trusted Parker Gilbert, who held out hopes of a considerable reduction of Germany's obligations. (I have no doubt that Parker Gilbert himself originally thought he could do it.) The scaling down would have had to be very considerable to offset the risks of scrapping the Dawes Plan, under which Germany herself could not be held responsible if her creditors had to áccept blocked marks in place of foreign currency.

On a visit to London, I had gathered the impression that the British Treasury favored a waiting attitude. But in Germany both political and financial interests were keen on a change. I wrote a series of articles in the *Berliner Tageblatt* trying to dissuade the authorities from attending a conference the possible outcome of which was not yet clear. I had learned by that time that weaker partners cannot break up a conference and refuse a compromise the stronger members consider reasonable. Germany was free to go to a conference; she was not free to leave it. Schacht's optimism, doubled by vanity, got the better of his natural shrewdness. He was sure that Parker Gilbert would deliver the goods. Since the Treasury had almost eliminated itself and the Foreign Office was not willing to shoulder responsibilities of a technical character, Schacht was to be the chief delegate and would make the new plan. He saw himself as the liberator of Germany and founder of a new world economic system. The friendship of the governor of the Bank of England, Montagu Norman—not unlike President Hindenburg's almost paternal affection for Papen—greatly enhanced Schacht's sense of importance.

The conference assembled in Paris early in January 1929. As one of Schacht's experts I visited him in March. He had had a very rude awakening. The reductions offered to him were far below his expectations. He resisted very courageously but to little avail. The rapid loss of gold by the Reichsbank showed him that the breakup of the conference would bring about a financial disaster. He bravely made up his mind to accept the inevitable. But one of his fellow delegates, Dr. Vögler, the representative of the heavy industries, formerly Stinnes's right-hand man, refused to sign the plan. The men behind him meant to use the new plan for whipping up national passions and for getting the masses behind their groups. Schacht was frightened. So far he had been a good republican, but he was very ambitious; I am sure that he hoped to be president of the Reich. He needed the blessing of the Nationalists and the votes of the republicans in order to reach his goal. By choosing Vögler as fellow delegate he had planned to make both him and his party share the responsibility for the outcome of the conference. He had been outwitted.

The plan drafted by the experts had to be adopted by the governments. They met at the Hague in the summer of 1929, and again in January 1930.

In the meantime the bubble had burst. Permanent prosperity had vanished. Prices were falling in the world markets, and the long delayed permanent adjustment was overdue. In Germany, Nationalists and Nazis outbid one another in denouncing the plan. Payments would not terminate before 1989 and would enslave generations of yet unborn grandchildren. It was useless to show that payments falling due after fifty years had next to no present-day value; that creditors, not debtors, should worry about such distant prospects. People would not understand, for Nationalist businessmen and Nazi agitators did their best to muddle their minds. Schacht got cold feet. He feared for his political career and tried to wriggle out. He pounced upon some unfavorable minor modifications inserted at the Hague and loudly proclaimed his inability to accept a fundamentally changed plan. The Foreign Office now accused him of interfering in foreign affairs. Greatly incensed, he decided to blow up the Young Plan at the second Hague conference.

I had gone to Paris for a meeting of the European Committee of the Carnegie Foundation. I had seen Pierre Quesnay at the Banque de France. "I know Schacht's game," Quesnay said to me. "He will try to block the plan by handing in his resignation as president of the Reichsbank. It will be accepted. A successor will be appointed, and the plan will go through."

On my return to Berlin I managed to get hold of Schacht. I repeated to him Quesnay's warning; I implored him to take heed of it and not to sacrifice his position. He would not listen. He was convinced that his resignation would blow up the conference and prevent the adoption of the plan. He had miscalculated. A successor was immediately found in the person of Dr. Luther, who was a firm believer in the old German proverb, "If God gives you a job, he will give you understanding for it."

Attacks on Schacht from the Foreign Office and its press increased in vehemence. He was furious. He went to the United States on a lecture tour attempting to justify his action. He had one very good card to play. He could have told his audiences that he had signed the Young Plan on the assumption that prosperity was permanent. He had been mistaken, but he was in very good company. For the leading United States financial experts on the Young Committee, Mr. Jack Morgan and Mr. Lamont, had been equally fooled. He did not take this line; he merely quibbled. He always had a tendency toward an aggressive, sentimental nationalism; it made it easy for him to change sides. The Weimar Republic had been ungrateful; it had disowned him in spite of his great merits. He had done with it. Now he was grooming himself for the role of economic savior of Germany by joining the Nationalists, and finally the Nazis.

## 5. Enter Brüning: Exit Respublica

Schacht's resignation was the beginning of the end of the Weimar Republic. Its financial management had never been wise. Even in the days of prosperity it had had a deficit, because its so-called experts insisted on financing capital investments, even battleships and guns, by loans. The deficits were covered by treasury bills; naturally when prosperity began to ebb, the size of the floating debt had become threatening. An effort was made to reduce the deficit by cutting down unemployment benefits. The Socialist trade unions would not accept this proposal and left the coalition. From the cabinet crisis a new chancellor, Heinrich Brüning, emerged.

Brüning's intellectual qualities were far above those of any of his predecessors. He understood economics, and as a leader in the Roman Catholic trade union movement he had acquired firsthand knowledge of social problems. He had traveled widely and was familiar with English conditions. In the war he had distinguished himself as an officer of the reserve; he was full of pride in the military achievements of the German army. He possessed the subtle intellectuality of the great medieval schoolmen. He looked very much like one of them, his face being all profile and intellect. Yet there was a strong passionate streak in him, well controlled and well concealed under an almost frigid impassivity; he may even have had a tinge of romanticism. "He is," I once said of him, "a great priest who has unfortunately never sat in the confessional." For he had none of that mellow understanding which has made so many servants of his church, whose intellect was far inferior to his, great forces in human affairs.*

At bottom Brüning was an authoritarian conservative. Yet he was intelligent enough to rule within democratic forms and to accept changes he could not prevent. He came into power as the exponent of an authoritarian doctrine. He had no majority in the Reichstag, and he would try to rule without one, basing himself on Paragraph 48 of the Constitution, which empowered the president to issue provisional decrees without the consent of the Reichstag. Brüning, wanting to break the Socialist opposition, flaunted this paragraph in its face. If the Reichstag did not accept his budget, he would by decree under Paragraph 48. The Socialists accepted the challenge. Brüning had to submit his decree to the Reichstag "without any delay"; he did not secure a majority. He had either to resign or dissolve the House. He chose the latter alternative, with the result that 107 Nazis were returned among 577 members. He had succeeded neither in breaking the Socialists nor in winning over the bulk of the Nationalists to a constructive policy. He had merely opened the road to a dictatorship by claiming power for a president who was but a kind of political robot.

* Dr. Brüning has told the story of the rise and fall of his government in a long letter to the *Deutsche Rundschau*, July 1947. It is but natural that a chief actor and a detached observer do not fully agree in their interpretation of events. This is particularly true as Dr. Brüning has been more than generous in explaining both President Hindenburg's and General von Schleicher's actions and motivations.

# XVIII. The Cross of Gold
# (1930-1931)

## 1. The Gold Scare

THE HEAVY fall of prices of foodstuffs and raw materials after the middle of the twenties had undermined the prosperity of agricultural countries. They could no longer pay their debts and finance their imports. For some time they managed to settle old debts by borrowing new money, but finally they defaulted in some way or other, reducing the income of foreign investors and with it their purchasing power, and paralyzing their banks. The financial crash in New York had worsened the situation. In every country, price levels were rapidly declining, yet manufactured goods remained relatively stable. Monopolist industries reduced output rather than price. Organized labor generally preferred unemployment to lowering money wages. Thanks to the dole, the working class as a whole was able to bear large-scale layoffs, though the impact on public finance was disastrous.

In the early twenties a decline of production of gold had set in; its continuation (actually production had risen again after 1923) might contribute to the depression. Once more the specter of a gold scarcity began to haunt the world. The Financial Committee of the League appointed a gold delegation to inquire into the matter. I was invited to join it.

I had been an ardent supporter of the League of Nations, but I did not care very much for what I might call the spiritual climate of Geneva; it was sometimes emotional, sometimes flabby.

Earlier the League had invited André Siegfried and myself to write a report on the economic causes of war. We had worked independently of one another but had reached the same conclu-

311

sions. We were called to Geneva and asked to incorporate our separate papers into a joint report. For three days we were closeted and, assisted by Sir Alfred Zimmern, labored hard to produce a joint report; we merely succeeded in turning two readable essays into a dull government paper. Finally we were allowed to write a short introductory note and present our views in their original shape. They were very well received everywhere. They started the discussion on the economic causes of war that has ever since been going on. It has become the favorite plaything of noneconomists who discovered, somewhat late in the day, what they thought was the Marxist economic interpretation of history, and claimed that all wars were the result of economic forces, especially of the capitalist system. Their discovery was a godsend to budding instructors. If the decisive causes of all wars were economic, the particular non-economic circumstances in which particular wars had started need not be carefully studied.

The League secretariat was not really pleased with us. It was developing an international civil service—the best civil service the world has ever seen—and had caught the spirit of caution which numbs the activities of every regular civil service. An international bureaucracy that had five to seven big masters and about fifty small ones to serve needed very much more tact than its national counterparts. It disliked dissension almost as much as conflict, and covered up discords in fundamentals by concords in formulas.

The gold delegation met in the early summer of 1930; it concluded its deliberations in the spring of 1932. Our number was small; our most brilliant member was the late Sir Henry Strakosch. He usually worked in close co-operation with Gustav Cassel; the latter rarely honored us with his presence, but when he did, he was pontifical. He never replied to an argument, but attempted to eliminate it by quoting from his well-known books with that authority to which his accomplishments entitled him.

Our president was an amiable Belgian, Janson, partly professor and partly businessman, who later, I am sorry to hear, fell a victim to the Nazis. He frequently dozed during the discussions, which were generally conducted in English. When he awoke from his slumbers, he asked for a French translation and recovered the threads. I disliked our first interim report drawn up in the summer of 1930, just after I had left for the United States. It did not destroy the myth of an impending gold scarcity. I had signed it, for it seemed unwise to resign on an interim report that could be corrected later on. I should, however, have made a personal reservation.

I went straight across the States to Stanford University as visiting professor. In many places things did not yet look very black outwardly, but gloom was descending everywhere. The golden age of permanent prosperity was vanishing beyond recall. The skepticism I had bashfully voiced in 1926 had been justified. Government of businessmen, by businessmen, for businessmen was perishing from the face of the earth. I set down my impressions in a small book called *Prosperity, Myth and Reality in American Business Life,* which my American publisher, somewhat overdoing it, called *The Crisis of Capitalism in America.*

World economics, slithering down rapidly, would inevitably drag the reparation settlement along with them. Germany would not be able to fulfill both political and commercial obligations. The question, Will the German government demand a moratorium or will private debtors have to do so? was on everybody's lips. Business naturally preferred a moratorium on political debts. It could not be had without the consent of France. Her consent could not be won without a previous moratorium granted to her by the United States. Everybody recognized the need for action, but nobody took it. Had the Hoover moratorium been prepared in the autumn of 1930, it might have saved the situation.

On my homeward journey I went straight to Geneva from Cherbourg to another meeting of the gold delegation. It was now getting its second wind. The fall of prices, which I had predicted as early as 1926, made possible the working of poorer gold mines and had automatically increased gold supplies. The problem now was the so-called maldistribution of gold, caused mainly by the violent changes in the international debt structure that war and peace settlements had brought about. Gold was concentrating in the United States, in France, and in a few other countries. They were creditors who were unwilling to accept payment in goods; the movement was accentuated by capital flights from weaker currencies—from real or imaginary political dangers. The problem was not technical, not due to a faulty monetary mechanism, but the result of unstable political and economic conditions; no monetary system in the world can be devised that can successfully withstand political shocks and large-scale economic miscalculations. The delegation was split into two sections. One section, for which Sir Henry was the spokesman, explained the rapidly spreading depression more or less exclusively by monetary causes, and proposed mainly monetary remedies. The other group, whose views I shared and frequently voiced, interpreted it as a much wider phenomenon for which political, economic, and monetary causes were jointly responsible.

My French, Polish, and Czechoslovakian colleagues frequently joined me in opposing Sir Henry's monetary dogmatism. Bandying arguments with Gustav Cassel was dull; to pit oneself against Sir Henry was fun, for he had great experience, a nimble mind, and what was perhaps more important, a very efficient secretariat.

"You should not be frivolous," he once reprimanded me as I tried to enliven the atmosphere a little, "when dealing with such important subjects."

"I see no reason," I retorted, "why I should be dull when I am right."

Our publications are monuments to the indefatigable and painstaking industry of the permanent staff of the League secretariat. They often turned our vague generalities into clearly defined, practical proposals.

## 2. *The German Crash*

On my way to Berlin I stopped in Frankfort for a few days to visit my mother, who was celebrating her eighty-third birthday. It was the last time I saw her alive.

In Berlin everybody was interested in my views on the American situation, but nobody seemed prepared to face the moratorium issue. The Chancellor was engrossed in grave political problems. His policy had landed him in a situation where he must work either with the Nazis, whom he loathed, or with the

Socialists, whom he did not like. He had left business affairs to the business world and the Reichsbank, and had concentrated his energies on balancing the budget and remaining precariously in power. By that time the domination of finance capital, if it ever existed, had come to an inglorious end. The banks never recovered their strength after industrialists had eviscerated them in the great inflation.

Dr. Luther, Schacht's successor as head of the Reichsbank, was not a trained banker. He had balanced the budget and put an end to inflation. But he had little vision, and not much *savoir faire*. Had he fully grasped his responsibilities, he would have made the banks put their house in order in the autumn of 1930. At that time the spirit of international co-operation was not yet dead. He could have secured credit support in case of emergency from the three great national systems outside Germany. When the crash caught him unawares, he chartered an airplane and toured the capitals; as the political situation had become unfriendly, results were negative. Velocity, after all, is not an alternative to foresight.

The actual crash came, as crashes always came in the German Republic, through bad teamwork between departments, arbitrary action of relatively subordinate officials, and ambiguity on the part of their heads, who let them act independently.

In March 1931 I was giving a series of lectures at the Royal University of Ireland. I learned from the Dublin papers that Germany and Austria were planning a customs union. The peace treaty had—very foolishly—forbidden their union. I had strongly favored it, for Austria could hardly be self-supporting. Her political parties, moreover, both Socialist and Roman Catholic, would have greatly strengthened the Weimar Republic. But this latest move horrified me, for it was as bad an improvisation as the Rapallo Treaty had been. The French immediately denounced the plan as a breach of the peace treaty; in their eyes, a customs union was the first step toward political union. They were probably wrong from an abstract legal point of view (notwithstanding the decision of the Hague Court to the contrary). But once more, the German Foreign Office had committed an act of criminal folly by imagining that the world is run on legal subtleties. Once more they forgot that one must never provide one's opponents with convenient pretexts.

Passing through London, I met Sir William Tyrrell, at that time undersecretary at the Foreign Office, in the house of my cousin the late Sir Max J. Bonn. He let me know in very plain language the very unfavorable impression the attempt had made upon his government. Once more I was used as a speaking tube to convey hints for unscrambling history.

I stopped a day in Cologne, where I had to give a lecture. Next day I left for Berlin; as I sat in the dining car, a few passengers entered, among them the temporary secretary for commerce in Brüning's cabinet, Dr. Trendelenburg. He joined me at my table, and I naturally told him of my meeting with Sir William. "Do you know," he replied, "that I was quite as much surprised by the proposal as any newspaper reader?" Bülow,* to whom I reported, assured me that neither he nor the Chancellor had been in the know. I could have believed him had the foreign minister been dismissed and his irresponsible counselor discharged.

The French withdrew their credits from Austria and Germany. This would not have mattered much (for they were not large) but for the crash of the Austrian Credit Anstalt, the leading Austrian bank. Great Britain came to the rescue—the French imagined—not so much for love of Austria as from hatred of France. For the governor of the Bank of England had managed to convince French public opinion, and what was worse, his French colleagues, of his dislike of them.

A few days later a great German textile concern, Nordwolle, smashed as a result of gigantic fraudulent manipulations. It dragged its bank, the Danat Bank, with it. Soon the Dresdner Bank followed. A run on the banks started such as the world had never seen before. Foreign credits, many of them short-term, were called in. The Reichsbank rapidly lost its gold; its raising of the discount rate to 15 per cent did not help much; high interest rates do not work when people fear the loss of their capital. London, familiar with the technique of international banking, stood by its debtors; the United States did not, and cleared out. The French were delighted to let Germany

---

* Bülow was secretary of state at the Foreign Office under Foreign Minister Curtius. One of the latter's subordinates was supposed to have sprung the Austrian customs union agreement on his unsuspecting chief.

feel their financial power. Luther flew to Paris and begged for help. He was turned down.

For a few weeks Germany was a financial pandemonium. All banks were closed. When they opened again, depositors were allowed to withdraw only very modest amounts. Severe exchange control was imposed in order to prevent a gigantic flight of capital. Ever afterward this control continued; it greatly facilitated the plundering of the Jews by the Nazis, and made possible much later the astute bargaining system devised by Dr. Schacht.

A decline of the mark, measured in foreign currency, presented to the German people the dread specter of a new inflation. The people were willing to undergo the most grueling privations, provided the stability of the mark could be maintained. By heroic efforts the government succeeded. The strain was terrific; the shock given to public confidence in the stability of the existing political order, stupendous.

Once more German industrialists had upset the applecart. This time they had not meddled directly with politics. They had merely shown their inability to run their own concerns in a businesslike way. The nation paid a heavy price for the irrational rationalization they had indulged in. To the public, the banks appeared the culprits. They had crashed, and they had dealt harshly with their customers; they had not had the foresight to check the boundless expansionist activities of self-appointed captains of industry. I often used to quote in those days a modification of Clemenceau's statement, "War is far too important an affair to be left in the hands of the generals"; I phrased it, "Business is far too important an affair to be left in the hands of businessmen." But the mass of the people, who had no inside knowledge, charged the new calamities to the government and to the republic. I can very well imagine Dr. Schacht gloating over the failure of the successor who had dared to replace him.

The Chancellor, fundamentally a conservative, had believed in the ability of business, and in particular of his business supporters, to run their own affairs. He saw that he had been mistaken. Yet Germany weathered the storm. The German people are always at their best when passing through weird tribulations. They have learned how to suffer frustration. They cannot stand prosperity.

## 3. *The End of the Gold Standard*

On the afternoon of Sunday the twentieth of September, I was in my country house in Parsch near Salzburg when a long-distance call came through. My former pupil Dr. Palyi, then adviser to the Deutsche Bank, informed me that the Bank of England had gone off gold. When I had recovered from the shock, I knew that we had passed a milestone in history.

September 20, 1931,* was the end of an age. It was the last day of the age of economic liberalism in which Great Britain had been the leader of the world. She had built a mighty empire in five continents by political domination and economic development. She had striven hard to keep it open for all nations. By protecting her own political and economic interests she had, at the same time, served as trustee for all nations, especially the smaller ones. The First World War had somewhat indented her system of free trade; she had clung to it tenaciously and tried hard to win new adherents in all parts of the world. She had failed; yet she had kept the door open. She had returned to the gold standard, though it involved serious risks, and in collaboration with the United States she had once more established a world economic unity based on it—though its foundations were much more brittle than they had been in the past.

Now the whole edifice had crashed. The slogan "safe as the Bank of England" no longer had any meaning. The Bank of England had gone into default. For the first time in history a great creditor country had devaluated its currency, and by so doing had inflicted heavy losses on all those who had trusted it. The British themselves seemed barely aware of what had happened. An English businessman who regularly visited Holland was greatly puzzled when his sterling notes no longer bought the customary twelve Dutch florins but fluctuated between eight and ten. "What has happened to the Dutch currency?" he exclaimed indignantly, "it has lost its stability."

* It was two days after Japan began the war in Manchuria.

At a meeting of the Gold Delegation Sir Henry Strakosch explained to us: "We had to do it because we had to relieve our sterling debtors."

"What difference could it make to them—for example Chile or Brazil," I replied, "whether they repudiate in good or bad sterling?"

Hitherto devaluation had been the prerogative of improvident debtor countries. Great Britain was a powerful creditor country, yet she had sacrificed, with apparently little regret, the fundamental principle of an international capitalist system, the sanctity of contracts. She had broken the economic unity of the world, which had survived the war, and opened the way to violent economic nationalism. One by one, financially strong countries followed her on the road to devaluation, while the weaker ones clung to exchange control. Unfortunately she had just discovered the use she could make of a fluctuating currency for widening temporarily her foreign markets and for strangling imports from abroad. Her statesmen were sincere in their advocacy of collective security in the political field; at the same time, they gloated over the economic anarchy their newly acquired monetary nationalism was ushering in.

Great Britain's repudiation of the gold standard might at first have been looked upon as an inevitable calamity to be remedied later on by stabilization at a new parity. Her refusal to stabilize, which she practically maintained until the United States had also gone off the gold standard, was evidence of a complete reversion of policy. It signified her withdrawal from the world's economic leadership in return for a partnership in a closed empire. The friends of England, all the world over, registered with deep grief this tragic act of abdication.

## 4. The Cross of Gold

The British consoled themselves by creating a legend. They made the gold standard the scapegoat for all their troubles. It was held responsible for the flight of capital that had led to the panicky outflow of gold, and which even generous American and French credits (£130 million) had been unable to stem.

The gold standard was the victim, not the cause, of this flight. Great Britain held huge funds of foreign short-term money, a large part of which she had invested in long-term ventures. The precarious balance between her long-term assets and her short-term liabilities depended entirely on the confidence of her creditors. The advent of a Labour government had weakened this confidence, both in France and in the United States. The growing deficit due to spreading unemployment shocked naïve bankers, who still saw in the dole a sign of moral depravity and in an unbalanced budget the beginning of financial perdition. The refusal of the bulk of the Labour party to accept the recommendations of the May Committee for cuts in salaries and social services seemed to justify their fears. The bank had not raised its discount to stop the outflow of gold; it had fought the depression with cheap money, and had failed to stay it. The Treasury needed cheap money in order to convert the 5 per cent war loan to 3½ per cent. It reversed its policy too late (end of July), when distrust had been widely spread.

Conservatives, moreover, had been unable to withstand the temptation to discredit the Labour government. When they joined a coalition under its leader, they knew how utterly innocuous Mr. MacDonald was, and how thoroughly trustworthy was his chancellor, Mr. Philip Snowden. But only the complete disappearance of all Labour men might have reconciled American capitalists. When the capitalist animal is once thoroughly frightened, it says good-by to reason and bolts. Its terrified imagination enlarged an unfortunate incident in the navy, due to a reduction in pay, into a mutiny of revolutionary Communist forces. The flight of capital and the outflow of gold could not be stopped.

The result would not have been very different had Great Britain been on a paper standard. Whenever a country cannot mobilize its foreign investments when its foreign loans are called back, either its currency goes to the dogs or it defaults on its creditors by means of exchange control. The gold standard became a handy scarecrow. Protectionist conservatives gloated over their unexpected good fortune. For its breakdown severed the British from the international price level far more thoroughly than any tariff policy could have done. It made possible both the return to protection and the closing of the empire by the Ottawa preferential arrangements. The gold standard, they argued, being international, must never be resumed.

Labor, rightly sore at having been maneuvered out of power, regarded the crisis as a wicked plot: an attempt by foreign capitalists to eliminate the Labour government by dictating to it a balanced budget at the expense of the wage earner and for the protection of gold bond creditors. It would never again permit the return to a currency system that made national labor the slave of international capital. The most brilliant modern economist, Keynes, had mercilessly damned the gold standard. His supposedly revolutionary doctrines invested the myth with the character of a scientific truth.

I had first met Keynes on a cold November evening in Rotterdam (1919) when a journey to England had come to nought. There and then I had undertaken the German translation of his *Economic Consequences of the Peace.* In that book he had shown himself a *political*, not an *academic* economist, for he was not profoundly interested in abstract, scholastic truths. He deduced his theories, not from the textbooks of his predecessors, but from the problems of the day. He wanted to find solutions that could be applied to urgent actual situations, not answers to eternal questions. His well-known dictum, "In the long run we are all dead," demonstrated this clearly. He preferred the role of the surgeon, who tries to save life by a bold experimental operation—though he sometimes sacrificed it—to that of a professor of anatomy who cuts up corpses. The value of a doctrine to him lay not so much in its truth as in its successful applicability. Keynes's mind was so much more nimble and quick than those of any of us that he usually detected the flaws in his arguments long before his most bitter critics had found them out, though not always before they had done harm. A creative artist such as he had to look forward, not backward. He was not always aware that the new gods whose worship he advocated were but ancient idols in modern disguise.

On the visit to Berlin when he launched his world-famed attack on economic liberalism in the lecture on "The End of Laissez Faire," he and his wife had tea with me before he delivered it. "Why," I asked him, "do you come here to preach the new gospel to us? In this part of the world we have never had genuine laissez faire; its only thoroughgoing advocate has been of British origin, by name Prince Smith." He was a little puzzled. He prided himself on the boldness of his onslaught on the gold standard, calling it "a barbaric relic." Yet fifty years ago his heresy had been the cardinal faith of American populism, "without which no man can be saved, that money may be created by the government in any desired quantity, out of any substance, with no basis but itself." One of its leaders had looked forward to the time when gold and silver would be discarded, and an international legal tender money be established—"but that is a vast reformation, which the world is not yet ready for; the greater part of mankind have never yet heard of it." * After Keynes had taken it up, mankind did hear of it. His loss is irreparable. For only his authority could have had held in check the noisy sect that is applying his doctrines to situations for which he had not designed them. For to him economics was an art to be practiced with all available scientific knowledge, not a book of rules from which medieval-minded scholars could pick dehydrated fruits of wisdom.


## 5. The Triumph of Populism

Great Britain's repudiation of the gold standard very nearly broke the back of the Weimar Republic. It had to cut prices on exports, otherwise imports could not be paid for and would shrink below what was bearable. It could do it either by internal deflation, which meant growing unemployment, or by following Great Britain and devaluating the mark. Unofficial advice from Great Britain suggested the latter. I opposed it. The British had no experience of inflation; by a curious combination of good luck and skill their home prices had not been inflated. To the average German, devaluation and inflation were identical terms. The government could not afford a second panic after the one it had just managed to survive. By devaluation Great Britain had greatly reduced her foreign obligations, for most of them were sterling debts. Scarcely any of Germany's debts were mark debts; their burden would increase with the decline of the mark. She would have to make new agreements

* John D. Hicks, *The Populist Revolt*, pp. 316, 317, 338.

with her creditors, and she would be endangering the final settlement of reparations, which had just hove in sight. Devaluation in Great Britain had facilitated balancing the budget. In Germany, the forces that had been at work during the heyday of inflation were already waiting for their chance to upset the precarious balance for which Brüning was striving.

The sacrifice of a stable mark might moreover be in vain; it might merely lead to competitive devaluation all round. Brüning decided—rightly—on a policy of deflation, and reduced prices, wages, and interest rates by government decrees. This enhanced and prolonged the strain almost beyond the limit of endurance. Yet his policy began to bear fruit. At the Lausanne conference (June and July 1932) the reparation debt was practically scrapped—the scrapping being made conditional on the United States' canceling inter-Allied war debts. Germany was to be let off with a final payment of 740 million dollars. A world economic conference was to follow, to face the problems of restoring currencies to a healthy basis, removing tariff difficulties, and reviving international trade.

By that time the British had learned that devaluation had to be a recurrent process if its benefits were to endure. One could not imagine that the United States, where a cheap money tradition was endemic, would continue to look on and let its rivals reap the rich harvest of financial dishonesty. But Great Britain could not afford to stabilize before she knew where the United States stood; and the United States did not know where it stood as long as Britain was unwilling to declare for stabilization.

A preparatory world economic conference was called in Geneva to clear the ground for the coming assembly in London. One of the two German delegates was appointed by the Reichsbank. I was asked to accompany him as adviser, and within the German delegation was to rank on a par with the delegate.

The conference first sat from October 31 to November 13, 1932. The delegations were small. Most members knew each other from previous meetings. There was very little politics and scarcely any intriguing. My relations with my chief were excellent. But there was an air of futility about it.

For a few days after we met, the election of Roosevelt had added a new element to a complex situation. The Democratic party had frequently advocated cheap money; it had been the debtors' party and had often shown an anti-gold bias. The President-elect was surrounded by advisers with strong leanings to money manipulation, or even inflation. He was known to be an experimentalist in economic matters, without profound theoretical convictions; but he might be more tractable on inter-Allied debts than Hoover. Sanctity and inviolability of contracts could not mean much to a man who was prepared to tamper with them at home. Keynes's monetary theories represented a scientific elaboration of populist slogans and a justification of Bryan's emotional imagery. Populism had been a revolt of debtor masses against creditor classes. The great depression might be explained as a rising of debtor nations against creditor nations—a kind of collectivized populism.

The members of the British delegation were as close as clams, even when I met them privately. We did not know where we stood.

The American delegates, John Williams and Edmund Day, newcomers to Geneva, were cautious. They had been appointed by Hoover and could not be certain to what degree the President-elect was willing to co-operate. The conference adjourned.

It met again from January 9 to 19. By that time the French had withheld the December payment due to the United States, relying on an assurance of President-elect Roosevelt that non-payment would not preclude negotiations. The British delegation, moreover, had become more articulate. The American experts had thrown out hints that early stabilization by the British at a reasonable rate might facilitate a settlement of the inter-Allied debt and further the liberal trade policy to which the new United States administration was pledged.

The British had sacrificed both free trade and monetary internationalism. They had gained complete freedom of action for an independent national price policy, but they knew that similar action by the United States would lead to chaos. They could only prevent it by showing their willingness to forgo in the future by stabilization the unilateral benefits they had been trying to retain. An offer on their part might tempt American producers, and especially the farmers, to agree to a reasonable debt settlement.

Apart from the difficulty of determining the new rate of exchange, there was the risk that devaluation by the United States might upset the new parity. Yet the risk of providing for it a justification for going off the dollar was very much greater. President Roosevelt would be quite willing to experiment, regardless of remote consequences, should internal emergencies seem to make it desirable. Influential members among his adherents were small-town-minded economic nationalists, and some of his most trusted advisers were primitive, dyed-in-the-wool inflationists. They were prepared to force their country off gold, partly to raise internal prices and to solve the farm debt problem, and partly because devaluation would be a valuable instrument of pressure in Anglo-American negotiations.

Since Great Britain had turned populist, her policy had become both timid and aggressive. Yet finally her delegates agreed to an agenda, unanimously accepted by the committee, advocating both stabilization and the restoration of the gold standard. It opened the road to economic world peace, and prepared a detailed program. But it could not transform it into a policy.

I thought the preliminary conference had done well and had laid the foundation for a final settlement. If Great Britain approached the United States government with an offer of stabilization in return for debt settlements and improved trade facilities, the impasse might be overcome.

I still believe that a bold policy would greatly have influenced developments in the United States. I recognized the need of easing the burdens of debtors the price of whose products had fallen through no fault of their own. It need not have been done by monetary experiments that were bound to benefit especially those producers who had no debts. I had always maintained that the capitalists' right to profit from sound investments is counterbalanced by their duty to take losses from faulty operations. But I objected to indiscriminate collective bankruptcy. I advocated individual proceedings. I never could see why a solvent railroad should be relieved of its debt charge because an insolvent one could not meet its obligations. In a world of so-called free enterprise, bankruptcy as well as success should be individualist. I was of the opinion that the crisis was originally a parity problem—the prices of agricultural and of industrial products diverging widely from one another. This discrepancy could not be remedied by monetary inflation and all-round price raising. The results of the American experiment have fully justified my view. Had the money wizards had real faith in their purely monetary nostrum, they would never have passed the complicated Agricultural Adjustment Act or the several price parity acts.

The very fact that the President-elect had no deep-seated monetary views would have enabled him to stick to a stable dollar, if by doing so he could have secured important concessions. The British played a game of watchful waiting, and they lost.

When the conference finally met in London (June 12), the United States had gone off the gold standard. It was naïve to expect them to retrace their steps immediately and go in for rapid stabilization. If the fruits of devaluation were actually as sweet as Great Britain's protracted refusal to stabilize had made them appear, the United States could not be asked to return to a stable dollar before it had had its fill. In these circumstances a conference for the immediate stabilization of all currencies was futile. The President, who had been unable to hold back the inflationists before they plunged him into the great experiment, could certainly not stop them from exploiting their success when even a hint of a return to some sort of stability led to a crash in speculative prices.

# XIX. Exodus (1931-1932)

## 1. *Rector Magnificus*

ON THE first of October 1931, eighteen months before Hitler assumed office, I had become Rector Magnificus of my college. In that year the college was celebrating the twenty-fifth anniversary of its foundation. My colleagues had elected me in the hope that I could perform with success the multifarious social obligations one has to submit to at a jubilee.

A rector in Berlin was a bigwig. He was addressed as "His Magnificence." At the openings of schools, museums, and other institutions he strode about in a velvet gown with a huge gold chain around his neck. At the innumerable social gatherings he had to attend he wore the chain over his dress suit. I found it very hard not to laugh at myself when I went to a government reception adorned with this chain from which dangled a huge plaque showing William II wearing the helmet of his cuirassiers. I could not help remembering the home-coming of the kine from the mountain pastures in the Austrian alps, when the best milker proudly marched ahead with a crown of wild flowers about her horns. The rector's wife shared his social grandeur. By courtesy she was called "Her Magnificence." Girl students curtsied and kissed her hand at student balls.

I had accepted my colleagues' choice with a heavy heart. I would have to live in the public eye; a good deal of my personal liberty would be gone. Yet the short quarter of an hour in which I delivered my inaugural address was worth the sacrifice. When I mounted the platform after the trite loquacity of my predecessor had consumed far more time than had been allotted to him, I had reached the high-water mark of an academic career. This did not mean much to me; I could have been rector at any time in the past ten years. But at that moment I embodied the success of an institution that twenty-five years earlier had not been much more than a purely technical training school for future businessmen, and which within that short period had achieved equality with the universities. It played a much more important part in the national life than was justified by its size. I had contributed my share to its development—especially in so far as its international reputation was concerned. I felt a curious, almost physical exaltation, as if I had been wafted far above myself into altitudes hitherto unknown to me.

Once before in my life had I experienced a similar sensation: in my last school year, at that gala performance of our boys' riding club for which I had unforgivably neglected a family funeral. I rode into the hall at the head of the cavalcade that was to perform the quadrille, dressed up in a jockey's red and white blouse. I rode a rather temperamental chestnut mare called Satanella. I was never a first-class horseman, but I have always been able to get on with thoroughbreds, animal or human. She was as excited and as puffed up with vanity as I was, and I knew she would not let me down. When the gates opened, and the band started playing, she just stepped up and showed the crowd what she could do. I merely gave her her head. I was on top of the world. But there was a fly in the ointment; I was at that time passionately in love, and I searched for the face of my well-beloved among the spectators. For some quite paltry reason, she was not in the box I had carefully chosen for her. That gap made all the difference.

Curiously enough, forty years later fortune played me a similar trick. My wife had broken her hip and could not be present at my inauguration. When it was all over, ending with a reception given by the trustees for the recipients of our honorary degrees—the American ambassador, the late Mr. Sackett; Sven Hedin, the explorer, and Theodor Leipart, the head of the German trade unions were among them—I went home. There I sat in the large new apartment I had taken in order to carry out my social duties as rector and pondered over man's intense spiritual loneliness; self-satisfaction and glory had turned to gall and wormwood.

Next day my work began. I found it easy; I had an excellent staff, and since I had no desire to butt in as long as the work was well done, my business load was light. I quickly learned the necessary social tricks. Fortunately I had a good press. Newspapermen generally treated me as someone who might have become a not too unworthy member of their craft, had he been intelligent enough to enter it early in life. They always mentioned my being present at functions, which was all that was needed from the point of view of the college. I used to turn up very early, when my hosts were not yet too much occupied and could take cognizance of my presence. After I had shaken hands with everybody I knew and had been introduced to those I did not yet know, I disappeared and bobbed up at another function, or went home and spent a quiet evening. Thanks to my newspaper friends I got much greater publicity than the heads of the university or the Technical High School, who represented far more important institutions than mine.

## 2. Nazi Professors

A hundred years before, university professors had functioned as leaders of the national opposition. By now, most of them had become thoroughly domesticated. They were appointed by the government, generally on the proposal of their own departments. They had become civil servants who were not yet aware of their bureaucratic position. As they advanced in years, they advanced in rank. They were given titles, such as Privy Councilor, that sounded impressive, but with which no actual advisory duties were connected; they received decorations according to rank, seniority, and sometimes even merit. Some of them, though not their wives, were received at court.

The academic world rather resented the advent of the republic. It ceased to be a privileged estate when its head, the minister of education, had merely a primary school education. In the early days of the revolution, some ministers were not even safe on spelling and grammar. Professors who had to serve under them felt thoroughly humiliated. The power of the faculty departments was broken. They were no longer able to keep out some of their more brilliant younger colleagues who held radical opinions, or were Jews, or in Prussia Roman Catholics, or in Bavaria non-Bavarian Protestants. Worst of all, the republic had abolished honorary titles and all decorations. It did not mean much to those who already had a reputation, but it greatly irritated their less prominent colleagues. It was of no comfort to them that the disappearance of imperial and royal titles left the field of honors to the universities, who could grant honorary degrees. Many were the stars and ribbons available in the twenty-two monarchies of the Bismarckian empire. Under the Weimar Republic, only a doctor's gown was available to hide the unadorned breast of an ambitious businessman.

One day one of my junior lecturers approached me and suggested the name of a Jewish banker to whose institution he acted as economic adviser. His chief was a very worthy man; but to confer a degree that could not be justified by any accomplishments on his part would have damaged the standing of the college. "I quite understand," said my young friend. "I am sure he is willing to make ample compensation." "Is he really?" I asked; "I need about two hundred thousand dollars to establish two new chairs in the social sciences, if the reputation of the college is not to suffer." "Two hundred thousand!" he gasped. "I thought fifteen hundred would do." They did, at a neighboring old-established university. A few months later the same young man who had been so solicitous for his Jewish chief revealed himself as a Nazi of long standing.

Our faculty comprised representatives of all political shades. We had a few ardent old-fashioned nationalists; but they were honorable men, who stood by me in the days of crisis when liberals proved far less reliable. Economics and law were in the hands of men with wide views, who with few exceptions were good republicans—at least as long as the republic was safe.

My most brilliant colleague was Dr. Carl Schmitt, a fervent Rhenish Roman Catholic. He was generally considered the most able of the new school of political scientists. I had given him his first innings in my Munich days; I finally succeeded in calling him to Berlin. I knew the instability of his temperament, but I had faith in his genius. I hoped the political responsibility he could shoulder in Berlin would sober him. I underrated his boundless vanity, his intellectual waywardness, and the influence of his Serbian wife, whose ferocious Balkan nationalism led him astray. He had not played the part he had hoped to play with the republican government, not even when the Roman Catholic party was in power. So he got in touch

with the intriguers round General von Schleicher, and finally
he was ready to join the Nazis. A few weeks before Adolf Hitler
became omnipotent, Schmitt had a call to Cologne. He justified
his accepting it by telling me that he had better clear out, since
our political views no longer coincided. "That is no reason," I
replied. "You know I am a liberal. I do not burn heretics; I
leave them to the tortures of their bad consciences." He had no
answer. A few months later he became Göring's adviser on
public law, denouncing the Weimar Constitution more fervently than he had praised it before, foaming at the mouth
against democrats, liberals, republicans, and Jews. But he did
not prosper. A man of ideas, he tried very hard to impose them
on his Nazi friends; but they had no use for original thinkers.
They wanted learned men with international reputations to
sell the Nazis' official intellectual crudities to the world as profound discoveries. Schmitt was soon sidetracked. The Nazis
gave him a lesson in gratitude. They justified his elimination by
pointing out that his career had been due primarily to people
like myself.

A similar fate befell Werner Sombart. Many years before, he
had found refuge at the Berlin College of Commerce when the
universities would have nothing to do with him because of his
supposed radicalism. He was certainly one of the most brilliant
of German economists. To a wide though not very profound
learning he added a great gift for salesmanship. He had played
the wild man very successfully at a time when it appealed to the
coming generation. He was the type of calculating bohemian
who manages to get an evil moral reputation, partly because he
means to have some extramarital fun, but chiefly because he
wants to shock the philistines. Yet the liberal philistines who
founded the college twenty-five years earlier had had the courage to appoint him in spite of his exhibitions. He had proved
a great attraction to the students. When the old regime in Prussia was on the decline, he was appointed to the university; he
still continued with the college, partly from habit, partly from
gratitude, but above all because it paid well. A few weeks before my resignation he celebrated his seventieth birthday; I
organized a banquet in his honor. He did not like my telling
our fellow guests the story of his early appointment, and my
mentioning the debt he owed to the despised liberals, for he

was getting ready to inspire the Nazis. By temperament a prima-donna, he had played the role of the socialist infidel when monarchy and religion were fashionable; when the republic was in power, he turned monarchist and reverted to God. He knew there was no real risk in his spectacular tergiversations. The Nazis, however, disappointed him. Like Schmitt, he was quite prepared to eat all his Jewish friends alive, though he owed a great deal to them, but he wanted to remain a prima-donna. He meant to inspire the Nazis with his own ideas, over-looking completely the fact that Adolf Hitler specialized in intuition and would brook no rivals in his particular trade. I had known Sombart for many years, and we had got on ex-tremely well, though I sometimes hurt his vanity badly. "You are just the opposite of Bernard Shaw," I once told him. "Shaw is a profound social thinker, who cannot help being brilliant; he regrets that the British do not take him seriously. But you try very hard to impress people as an amusing cynic, and you do it by throwing cumbersome volumes full of abstruse learn-ing at their heads."

## 3. Nazi Students

Students all over Germany had been greatly unsettled ever since the war. The new regime was tearing down obstacles that had impeded the poorer classes from entering universities. It tried to carry out the slogan "Open roads to all talents." It was not very successful as far as manual workers were concerned; but it thoroughly frightened the beneficiaries of the previous system. In the winter term 1913–14 there were 78,000 university students registered in all Germany; in the summer term of 1931, their number had grown to 104,000 men and over 20,000 women. Jobs had not multiplied as fast as applicants. The specter of unemployment frightened students.

The more brilliant ones had little to fear; but the mediocri-ties were terrified by the increasing severity of the struggle for life. In many cases their families' financial position had wor-sened. Inflation had not killed capitalism—in fact, it had greatly strengthened the position of aggressive entrepreneurs, who were making profits at the expense of their weaker brethren. But it had destroyed the financial background of the educated middle class, who had supplemented their professional incomes by investments in government bonds and mortgages. They blamed the loss of their modest fortunes on the new order. Students saw with great displeasure that many of the choicest plums in the administration were given to men without academic training as rewards for past political services. The smarter ones quickly sized up the situation and affiliated themselves with mass parties, either the Socialist or the Roman Catholic Center, which could be expected to have a hand in the government of the Reich and the states in nearly all imaginable combinations. They became good forecasters of party prospects, if not firm believers in party programs.

The smaller fry had neither the same clarity of vision nor the same opportunity. They had no luck with the powers that be, with whom smart Jews and equally smart Gentiles were collaborating. The regular opposition, such as the Nationalists, did not attract them, since it drew its recruits from the higher social ranks.

Only the Nazis offered them a really good chance. They promised to clear out every wicked jobholder whom the republic had put in, and to distribute the spoils.

In the autumn of 1932, when Hitler's chances were rapidly declining, Nazi students were deeply depressed; they openly talked to me about their troubles. "Our hopes have gone—we thought the party would be in very soon. The Jewish professors would have been eliminated, exams would have been made much easier, we would have passed with flying colors and got the jobs for which we have been designated." These feelings were frequently nursed by equally disillusioned professors.

The Nazi party took good care to organize the students. Its appeal to patriotic and militarist emotions naturally found an eager response from a generation which had not seen the horrors of war, but which knew, and feared, the terrors of peace. Its members loved to join secret bands and to train for a war of liberation. The party denounced the sterile intellectualism from which Germany was supposed to have suffered, and taught its followers that brains mattered little, provided they were bred from brawny sires.

In 1931 and 1932 student riots were the order of the day.

They were always organized by students from another school. Academic authorities could discipline their own students—they were powerless against intruders from outside. They did not want to call in the police, for the universities had always been sanctuaries that the minions of tyranny must not invade. The only way to deal with such disturbances was to close the institution for a day or two and to admit no one to its sacred halls without a proper identification card.

Fortunately my college had not had much trouble, though friction between rival political groups was inevitable. A small, numerically unimportant Communist group made it their job to defend the college, the Reich, and the world against fascists. The Nazis, on the other hand, tried to save civilization from the Communist dragon. It all went on in a fairly harmless way. The several groups met between lectures, in corners of the great hall, and did a little joshing. The Communists, who expected the downfall of capitalism in the next few months, as the Moscow clairvoyants had predicted, waxed very aggressive and one day tried to oust the far more numerous Nazis from their pet corner. A free fight was in sight.

I got in touch with both groups. I had just settled the problem on Solomonic principles with the leader of the Nazis, by allocating separate days for the meeting of each group, when a wild commotion started in the hall, followed by the intonation of the "Horst Wessel Song," the Nazis' battle hymn. I rushed out, dragging my Nazi student leader with me. Groups of excited students crowded the place, dominated by a Nazi band, which evidently had come from other colleges and was ready to start a free-for-all fight. When they saw me, they stopped for a minute. I have had scant opportunity for using really bad language since my African days; now I let myself go. I called them despicable curs, who could not even be loyal to their own men. I shoved my Nazi student in front of me, and, to his honor be it said, he was terribly ashamed of his comrades. "Here," I shouted at them, "is your leader; I have just made an agreement with him, now you stab him in the back and make him break his word, which he gave a few minutes ago. You are swine and cowards; I know how to deal with you; I don't have to shut you out, I'll shut you in. All doors will be closed immediately. Nobody will leave the house who is not registered as a student of this college."

Consternation was rapidly followed by a stampede. My janitors were closing the doors; but the windows on the ground floor were open, and the invading host jumped through them as quickly as it could. A few managed to get away by borrowing identification cards from our own students. I did not catch any of them. I could not have punished them anyway, since they were not under my jurisdiction. But I did round up a number of my own students who had given away their identity cards. I have never seen more miserable sinners. Each one started by denying everything; but as they had been caught red-handed, all finally broke down. Only one of them had the courage to say that he was bound by loyalty to his party. "Very well," I replied, "are you not also bound by loyalty to this college? Didn't you agree to obey its laws and to uphold its honor when you first registered? You have to choose. If loyalty to your party comes first, there is no place for you in this institution."

The worst of all was a girl—one of those fanatics whose mad rage stares at you through their eyes, and she was a stubborn liar. It ended in an awful wail. When she had calmed down, I told her that I was not going to punish them. "I know you now," I said, "and I know you are a despicable lot. You have neither honor nor courage. I am not going to let you pose as martyrs and present your party with a cheap triumph. I despise you. If you want to go on in this institution, in spite of my contempt for you, you can stay. Anyhow, you have learned that I can keep order in this house without having to call in the police." None of them left the college.

Somehow the story leaked out. The papers gave me headlines and wrote me up as a hero who had single-handed beaten down a Nazi rebellion. It was very useful. From that time on until my resignation, I had little trouble with my Nazi students. I had spoken a language they could understand.

## 4. Von Papen

The summer of 1932 saw the downfall of the Weimar Republic. A palace revolution, engineered by von Papen and his Nationalist friends, ousted Brüning and made Papen chancellor. It was the beginning of the end. True to its pacifist traditions, the German Republic did not fight; up to the last moment the working class remained law-abiding. I was credibly informed that the Democratic and Centrist members of the Prussian cabinet, which Papen was illegally removing, were prepared for a call to arms and were ready to have him arrested by the stanch republican Prussian police. The trade union leaders held back. They had to face a struggle on two fronts. They never knew whether or not the Communists would stab them in the back; they could not come to terms with them because they were mere puppets who took their orders from Russia.

The Russians recognized a kind of spiritual affinity between German Communists and German Nazis; they knew that a few million votes had repeatedly shifted from one group to the other. They had no objection to civil war in Germany. It would undermine the Weimar Republic, and with it the capitalist system. In the summer of 1939 they expected to emerge as the happy survivors of a European conflict in which the Western capitalist powers and the Nazis would devour each other. Seven years earlier in the summer of 1932 they did not mind the slaughtering of the Weimar Republic by Nationalists and Nazis, for they naïvely assumed that they would be the Nazis' heirs. The republicans contented themselves with an appeal to legal arguments before the Supreme Court.

I had known the new chancellor, von Papen, very well during part of his American career. I had never had a very high opinion of his political abilities. I appreciated his personal attractiveness. He was a charmer. He did not, like old Prince Bülow, make a business of this art—it was second nature to him. He is probably one of the most consummate liars who ever lived, but he rarely lied with the object of misleading one; he merely wanted to impress one favorably. He made promises over and over again, believing in his ability to carry them out. He usually forgot them as quickly as he had made them. He had not the slightest feeling of responsibility. As a dashing cavalry officer he boldly took risks, not so much because he was a hero as because he lacked the foresight to anticipate what he was in for. With the resilience of the daring horseman who has fallen off his mount over and over again and who has broken many bones, he somehow managed to get on his feet again and to climb back into the saddle. He joined to these qualities a good deal of cunning, a love and a gift for intrigue, and an unbounded ambition, in which there was more vanity than desire for power. His American exploits had given him a great deal of publicity. They showed an odd combination of astuteness and naïveté; yet he possessed a good deal of common sense. He had seen the American situation in its true light and had reported truthfully on it, which had not endeared him to Ludendorff.

A faithful Roman Catholic, he had married into an influential Roman Catholic industrial family of the Saar. He entered politics under the Weimar regime as a member of the Center party. The majority of the Prussian Center party were republicans. But Papen represented a conservative Westphalian constituency in the Prussian diet. He tried (unsuccessfully) to push the party toward the right. Finally through his financial resources, he managed to get a controlling interest in the great party paper, the *Germania,* to the disgust of its editors. One of them, my friend Dr. Kuenzer (murdered by the Nazis in 1944) poured out his heart to me in the twenties and enlisted my help in getting rid of Papen. "We must get him out of Berlin and give him a job which appeals to his vanity, but in which he cannot do much mischief. The Berlin government has to appoint a commissioner to the Bavarian government, a position not unlike that of an ambassador. The Bavarians have a strong reactionary tilt; they would love Papen, and Papen would love them. Neither of them can do more harm by joining the other than by standing apart. If we propose it, the government will see in it merely another example of jobhunting by my party. Cannot you do it for us?"

I did my best. But my Socialist friends in the government were adamant. They would not entrust a diplomatic post to a man with·Papen's bad international reputation. So he stayed in Berlin, and as his ambitions were far from satisfied, he very cleverly trained himself for the role of gravedigger of an ungrateful republic.

His appointment as chancellor amused those who knew him; no one, except Papen himself, had a high opinion of his states-manlike qualities. When Frau von Papen was told of his appointment, she is supposed to have broken out into the words, "My poor little Francie!" Her pitying sympathy was thoroughly misplaced; she should have said, "Poor Germany." We all underrated his capacity for doing mischief. For President Hindenburg loved him. The old man, who always looked upon civilian affairs with the eyes of a professional soldier, was charmed by this dashing cavalryman. Papen, moreover, was on intimate terms with the President's son, and was the friend and candidate of General von Schleicher, the archintriguer in the war office. All those who disliked the republic for one reason or another concentrated behind von Papen—with the exception of the Nazis, who had no desire whatever to contribute to his success. I happened to meet Schacht, for the last time, the day after Papen's appointment. Everyone present was poking fun at the new chancellor. "There may not be much to him," said Schacht. "What matters is the men behind him." Schacht was evidently getting himself ready for the role as economic savior of any regime opposed to the one that had been unwise enough to dispense with his services.

Events rapidly showed that Papen's capacity as a statesman did not measure up to his own opinion of himself. He could neither make the Nazis join him as subordinate supporters of a national coalition nor reconcile the republican majority he had so deeply offended. In the autumn Papen was through. He had to hand over power to his hitherto intimate friend and fellow intriguer, von Schleicher. He thought that Schleicher had betrayed him and breathed vengeance.

Kurt von Schleicher was the only chancellor of the republic I never met. He had been pulling wires for many years in the war office, but had been wise enough to keep in the background. When his candidate Papen had made a mess of it, he came into the open. I greatly disliked the advent of a soldier into the political arena, and I took no trouble to make his acquaintance. On his side, there was not the slightest reason why he should want to meet me. I did not have a good reputation among the literary crowd surrounding him, especially the group connected with the review called *Action*. They printed a very scurrilous article accusing the College of Commerce of being the center of the opposition, where "the spider's web was spun." Spider in German is *Spinne;* by some misprint they used the word *Spion,* spy, which gave me my innings. I wrote to the editor demanding an explanation for his accusing us of being "spies." He excused himself by calling it a misprint; it should have read "spider." "I am delighted," I retorted, "to be able to attest to you that your proof reading is as inaccurate and as irresponsible as your statements." My lawyer implored me to withhold the letter; I would certainly be sued. I told him these people would never attack anybody who hit hard; and I was right. They did, however, try to get even with me a little later. As soon as I had been retired by the Nazi government, they demanded in a leading article that I should be deprived of my passport, as I might do mischief abroad. I read this outburst on Austrian soil with a good deal of satisfaction.

The year's big social function was the *Presse Ball,* a huge feast given by the metropolitan newspapers to their friends. Everybody from the Chancellor down, who was or tried to be anybody, was invited and expected to be present. I had to turn up on Saturday, January 28, in the restaurant of the Zoological Gardens, the only hall that had room for so many celebrities and their hangers-on. I wore full regalia, adorned with my gold chain (it was rather light gold). I shook hands with acquaintances, passed along the different stalls, and managed to be photographed arm in arm with Maffalda Salvatini, a famous opera star, and with an equally popular film star. Having done my duty, I might have gone home, but I felt a curious tension in the crowd.

The Chancellor had not turned up; he was detained by an audience with the President. He wanted to dissolve the Reichstag and break the Nazis, whose power was already on the decline, as the last election had shown. Suddenly the news spread that Hindenburg had refused his demand; Schleicher had resigned, and Adolf Hitler might be entrusted with the formation of a cabinet. "Poor little Francie" had turned the trick. Nothing definite was yet known except that Field Marshal Hindenburg, true to form, had betrayed another government without realizing what he had done. The excitement among insiders was intense. I ran into the minister of agriculture, von Braun, a

Prussian Junker whose protectionist policy I had violently attacked; we had scarcely ever spoken to one another. He took me aside, and bursting with indignation, said, "We have been betrayed!"—giving voice to a sentiment that animated many a decent conservative in those days.

## 5. The Advent of Nazism

After the advent of Adolf Hitler, I immediately sent for my Nazi students. "Your party is now in power," I told them. "This means that you have to support me in maintaining order in the college. Nothing in this house is changed. I have always acted on the principle you profess: I give orders, you obey."

"Yes, Your Magnificence," they replied, clicking their heels. "We obey until we receive counterorders from the government." Until after the burning of the Reichstag and the new election, I had little trouble with them.

After the new elections had shattered Papen's dream of a strong nationalist non-Nazi party, the Nazis began to show their true colors. They had no majority; they had polled only 44 per cent of all votes, while 7 per cent had gone to their Nationalist allies. Yet they considered themselves entitled to domination. All universities and colleges were immediately enjoined to hoist the Nazi flag for three days. My trustees instructed me to carry out the order. No Nazi flag was available. So I sent for my Nazi students and asked them to lend us their flag. They were delighted. I told them that they might be present when it was being hoisted; it would be returned to them after three days. They were in no hurry to claim it; they were, they said, quite sure it was safe in my hands.

Tempers did not remain as gentle. A few days later, a deputation of Nazi students turned up and clamored for the suppression of the Communist party in the college. I was to take down the blackboard in the central hall on which groups used to make their announcements. I refused to do so. "As long as the Communist party is a legal party, I shall maintain its rights. It is not the task of an academic institution to persecute student minorities. You know very well that I have protected you from outside attacks as long as you acted within the constitution. I

have not changed my principles." They withdrew, somewhat
disgruntled. A few days later they sent word that they would
suppress the Communists by physical force if I did not take
down the blackboard. There was only a handful of Communists
in the college—they would have been beaten to a pulp if they
had tried to resist.

I sent for the Communists and explained the situation.
"Write me a letter," I suggested, "in which you insist on your
constitutional rights; but express your willingness to avoid a
fight within the college. Hand over to me your blackboard for
safekeeping until things have quieted down." They promised
to think it over. Their answer was in keeping with their usual
attitude. The chairman of the group, they replied, had gone
abroad (a wise precaution). They did not dare to make a decision in his absence.

This being the case, I took down the board on my own responsibility. I was not going to have a fight within the college
to protect a group who could not even muster enough courage
to make up their minds. I have always respected Communist
workingmen who were ready to shed their blood and die for
their ideals. Ever since my Munich experience I have taken the
measure of the "Pinkie Winkies," the half-baked minor intelligentsia who clamor for blood as long as there is no danger
and who faint from fright when they see a slight red trickle.

A few days later a member of the moderate Socialist party
came to my office half blinded, with blood running down his
face. He had been attacked without provocation on his part
by a Nazi student. The attack had evidently been well prepared;
the aggressor, medical evidence showed, had put brass knuckles
on his hands. The onslaught had taken place in the street,
where I had no jurisdiction. Neither the police nor the law
courts, I was sure, would do anything. So I sent for the Nazi
student, who fortunately had enough discipline left to turn
up. He was a very unprepossessing individual—a perfect specimen of that low yet cunning type which can be found in faraway border districts like upper Silesia, where he came from.
He rolled off the customary lies about provocation, but I had
no difficulty in eliciting the essential facts. "Witnesses," I told
him, "will make it pretty hot for you. You will be sued in court,
found guilty, and condemned to pay a heavy penalty. Moreover,

after your conviction you will have to be expelled from the college. I do not want the college to be involved in a scandal. Perhaps I can persuade your victim to accept your apology with suitable compensation for the injuries you have inflicted upon him."

"I cannot pay a cent," he yelled, "I have no means of my own. I am here on a scholarship."

"You have certainly made excellent use of that scholarship. Maybe I can arrange matters anyhow. I will use my influence with your victim to get you out of the scrape on condition that you make proper apologies."

"I have to discuss it with my party," he replied. Next day he turned up again. The party was evidently not pleased with his achievements.

"Well?" I inquired.

"I have got no money."

"Are you willing to apologize?"

"Yes," he said. So I dictated a statement in which he acknowledged having deliberately attacked in a cowardly way, without the slightest provocation, an innocent fellow student. He expressed his deep regret for this indefensible action, especially for having hurt him badly, and offered his humble apologies to the victim and to the college. But for his poverty, he would have compensated him, and he was very much distressed at his inability to do so. He signed the paper, which was duly witnessed, and disappeared. It was my last victory.

By that time the Easter vacation had begun. Usually I spent it in my country house in Parsch, near Salzburg. My wife had gone to Bermuda to stay with her brother, who was at that time governor of the islands. I decided to go to Baden, near Zurich, to take a cure for rheumatism. I had a premonition that my German days might be numbered.

Instead of going by train, I went by car to have a last good look at the sights of Germany. I spent a night in Jena, having passed through Naumburg with its great cathedral; another night at Bamberg, the Romanesque beauties of which I had never seen before. I stopped at the lovely old monastery of Fourteen Saints (Vierzehn Heiligen), and finally reached Stuttgart. Next day I drove across the Swabian Mountains, covered with fresh snow, through Donaueschingen across the Swiss frontier. At lunch at Donaueschingen, I listened to the broadcast describing the meeting of the Reichstag in Potsdam that gave full powers to Hitler.

A few days before leaving I had attended what was to be my last public function. A day of mourning in memory of the dead in the great war was regularly observed in March. A solemn meeting in the opera house inaugurated it. I sat in the President's stall, not far from Hindenburg and Hitler. I had ample time to study closely the Slavonic features of the two master gravediggers of Germany. The former showed the drowsy, immobile mask of a man whose mind has died long ago; the face of the latter twitched with the suppressed intensity of the neurotic. After the ceremony we went to the balcony to see a parade of the troops and of the Nazi hosts. I stood in front of Josef Goebbels; he resembled an intensely intelligent, very wicked monkey; his face lit up with joy. "Is it not a miracle?" I heard him say. "Who would have thought it possible a few months ago!" The regiments marched past us with the perfect goosestep for which the Prussian army has always been famous. Behind them came the Black Shirts and the hordes of Brown Shirts, with a loose swinging gait quite alien to Prussian military drill. I suddenly realized its meaning; it was an imitation of the swing of the Deutschmeister, Vienna's crack regiment.

I was witnessing the end of old Prussia: the advent of a new order, none of whose masters were Prussian. Goebbels was a Rhenish Catholic, Göring hailed from Bavaria, and Adolf Hitler came from a corner of Austria where the darkest superstitions of the Middle Ages are said to survive. After the Prussians had defeated the Austrians in 1866 at Königgrätz, otherwise called Sadowa, Austrian patriots and anti-German French breathed "vengeance for Sadowa." It had not materialized for sixty-seven years; now it was coming. Adolf Hitler was Austria's revenge for Sadowa.

## 6. *The End of the Trail*

My cure at Baden did not greatly prosper. News from Berlin was very disquieting. Laws were passed for the dismissal of Jews and Communists who had crept into the civil service without proper qualifications. Those who had been properly established in the hierarchy before 1914 were to be retained. The universities were to be included in this cleaning-up process. My trustees got very worried; they sent me letters and telegrams but did not ask for my return. I realized that I could do little. I was pretty sure I would have to resign as rector. I knew that after my resignation I could not do much for any of my colleagues. I meant to stand pat and to sell out on terms.

I assumed that the government would not yet be willing to depose a rector against whom they had no case. By offering my resignation I might be able to wangle benefits for some of my colleagues who were threatened with dismissal. Some of them argued differently. They hoped that their own positions might be safe, if only they could get rid of me. One of them, who was not an Aryan but who pressed very hard for my resignation, was allowed to remain in office two years after retiring age. He had been a liberal political economist; he did not find it difficult to justify the economics of the Third Reich.

While I was deliberating whether or not to break off my cure, the Nazis acted. They organized for April 1 a nation-wide anti-Jewish boycott. An immediate stampede across the frontier followed; yet not everybody got away. A few wealthy men were held up at the frontier and had to pay a very heavy ransom, if no worse fate befell them. In these circumstances I had to go back and use my official position for the protection of my colleagues. I might have spared myself the trouble.

I crossed the Rhine near Bâle and took the night express to Berlin. It was a weird journey. The long train, composed almost exclusively of sleeping cars, was nearly empty. I was probably the only first-class passenger on it. I reached Berlin without a hitch. The face of the city did not seem much changed. The pogrom was over; the Nazis had duly informed the world that they had not harmed anybody.

I immediately got in touch with my colleagues and my trustees. The chairman, a good Aryan who had never taken much interest in the college, had remained. A new commissioner, till then a subordinate clerk in the accounting department, had assumed control of the college; he was now inflated to bursting point with the sense of suddenly acquired power. He met me in the presence of the chairman and asked bluntly,

"When are you going to resign?" "I shall consult the authorities," I replied, "and make sure of my legal position. Having done so, I shall act accordingly." He was furious. He had evidently wanted to tell his cronies that he, singlehanded, had compelled me to retire. I had to resign in any case, but I did not like to quit without a fight. Having put my neck in the noose by returning to Berlin, I might as well continue to play the hero. I fortunately found a loophole by the use of which I could uphold our independence.

Our financial year ran from April to the end of March; the rector's term of office from October through September; this discrepancy had involved us in some incongruities—we had often discussed a modification. I handed in my resignation, justifying it by the needs of administrative consistency. It would leave a vacancy. The vice-rector who would automatically take my place might not be recognized as an Aryan, and what was worse, according to our constitution we had to elect my successor in June. The college could not be without a head for over three months. So I resigned on the understanding that we would be allowed to antedate a new election. The authorities gladly consented; they were eager to get rid of me.

We duly elected a new rector and performed, without being aware of it, an act of some historic significance. For my successor was the last rector elected by his colleagues in accordance with the ancient tradition of German universities. Everywhere else, the rector was appointed by the Nazis; he no longer represented his colleagues, but became an agent of the central government.

Once I had made up my mind to resign as rector, I wanted to clear up matters completely and send in my resignation as professor of the college. This post was a lifetime appointment. The same people who had wanted me to resign as rector now objected to my doing so as professor. If I retired of my own free will, I would create a precedent. What would happen to them? The Department of Commerce informed me, moreover, that it would not accept my resignation. I was unwise enough to let myself be persuaded. My not having taken the initiative involved a certain loss of personal dignity.

The last fortnight in Berlin was a nightmare. Many personal and political friends had fled. I was completely isolated. My wife had spent the winter in Bermuda. She had started back as soon as the situation became serious, but she had not yet arrived. My telephone was tapped. Every day one heard of people who had been arrested and had disappeared in concentration camps. I lived alone, with a reliable but not very bright housekeeper. I was terrified but tried not to show it. I went about town as if nothing had happened, and nothing did happen to me. I do not know whether I owe this good fortune to my having acquired the reputation of a hero whom the Nazis respected—if so I was a hero in a blue funk—or to some unknown supporter who was able to protect me. The only precaution I could take was an arrangement with a friend who had access to Hindenburg. I was to be called up every morning. If I did not answer, and if the housekeeper could not give an adequate explanation of my whereabouts, immediate steps were to be taken with the President. It was not necessary. As soon as my resignation was accepted and made public I was able to secure a visa for going to Austria. The press was still fairly free. I had a good send-off. I settled my affairs as well as I could and got ready to leave. On the last Sunday, I took my secretary, Grata Schlomka, for a drive to the one beautiful ancient building within the radius of Berlin, the Monastery of Chorin. On a small lake, in a forest of pines, stand the red brick remains; from this center, the Cistercians had spread civilization in these pagan lands. The monastery is a ruin; the heathen had returned.

Once again I traveled the length and breadth of Germany. I spent the first night in Erfurt to look at its Gothic dome; the second night at Würzburg, the center of German baroque. I passed through Nördlingen and Dinkelsbühl, the latter perhaps the loveliest of South German medieval cities, and got as far as Augsburg. In Würzburg I learned by telephone that I had been compulsorily retired as professor. I led the long list of those who were kicked out. The list was cabled all round the world; my wife learned of it when her ship touched Vigo. She was told that I was among the earliest victims of Nazi brutality. She had an awful time till the true facts leaked out. I had managed to send her a wire to Paris, to the house of friends where she was sure to call. By bad luck they were out, and she had to hurry to catch the train to Salzburg.

Those who were compelled to retire were guaranteed a pension. Jewish pensions were reduced by one fourth; pensions of politically dangerous people by one third. I had the honor of being classified among the latter. It did not make any difference, since I never saw a penny of it; the Education Office stopped it by insisting that I had no right to live abroad. The Foreign Office, the Finance Ministry, and the Reichsbank saw no objection to my doing so; the Education Office stuck to its views, even when a pamphlet was shown it containing a not very flattering portrait of me with the caption, "Very dangerous, not yet hanged." I have always accepted it as a compliment paid to my activities in republican days. The Education Office evidently hoped that my desire for a measly pension might be strong enough to make me return to its benevolent tutelage.

From Augsburg I went to the mountains. I passed through Oberammergau. I wanted to see once more the Lake of Roses, where we had spent three happy summers. I knew I was taking a road that had no turning. It was a bright early spring day. The lake lay quiet under the towering peak of the Zugspitz. Nothing had changed much in the twenty years which had passed. Silently I took leave of everything that had tied me to this land. I spent the last night at Feldaffing on Lake Starnberg, at the house of my cousin Emma Bonn. She had been an invalid for many years, but her intellectual activity had never ceased. She had written a number of novels. One of her books, *The Silver Key*, was a charming autobiography; it well deserved the English translation it received. She never left her sickbed until the autumn of 1942, when she was deported with other victims of Nazi brutality and died two weeks later in Theresienstadt.

In Munich, I had lunch and saw a few old friends. The husband of one of them, the perfect type of aristocratic skunk, was in high spirits. He thought his time had come. The other, General Max Montgelas, the foremost German authority on the responsibility for the war, and a man of superior intellectual and moral standards, did not quite know where he stood. As an old army man he welcomed the advent of the Nazis; it represented to him the vindication of Germany's military morale. As a philosopher and a very human being, he was horrified. His wife, on the other hand, was almost mad with enthusiasm—though she was Austrian born and a very fervent Catholic. An impassable wall was rising between us. It was not hard to say good-by to them.

The drive from Munich to the Austrian frontier takes about three hours. We went along a road which I had traveled many times. Far in the distance was the knoll on which stood Sonnenleiten, where we had lived for five years. A little later we passed Freilassing, the last station in Bavaria. What would happen at the frontier? Would they let me pass?

A few hundred feet from the Bavarian customs I stopped for gas. It was Sunday, but as the attendants told us, there was little traffic. We drove slowly toward the customs. They turned out as usual, looking at me and at the car, which they knew well. Then came the passport authorities. Here, too, little was changed. The same faces were there, but a few élite guards were hovering in the background. The inspector looked at my passport, asked the usual questions about currency, which I could truthfully answer, and let us go. The car started slowly toward the river Saalach. The frontier is in the middle of the bridge. A few seconds and we had passed it. The danger was over. I was in Austria.

The sun was setting, and it was getting cold. We stopped at the next inn, and I telephoned to my house that I was coming. The servants were astonished, for they had not the slightest idea of what had happened. They said they would start the furnace, for the house had not been lived in for the last three months. It was odd to feel safe once more, not to have to worry about every step one took, to be able to telephone without fear. But I was terribly tired and played out. The long trail was over; journey's end seemed well in sight.

# XX. On the Fringe of History

## 1. *Austria*

NEARLY THIRTY years earlier, we had gone on a short vacation to Salzburg. The place was almost deserted; we were the only guests in the hotel. It was bitter cold. A thin layer of snow covered housetops and hills. Town and country sparkled in the sunlight like a city of fairyland. We drove in a sledge to the Königsee, and though we almost froze to death, my wife fell in love with the place. Twenty years later, we were looking for a home to which we could retire when my active career was over. We had hired a farmhouse in the Bavarian mountains called Sonnenleiten, planning to buy it later. But we failed to do so, and had to look elsewhere. Sonnenleiten was only an hour from the Austrian frontier; we made many excursions to find something in or near Salzburg. We wanted neither a town house nor a farm—milking cows is not a suitable occupation for a decrepit couple. Nor did we aspire to an old castle with moat and ghost, or to one of those charming rococo or baroque creations, flanked by one or two graceful turrets topped by a bulbous roof, that dotted the valley. We found nothing that suited us. One day when I had almost given up hope, I was driving about with the agent and spotted a little rise above the village of Parsch. On it stood a decrepit structure, overshadowed and surrounded by trees, which a Salzburg lawyer had built for himself. His heirs had let it go to rack and ruin, camping in it for a few weeks in summer. It was for sale. A local architect advised me to pull it down; nothing could be done with it as it was. It had a superb view. Directly in front, in the center of the landscape, rose the citadel of Salzburg with its bold profile, and in the background towered the steep Untersberg; at its foot Tannhäuser is supposed to have rested on his return from Rome. A tremendous ash leaned over the roof of the house, and the branches of tall firs seemed almost to suffocate it. The building sprawled on a narrow ledge on the flank of the Gaisberg, Salzburg's most famous viewpoint. A row of old yew trees screened the main entrance facing a small wood of beeches and maples interspersed with firs, which stretched up the slope of the mountain and was part of the property. I immediately knew that this was the right place for us, and my wife agreed enthusiastically. I was sure that the local architect was wrong. The ground plan of the house was excellent; the foundations were solid. So I went to Munich with a rough sketch I had made and showed it to the architect friend of ours who had built our Munich house. "Let's take the next train and have a look at it," he said. On his advice we bought the place, and commissioned him to reshape it; he made an excellent job of it. It had its own water rights, and we could indulge in modern plumbing based on our American experiences—our wastefulness horrified the parsimonious natives. We moved into the house in the early spring of 1926. The property had been originally named Ringlschmidt Gütle, the "chain smith holding"; the house, built shortly after the Franco-Prussian War, when a wave of Pan-German emotionalism swept through German-speaking Austria, had been misnamed Wilhelmshöhe after the old emperor. We de-Prussianized it and spent twelve happy years in it, my wife living there all the year round, and I in the university vacations.

The Salzburg of the festivals has often been described by Anglo-Saxon pens. Its odd mixture of peasant naïveté and Hollywood sophistication was no doubt a fascinating theme, but it was only a kind of varnish that for two months in the year overlaid a much more solid substance. During those feverish weeks the residents, bourgeois and aristocratic, blew highly remunerative soap bubbles, for the benefit of their visitors, which danced gracefully in the blue air. This started on the first of July and ceased on the first of September, when one assembled in the Café Bazar and recounted to one's friends the material blessings the P.G.s (paying guests) had left behind, and said, "Thank God, it is over."

Though closely united by common interests, city and county were socially divided. City society, led by the professions, was middle class. Incomes were moderate and the style of living simple. Most businesses were conducted in what might be called

Biedermeier style. It was more important to maintain one's accustomed ways of living than to get rich; the rhythm of life was very even, not to say slow. The Church had been the dominant factor in bygone days; its power was still visible in its monasteries and palaces, and in the cathedral in the heart of the old city. The prince bishop of Salzburg had once been both primate of all Germany, and temporal ruler of the city and the surrounding counties. The days of his splendor had gone. The prince bishop I knew was a shrewd peasant from Vorarlberg, who was to show great courage in the days of the Nazi invasion, but who wisely did not try to play the part of prince of the church. I met him the last time at a party given in his honor by an American lady of means. I managed to place myself at a corner farthest away from His Excellency, for I was well aware that we were expected to pay for the honor of sitting down at the same board with him. And sure enough, he produced a plan for an expensive new organ for the cathedral, for which gifts from nonbelievers would be gratefully accepted. I have never refused an appeal for charity from members of another creed, but I do believe that every denomination should pay for its own organ pipes, and I managed to "vamoose."

As in almost every exclusively Catholic country, the people were split into clericals and anticlericals. The clericals embraced the mass of the plain folk, even though socialism had made a deep inroad on them. The professions and the intelligentsia were predominantly anticlerical. They saw in the church and its adherents an organization for keeping men in ignorance and subservience. They called themselves liberals, but their liberalism was almost exclusively anticlerical. Clericalism had once more become a policy under the Dollfuss regime. It attempted to exclude from office nonchurchgoers, whether they were aggressive socialists, atheists, or mildly indifferent bourgeois. It furnished its opponents with ample grievances. Many of them looked upon the Nazis as their liberators and had enthusiastically joined their ranks; for the Nazis stressed their hatred of the church beyond anything the Socialists had ever done.

While a large part of the city was bourgeois, Pan-German, anticlerical, the county was aristocratic, churchgoing, Austrian in the sense that it believed in a kind of Austrian nationality that, apart from the language, had little in common with Germany. Its views were shared by farmers, small artisans, and shopkeepers in the city. It lived in the afterglow of feudalism. In the castles and turreted mansions dotted over the hills and valleys dwelt an impoverished aristocracy, who had lost their fortunes as a result of the breakup of the empire and inflation. They lived a modest, even penurious life in their country residences, which fortunately had been built in the good old solid days of masonry and were comfortable all the year round. All these noble families were related or connected with one another, while their racial origin was very mixed; Czechs, Poles, Magyars, Italians, even Greeks and Rumanians were among the ancestors of the Habsburg nobility. They all called each other "thou," the men having served in the imperial army in which every officer from field marshal to lieutenant used this form of address, while most of the women had been educated in the Sacré Coeur. With few exceptions these ladies were not very learned, but thoroughly cultivated. They were all very religious, but rarely bigoted; being quite sure of salvation, they could afford to indulge in a good deal of tolerant worldliness. They were born hostesses, even when they could no longer entertain beyond offering one a cup of tea. They could all make conversation which never bored one, though it gave one not much to remember, except perhaps an occasional naughty bit of scandal. It seemed fitting that so many had retired to Salzburg, Mozart's playful, gay home town, where city and scenery continued to exhale the spirit of rococo, which even the heavy baroque cupolas of the cathedral had been unable to suppress. To one like myself, who had to study man's problems in the great pulsating urban centers, the few months regularly spent in Salzburg were a vacation in a smiling yesterday. When one had listened to the heavy tramp of revolutionary and antirevolutionary battalions, the rhythm of life in Salzburg was that of a perpetual capricious minuet.

Pauline Montgelas, who was born in the old imperial Austria, had given us an introduction to her friends the Revertera sisters. These two elderly ladies lived in an old spacious mansion in Parsch village; it was almost the only possession left to them. Their father had been ambassador to the Holy See. They had shared the gay life of Rome at the top of the social pyramid.

Countess Paula had somehow missed her true vocation by not entering a convent. Countess Anna lived in the world and loved it. She had played a courageous part in the First World War. Having close connections with Czarist Russia through her mother, she went on a Red Cross mission to Siberia to look into the conditions of the Austrian prisoners of war. She survived a terrible ordeal. When she reported to Francis Joseph, the Emperor commanded her to tell him the full truth of what she had seen and heard of his troops. After listening in silence, the hard old man broke down and wept.

The two ladies were mothering a charming lad, the son of their youngest brother and a beautiful Dutch woman whom he had met and married in South Africa. The boy had inherited his mother's good looks, and had developed an un-Austrian strength of character. Both endeared him to my wife, who after the death of the two countesses looked upon him as her godson. As a native of South Africa, he could claim British nationality. He managed to escape from Austria after the Nazi invasion. At the beginning of the war, he enlisted as a private in a crack regiment, and rapidly rose from the ranks, seeking, it seems, death on the battlefield. For he felt deeply the tragedy of having to fight for the land of his birth and his choice against his father's people. He succeeded; somewhere in the Italian mountains, a hero's death healed the breach.

The Reverteras received us with open arms. Very soon my wife was part and parcel of this last remnant of the once gay and grand European world. As usual I remained an outsider. My wife's friends liked me as much as I liked them—but I was a guest, not a resident. A peasant neighbor who directed a visitor to our house summed up my position correctly: "I am told she is a countess, but he is merely a professor." Still, I ranked above the summer guests, who were not much esteemed, though our social life depended on them. Punctually on the first of July, our friends opened their houses to paying guests whom the festival attracted. The bigger places whose owners had connections with France, Great Britain, or the United States generally had a kind of waiting list of distinguished people. But broadly speaking, on the first of July everybody put away his or her social prejudices and offered hospitality to those willing to pay for it. Few of the great ladies were good businesswomen. They did not charge extra to British and American snobs for the pleasure of living with princes, dukes, and counts. They treated all as welcome members of a large, gay house party. For eight weeks their rooms were once more filled with joy and laughter as in the good old days. One sat down to an early dinner before the performance or a late supper when it was over. Countess Paula disapproved rather mildly of this inroad of worldliness into her quiet life, but Countess Anna was rejuvenated. Once more she was a gracious hostess, directing conversation in three or four languages, mixing her guests as she had been wont to do in her father's ambassadorial palace. Her eldest brother, Count Nicholas Revertera, who frequently visited them for a few weeks or months at a time, was the perfect image of an ambassador of a ceremonious age, when charm and dignity complemented one another. Many a time we compared notes on the opportunities statesmen had missed for making a better world.

When my vacation was over, I had to tear myself away, and pass within twenty-four hours from the eighteenth to the twentieth century.

The triumph of Hitler in Germany had profoundly affected the Austrian atmosphere. The Socialists and the liberals had been the champions of the Anschluss. The former now recoiled from it, while the latter were converted to a kind of exalted Nazism. The Austrian chancellor, Dollfuss, met the danger by establishing a kind of gentlemanly fascism under the protection of Mussolini. Instead of joining hands with the Austrian Socialists, who were by now beginning to understand that greater issues were at stake than the fight against local clericalism, he used the opportunity for establishing after Mussolini's pattern a one-man, one-party government—knowing very well that his party had barely a majority. Having goaded the Socialists into a futile rising, he easily defeated them and court-martialed those leaders he could lay his hands on. He had knocked out the most reliable defense force against Hitlerism, for the Socialists represented more than two fifths of the Austrian population. A little later he was murdered at Hitler's instigation, paying with his life for the criminal blunder he had committed. The Nazi rising failed, for Mussolini came to Austria's rescue.

It was pretty clear that sooner or later I should lose German citizenship. I could easily have been naturalized in Austria; I was Austrian on my mother's side. I knew the ways of the people from long years of residence. My wife, notwithstanding her English descent, had been almost completely Austrianized. Yet I refrained from taking the necessary steps. Austro-fascism was mild; the new chancellor, Schuschnigg, tried his best to undo the harm Dollfuss had done. As a mere visitor I could accept a political situation that greatly distressed me; as a citizen I would have had to take a part. I had little in common with the provocative acidity of some Socialist leaders, but I had even less sympathy with a policy of sentimental medievalism that established a narrow-minded, spoils-hungry, one-party regime. Moreover, I sensed very clearly that after the smashing of the Socialists Austria was tottering. Mussolini had saved her after Dollfuss's murder. He would scarcely wax enthusiastic about an Austria that had mended her ways and reconciled the Socialists. Had Great Britain and France consented to the Ethiopian adventure, he might have been counted upon. When they tried to inconvenience him by sanctions, they lost his support. They did not attempt to snuff him out, a policy the success of which would have intimidated Hitler, who at that time was still pretty weak. They allowed Mussolini to play both Great Britain and Hitler. Naturally Hitler won. The possibility of a Nazi invasion confronted us all the time. We were always in a precarious position, for we were only a few miles from the frontier. But we gambled and we finally lost; fortunately we were not caught. When the Nazis invaded Austria, we were both in London.

## 2. A Road That Has No Turning

When I crossed the Saalach bridge on that cold April day in 1933, I had thought that my active life was over. I could never return to Germany, for the Germany of which I had been, I hope, a not unworthy part had irretrievably gone. The Hitler regime might collapse within a few years; it could easily have been checked in its earlier stages by a high-principled, courageous policy of the Western powers; the wounds it was inflicting on Germany would not heal within my lifetime. I did not share the illusions of many of my countrymen—Brüning among them. The last time I saw him, in summer 1934, in London, he had high hopes of a speedy return. It was just before the June purge. "And what about you?" he asked me. I answered, · "I shall only return under the black, red, and gold flag," knowing well that it would not be hoisted after Hitler had vanished. I had felt no bitterness or vindictiveness—one of my shortcomings is that I am not a good hater. But it was a matter of personal dignity. I was not prepared to accept a belated, lukewarm apology after I had been told that I was not wanted. I could never again do useful work in Germany; my roots had been cut. The republican colors meant little to men like Brüning, who in his innermost heart was a conservative nationalist. I was not a fervent republican doctrinaire. I had early seen the ludicrous side of the republicanism of '48, yet somehow it had got a hold on my emotions. I had never understood why the Weimar leaders had not made Freiligrath's stirring flag song the official republican anthem.* The ditty that had run through southern Germany, after the Revolution of '48 had failed and the flag had been hauled down, faintly tinkled in my memory.

> The tie has been sundered,
> 'Twas black, red, and gold—
> Why God let it happen
> I have often wondered.

I had reached the parting of the ways; the road I was taking had no turning.

But work was not yet over. A few days after my arrival in Parsch Sir William, now Lord, Beveridge, rang me up and invited me to the London School of Economics; not much later the universities of Manchester, California, Pennsylvania, and Ohio asked me to join their faculties. Most enticing in many ways was Alvin Johnson's offer to undertake the organization

* In sorrow and obscurity,
  So long we had to fold them,
  But now at last we have set them free,
  The grave no longer holds them.
  Hark how they rustle, brave and bold,
  The glorious colors, black, red, gold.
  Powder is black,
  Blood is red,
  Golden flickers the flame.

of the University in Exile he was planning, and which became part of the New School for Social Research.

The decision was not easy. Berkeley had been a haven of peace to us twenty years earlier, and many personal friendships bound us to members of the department of economics. We loved California, and we knew that once we had turned toward the Golden Gate, we would soon forget the troubles of Europe. It meant cutting the ties with the old world. We could not keep up our house in Parsch six thousand miles away. It had become my wife's real home; I had no right to uproot her. We might have maintained it from New York. But I did not feel equal to the task of establishing a first-class institution in a foreign land. I had spent a large part of my life in organizing or running colleges and departments; I almost felt a kind of gratitude to Adolf Hitler for having put an end to the administrative side of my career. I was not going to resume it of my own free will. I may have missed a great opportunity, but missing it was far better than not being equal to it. I deeply felt the infectious charm of American life, yet somehow I was always a better European in New York or even in Berkeley than in Berlin or London. I was of the old world, and belonging to it I could interpret it to an American public. But I could not continue to do so once I had lost the intimate touch that depends on permanent residence. My duties at the London School would be light; I could easily go to the States from time to time as a visiting professor; the reverse move was hardly feasible. Last, but not least, England had always been a second home to me. Her institutions and her basic ideas had helped to shape my views in my formative years. Nature may have given me a Latin mind; it was trained in British empiricism. Both my wife and I had close family ties; my work on reparations had brought me in contact with the City and the Treasury. We had personal friends in many different social circles, and in all political camps. I never felt like a refugee or an exile.

England received me with greater kindness than I could have expected. Old and new friends rivaled each other in making life easy for us. Yet I was not really happy. I was no longer a guest in my own right, so to speak. I had slowly graduated from the position of a "bloody foreigner" to that of a "distinguished foreigner"; I now had become an alien. I have no complaint to make; I was treated with the utmost consideration—even the police at Bow Street, to whom I had to report regularly until I became naturalized, were very friendly. Unlike other emigrés, we had no serious financial worries. I had many activities, and I was not torn by divided loyalties. The one and only way to keep the faith was to transfer to Great Britain the loyalty that had bound me to pre-Nazi Germany. Germany, not I, had changed. But my life's work had gone. My chief task had been to interpret the Anglo-Saxon peoples to the Germans, and the Germans to the Anglo-Saxons. Thanks to a number of fortuitous circumstances, I had been fairly successful. Both sides had trusted me. Now the door had been shut.

I could, of course, continue to explain Germany, and there was greater need for this now than at any previous time. But I was no longer on the spot, even though Austria was a point of vantage for observation. Many of my English friends, chief among them the late Lord Lothian, felt some sort of responsibility for what had happened in Germany; they wanted to atone for previous mistakes. "You have refused a permit for carrying a gun to a worthy citizen," I used to say. "After he has been killed by a gangster, you have given it to the murderer." They meant well, and they did not want to have their opinions upset by an anti-Nazi. It was more natural to them to assume that I was prejudiced than that they were blind. When I warned them that "you cannot play cricket with people who bowl with stink bombs," they smiled. After all, I had never played that noble game. Cassandra is a boring female wherever one meets her. Knowing this, I refrained from acting her part. I shut up. I only stated my opinions when challenged. Life in those years was often very pleasant, but somehow it no longer seemed very real.

In those years I roamed through more academic institutions than I had ever done before. Though we settled in London and became British subjects, nearly half of my time was spent in Canada and the United States. My work continued, but my position was greatly altered. I was no longer located in the prompter's box; I had become at best a member of the chorus who could accompany the performance with lugubrious admonitions but was no longer in a position to prod the actors.

I had moved to the fringe of history. The fullness had gone out of life. I had never played a prominent part on the political stage. By temperament and training I was not made for it; I knew my own limitations very well. I had never been an indispensable adviser on technicalities—there were many who knew them far better than I did—but I had a flair for what was essential. When given a chance, I could persuade those in responsible positions to take the right action at the right moment. That was over. It was but natural that an outsider's view in a foreign land had not the same weight as an insider's opinion at home. It was but human to treat an exile's suggestions about his former country with a certain amount of reserve.

I had been bilingual for years; I spoke and wrote English as fluently as my native tongue. Yet I was always under a heavy handicap when I had to express my innermost thoughts in English. I had had a style of my own when writing German; it was accepted and praised as such by readers and reviewers. My English was probably better than that of most translators, for I knew better than they what I meant to say; at its best, it was adequate. I rarely ever again experienced the creative joy that is the reward of a writer who has succeeded in saying what he meant to say in words that perfectly render his thoughts.

As long as we lived in Austria I was not cut off from German thought expressed in German literature. But I had no public in that semi-fascist Austria hanging, so to speak, over the abyss; I do not remember having written a line in German since I left Germany in 1933.

### 3. The Spineless Era

There was a deeper reason for my disenchantment. The England of 1933 was no longer the England of my youthful enthusiasm. She was passing into the spineless era. She alone among the nations of the world had been Rome's successful heir. She was far less Latinized than France, Italy, or Spain, but she knew how to rule in Rome's way. The Roman bearing of her statesmen, not the resemblance of her institutions to those of her great predecessor, had impressed me in my early days. Frenchmen and Italians had "Senates"; they used many institutional

Roman terms. Yet none of their leaders could have worn the toga of a Roman senator as Gladstone, Grey, and Dilke among the politicians could have, or Milner and Cromer among the imperial proconsuls.

The classic fiber in British political life was intertwined with a very different strain—Nonconformity. It had none of the graces that the humanists had salvaged from the barbarian invasion, and which may not survive the age of the technocrats. It did not possess the steel-like flexibility of Rome, but it had even greater strength. It drew it from man's close union with his God. Its exalted fanatic individualism bordered almost on anarchism, for the world might perish if true believers could but save their souls. Had Nonconformists ruled England—as their ancestors had done for a short spell in the seventeenth century—her cultural glories might well have faded; life under their domination would have been void of color and charm. Fortunately the Nonconformists were a minority. As such, they were compelled to fight for human freedom in temporal as well as in spiritual matters, and thus won a liberty they might have denied to other minorities. Nonconformity gave a harshness to British liberalism that the humanist rational liberalism of other countries never possessed. For those who professed it feared Hell more than the temporal power; they were willing to go to the stake for liberty. The Nonconformist conscience, with its horror of arbitrary secular power, had laid the foundation on which laissez faire gained its popular support. Its chosen spokesmen did not always belong to the dissenting churches; John Bright was a Quaker, John Morley a Secularist.

Both temporal Roman classicism and rigid spiritual Puritanism had gone. The latter sometimes revived in fits—about Edward VIII's marriage or a temperance issue. Sir Stafford Cripps is probably its one surviving representative. The last of the Olympians was Lord Asquith. I have known a good many leading statesmen in a number of countries. Some impressed me, others depressed me: I had always been able to meet them on their own level. Asquith in his old age affected me differently; he seemed to have that benign aloofness which we usually associate with the immortals.

I had encountered a similar classic stateliness among the merchant bankers of the City. They wore their frock coats and top hats with the easy dignity of Roman patricians. They were not tied up with local industries like their German and French colleagues. They had been empire builders. Their credits had made goods from all the corners of the earth flow to the London emporium, and their overseas investments had nurtured the dominions and weaned the dependencies. They too had gone. In the crash of 1931 their empire had disintegrated. By now, the short jacket has replaced the double-breasted frock coat; in occasional combination with a top hat, it looks like a symbol of uneasy compromise between old and new.

The emotional strain in Nonconformity had survived in Lloyd George; especially in his opposition to the Boer War and in his hatred of the infidel Turk. But the Welsh wizard was almost as much a spiritual alien in the land he ruled as Disraeli had been. I had come much closer to him than to Asquith. His versatility was dazzling. Yet I never thought that he was betraying his cause, notwithstanding some of his puzzling political somersaults. His political faith was very primitive; he loathed oppression in every form. His stock of learning was slender, but he had an almost eerie flair for "situations." When things could not be done in the right way, he did them in the wrong way—since they had to be done anyway—trusting to time, luck, and his own adroitness for putting them right later on. Something was bound to turn up, and it always did, though not always at the right time or at the right place. His seeming contradictions, his legerdemain, his inclination to be too clever, disgusted many and made them distrust a fundamentally simple personality that had the fatal gift of shining in many colors. He often acted like a chameleon; one should not forget that the chameleon is quite a respectable sort of animal: it never changes its ways of life, it merely varies its purely superficial iridescence when circumstances demand it.

My several encounters with Mr. Lloyd George during the early phases of the reparation discussions had evidently made him overrate me. One day, when I was on a private visit to London, he sent for me. I was introduced to the committee working on the Liberal industrial program as a great expert on coal and steel questions. I tried to wriggle out, but Mr. Lloyd George took me gently in hand. He asked a number of apparently innocuous questions, to which I thought I had cautiously replied.

After an hour of pleasant quizzing, he thanked me solemnly in the committee's name for having furnished them with all the information they had been in need of. He handsomely atoned later on. At a luncheon for the delegation attending a congress of European liberals, he made me sit on his right hand. For the benefit of posterity we were all photographed. My own copy was in my home in Parsch when the Nazis invaded it. It must have been valuable evidence to them of the treasonable activities I was engaged in. I had an inkling that my privileged position was not due entirely to my merits. Putting me in the seat of honor got Mr. Lloyd George out of the difficulty of deciding whether the French or the German delegate was to take it. "He is an old friend of mine, I need him as an interpreter," he said. "I know no German and my French is not very good." To the latter I could attest, for during a committee meeting I had acted as interpreter between him and Daladier.

With all his faults, Lloyd George was Britain's last great prime minister until the advent of Winston Churchill. Those who came after him were either unimaginative businessmen, like Bonar Law and the unfortunate Neville Chamberlain, or political crooners like MacDonald and Lord Baldwin. The former naïvely believed that the airs he warbled were really high-class music; the latter, being a very astute politician, produced them because the people liked them. He kept his ear carefully to the ground in the way American presidents are apt to do. They are accustomed to take their policies from the men and women they are expected to lead, but a British prime minister was supposed to have a policy of his own to offer to the country.

A curious torpor seemed to have seized the British people. A highly emotional flabbiness prevailed. The classic representative of this spinelessness was Ramsay MacDonald. My active sympathies belonged to the Liberal party, but I had been on very friendly terms with British Socialism and the British Labour party since my student days. My personal contacts with MacDonald were few; my superficial impressions were, however, corroborated by the reflex of his personality on his close associates.

Lord Baldwin, leader of the Conservative party, had undertaken the social education of Ramsay MacDonald, who naturally preferred his mentorship to the support of Lloyd George or Asquith. Like many socialists, he hated liberals more than conservatives. Genuine conservatives, after all, sympathize with the collective, not to say coercive, conception of society inherent in all forms of socialism. Liberals, being individualists, loathe it. At the same time, liberals, especially their more radical wing, are serious competitors for votes. In nearly every country the growth of socialism has taken place at the expense of radical liberalism, with the result that the actual strength of progressivism was lessened. Baldwin possessed that mellow seductive lack of principle which is so disconcerting to non-Britishers, and MacDonald was, after all, a glum Scot. Society, moreover, opened its doors to a prime minister whose political harmlessness was guaranteed by his friendship with Baldwin. He was an impressive figure who looked particularly well in evening dress. Society took him to its bosom and made him feel at home. His colleagues saw very little of him.

Baldwin's taming of Ramsay MacDonald was a political masterpiece—though it is true that the animal, never very ferocious, had yearned to become domesticated. For MacDonald as coalition prime minister did not abjure socialism; he let himself be used for conservative policies and purposes. By abandoning free trade, he was instrumental in destroying Great Britain's leadership in international economics. He surrendered it just when the United States was getting ready for a profound change in its hitherto restrictive policies. He never understood that collective security in the political field, to which he was sincerely attached, could not be won when counteracted by economic anarchy, the result of competitive currency manipulation and high tariffs.

No man was perhaps a more passionate friend of peace than Lord Baldwin—being an iron master, he should have been a warmonger according to the pink intelligentsia—and no man was more responsible for the coming of the war. He saw the danger, but he did nothing to make color-blind pacifists visualize it. The specter of class war at home and the threat of totalitarianism abroad were throwing their shadows over Britain. Baldwin tried to disperse them by kindness at home and by pretending not to see the threat abroad. At home he succeeded, notwithstanding the belated infection of the British mind by the Marxist measles, which was as severe as infantile diseases usually are when the patient is of mature age. Britain continued to abhor violence of all kinds. With the exception of a small group of intellectuals, who played with it as with a newly found plaything after the manner of their kind, she repudiated class warfare at home. She loathed foreign war; she was almost ashamed of having won the war and morally disturbed by her holding of an empire. Young England, in particular, saw in imperialists of Kipling's type nothing but blatant music hall performers. A wave of pacifism was sweeping the country. It was willing to let justice go by default rather than risk the ordeal of battle. The minor lights absolved their consciences by charging the responsibilities for the last war to armament manufacturers, and philosophers advised their people to let go everything aggressive nations coveted; once they were saturated with spoils, they would leave the British homelands alone, which could not be defended anyhow against air attacks. In the early thirties the British were probably in a more kindly frame of mind than they had ever been before. They were willing to atone, to forget, to make allowance for anything and anybody as long as they were spared war. They did not mind treaties being broken, provided some plausible justification could be invented. Having given up the guardianship of economic internationalism, they put their hope for an enduring peace in the League of Nations. Lord Baldwin, appealing to this widespread popular feeling, won an overwhelming Conservative victory at the 1935 elections.

Yet all the time the danger was growing. It did not so much consist in German rearmament, or even in the Nazi party, as in Adolf Hitler's make-up. Both Baldwin and Chamberlain inflated the ego of a man to whom everything was personal. One could discuss business with Mussolini, for notwithstanding his megalomania, he had some remnant of Latin common sense —proved by his coming into the war only when he thought it was over. With Adolf Hitler one could not talk, one had to shout him down. He had originally shown great respect for the might of the British Empire. Ribbentrop's report on its spinelessness made him believe in Britain's decay. He did not see the difference between sleep and death.

In the United States a legend was widely spread explaining

appeasement as the desire of capitalists to save their businesses from the impact of war; it was eagerly believed in by the same people who held monopolist capitalism responsible for all wars. Unfortunately the slogan, "peace at any price," was accepted by all British parties—Labour, Liberal, Conservative, with a few honorable exceptions. The former chancellor of the exchequer, Hugh Dalton, was one of them, but not so the prime minister, Mr. Attlee.

But for this insipid pacifism, the danger of war during the first years of Hitler's regime was slight. Had Great Britain informed him early in the day that his anti-Jewish policy must not inconvenience Britain's position as the mandatory of Palestine, Hitler would have fumed and raged, but he would have drawn in his horns. At that time he could only bark, not bite. Had Britain and France withdrawn their ambassadors after the murder of Dollfuss, in which Hitler was implicated—as Great Britain had done in Serbia a quarter of a century earlier—the shock to Hitler's reputation would have been very great. Had Great Britain told the world that she was prepared to rediscuss all German questions with any civilized German government, she would have undermined Hitler's internal position. By withholding absolution from men who broke treaties, she could have made it very clear that the issue was not remilitarization of the Rhineland, or Czechoslovakia or Poland, but the foundation of international life, the sanctity of treaties. There was little sense in upholding the Covenant when one was ready to condone the violation of treaties the Covenant was supposed to uphold.

It is unfair to throw all responsibility on Neville Chamberlain; most of the sins of omission had been perpetrated before he came to power. But he was a leading member of the cabinet that had condoned them. It had never realized that Britain's concessions were consolidating Hitler's position in Germany. The millions who had voted against him were shocked when they saw him treated with deference by the powers who had often humiliated republican statesmen. They were given no chances of pointing to the failure of the new regime, when the Allies were providing it with easy triumphs. Those who express astonishment at the absence of a powerful underground movement in Germany should remember that their own policy deprived the opposition of all trumps. It is not easy to revolt against a government that is successfully re-establishing a nation's international position.

I had never met Chamberlain in person, but I knew Sir Horace Wilson, his trusted adviser. I had seen him at my cousin's, the late Sir Max Bonn, who shared his interest in youth problems. Sir Horace had little if any experience in international affairs. I met him the last time at Whitsuntide 1938, before the Czech crisis, at Sir Max's quaint Surrey cottage, Ifold. He took me aside after tea. "The Prime Minister," he began, "is a very solitary man. Can you make a suggestion that I can pass on to him?" I replied, "Get an unexpurgated translation of *Mein Kampf* and make him read it." I am sure he never did.

I happened to be staying with the late Lord Tweedsmuir, then governor-general of Canada, who was convalescing in a Welsh sanatorium, when the papers announced Chamberlain's intention to call on Hitler. The mere fact that the British prime minister asked for an audience—for this was the way Hitler saw it—was bound to inflate the ego of this neurotic weaver of crude Caesarian dreams, and make him lose all sense of proportion. When the message reached him, he is reported to have said, "But surely this is impossible." It did not matter whether or not Chamberlain lost a little prestige. What mattered was that Hitler, who had hitherto admired the British Empire, saw its premier groveling at his feet.

Chamberlain, decent and apparently modest, suffered from personal overvaluation. He saw himself as the man capable of taming this wild beast, armed only with good will and a well-advertised umbrella. His self-confident naïveté surpassed all bounds; he evidently did not even bring his own interpreter. I implored Tweedsmuir to warn the Prime Minister that Hitler would misunderstand Great Britain's basic attitude if the meeting did not take place on neutral ground. The Prime Minister's self-deception was incurable: it survived even the Munich conference. When he returned from the ordeal he was evidently convinced that he had saved the peace of the world.

One day in that dismal winter I had been pressed into a discussion on foreign affairs at the English Speaking Union. "I am not going to give you my opinion," I said, "but I am going to tell you a story. It runs like this: I am informed that Mr.

Neville Chamberlain had invited Adolf Hitler to come over for a few days' fishing. Hitler accepted, and managed to arrive safely in a secluded spot in Scotland, without having been mobbed by an honest British crowd. The weather was fine, the guest was in good humor and put his best foot foremost. He was given a rod, and a gillie conducted him to a pool where he was bound to make a strike. The P.M. was delighted: his method worked. He was just casting a fly, when he heard a loud detonation. An attempt on Herr Hitler! He rushed to the spot, and to his great relief saw Adolf Hitler staring gleefully down on the water. A number of dead fish were floating on the surface of the pool. Adolf Hitler had dynamited them. The P.M. was shocked. He was torn between his duties as a host and the ethics of the complete angler. He tried to explain to his guest, who seemed rather proud of his exploit, that things were not done in this way in the British Isles. But Hitler merely yelled at him, 'But I do them, have you not read my book?' "

My audience was delighted. After the meeting, a distinguished elderly lady addressed me. "That was a good story. I am going to Scotland tomorrow to fish with the Prime Minister."

# XXI. The Guardianship of the Western World

## 1. *Disillusion*

TWICE WITHIN barely thirty years I have been in a position to watch the attempts of the United States to advance from the stage of timid, self-satisfied provincialism to that of the leading world power. Twice it fought obstinately against greatness thrust upon it. The transition, not being the result of organic growth, but of two wars, both of which the American people had tried hard to avoid, was painful. Fortunately the United States was strong enough to carry the burden, though its people deeply resented the responsibilities involved. Woodrow Wilson, their leader in the first war, had had a vision of the City of God among men. He had managed to impart to his countrymen the fiery passions that burned below a frigid surface, and had turned the war into a crusade. But he had failed to reach the goal, for the scale of the adventure had made him lose the solid ground under his feet. He knew mankind better than men. When he succeeded in creating the framework of a better world in the League of Nations, his own people refused to dwell within it. Both the downfall of the marvelous edifice they had attempted to build and their actual experiences had disillusioned them. The American armies that had fought in France and entered Germany found to their dismay that they had much more in common with the detested Hun than with their gallant French allies. "Thank God we are in a clean land," two American newspaper boys exclaimed, who had managed to run into Munich ahead of their formation immediately after the armistice. They had slipped away without any extra clothing, and knowing our name, had come to ask for help. We gave them the horse blankets left over from the days when our horses had been commandeered.

The American people at large just could not understand the European mix-up. Both European history and geography are complicated when compared with their massive counterparts on the American continent, where the actual meaning of a frontier is fortunately unknown to many. Americans saw in the intricacies of European affairs a wicked game played by power politics; political Europe was a body in decay; the mere contact with it might poison America. Yet economic ties had to be forged, for trade, properly protected, was an antidote to political entanglements: President Coolidge had solemnly impressed this rather doubtful doctrine upon me in 1924. His party had accepted it with enthusiasm, and had encouraged its countrymen to pour out their wealth in loans to Europe. But Europe had defaulted (so had Latin America); she had shown that she was as little trustworthy in business as in politics. All European nations, Britain and France as well as Germany, had welshed. Only gallant little Finland had punctiliously discharged her obligations. The outcome of it all was a neutrality legislation, a scrapping of the principle of the free seas, for which peace-loving Thomas Jefferson had almost gone to war, by those who claimed to be his heirs. Wars were the curse of Europe; peace was the privilege of the Western Hemisphere. The farther apart the two were drawing, the better it was for the future of mankind. While Europe might destroy herself, the United States in splendid isolation would prosper, and fulfill mankind's glorious destiny.

## 2. *It Is No Crime to Be Young*

I crossed the Atlantic late in October 1939 to fulfill earlier lecturing engagements in the United States and Canada. I had planned to return after three months; I stayed for six and a half years. Thanks to the Rockefeller Foundation and to the Institute of International Education, a number of visiting professorships were offered to me. I accepted them on the advice of Lord Tweedsmuir and Lord Lothian; both were of the opinion that such qualifications as I possessed were more useful in the Western Hemisphere than in England. I spent terms at Bowdoin College, Maine; McGill University, Montreal; the University of Pennsylvania, Philadelphia; Occidental College, Los Angeles; Hamilton College, Clinton, New York; Carleton College, Minnesota, and Colorado College, Colorado Springs. As my academic duties were usually not very heavy, I had time to address popular audiences, Lions, Kiwanis, Rotary clubs, church meetings, and institutes of all sorts on my particular subjects. I spent little time in the big cities, among skyscrapers and screeching trolleys. Once again I lived the life of the small communities with which the United States is dotted. I enjoyed the tranquillity, the friendliness and good will I found in their midst; they have none of the churlish arrogance of the European small town. They represent democracy at its best; they do not impose on everybody a rule of hard, leveling-down equality, but give a chance to all their members to live a decent life. I had shared to some degree the haughty attitude of the intelligentsia, most of whom have come from a small town, who look with scorn upon the Babbitts they have left behind and make Rotarianism and what it stands for the butt of their wit. I have sometimes been amused by some of the quaint ceremonies local Rotarians, Kiwanis, and Lions indulge in. Like many of their countrymen, their members have an almost childish delight in masquerade and mummery; and I must acknowledge that their musical performances frequently gave more joy to the performers than to detached listeners. But after all, it is better to be grown-up and feel young, than to be young in years and old in mind, as many intellectuals are. I have watched the transition in the United States from stern Puritanism to cheerful Rotarianism for over thirty years. It is not a change for the worse. I prefer the naïve inquisitiveness of the plain people to the sophisticated querulousness of more intellectual groups who show their progressiveness by asking "Marxist" questions that I first heard answered in my Vienna student days nearly half a century ago. I remember with particular pleasure the Christmas dinner of the post office employees in Northfield, Minnesota, where I was the guest of the evening, and had to give a talk on continental European problems. I was plied with pertinent questions. Whenever I met one of my hosts on his rounds, he stopped me to discuss the latest news or the most recent books on foreign affairs.

In the autumn of 1939 the American atmosphere did not differ much from that of Europe during the spineless years. The same color-blind pacifism prevailed, particularly among progressive elements. It was greatly strengthened by that naïve moral superiority complex of the masses, who look upon the European peoples as cursed with a double dose of original sin, and are apt to forget that the only total war in the nineteenth century was the War between the States. This primitive, somewhat antiquated Puritan pacifism was blended with an equally primitive Marxism, which had infiltrated the United States after the Russian Revolution. It had had a little influence on the working classes; it fitted in beautifully with the moods of the minor academic intelligentsia. It taught them that war was the inevitable result of the capitalist system, which could not survive but for an expansion of markets through war. The part the "merchants of death," the armament industry, was supposed to have played in dragging the United States into the First World War seemed to prove this thesis. A people that felt secure in its geographical isolation, whose history was mainly economic, and whose successful assimilation of many races seemed to prove the relative unimportance of nationality could easily overlook all noneconomic causes of war. By mixing a little isolationism with a lot of so-called Marxism, history became simple and convincing. All facts easily fell into line, and one did not have to worry about what otherwise was very much like a complicated jigsaw puzzle. Teaching history was made easy, and so was learning it; it did not matter whether the information came from broadcasters, columnists, or junior college teachers. The fact that Russia had turned her back on the Western powers, and had, so to speak, blessed Hitler's adventure in advance, in return for a very large share of the spoils, was ample proof of the correctness of this reading of history. The war was nothing but an imperialist war between the decaying capitalist powers in Europe; its outcome would not matter much to true civilization.

Behind it all lurked the fear of war. Under modern conditions war meant the draft. Both American mothers and American youths, especially in the big cities, loathed it. The soothing comforts of a mechanical age had damped youth's adventurous spirit for the time being—just as in England. The movies provided all sorts of romantic excitement at very little expense, and for those whose imagination rose to higher planes, there was the great Bolshevist experiment to be admired, and if possible, imitated. Facts are often more weird than fiction, but facts established by fiction are just irresistible.

I happened to be present at the Republican convention in Philadelphia that bolted from the safe, standpat Republican leadership and nominated Willkie. Groups of boys and girls were parading outside the hall carrying placards—"The Yanks are not coming," and "It is no crime to be young." "—It certainly is not," I said to one of them, "but is it a merit?" She scowled at me, for she saw in it a kind of supreme personal accomplishment, which not only entitled her to special personal consideration, but gave her an unerring insight into the world's working mechanism. She was a spirited representative of many progressive groups, who were all for clamping down salutary regimentation on the wicked capitalists responsible for the great depression, but who were terrified that the coming of war might subject them to similar disciplinary injunctions.

Britain's ways, moreover, in the spineless era had estranged many of her friends, even though there were ardent appeasers for their own country among them. The course of the war in the first months did not win much sympathy. While Poland went down like a house of cards—which scarcely astonished those who were conversant with the heroic dilettantism of this gallant nation—her allies seemed to seek shelter behind the Maginot line. The war was "phony." It was galling to war correspondents who had nothing to report, and disappointing to a public that had nothing to read.

The fall of France, in June–July 1940, changed the picture completely. For the first time, the masses sensed the actual danger of a Nazi victory to the United States. The British stand at Dunkirk, the skill of the evacuation, the speeches of the new prime minister thrilled the country. This was heroism on a scale that did not merely satisfy the cravings for headlines; It touched the heart of the nation. For a short time the British were more popular than they had ever been. Yet admiration was mixed with almost pitying sympathy. Britain could not last. I spent those critical weeks in Bowdoin College, Maine, and in Montreal among true friends of England. Almost all of them were convinced that the end was in sight. They smiled at me when I assured them that this was only the beginning.

The blitz raised both British credit and American fears. The almost fantastic victory at Sidi Barrani showed the pitiful weakness of Italian empire builders, and damped the ardor of the by now no means negligible fascist elements among Americans of Italian origin. But the Greek tragedy, which entailed the sacrifice of the African success, evoked criticism rather than admiration. The sending of troops in an almost forlorn hope to save a gallant ally seemed silly; in any case it was "too little and too late." Thermopylae touched no string in the public mind. The rasping yells of Muscovite fellow travelers, who continued to call the war imperialist, drowned the humanist traditions that the best in the United States had shared with Europe.

## 3. Slag in the Melting Pot

American foreign policy is complicated by foreign-born pressure groups. Their members are loyal American citizens. Nothing on earth could induce them to return to the lands of their birth; yet they feel it incumbent on themselves to act as their spokesmen, even when their interests are by no means those of their new home. There have been Irish, German, Italian, Czech, Hungarian, and Polish pressure groups. Those of their members to whom success has been denied, and whose assimilation has been incomplete, resent the time-hallowed ascendancy of the Anglo-American strata. They see in them a kind of spiritual British garrison on that otherwise free continent of theirs, through which a socially backward country like monarchist Great Britain exercises a kind of domination over them all, using the wealth and the strength of the American people for sinister, purely British interests. Sentiments of this sort have prevailed among the Irish for a long time.

All through its history "ascendancy" has been split. Its New England branch spread all over the continent. Only a relatively small remnant has stayed in its native haunts, where it forms a thin crust overlaying large Roman Catholic masses: Irish, Italian, Polish, and Portuguese immigrants in the big cities,

French Canadians in the textile and lumber towns. In the South, the English stock continues to prevail, for the presence of the Negroes has prevented mass immigration. The South has always been more pro-British than New England, which never completely forgot its early revolutionary doctrines; but it has played a far less important part in the nation's intellectual life. Unlike the fellow traveler whose sun rises in Moscow, neither the Irish nor the Czechs nor the Poles have had a doctrine to rival "the American way." At one time the German-Americans possessed one, which found expression in the elder La Follette's Wisconsin idea. Its mild state socialism had been incorporated in national policies through the New Freedom and the New Deal. By now neither Irish nor Germans were particularly articulate. The Catholic church, very influential among the Irish—or one might even say, the Irish were very influential in its hierarchy—had no particular love for the Austrian paperhanger, as one of the princes of the church had dubbed him. The neutrality of the Free State offended the generous fighting spirit of many an Irishman. The German-Americans lay very low. Intense anti-German feeling, such as I experienced during the First World War, was absent. One could speak German everywhere without being molested, and could use it freely over the telephone without the risk of its being tapped. The fear of a strong German-American movement had vanished. The last twenty-five years had almost completed the Americanization of the millions of old immigrant Germans; the frantic effort of Nazi newcomers only touched a narrow fringe of disgruntled fanatics.

There was no Russian pressure group proper, for there was no regular emigration from Soviet Russia. But a certain nostalgia for things Russian had never died out among the Jewish victims of former Czarist persecution, who had found Zion in New York and other big cities. Their sons and daughters have risen in the world and are playing an influential part in American life. Many of them saw in the Bolsheviks avengers of the wrongs done to their parents and grandparents, and found it easy to sympathize with them. Highly gifted intellectuals are among them, who enjoy the dogmatic subtleties of the new faith. The minds of a people whose ancestors have been engaged in finding eternal truth by defining words and splitting

hairs are well prepared for its dialectic theology. Deep down
in their souls, the messianic belief in the coming of a Re-
deemer is slumbering. The young generation have long since
been secularized in American schools. But their craving for
redemption has survived; it has been turned into philosophic
materialism. The coming of Marx-Lenin was to them the beginning of the millennium. They have no inborn love for the
spiritual inheritance of the Anglo-Saxon people, which they
have had to share in an alien language, and which they will
have to fashion in their own particular way before it really
becomes their own. Its direct heirs are privileged rivals, who
start the race from a favored position, and who exact con-
formity from those born outside the pale. The latter naturally
resent this. There is a good deal of social anti-Semitism in the
United States, which does not distinguish between western and
eastern Jews, though they are as distinct from each other as the
hosts with whom they had lived. These groups had no intellectual alternative to the Anglo-American way until the advent of
Bolshevism. They now have a rival creed.

The number of actual Communists in the United States is
very small; but Bolshevist slogans were eagerly taken over by
numerous less privileged groups who have not won complete
assimilation on the basis of equality. Pacifists, isolationists,
foreign pressure groups, and native Americans were all anti-im-
perialist. The mere fact that the British hold an empire con-
demns them in the eyes of even friendly Americans. For empires
were won by force, and imply the subjugation of one nation by
another. It does not matter whether their rule is good or bad,
or whether those governed are fit to govern themselves by
democratic methods. Empires are wicked anyhow, and those
who hold them should not expect support from American democracy. The British Empire, moreover, is far-flung and brittle.
It is full of danger spots where war might break out any day.
The United States must not allow the Anglo-Saxon minority
among its people to draw it into a war for salvaging a tottering
empire. Lenin's definition of imperialism as the final stage of
monopolist capitalism, and his assertion that capitalism as such
could only survive by the conquest of new markets, gave a
common platform to antimonopolists, pacifists, nationalists, isolationists, and Communists. The same people who accused Cham-

berlain of having sold Czechoslovakia in order to save British capitalists from the impact of war now turned round and blamed the war on capitalists.

The situation changed with Hitler's attack on Russia, when the war between two partners who had agreed to partition Europe had in fact become imperialist—a war for huge territorial spoils. Overnight all pink peacemongers became red warmongers. The new Jerusalem was being menaced, and all mankind must come to the rescue. The relief was great, though Russia's military accomplishments during the first war year were by no means spectacular. She had armed feverishly for sixteen years; she possessed overwhelming manpower and unlimited natural resources, yet she had lost the richest part of her territories. Had not Adolf Hitler himself interfered with his generals, the Germans might have won.

### 4. *The East Saves the West*

President Roosevelt had foreseen the grave danger to the United States of a Nazi victory. He had done everything in his power to prevent it—but his power was limited. He could not declare war on Germany; this was the privilege of Congress, and public opinion would not permit Congress to do so as long as vital American interests had not been ostensibly violated. The concept of a preventive war is repulsive to the American people. They might not even authorize the use of their atomic bomb in a future crisis before the enemy's atomic bombs had wiped them out first. The Germans were wise enough not to perpetrate too many flagrant anti-American acts. They deliberately ignored the attitude of the Roosevelt administration in support of Great Britain. As long as Great Britain was in the war, America's potential strength was a menace to Germany. Once she was out of the way, the United States could safely be flouted in Europe; for without a bridgehead to the Continent, the Americans could not deploy their power. The President, rightly banking on the Germans' disinclination to declare war on the United States, was on safe ground. United States assistance to Great Britain did not involve the threat of war.

His policy was acclaimed by powerful groups in the United States, by no means exclusively of Anglo-Saxon descent, who realized the danger of a British defeat to America. The organization "Defend America by Help to the Allies" did very useful work in clarifying the issues, which the peace-at-any-price groups—whatever their motives—tried hard to becloud. Though some of my intimate friends were very active in the movement, I kept away from it. There is no sense in preaching to those who are already converted. I knew, moreover, that noncitizens should leave American issues alone. Nobody in the United States minds national pressure groups and national propagandists; the national political system is run in this way. But foreigners must not butt in. Having neither a British birth certificate nor an Oxford accent, I was less suspect than a native Britisher. I used the platforms to which I was invited for discussing issues from a European point of view. I have always objected to those Europeans who think they can serve both Europe and the United States by telling an American audience things they wanted to hear in the way they liked to hear them. The misunderstanding of Europe by people in the United States is often enough due to speakers who desire to ingratiate themselves with their audiences by describing their overseas countrymen as near Americans who only need a little push to become real Americans. I imagined my audiences liked me best when I told them facts they did not care to hear, provided I could prove them. I was rewarded for my reticence when Hamilton College, Clinton, New York, asked me to take charge of the political instruction of the two hundred army men who were to be prepared for service on the European continent. It was perhaps the most interesting appointment I have held. I hope that our teaching made their vision a little clearer, and their burdens a little lighter, when they had to face the final test.

Neither the President nor the groups who supported him could have gone beyond what might be called belligerent neutrality. Their help might have prevented Hitler from winning the war, but they would not have been able to secure his complete defeat. At the decisive moment, the East saved the West.

By the autumn of 1941 the Japanese were evidently as convinced of a German victory as the Italians had been in 1940. The treacherous assault on Hawaii and the Philippines was in keeping with their national tradition, yet it roused the people in the United States to spluttering rage and indignation. They felt insulted rather than threatened. A nation, inferior in everything they valued, had caught them napping. It could not be tolerated. "I expected Germans or Italians to behave badly," a California socialite complained after Pearl Harbor. "One cannot expect manners from Dutchmen and dagos, but that a race of perfect housemen could do this to us is beyond me."

The Japanese surprise attack finished Germany's chance of victory. It finally forced world leadership on the United States. It nearly killed pacifism and isolationism. One cannot argue whether or not one should fight when the other fellow is bombing one's harbors, and one cannot insist on isolation after one's possessions have been invaded. After Hitler had declared war on the United States, even the most fanatic advocates of peace at any price could no longer clamor for a negotiated peace in Europe. His action had prevented the United States from limiting their effort to the Pacific, a policy that would have been very popular. As it was, even the frantic demands of the Reds for a second front in Europe in order to save Russia did not arouse the nation, though her collapse would have provided Hitler with unlimited natural resources and huge reserves of manpower that would have made him almost invincible. The war in Europe never became truly popular. The national war was the war against the Japs, in which insults had to be avenged and the wrongs done to China would be righted. The United States, a preponderantly continental nation, gloried in the terrible war on the islands waged heroically by the navy and the marines, though a good deal of the spotlight fell on General MacArthur. This was its own war. It almost resented the cooperation of the British navy, and complacently ignored the greatest land effort made in it—the Burma campaign, fought almost exclusively by British imperial forces.

I happened to be in Los Angeles at the time of Pearl Harbor. The feeling on the coast was a blend of blind fury and panicky fear. Stories of Japanese warships bombarding the cities were current; rather ineffectual blackout means were improvised— the necessary materials were not obtainable. I had to address a meeting of the Conference of World Affairs at the Riverside Inn, about two hours' drive from Los Angeles. Five minutes before it started, a blackout drill was announced. All the lights went out, for there were no curtains. My anxious hosts asked me whether I could speak in utter darkness. With the help of a flashlight I climbed onto the platform, and let myself go to an invisible audience. It could not see me, I could not see it, but somehow I managed to get in touch with it. When I felt that it had had enough, I climbed down again amid vociferous applause. A little later the blackout was lifted, and everybody seemed to have enjoyed the situation. But I had to spend the night in the inn; as our car had no "blackout lights," we were not allowed to leave.

After Pearl Harbor, isolationists and pacifists concentrated their efforts on trying to prove that Roosevelt's tricky political methods had left no other alternative to the Japs than to load their bombers and release them on Honolulu. It needed both the President's political skill—he was probably the greatest living master of the art of manipulating public opinion—and General Marshall's professional clarity to direct the major effort to the European theater.

The President thoroughly understood the missionary temper of his countrymen; they prefer to fight for abstract principles rather than for a concrete cause. He had to show them a goal on which they could focus their enthusiasm. So he drafted the Atlantic Charter.

The European nations did not need it. They fought desperately for their lives and for national survival. They had no urge for combating "sin." The Atlantic Charter, unlike Wilson's fourteen points, was a confession of faith, not a program; even the nonbelieving Soviets had been made to sign it. Yet it was hard to imagine that victorious Russia would disgorge the spoils she had secured by her treaty of partition with Hitler, and by her war on Finland. Her leaders would have been saints had they agreed to surrender what once had seemed so cheap, after they had had to pay for it the terrific price of the German invasion. The Atlantic Charter was not made the basis of the coming peace treaty; it did not expressly bind the Allies toward Germany, as Wilsonian principles had done. It will not be easy to explain by it the map of the world emerging from the treaties. Even the United States did not feel constrained to observe its spirit too literally when dealing with the islands formerly mandated to Japan.

American public opinion, moreover, seemed far more interested in the application of the charter to the Pacific than to the Atlantic. Anti-imperialists saw in it a justification of their attitude. The liberation of Holland and Belgium or of Denmark and Norway from Nazi dictatorship seemed to them far less important than the independence of India, Malaya, and Indonesia, or the return of Hong Kong to the Chinese.

I had been in the vanguard of colonial reform for most of my life. Only a year before the war, I had published a volume, *The Crumbling of Empire*. Being convinced that for the time being an age of countercolonization and of empire breaking was superseding empire making, I could scarcely be described as an old-fashioned imperialist. But it seemed to me hardly opportune to make the struggle for survival of Western civilization more difficult by an immediate dissolution of the colonial empires on which part of its strength depended.

It was natural for Indian politicians to see in England's difficulty India's opportunity. There was no reason why American public opinion should at this moment join them. British rule in India was no threat to world peace; a Nazi or a Japanese victory was. Whether or not India was freed immediately or ten years hence did not much matter in those critical days. Her mighty military effort did not depend on immediate independence. One does not swap horses when crossing a stream, and here was a team of horses that had little inclination to pull together, once the rider let go. Fortunately for the cause of the Allies, the Indian government was strong enough to stop sabotage. India's fighting races flocked to the colors in large numbers, and helped to win the Burma campaign.

## 5. *The Shadow of Appomattox Courthouse*

By the end of 1942, after the battle of Alamein, victory was clearly in sight, even though it was a very long way off. What would the pattern of the peace be?

Alluring aims had to be put before the people, for the national effort had to be speeded up. Casualties were bound to be heavy, and the burden of the war was slowly being felt; when measured by European standards, it never was very oppressive.

The masses were better off than they had ever been, though real wages lagged behind money wages. But labor everywhere is money-conscious and rates high money wages above high real wages; it can hardly ever be convinced of the danger of inflation as long as it is able to even up price rises after not too long an interval by corresponding wage rises. Yet price rises had been kept fairly well under control. The transition from peace to war production was a gigantic accomplishment, of which the United States could justly be proud. The "wasteful capitalist system," so often held up to derision by Moscow's disciples, had turned out goods on a scale that completely dwarfed Russia's sixteen years of concentrated prewar effort, and greatly contributed to her military survival. War profiteering for once had been democratized, organized labor having become one of its main beneficiaries. It was almost a golden age for many people who were not yet worried by their sons' and brothers' being sent overseas.

A large section of public opinion did not trust the President. His repeated re-election violated the unwritten law that no president should have a third term of office. The foresight he had shown, the skill with which he had handled his incongruous coalition majority, the adroitness with which he had split the Republican party, and not least, the attempt of his New Deal followers to perpetuate the presidential war emergency powers for all time to come had embittered the opposition. It saw in the President a betrayer of his own class, and distrusted his political honesty. The foreign visitor was often enough embarrassed by the vituperative attacks on the head of the state that his Republican friends indulged in in his presence.

The American forces on land and sea had given proof over and over again of their great fighting qualities. But the nation visualized the war as a mechanical rather than a military issue; logistics seemed to be the master, not the servant, of strategy; the war was an engineering feat rather than an instrument of policy. The people of the United States, having taken up the challenge very much against their will, wanted a peace that would rule out war for all time to come, and stop once and forever the recurrence of the hateful call to arms. Twice "the Yanks had come" to save Europe; it must never happen again.

The President formulated the slogan that promised fulfillment of this demand—"Unconditional Surrender." It had made a chord vibrate in many an American's heart. The War between the States had culminated in the "unconditional surrender" of Lee's army at Appomattox courthouse. This had spelled the end of the Confederacy, and had consolidated the Union for all time to come. With the surrender of its armies the rebel government had passed out; the Confederate states were automatically returned to the Union as beaten rebels. The way was free for reshaping their state governments according to the ideas of the victorious northern democracy, before they were handed back to their own people. Lincoln's death enabled the zealots in its ranks to punish the rebels for their crimes, and to exact the wages of sin from a disarmed adversary. Here was an excellent pattern to follow in dealing with a fallen nation that was evidently cursed with a double dose of original sin. It gave a chance to American blueprinters to reshape the life of an entire nation according to their own universalist ideas. They would eradicate "sin" and when their victims were properly purged, endow them with those institutions that had blessed America. It was the most ambitious planning venture, the most daring piece of social engineering, ever undertaken. It appealed to a nation that prefers simple abstractions to complicated reality. Insistence on unconditional surrender was moreover meant to impress Stalin. He seemed to doubt the willingness of his allies to destroy the false friend with whom he had planned to partition Eastern Europe.

But the German situation bore no resemblance to the case of the Confederacy. The legitimacy of the Hitler government had unfortunately never been contested. It had been accepted in peace and in war as a sovereign government. Neither Hitler himself, nor any of the Nazi leaders, could surrender unconditionally; they knew what their fate would be. They would either escape or die by their own hands. If Hitler could not vanish like Lohengrin, he might at least dramatically perish in the flames of Valhalla. Hitler's disappearance would leave Germany without a government. The Allies would have to take over and rule nearly 70 million Germans in Germany and Austria; for no genuine German government could be formed, since its first task would be self-extinction by unconditional surrender. As was to be expected, none of the three Nazi arch-criminals met his death at the hands of an Allied hangman.

The President had made his allies accept his slogan—it naturally crystallized into a policy. Nobody can prove or disprove whether or not it prolonged the war; it certainly created a vacuum. The Allies could not very well recognize Admiral Doenitz as the ruler of Germany and thus acknowledge Hitler's right to appoint a successor. Once the German army was in prison camps, there was nobody with whom to deal. The Allies had to run the country through armies of occupation. Such a task had never before been attempted. Even in colonial regions, no army of occupation had ever acted in lieu of a national government, but always through one—as General MacArthur is doing now in Japan.

No condominium in modern times has really been successful, and a condominium exercised by two capitalist and one anti-capitalist power could hardly harmonize outside military matters. Even in the most critical phase of the war, Russia had not co-operated wholeheartedly with the Allies' Supreme Command.

The Allies, moreover, were not taking over Germany as a going concern. They had agreed to cut off part of it, to transplant its inhabitants and turn the remainder from a highly industrial community into a pastoral country. They were deliberately planning a social revolution, though, apart from the Soviets, they had no definite ideas about its nature—whether the new social structure was to be capitalist or socialist, or a hybrid of the type of Britain under a Labor government. They meant to build a new spiritual Germany by exterminating the Nazis, and by educating its people, under the protection of the bayonet, to true democracy. It was not decided whether it was to be democracy of the American or the Russian type. Finally they were going to make them frame a constitution, under which they would get a national government with which the Allies could conclude a peace.

The experiment in remaking the American South had, however, been neither very successful nor very creditable. The planners forgot the salutary lesson it could have taught them. To imagine that a blueprint for a new democratic Germany could be drawn that would satisfy both Russia and the United

States was either naïve or irresponsible—or perhaps a combination of both.

The President probably realized this. He by-passed the issue by creating an even more difficult one. At Yalta he had advocated the dismemberment of Germany. The Potsdam scheme split the country in four zones of occupation; France was to get one of them. The British government agreed to it, though it managed to preserve on paper the economic unity of Germany; identical economic policies were to be pursued in each zone. But economic unity does not so much depend on a free flow of goods and men between the zones as on the economic structure of each region. It soon became apparent that Russia very deliberately, and from her point of view naturally, was bent on laying the foundations of a semi-Communist order in her zone in the hope that the seeds of Communism sown in it would infiltrate the West, once administrative barriers no longer held up their transmission. When she had partially achieved her object she turned round and clamored for the restoration of the unity of Germany. She played up to German desire for unity and tried hard to be admitted to the control of the Ruhr.

It was not very difficult to foretell the catastrophic implications of this superb piece of irresponsible planning. The tragic story since 1945 was to prove them. As soon as the scheme was being discussed, I wrote a paper (autumn 1942) predicting some of the inescapable consequences. I sent it to both English and American friends high up. The response was, "Do not publish it, or you will be very unpopular." Had I known at the time that General Eisenhower and his staff held similar views on unconditional surrender, I would not have minded unpopularity.* But there is no sense in speaking up when nobody will listen. Whatever its implications, the success of the

---

* Captain Harry Butcher, U.S.N.R., *My Three Years with Eisenhower*, p. 518. "Can unconditional surrender be unconditional? . . . Any military person knows, that there are conditions to every surrender. There is a feeling that, at Casablanca, the President and the Prime Minister, more likely the former, seized on Grant's famous term without realizing the full implications to the enemy. Goebbels has made great capital with it to strengthen the morale of the German Army and people. Our psychological experts believe we would be wiser if we created a mood of acceptance of surrender in the German Army which would make possible a collapse of resistance similar to that which took place in Tunisia. They think if a proper mood is created in the German General Staff, there might even be a German Badoglio."

American plan depended on the United States' staying long enough in Germany to see it through. In the hour of victory, the people of the United States seemed to forget it completely. Both public opinion and the army in Germany bolted.

The army was homesick; all over the country irate mothers badgered congressmen and senators to let the boys come home immediately. Acts that in any other army would have been called mutiny had to be condoned. The victorious host disintegrated in a kind of huge stampede and helter-skelter made for home. During the war railway travel and hotel accommodation in the United States had become increasingly difficult, but with a little foresight one could nearly always manage. After V-E day the maelstrom of veterans rushing home to Mom clogged all communications and nearly broke the transport system. Having victoriously asserted its position as the greatest world power, the United States seemed to throw it away lightheartedly because the boys in Europe, no longer confronted by death, were homesick. Friends and foes had to assume that America was not a partner to be reckoned with.

## 6. *The Blessings of Fear*

The release of the atomic bomb ended the Japanese war. It did so at a time when Japan's power of resistance was visibly waning. The use of the atomic bomb no doubt saved many American lives. Its repercussions were to determine American foreign policy for good and all. Its possession raised the military pride of the nation, though it was an engineering accomplishment rather than a soldier's triumph, and soldiers as well as civilians felt not quite easy about its having been used. Yet it gave confidence to the masses in the country's overwhelming strength. At the same time it dealt a decisive blow to isolationism. Neither the oceans nor the Monroe Doctrine—the latter was based on the wide expanses of the seas—could any longer protect American homes from destruction. From now on, Des Moines, Iowa, was almost as vulnerable as New York and Washington. The European nations had always lived under the shadow of fear. The blitz and its counterparts on the Continent had surpassed their worst expectations. They saw in the atomic bomb a multiplication of the horrors to which they had been subjected. To the people of the United States it was the end of a dream. Security could no longer be entrusted to the kindly elements, which had lovingly sheltered the United States from all possible dangers. From now on, the risks of destruction were more or less equalized among all nations. The United States was not even the most favored; New Zealand and Australia or Argentina and Chile were probably safer. The bomb had brought to the United States the blessings of fear. Public opinion was deeply stirred. It realized the decisive change far more rapidly than England had recognized the loss of insular security in an age of airborne attacks after the earlier war. From now on an active, realistic policy had to be pursued; contracting out was no longer possible. Even before the bomb fell on Hiroshima public opinion had realized dimly that it could no longer wriggle out of European or Asiatic danger zones. For this reason, it had enthusiastically sponsored the foundation of the United Nations. It had seen in Japan and Germany the only potential disturbers of the peace. Once these nations were defeated, a world alliance would keep them in check—even though they might be admitted to it later on after having been rendered innocuous. By offering three votes to Russia, and by accepting the veto, the United States had made the U.N. universal.

But the U.N. was as much a concession to isolationism as a triumph for internationalism. Isolationists had balked the United States' entry to the League of Nations because it had threatened to saddle it with non-American responsibilities; they saw in the U.N. an instrument that would lessen them. They could no longer assert that the United States could live happily within its own shell, even if that shell were to encase, for protective purposes, a by no means overenthusiastic Latin America. The United States could not be secure in an insecure world. By associating itself with the entire world, it would achieve more safety than by standing by or concluding entangling alliances; and without such alliances it might even become encircled by a hostile world. Wealth always causes envy, and if potential material strength is sapped by spiritual weakness, a rich country is in grave danger from poorer, covetous neighbors. The isolationists who supported the U.N. saw in it a kind of powerful international fire-insurance company, whose excellent supervisory services would diminish fire risks and thus reduce the expense of a national fire brigade. The veto, moreover, reassured them that no attempt on American sovereignty could be made. The internationalists had accepted the U.N. since they could not secure a world state, which would have to be a replica of the American federal constitution on a world-wide scale. They imagined that pooling sovereignty among the federated members would put an end to the danger of war; they forgot that the only war in the nineteenth century that might be called total war had been the American Civil War. It had split the pooled sovereignty of the United States of America. Curiously enough, the most peace-loving nation on earth, which experienced a civil war not quite a century ago, is always ready to overlook the horrors of internal strife, while recoiling with loathing from the smallest border warfare.

The United States had discovered but slowly that it had helped to destroy Old Europe. The First World War had apparently ended in an overwhelming victory of Western civilization. The two great non-European powers that had threatened it in the past, Turkey and Russia, had been driven back. But the peace had been a triumph of Slavs over Germans. Poland and Czechoslovakia had been re-established as independent states. Their religions tied them to the West; descent and sentiment to the Slavonic East. The eastward moves of Germans in the north and Italians in the south had been checked. The Bolshevik Revolution, moreover, was a challenge to everything the West stood for. The second war definitely destroyed the work of both Italian and German colonization.

Of the six great powers that controlled Europe in 1914, Austria has vanished completely; Italy, never really strong, is weaker than ever; France can hardly be a great power as long as her policies are dictated by fear (courage, not war potential, makes a great power). The Potsdam agreement has both mutilated and split Germany. The provisional transfer of four whole and two half eastern provinces of Prussia to Poland and Russia has wiped out Old Prussia, the military backbone of Germany. This can hardly be undone, since the Western powers have consented to the expulsion of 2½ million Germans from New Poland, the residue of 9½ millions who once inhabited these lands. No countercolonization movement on such a gigantic scale has ever happened in history. Woodrow Wilson would turn in his grave if he saw how his heirs have handled the self-determination of nations and the protection of minorities.

England has survived, but she is not strong enough to hold by herself the guardianship of a Western world, which is menaced by Soviet Russia, the main beneficiary of the war. Russia emerged with a much greater power potential than she ever possessed. Thanks to the collaboration of her Western allies, Germany had been broken, and thanks to the American victories in the Pacific and British successes in Burma, Japan is no longer a threat to her. The picture of two great continental powers, the United States and Russia, holding the peace of the world in their hands, appealed to American imagination, which is always impressed by size. It saw the United States in the role of a moderator, effectively damping the acquisitive ardor of its not too squeamish allies.

But Great Britain was more interested in divesting herself of the burden of empire than in acquiring new possessions. Her withdrawal from Egypt, India, and Burma might upset the balance in the Far East; Russia was pressing forward everywhere. American policy toward her had alternately shown fear of her weakness and of her strength. It had made her accept the Atlantic Charter, but had admitted an interpretation of it that brazenly ignored its principles. At Yalta it had sacrificed China's interests in Manchuria in return for Russia's participation in the Japanese war, when this participation was no longer of importance. The U.S.A. had never been sure whether Russia would not quit and let it finish the German war under much more difficult conditions. When all was over, the fear of Russian weakness suddenly turned into fear of Russian strength. It let Russia dig herself in on the Continent, create a shelter belt of subservient states, and entrench herself between Oder and Elbe. It was opposing her in Korea, and was very much irritated by the support given by her to Chinese Communists. The dream of a united democratic China guarding the peace on the Asiatic continent as the United States did in the Americas was vanishing. Public opinion distrusted Russia but was afraid of irritating her. "You should not make these statements," I was told in a debate on the future of Europe, when I had alluded to Russia's incorporation of the Baltic states. "Are my facts wrong?" "No," came the reply, "but we must not say anything that might provoke Russia, and drive her into war."

But for Molotov's speeches and Russian underground activities, United States policy might have continued on the assumption that peace with Russia, at almost any price, meant world peace. The United States had been in the habit of lecturing the world at large on the merits and duties of democracy —following, in this respect, earlier British precedents. In the Russian representatives in the U.N. it met aggressively pedantic schoolmasters whose boring dialectics wasted time and patience. The Russians used terms familiar to Americans, but gave them an entirely different meaning, thanks to which all aggressive acts of Russian policy were justified, while every defensive move of the Western powers was condemned. A nation of born world improvers does not take kindly to the activities of a rival sect that not only invades its territory but derides its methods and blackens its motives. The Western world owes a debt of gratitude to the Russian spokesmen who hammered into men's minds that the ways of Russia are not the ways of the wicked West. They have forced the United States to accept the challenge, and to stand firm on all essential points.

Germany lies in the center of Europe; if she were to become a Russian satellite state like Poland and Czechoslovakia, Russia would dominate the Continent, and with it all Europe. The mountains that hold up an invasion of Italy and Spain cannot stop the infiltration of doctrines. The attempt to oppose Russia only at the White Cliffs of Dover would not be as successful as the retreat from Dunkirk.

Within three years after the disastrous Potsdam conference, the United States has learned its lesson. It has scrapped the policy of planned destruction and is earnestly engaged in rebuilding Europe. Much has been lost that cannot be recovered. It may be possible to re-establish the unity of Germany. This will imply an internal struggle within Germany between Western and Russian conceptions of the good life. The mere fact that Russia can always count on the support of a Russian party— the German Communists—while there is no British or American party in the country will favor Russia. Yet Russia's inherent economic weakness, well known to governments if not to the public, will give a breathing space for building up Europe and securing peace.

In the summer of 1945 the future of Europe looked very black. Large sections of the United States did not yet see the danger of leaving a shattered Europe to right herself politically, while other sections were as frightened of provoking Soviet Russia as European appeasers had been of irritating the dictators. Fortunately Russia's threats and bluffs in the U.N. converted public opinion. The country that possessed the atomic bomb and the most efficient economic war machine could call Russia's bluff.

Half a year later I had the good fortune to be on the same platform with Mr. Henry Morgenthau Jr., the author of the pastoralization plan. He outlined its history, and wailed that things had gone wrong because his policy had not been carried out with sufficient energy. He read a carefully prepared document, while I had to rely on a few notes, for I had been called upon suddenly as a substitute for another speaker. The applause with which the large audience greeted my reply showed me that the tragic period was ended in which public opinion had accepted the blueprints of vindictive, frightened amateurs. A few weeks later, when I left the United States, the nation was getting ready to relieve Great Britain of the guardianship of the Western world.

# XXII. Summing Up

## I

AFTER SIX and a half years living in trunks, my "Wanderlust" has somewhat abated. For the time being, I am grateful for not having to plan ahead for another move; though we are no longer camping, my books, or those, at least, that have not been destroyed by bombs, are still scattered. But whether this is a mere interlude, or the beginning of passing out, it is an appropriate time for summing up.

The outward results of my activities are not impressive. The world would have been just the same had I never set foot in it. Once or twice I was in the center of the marshaling yard and did a little shunting of my own, which, for the time being, was quite successful. Somewhat later, however, the train took the wrong track, and as I had predicted, went off the rails.

I suppose I was a fairly good teacher of intelligent students. The unimaginative, plodding type did not get much from me. I tried to teach them how to think, not merely what to know, and they usually resented it. A few men and women whose minds I had influenced were and are holding important positions in Germany and the United States. I have written a number of books, some supposed to be good, others being actually popular. None of them was as good as it ought to have been, partly because my physical capacity for work was limited, partly because I usually dealt with current events from a long-term point of view. One has to hurry to keep abreast of them; if one ponders too long and too deeply, they will have slipped away before they have fully revealed their meaning. Though my method was not always satisfactory, it enabled me to become a fairly good forecaster, as shown by my publications. But I was not cut out for the part of a prophet. I am by no means overmodest, but I have found it hard to believe that I could see trends hidden to other equally intelligent, often more advantageously placed, observers. It seemed unlikely that my intuition should be more trustworthy than their information; it sometimes was. Yet I never trusted my own findings completely. The trade of a prophet demands a firm belief in his own infallibility; conflicting, contradictory facts must either be explained away, distorted, suppressed, or ignored. I do not own sufficient will power for the performance of this feat. I cannot work myself up into a trance in which truth is what one believes, irrespective of facts or proofs. Nor do I possess the physical vigor for delivering a message in season and out of season, from pulpit or platform, soap box or stage. I tried to get knowledge, not to sell information. I may have been a good digger for truth; I was a bad salesman.

But had I wailed like the prophet Jeremiah, my wailings would not have diverted the course of history. Those who swim against the current may occasionally reach dry land; eventually they may even discover the source of the river. But they cannot turn the flood.

In retrospect, much of what I have done looks pretty futile. Yet I probably would do most of it again, were I given a second chance. For the fun of the race is not in the winning but in the running. I thoroughly enjoyed it. The life I have led suited me; it gave me the priceless gift of being my own master. I would of course like to bypass a few years and to forget a few ugly spots.

People of my type are rarely ecstatically happy, for they try to look at the procession whilst they are marching in it. It spoils the fun. The mere thought, moreover, that the show will be over soon in any case makes it hard to enjoy it unstintedly. They sip life, they cannot gulp it. But they are capable—if outer circumstances favor them, as they have done me through most of my active years—of deep, lasting content. This has been my lot.

## II

There is no finality in human affairs. Even atomic warfare will not spell the end of history, though it may steepen the curves along which it moves. It is not beyond men's ability to foresee its hectic course and to anticipate the consequences of their policies. But consequences are a prolific and rather promiscuous breed. Their young ones, and certainly the young ones' own offspring, rarely come up to the expectations in which they were conceived. Their features frequently raise doubts about their legitimacy; impurities somehow have crept in; one cannot breed events as one breeds racehorses.

The Wilsonian program centered in the self-determination of nations. It was the decisive factor in the disintegration of Eastern Europe and the break-up of the Habsburg empire. Its author visualized a number of virile young nations who, born in freedom, would dedicate themselves to the cause of freedom and not merely to their own sectional interests—President Masaryk was the embodiment of these dreams. But Wilson did not perceive that people who had lived long under Turkish rule and Russian domination, or were influenced by close spiritual or geographical contact with them, could not fully accept the values of the Western world; even the peculiar features of the Junker's Prussia can best be explained by its vicinity to and its affinity with absolutist Czarist Russia. On a cultural map Topeka, Kansas, or St. Paul, Minnesota—not to mention San Francisco—are much nearer to Europe than Bucharest, Belgrade, or even Budapest.

Both Great Britain and the United States have frequently overlooked this. The manly bearing of the eastern and southeastern peoples, their heroic struggles against their oppressors, in which the ethics of patriotism and the romance of banditry were often inextricably interwoven, appealed to Anglo-Saxon love of liberty. The orderly, drab civilizations of the machine age look with longing eyes to colorful near-Homeric folkways, especially when their fundamental crudities can be toned down by sociological explanations.

The newly established nations could not fulfill their founders' hopes. They did not become in Eastern Europe the counterpart of Switzerland and the Low Countries in the West. Jammed in between Russia and Germany, they were at the same time too weak and too proud to take over Austria's mission and to serve as a bridge between East and West. They finally provided Hitler with plausible pretexts for his nefarious schemes. At a time when Germany had forfeited the right to speak as a part of Europe, she had almost established her domination over it. But for the stupendous effort of the United States, Hitler might not have failed.

Hitler's collapse unfortunately has not saved Europe. It has changed the course of European history. The expulsion of about 12 million Germans from east of the Oder-Neisse line, Czechoslovakia, and Hungary, has completely reversed the trend of nearly a thousand years of eastward migration. A new frontier of Europe is being established. It runs through the heart of Germany. It has shifted Western and Southern Slavs, Hungarians, and Rumanians from dependence on the West to domination by the East. They have passed from Austria's sloppy imperialist despotism, which they had been allowed to denounce freely, to ruthless Russian dictatorship, which they are not permitted to criticize.

In the lecture rooms in Königsberg, where Kant discoursed on Perpetual Peace, and where the doctrines of Adam Smith were first proclaimed outside his native country, Marxist pedants will preach their crude gospel in the near future. If Goethe's residence in Weimar were not of a rather modest character, a Soviet commissar might make it his Kommandatura. Yet Kant, Smith, and Goethe are not bound by space. They live wherever thought is free. But Vienna is a physical reality. She had an atmosphere which one could breathe, a way of living one could share, she was not an abstract idea. Can she survive the tribulations ahead of her? If things go well, she will become a frontier town precariously perched on the outskirts of Western culture. She will no longer be one of its main centers, whence radiated the roads from West to East, and where East and West could meet and mingle. The last words of a hundred-year-old dirge rise in my memory. It laments the fall of the city, stormed by Southern Slav regiments led by a Southern Slav field marshal. He squashed the revolution of 1848 and saved the throne:

> "Were strength left us for kneeling,
> On bended knees we'd stay;
> Could we still believe in prayer,
> For Vienna we would pray."

Europe has been cut in two; her frontier has been shoved back to where it stood nearly eight hundred years ago. Neither

France nor Great Britain can hold it unaided. History has taken another sharp turn. But Europe will survive, though for the time being she is mutilated. The United States has come to the rescue; the two continents which the American Revolution had separated are once more drawing together. The Marshall plan is the boldest scheme of international economic reconstruction ever conceived. Whether or not it will achieve all its objects, it has already become the symbol of Re-Union.

### III

The English people, it seems to me, got thoroughly accustomed to regimentation during the war; by now they no longer resent the rather inept multiple dictatorship imposed upon them under the name of planning. It is galling to a sincere liberal to see Prussian state socialism introduced in these isles under a new name, at a time when Prussia herself has gone. It almost looks as if the only booty the British army brought home from Germany were the placards *Verboten* that formerly dotted the German landscape and are now being distributed by government departments in Britain. I have never liked Marxism. I vividly remember the crippled little tailor who sat next to me at a housing congress over half a century ago, and who saw in me a promising subject for indoctrination. "Science tells us," he informed me during a pause in the discussion, "what is bound to happen in the social world, and nothing can prevent its happening soon." Yet it is just over a century since Marx and Engels prophesied the collapse of the capitalist world in the near future. Evidently their timetable was not very reliable. I have been close to many leading Continental Marxists, Eduard Bernstein, Karl Kautsky, Rudolf Hilferding, and on friendly terms with most of the prominent Socialist politicians. They often suggested my joining the party. Had I done so, I would soon have been given a safe seat in the Reichstag. I never was tempted.

When I became politically minded, the party had passed its heroic age—its successful struggle against Bismarckian persecution. Its rapidly growing parliamentary strength had made it wary. It still talked revolution, but it no longer dreamed of barricades and red Phrygian caps, to the great grief of some of its older temperamental leaders. Its ideas of the good life for everybody had become thoroughly bourgeois. Its Utopia was a lower-middle-class, comfortable, clean, well-ordered suburbia, not the dreamland of the highly emotional, untried intelligentsia, where everybody—except the detested bourgeois—could do as he liked. These intellectuals, not the proletarians, were the real enemies of the bourgeois; the conflict actually raged between philistines and bohemians, not between bourgeois and proletarians. For the well-organized proletarian trade unionist was as much a supporter of social order as his employer counterpart. He did not want to destroy the bourgeois world, he wanted to share it.

Suburbia has never appealed to me; I may have to spend the last years of my life in its uncongenial atmosphere. Yet after my student days were over, I had even less sympathy with advanced revolutionaries, who wanted to unhinge the world because it was drab and orderly, and order to them was the equivalent of boredom. They had been good company when I had sat with them in the Café Griensteidl in Vienna or the Café Stefanie in Munich and had heard them lay down the law on art, literature, and philosophy—and of course on Marxism, which then one could debate as something novel as one does existentialism today. Sometimes I hear the name of a survivor of those days and a shadow flits through my mind of an eager youth who firmly believed that he could easily surpass Samson, by courageously avoiding a barber's clip. A quarter of a century later I saw "the young men of the Café" swarm into the open and make the Munich revolution. They thoroughly justified the contempt in which Lenin held their breed.

As long as the Socialists were a minority, they shared the hatred of an omnipotent government with which I had grown up. They had, moreover, taken over all the cultural ideals that genuine liberalism had cherished in its creative days. But I could not swallow their concept of a determinist social mechanism, according to which the production setup of capitalism was to turn out Socialism as unfailingly as a trustworthy hen lays eggs. In the late nineties they expected the hatching of the socialist Phoenix within a few years. The approximate date was furiously debated at the party meetings. This determinism had given them great strength, for they were as sure of the end of the wicked world as a Seventh Day Adventist. Yet it led to a kind of fatalist quietism alien to my temper. Much later I greatly sympathized with their plight after the victory of Bolshevism. It had knocked their determinism on the head. Russia's production setup—which certainly was not capitalist—had not made the revolution; the Bolshevist revolution was creating the production setup by physical force. It just was too bad. The Bolshevists, moreover, had thrown overboard as "bourgeois piffle" the entire idealistic cultural superstructure that had made the German socialist working class the best-educated working class in the world, and had drawn toward socialism many who had no stake in it. In the eyes of my orthodox Marxist friends the Bolshevists had betrayed the true faith; both their teachings and their methods were heretical. They certainly were effective. Yet their brutal coercive actions were supposed to be emergency measures of a purely temporary character. When the transition period was over, a truly free society would airse, in which the State would wither. There would be neither bureaucrats nor ministerial decrees. It would be a world which would run itself. This Marxist final goal was an Utopia in which even a fanatic Manchester man might feel at home. It has not yet emerged in Russia, and I doubt whether it ever will. But it had a humanitarian glamour that could warm one's heart. The new planners do not plan to unplan themselves at any time; they mean to ramble on like Tennyson's brook, only much less gently.

Yet all hope is not lost. Even brooks sometimes dry up, when the sun has beaten down on them. The state in which we are living at present is certainly not the Marxist ideal state; it is a fairly faithful copy of the design of the leading German nationalist philosopher, Fichte's, "Closed Commercial State," with its blend of permanent austerity and permanent coercion.

For a contrarious mind like mine, this state of affairs has its blessings. Were the world nearer perfection, I might have chanted a "Nunc Dimittis." But my eyes have not seen the coming of the Lord, and are most unlikely to do so. Had it been otherwise, I might have retired long ago and, not having any hobbies, I would surely have been bored and would have become a burden to those near me. I would have sat for hours in my club and tried to catch the attention of younger members to tell them stories of the good old days, when everything was as perfect as it is imperfect now. I would have emerged from time to time to attend the funeral of a contemporary whom everybody apart from his cronies and the professional writers of obituaries, had forgotten, though once perhaps he held eminence. After the ceremony one would shake hands with an ever decreasing number of the Old Guard, each silently asking the other who would go next.

All this has fortunately been postponed. As long as the senses function, I can do some more kicking. When they fail, I shall have to rely on the greatest of gifts with which nature has endowed me, the ability to dream. I have been a dreamer all my life, and dreams have often been more vivid to me than things real. I have always controlled them, and I have never mixed them up with reality. I have learned to switch over from dreamland to life almost without friction. As the sphere of life contracts, as it is bound to do, the realm of dreams expands. It will no longer embrace hopes of things to come, but only reflexes of what has been and what a grateful memory has treasured. If I could but go on dreaming dreams until they fade insensibly into sleep eternal, I would bless the future as I have blessed the past.

# Index